Michelle

BETWEEN THE CRACKS
BOOK THREE

P.D. WORKMAN

 PD WORKMAN

Copyright © 2015 by P.D. Workman
All rights reserved.

No part of this book may be reproduced in any form or by any electronic or mechanical means, including information storage and retrieval systems, without written permission from the author, except for the use of brief quotations in a book review.

ISBN: 9781988390017 (IS Hardcover)
ISBN: 9781926500997 (IS Paperback)
ISBN: 9781774688267 (KDP Paperback 2 ed)
ISBN: 9781774688274 (KDP Hardcover)
ISBN: 9781926500621 (Kindle)
ISBN: 9781926500638 (ePub)
ISBN: 9781774688281 (Lulu Paperback 2 ed)
ISBN: 9781774685303 (accessible audiobook)

Also by P.D. Workman

FIND MORE BOOKS AT PDWORKMAN.COM

YOUNG ADULT FICTION:

Medical Kidnap Files:
YA Suspense
Mito
EDS
Proxy
Toxo
Pain
Fail
Pulse

Between the Cracks:
Gritty Contemporary YA Family Saga
Ruby
June and Justin
Michelle
Chloe
Ronnie
June, Into the Light

Tamara's Teardrops:
Gritty Contemporary YA
Tattooed Teardrops
Two Teardrops
Tortured Teardrops
Vanishing Teardrops

Breaking the Pattern:
Gritty Contemporary YA

Henry

Sandy

Bobby

Stand Alone Young Adult:

Stand Alone

Don't Forget Steven

Those Who Believe

Cynthia has a Secret

Questing for a Dream

Darkness before the Dream (prequel story)

Once Brothers

Intersexion

Making Her Mark

Endless Change

Gem, Himself, Alone

AND MORE AT PDWORKMAN.COM

To loved ones open to second chances

CHAPTER
One

Michelle was in her room with a book when her daddy got home from a long haul with Marcie. She listened to June greet Justin and Marcie. Kenny, sitting on the bed staring at his schoolbooks, got up and went out to the front room.

"Kenny, get out of here and back to your homework," June told him.

Kenny said nothing. He rarely had anything to say.

"Kenny..." she raised her voice warningly.

"Leave him alone, June," Justin told her.

"I told him no TV before his homework is done."

"Well then, I guess his homework is done."

There was silence for a couple of minutes, while they probably glared at each other, trying to decide whether to have an out-and-out argument over it.

"Where's Michelle?"

"In the bedroom with her nose in a book, like always."

A moment later Justin was in the doorway. Dark hair like Michelle and Kenny had. Like all of them had. Justin and June looked strikingly similar; slender, medium height, with fine features. And the same dark hair. "Hi, pumpkin."

"Hi, Daddy."

He walked in and sat down on the edge of the bed. "How are you doing, Michelle?" When she turned her face toward him, he saw her black eye. "Oh, sweetie. What happened?"

Michelle shrugged and didn't answer. She didn't need to. He knew what had happened. "I wish I was Marcie and could go with you all the time."

"Well, you need to go to school. Marcie doesn't."

Michelle nodded. "I wish I was like her."

Justin touched Michelle's bruised face. "You don't wish you had cerebral palsy."

June walked in. "What are you doing?" she demanded sharply.

"I'm talking to Michelle."

"Get your hands off her!"

Justin withdrew his hand and frowned at June. "What's the matter, June?"

"You think I don't know what's going on? Get out of here and leave her alone."

Justin stood up, his brow creased in consternation. "Do you think I'm hurting her? I would never do that. We were just talking."

"She doesn't need you in here, putting ideas in her head and touching her."

Justin walked out of the room. June also left. Michelle went back to reading her book. A while later, June yelled at her to come for dinner.

"I'm not hungry," Michelle answered.

"You have to eat."

"I don't want anything."

"Leave her alone," Justin told June.

"Fine, it's less money spent on groceries if she doesn't eat," June grumbled.

"June, have a drink and relax. You're usually happy to see me when I've been away on a long haul."

June said nothing. Michelle listened to the clinking dishes and glasses.

∼

Michelle was asleep when Kenny came in. She woke up and watched him slowly undress for bed. Justin had put Marcie to bed with

MICHELLE

Michelle earlier and her little sister was now fast asleep with Michelle's arms encircling her. Kenny was oldest and stayed up watching TV late as usual, waiting until long after dark when everyone had gone to sleep and the apartment was totally silent. June and Justin had gone to bed together an hour or two earlier. Michelle didn't know how they could fight and argue all night and then go off to bed together as if nothing were wrong.

"Goodnight Kenny," Michelle said softly.

He flapped a hand in her direction and climbed into bed.

Two days later, Justin was off to work again and Kenny and Michelle were left alone with June. June was quiet and easier to get along with for a couple of days, as she always was after Justin had been home. But it didn't last. It never lasted.

Kenny was in trouble at school again. Not for fighting this time, but because he was failing, and failing in everything. Usually, they advanced him a grade anyway, but they called home to try to motivate him to work harder.

"You are so stupid," June berated him. "How come you can't pay attention in class and make the teachers think you got something between your ears besides rocks? You're so dumb!"

"Leave him alone," Michelle protested.

June turned on Michelle. "You stay out of it, missy! This has got nothing to do with you."

"Kenny is good at school, he doesn't bother anyone. He's quiet…"

"And he's thick as a post! If I want to hear from little Miss A Plus, I'll tell you."

Michelle opened her mouth to argue and June raised her hand. Michelle ducked back and went to her room, shutting the door. She turned her radio on loud to drown out the sound of June's voice as she continued to castigate Kenny.

He came into the room later, avoiding her eyes as he went over to his bed and lay down.

"Are you okay?" Michelle questioned, and went over to him, sitting down beside him. Kenny covered his face. Michelle looked at him.

"I hate her," she muttered. She opened the door and looked around covertly for June. She couldn't see or hear June. Michelle went to the bathroom and was back a moment later with cotton and peroxide.

"Okay, let's see now." She held Kenny's hand away from his face and dabbed at the cuts. "Hold still. We gotta get you fixed up."

He let her clean the cuts and grazes without protest. When she was done, they just sat in silence looking at each other.

"Do you have any homework?" Michelle asked finally.

"Uh-huh."

Michelle looked around for his books. "Where is your bag?"

He looked away. "I forgot it at school."

"Oh. What were you supposed to do?"

"Dunno."

"You gotta bring your bag home. I can help you with your homework, but you gotta bring it home."

"Yeah."

"I'll help you," Michelle repeated.

He nodded. Michelle went back over to her bed and picked up her latest book. Kenny lay staring up at the ceiling in silence.

Kenny was ten and Michelle was eight. Only a year and a half apart, actually. He should have been one grade above her. It was pretty young to be on their own, but Michelle was considering it. Justin was rarely ever home and June wasn't getting any less abusive. Things weren't going to get any better.

Michelle honestly hadn't realized how bizarre June's behavior was getting. Justin got home after a long haul one day and June refused to even let him get close to Michelle.

"You just leave her alone. Stay away from her. You understand?"

Justin didn't get angry. He just looked at June. "You don't even know why you're doing this, do you?"

"Doing what?"

"I didn't figure it out last time either." June was looking at him like he was crazy. "How old is Michelle?"

"You know as well as I do she's eight."

"And what happened when you were eight?"

June stared at him, understanding flooding her features.

Michelle looked at them. "What happened when Mama was eight, Daddy?"

"Go to your room and let your mom and me talk."

Justin wasn't usually strict with Michelle so she pressed further. "What happened?"

"You heard me." His voice was firm and he raised one eyebrow.

Michelle went to her room, wondering what was going on.

June's place at the dinner table was empty. June was in her room with the door shut. The children all looked at each other.

"What's wrong with Mama, Daddy?" Michelle asked.

"Mama's got some things to think about. You just stay out of her way for a while." Justin was preparing to feed Marcie and didn't look at Michelle when he spoke.

"Daddy... can't we come with you when you leave this time?"

"Honey, you know I can't go dragging three kids around the country with me. I have a hard enough time with some of my bosses over taking Marcie with me."

"Why don't you ever take me or Kenny with you instead?"

"I have to take Marcie because June can't take care of her. There's nowhere else for Marcie to go." Justin inserted a spoonful of pureed peas into Marcie's mouth.

"What if Mama can't take care of us either?" Michelle persisted.

"You guys can take care of yourselves. Marcie can't."

Michelle looked pointedly at Kenny. He could take care of himself? "You don't know what it's like."

Justin finally looked at her, his face sad. "Sweetie, if I could be here all the time, I would. But somebody has to pay the bills."

"You don't know what it's like," Michelle repeated desperately.

He studied her. "You're a smart girl," he said. "Smarter than anyone I've ever met. You tell me what you think I should do."

"Is mama going to be better after this?"

"You know she's not going to get any better."

"Then I don't want to stay here anymore."

Justin was silent for a while. "You want to go to foster care?"

"Yes."

"I'll call Social Services," he said finally, after another long silence, during which he fed Marcie.

"They have to keep us together," Michelle said.

Justin nodded. "If we can," he said quietly, "but you gotta know, they could separate you. And even if they don't, there's no guarantee you'll like it any better than here."

"I know."

Justin looked at Kenny. "What do you think, Kenny?"

Kenny didn't look up from his plate. He shrugged.

"You want to come with me if I go away, right?" Michelle prompted.

Kenny nodded. Michelle and Justin sat looking at him.

"Do you understand what that means?" Justin asked.

Kenny didn't answer.

Justin went back to feeding Marcie, silent.

"I'd like to talk to the children separately," the social worker told Justin. She was on the short side, with tousled blond hair and a tough face.

"Marcie can't talk. Besides, she'll be staying with me. Kenny won't talk to you. But you are welcome to talk to Michelle."

Marsden looked at Marcie in her wheelchair and discounted her. She looked at Kenny and Michelle. "I'll talk to the boy first," she challenged.

She took him by the arm and led him into the conference room. She sat him down in a chair across from her. "So how are you, Kenny?"

He shrugged and didn't say anything.

"Why don't you tell me why you don't want to live with your mom anymore," Marsden suggested.

He didn't make any response.

"Do you want to go with Michelle?"

He nodded.

"Why do you want to go with Michelle? Is that what your daddy told you to say?"

She expected him to shake his head, but he didn't do anything. He just sat there looking at his feet.

"Does your mom hit you, Kenny?"

Again there was no response. His head sank lower. His eyes didn't leave his feet.

Marsden tried approaching it from several angles, but got no response. She abandoned the topic and tried to engage him in a casual conversation about himself or his interests. But Kenny just sat there as still as a statue, not looking at her. Eventually, Marsden gave up. She took Kenny back out to his father and motioned to Michelle.

"Come with me, honey."

Michelle followed her. She sat down in the chair, shifting uncomfortably.

"So maybe you can tell me why you don't want to stay at home anymore."

Michelle looked around. "I'd like it if Daddy was there. Mama's okay when he is. But he's not home very much. He's a trucker."

"Yes, he is. Why don't you want to stay with just your mom?"

Michelle looked down at her hands and scratched at the arm of the chair. "Mama can't take good care of us," she said cautiously.

"Why not?"

"She gets mad... and then she gets mean to Kenny."

"What does she do to Kenny?"

Michelle bit her lip. "Sometimes when he gets in trouble at school she hits him."

"Is that what your dad told you to say?"

"No. She doesn't do it when he's home."

"Does she spank him or hit him hard?"

Michelle shrugged. "Hard."

"Does she 'get mean' to you too?"

Marsden held her gaze and Michelle looked away from her. "Uh-huh."

"What does she get mad at you for?"

"Sometimes... I forget to help with dinner... or I try to stop her from getting mean to Kenny."

Marsden nodded. "Okay, Michelle."

"I get into trouble at school too, sometimes," Michelle added, "because I talk too much. The teachers say I'm disruptive."

"Okay. Let's go back out and see your dad."

CHAPTER Two

"Why are you taking away my kids?" June screamed, holding onto Kenny so no one could take him.

"Mrs. Simpson, there are allegations of abuse. We have to respond to them."

"I wouldn't hurt my kids!"

"Come on, Kenny," Marsden encouraged.

Kenny didn't move, looking at his mother, scared.

"Michelle."

Michelle looked at Marsden, who motioned for her to come over. Michelle went over to Kenny and took him by the hand. Kenny refused to move and June didn't let go. Michelle went over to Marsden without him and stood by her.

Justin pulled Kenny away from June and picked him up.

"Justin, you can't let her take them away," June insisted.

"June. It's okay. It'll be okay."

Kenny started to cry.

"He wants me, you can't take him away," June wailed. She tried to take Kenny back again. Kenny shook his head. Marsden took Michelle by the hand and took her out of the apartment and down to her car. Michelle obediently climbed into the car and buckled her seatbelt. Justin followed them out of the building with Kenny, who was still crying. He put Kenny down on the seat and buckled him in.

"Goodbye, guys. You be good," he said huskily.

Michelle held Kenny's hand and bit her lip, trying to hold back the tears welling up in her eyes. "Where's Marcie?"

"Marcie's with a friend for a couple of hours. I didn't want her to be in the way for this."

"I didn't get to say goodbye to her." There was a hard, hot lump in her throat that she couldn't swallow.

"I'll tell her for you. You be good, okay?"

"I will."

"Okay. Bye, sweetie."

Michelle was fighting for composure. "Daddy, you'll come see us? Right?"

"I love you, honey. You look out for your brother?"

"I will."

"I'll be in touch, Mr. Simpson," Marsden advised. Justin closed the door of the car and watched them leave.

Justin kissed June gently. "I have to go, sweetie. I have to work."

"Why did you let them take my babies?" she wept.

Justin hugged her. "I had to, June. They asked to be taken away. You were hurting them."

"I wasn't hurting them."

"I saw the bruises, honey. I know you hurt them. It's not your fault; you never had a good example of parenting. You don't know how to be a good mom."

"I'll change, Justy. I will. I just need a little help."

Justin winced at her use of the old nickname. It still made him feel guilty and protective of her. "June. Listen. They haven't started looking at our background yet. They just talked to me and the kids. But they will look into our backgrounds. You should find a new place before they come by asking more questions again."

"Where are we going to move to?"

"You can move wherever you want. Just take what you need. They might come back for some of the kids' stuff."

"Some of your stuff too?" June suggested.

"I've already got everything I need for me and Marcie in the truck. Just take what you need."

"We have to decide where to go."

Justin put his hand on her arm, trying to make himself clear. "I'm going to leave right now. I got a long run to do. I'll be back in a week, but you should probably move tomorrow early."

"How will you know where I move to?"

"I won't."

She stared at him. "How will you find me?"

"I'm not going to find you. We're going to say goodbye and go our separate directions."

Her face was pale and pinched as she finally understood his meaning. "You can't."

"It's time, June... It's time," he couldn't think of what else to say.

"No. Justy, I can't live without you."

"You can. You do most of the time already. You won't have to worry about taking care of anyone else but yourself."

"Don't leave me alone, Justy."

He kissed her, turned and walked out.

"Justin!" June called out, agonized. He tried to keep going and not be deterred by her desperate plea. "Justy, I'm pregnant."

Justin stopped. He turned and looked at her. June had become pregnant at key points during their relationship. Times he had become compelled to stay with her.

"If you're pregnant, it's not with my baby."

June just stood there looking at him. Justin turned away again and didn't look back.

Marsden knocked on the door but there was no answer. She looked at her watch, frowning. According to Justin and the children, June rarely went out, practically a recluse. Marsden rang the doorbell again. There was no response. Eventually, she gave up and went to her next few appointments.

She returned later on in the day, late in the afternoon. There was still no answer. Marsden called the police on her cell phone. An officer arrived a while later and talked to the landlord to get a key.

The officer knocked on the door a couple of times. He didn't expect an answer and didn't get one. He unlocked the door. Marsden thanked him and entered. It looked pretty much the same as it had when Marsden had taken the children the day before. She looked around the apartment quickly. Michelle said that Kenny had to have his teddy bear. Just a tattered old puppet, but one of those things that kids get attached to and can't change houses without. She found it in the bedroom and glanced around to see if there was anything else she should pick up.

"Miss Marsden?"

"Just a moment."

She heard the policeman talking and left the room to see what was going on. It wasn't until then she realized that they weren't alone in the apartment. The officer was talking into his radio and looking down at June, who was lying on her bed. Marsden hurried over.

"Is she okay?" she asked breathlessly.

He nodded. Marsden bent over and looked at her. June was breathing. Conscious even, her wide eyes red and bloodshot.

"Mrs. Simpson? Are you okay?"

June just turned away from her, still crying.

"I was afraid," Marsden said, "I had a mom once who killed herself when we removed her kids."

He nodded. "I called for an ambulance."

They said little while they stood there waiting. June suffered in silence.

It was late when Marsden made it to the house to see Michelle and Kenny. Mrs. Antonio let her in and directed her to the family room, where Michelle and Kenny cuddled together like two hostages in front of the TV. Kenny brightened a little when she handed him the teddy. Marsden was surprised that at ten he still needed it. But it was the first time he'd been away from home and Marsden was beginning to wonder about his mental abilities. Kids didn't fail grades in elementary school for no reason at all. Maybe it was the pressure of the situation at home, or maybe it was a developmental problem. He'd cried when he was taken away too. She hadn't heard him say a word yet.

"How's it going?" Marsden asked Michelle.

"Okay."

"Good. I brought you a few things too."

"Thank you."

Marsden struggled with what she should say about June, but decided that now was not the time. She ruffled Kenny's hair and went to talk with Mrs. Antonio.

"Has Kenny been okay?"

Mrs. Antonio shrugged. "Hard to tell. He's been quiet. Doesn't talk to anyone."

"Except Michelle."

"I guess. I haven't heard him say a word yet."

"I talked to the school on Friday, so they'll be expecting the kids tomorrow. I think I'm going to see if I can have them do some educational testing on Kenny, too."

"He doesn't follow instructions. I don't know if it's just because he doesn't know me, or what."

"Hopefully he'll open up a little once he gets used to the situation. Give me a call if anything comes up."

Michelle was glad that Marsden had found Kenny's puppet for him. Starting at a new school wasn't going to be easy for him. They had started at new schools before, they moved pretty often. The other kids always made fun of Kenny because he was sort of slow and didn't talk much. And Kenny defended himself the only way he knew—with his fists.

Kenny didn't usually go to bed that early, usually he stayed up late watching TV. But Mr. and Mrs. Antonio took him to bed even though he didn't pay attention to their instructions. Michelle lay in bed reading while they put him to bed in the other room. Then they came in to say goodnight to her.

"You all tucked in and ready to sleep, Michelle?"

"Yes."

"Ready to start school tomorrow?"

"I guess."

"You have a good sleep."

Michelle nodded.

"Okay, see you in the morning."

They left, and Michelle lay awake until they had gone to bed and were quiet. Then she went into Kenny's room.

She tiptoed into his room and crept over to the bed to see if he was still awake. Kenny's eyes were open and he clutched the puppet to his chest.

"Are you awake, Kenny?"

He nodded. Michelle sat down on the edge of the bed. "Do you want me to stay with you?"

He held her hand. Michelle lay down close to Kenny and closed her eyes, listening to his rapid heartbeat. Neither moved or said a word until they both fell asleep.

CHAPTER Three

Michelle's stomach was all queasy and her chest felt tight. When she had awakened in the morning, Kenny had been sucking his thumb in his sleep. He pulled it out when he woke up, but she knew he was stressed out too.

"School will be okay," she told him, knowing it wasn't true, "this one will be better. There's better schools here, 'cause people have more money."

He nodded, but his eyes were wide and scared. Neither of them could get much down at breakfast. They didn't normally eat breakfast anyway. Mrs. Antonio drove them to the school. Next time they would have to take the school bus, but the first time she would drive them. They all went to the office to check in.

"They're both in grade three," Mrs. Antonio informed the administrator there.

"Are they twins?"

"No, Kenny's been kept back."

The woman looked down at Kenny. "Why?"

He didn't say anything.

"He should be in my class," Michelle told them, "we won't talk."

"We don't put siblings in the same class."

"It might be a good idea this time," Mrs. Antonio suggested, "at least to see how it works. If they cause problems, we can always split them up later."

The woman shook her head. "I'll have to talk to the principal about it."

Things were fine until recess. The teacher didn't make them stand at the front of the class and introduce themselves or answer questions. Michelle and Kenny just sat down where they were told and were quiet. But at recess they had to talk to the other kids. The teacher assigned them both buddies to be their friends and show them around. Kenny's buddy was Harold Baker and Michelle's was Stephanie Bridger. Michelle watched Harold take Kenny off in the other direction and tried to keep an eye on them. But Stephanie demanded her attention, wanting to know where she was from and why she had moved in the middle of the year; all the important details. Stephanie toured her around the school and playground, pointing out the places that were out-of-bounds and where they were allowed to play.

After recess, Kenny had a bloody nose and Harold was nowhere to be seen. Michelle's heart sank.

"Kenny, you know you aren't supposed to fight."

He shrugged and tried to stop the nosebleed with a tissue.

"You got in a fight?" Stephanie said in amazement, "On the first day?"

The bell rang and they were all supposed to be in their seats, but nobody wanted to settle down, they all wanted to know what had happened.

"Everybody quiet down and take your seats," Miss Pepper ordered. She looked over everybody. "Kenny Simpson. What's going on?"

"He got in a fight," Stephanie contributed, wide-eyed.

"Have you been to the office?"

Kenny nodded. Miss Pepper looked around for empty seats. "Harold—where is he?" Nobody answered. Miss Pepper zeroed in on Kenny. "Is that who you were fighting with?"

He shrugged and she took it as assent.

"Is he at the office?"

Kenny nodded.

"Don't you know how to speak?"

Kenny didn't respond. He tried to hide behind his desk and tissue, not wanting to be the object of scrutiny. She gave in and let it go.

"You can stay after class."

MICHELLE

"We have to take the bus," Michelle protested.

"Were you around when this was happening?"

"No."

"Don't you look after your brother?" she demanded.

"Yes."

"Well, next time make sure you keep him out of trouble. I'll call the Antonios and make sure they're here to pick you up after school."

Mrs. Antonio could not believe Kenny had gotten in trouble the first day of school. "What did you get into a fight over?" she asked.

"Leave him alone," Michelle pleaded.

"I'm not hurting Kenny. You can just let him answer."

"It's not Kenny's fault."

"Were you there?"

"No."

"Then you don't know what happened, do you?"

"I know," Michelle asserted.

"Michelle, would you go to your room while we talk to Kenny?" Mrs. Antonio tried to shoo her away.

Michelle shook her head and stood fast. "Just leave Kenny alone! It's not his fault."

"Michelle—to your room!"

"No!"

Mrs. Antonio grabbed Michelle by the arm and pushed her towards the bedroom. "Go to your room."

Michelle ran out of the room and went to her bedroom. She sat there waiting for the yelling and hitting to start. Everything was quiet. After a while, Michelle sat down with a new book and immersed herself in the pages.

Later, Mrs. Antonio came into the room. "It's suppertime, Michelle."

"Okay."

Michelle walked with her to the kitchen.

"I need you to stay out of it when I'm talking to Kenny, all right?

We can't have a good sense of discipline if you are always stepping in the middle."

Michelle looked at the table. There were not enough places set. "Who's not eating?"

"Kenny."

"Why not?"

"He won't talk about what happened at school. When he's ready to talk about it, he can have his supper."

"That's not fair!" Michelle was outraged.

"That's the rule."

"You're not fair! Kenny can't talk about it."

"I know you're used to protecting him, Michelle, but in the real world, Kenny is going to have to deal with these things like everyone else. He cannot be excused for fighting because he has trouble verbalizing. Sooner or later, he will have to answer for his own actions."

"The other kids pick on him and make fun because he's different."

"I'm waiting to hear it from Kenny, Michelle."

"You're not fair!"

"Wash your hands and sit down."

"No."

"I'm hearing that from you just a little too often, Michelle. Do what you're told."

Michelle left and went back to her room. If Kenny couldn't eat, she wouldn't either.

Mr. and Mrs. Antonio had dinner by themselves. Kenny didn't offer to explain himself and Michelle was on a self-imposed hunger strike. Kenny didn't stay in his room, preferring the familiar comfort of the TV. Michelle stayed in her room with the door shut.

After everyone was in bed, Michelle went in to talk to Kenny. "Are you okay, Kenny?"

He sat up. "I'm hungry."

Michelle nodded. It was not an unfamiliar thing. Sometimes June would go days and days without shopping, until there was nothing at all in the house to eat.

"I'll go find something," Michelle promised. She was hungry too. She tiptoed out into the hallway and waited and listened to see if anyone was around. The Antonios were quiet, gone to bed. Michelle slipped out to the kitchen and looked through the cupboards and fridge. A few minutes later, she was back in Kenny's room, her arms full of food. They sat in the dark filling their stomachs, and then lay down and went to sleep.

∼

"Maybe you can tell me this morning about your fight yesterday," Mrs. Antonio suggested to Kenny.

He just looked at her and shook his head.

"Sit down at the table, Kenny."

Michelle was watching and listening from the doorway.

"Can you tell me what the other boy said to you?" Mrs. Antonio prompted.

"No."

"He said something that bothered you, didn't he?"

Kenny nodded.

"Was he making fun of you?"

Kenny didn't answer.

"Tell me what he said, Kenny."

He shook his head.

"Leave him alone!" Michelle interrupted.

"Michelle," Mrs. Antonio said in exasperation.

"Kenny doesn't want to talk to you about it. He doesn't have to."

"I think you should stay out of this Michelle. Go up to your room."

∼

Marsden took the phone call from Mrs. Antonio and hung up slowly, thinking. Justin had insisted the kids be kept together. And of course, they always tried to keep siblings together. But sometimes, as Mrs. Antonio said, it was best for them to be separated, at least for a while. If Michelle was interfering with the Antonios' parenting of Kenny, they had to look after Kenny's interests. Marsden had already deduced Kenny was the more fragile of the two. Michelle's protectiveness bore that out.

Marsden opened her phone book and looked down the list of names.

After school, Marsden picked up Michelle and Kenny. Michelle was happy not to have to take the bus and put up with the other kids for another hour.

"I hear Kenny has been having some problems at school," Marsden commented.

"A little."

"Mrs. Antonio says you won't let her talk to Kenny about it."

"Kenny doesn't want to talk about it."

"Don't you think you should give Mrs. Antonio a chance to talk to him anyway?"

"I did. He didn't want to talk about it."

"Okay. Michelle—I'm going to put you with another family over the weekend and see how you guys do. It won't be permanent, but I think you might both need some of your own space until you get things sorted out. Okay?"

"But you're moving Kenny too, right?"

"No. I'm moving you and leaving Kenny with the Antonios. He'll be fine and you guys will still be going to school together, but I want you to have some time to yourself for a while."

"I don't want to go somewhere else."

"I know, Michelle. And I don't like to separate you guys. But I have to do it anyway. It will be okay."

"What if I'm really good? Please, can't I stay with Kenny?"

"This isn't just about you, Michelle. You should have let the Antonios take care of Kenny without interfering, but that's not the only reason you're being separated. I just think it is the best thing for now."

"I want to talk to Daddy."

"If you want to call the house and leave a message for him, you can. But he's working and there is no way for me to get ahold of him."

"Mama could find him."

Marsden sighed. "Your mom isn't feeling too good right now. She doesn't want to talk to us about your dad."

"Is she sick?"

"I guess she is, Michelle. She just can't help us out right now."

Michelle tried to think of what to do. That June was sick and not helping Social Services was no surprise. And Michelle didn't have to look after her this time, worrying about the groceries and the bills and dinner. But she knew Justin wouldn't just let them be separated like this.

"I want my daddy," she repeated.

"I'm sorry. He should call me when he gets back in town. But right now, I can't contact him."

Michelle sat back in her seat and looked at Kenny. He was staring out the window, apparently oblivious to their conversation.

CHAPTER
Four

Michelle packed her small bag slowly, not wanting to be finished. When she was done, Marsden would take her away and she might never see Kenny again. She desperately wanted to make them see what they were doing was wrong, but they just didn't understand. She couldn't make them see what they were doing. Marsden kept saying she was sorry, but that didn't stop her from taking Michelle off to a new home.

Eventually, when she didn't go downstairs with her bag, Marsden came up to get her. "Are you all packed?"

Michelle's eyes welled up with tears when she looked at her bag. "Don't take me away from my brother."

"It's not permanent. You'll see Kenny again in a few days."

Marsden took her by the hand and took her down the stairs, picking up Michelle's bag with her other hand. Michelle looked for Kenny. "Kenny, where are you?"

He came to see her a minute later. Michelle hugged him, tears running down her face. When Kenny saw she was crying, he burst into tears too. Marsden pulled them apart and took Michelle out to the car.

Marsden had said she would be on her own, to get things straightened out. But when Michelle got there, she found out she wasn't going to be on her own at all. The Lollers had five other kids, two of their own and three foster kids. She would be sharing a family and sharing a room with some of the other kids.

∼

Kenny eventually stopped crying and curled up in front of the TV, staring unblinkingly at the picture. He didn't eat supper. When it was time for bed, Mrs. Antonio went in and turned the TV off.

"No!"

"It's time for bed, Kenny."

"No!"

She reached out for his hand but Kenny didn't take it. Mrs. Antonio caught him by the arm to pull him to his feet. Kenny jerked back from her touch.

"The TV's off. It's time for you to be in bed. You can watch cartoons in the morning."

"No."

"No what?"

He looked at her for a moment without answering.

When she reached toward him, he slapped her hand. He was much stronger than she expected and it stung. When Mrs. Antonio tried to grab him to take him to his room, Kenny writhed away from her. He stayed on the couch, his face shielded by his arm, watching her for her next move. Mrs. Antonio saw his scared expression and tried to calm her anger. She sat down on the couch next to him.

"Kenny, we don't hit here. I won't hit you and I don't want you to hit me, either. If you're upset about something, you have to tell me with words, not hitting."

He watched her warily despite her words. Mrs. Antonio sighed. "Enough fooling around now. Let's go to bed."

"No."

"Why not?"

"I want Michelle," he said finally. It was the first time she had heard him speak more than one word since the kids had been dropped off there.

"Michelle had to go away for a little while. You'll see her in a few days. Okay?"

He shook his head. Mrs. Antonio put her hand gently on his arm. "Come on," she encouraged softly.

He struck out with his feet, knocking over the coffee table. Everything on it went spinning to the floor. Kenny darted away from her, anticipating a violent reaction.

"I want Michelle!"

Mrs. Antonio didn't go after him. He ran out of the room and Mrs. Antonio knelt down to pick things up. When she went down the hall, Kenny's bedroom door was shut. Mrs. Antonio decided it would be best to just leave him alone for the night.

In the morning, Mrs. Antonio found Kenny asleep in front of the quietly playing TV. Mrs. Antonio brushed the hair across Kenny's forehead. He stirred.

"Wake up, Kenny."

He opened his eyes and gazed at her for a few moments before any awareness entered his expression. "Where's Michelle?"

"Michelle isn't here. What do you want for breakfast?"

He shook his head and looked at the TV. His eyes focused in on it, tuning Mrs. Antonio out. She went to the kitchen and fixed a bowl of cereal for Kenny. She took it in to him, but Kenny wouldn't even look at it. He just kept watching TV and pretending not to see her.

Michelle looked for somewhere to read a book by herself. She couldn't read in the bedroom because one of the other girls had staked it out as her territory. The rest of the house was anything but peaceful. She didn't know where to go. She went outside to the backyard and sat on the pavement. It was cold, but she could live with it for a while. At least it was quiet.

She opened the book she had found in the study and started to read.

"How's Kenny been with Michelle gone?" Marsden asked.

"Not any easier to talk to. All he'll say is he wants Michelle. I'm hoping after a few days he'll loosen up."

"So he hasn't been able to talk to you yet?"

"No. How's Michelle doing?"

"Pretty withdrawn, from what I understand. Just goes off by herself to read. I don't want to keep them apart too long if we can help it."

"It's going to take a few days before Kenny gets used to the idea of being on his own."

"Okay. We'll let it go for a week or two and see if it helps communication."

"Sounds good. Have you had any contact with their father at all?"

"No. I haven't heard anything from him. I hope he'll contact us soon. Especially with mom in the hospital."

"Do the kids know about that?"

"I told Michelle she was sick. That's all."

Michelle hugged Kenny tightly when she saw him at school. She didn't hold him for long because she didn't want the other kids to make fun of them. When she pulled back, Michelle saw he was crying, his lip trembling. She wiped his face.

"Don't cry, Kenny. Don't cry around the other kids."

Kenny bit his lip, nodding. But one of the older kids had already seen. He was a dark blond, with longish, shaggy hair.

"Hey, cry baby, what's the matter?" he gestured to Michelle. "Little girl beating you up?"

Kenny rubbed his eyes.

"Come over here, baby. I'll give you something to cry about."

Michelle pushed Kenny in the other direction. "Don't listen to him," she told him, trying to get out of the situation. But Kenny resisted.

"He's bigger than you, Kenny. Come on."

"Listen to your girlfriend, cry baby."

"Stop it."

"Yeah? What are you going to do about it?" he shoved Kenny. Kenny kicked him in the shins. The other boy knocked him over. As he went down, Kenny managed a kick behind the knees and shortly they were both rolling on the ground trying to hurt each other. Michelle tried to get them apart, but only managed to get hit by both of them for her trouble. There were a couple of teachers there a few minutes later to do what Michelle could not and pull them apart

"What's going on here?"

"He started it," Michelle said, pointing to the other boy.

"Is that true?"

The boy didn't answer.

"Well, you can all go to the office and get detentions."

"I didn't do anything," Michelle protested.

"Tell it to the principal."

All three children were hustled to the office and sat outside of it in chairs along the wall. The older boy looked at Kenny.

"If you don't want to get beat up, you shouldn't cry." He looked at Michelle. "Or tattle."

"You should leave other kids alone," she retorted.

He grinned. "Wouldn't you rather have a boyfriend like me than like bawl baby here?"

"He's my brother."

"Oh," he smiled, pleased. "Then you *can* be my girlfriend."

Michelle snorted. "If I wanted to."

"You want to. All the girls do."

"You got a big head."

"Well, if you don't want the both of you to get beat up every day, you'll be my girl."

Michelle folded her arms across her chest. "I'd rather get beat up."

"I'm not so bad. You'll see. My name is Tanner."

"I'm Michelle."

Tanner looked at Kenny. "And...?"

"Kenny," Michelle advised.

"Kenny. Well, you're a decent fighter, Kenny. You start being a man instead of a baby and I might be interested."

"Interested in what?" Michelle demanded.
"Interested in recruiting him to my gang."
The principal opened the door and Tanner went in.

CHAPTER *Five*

Mrs. Loller picked Michelle up after school. The car was full of kids and Mrs. Loller looked tired. She sighed. "I guess you had some problems."

"It wasn't my fault. "

"Getting into a fight at school is not something you can blame on somebody else. What's up?"

"A kid was picking on Kenny."

"And how did you end up in a fight?"

"I was just trying to stop them."

"Well, I think you should try to just stay out of it next time. Okay?"

Michelle shook her head. "I take care of Kenny."

"Kenny is older than you, isn't he?"

"Yes."

"And bigger?"

"A little, but..."

"I think you should let Kenny fight his own fights," Mrs. Loller suggested.

"I take care of Kenny."

"I think you need to take care of yourself."

Michelle was quiet until they got home.

"You can stay in your room until supper," Mrs. Loller told her.

MICHELLE

Michelle went upstairs to the bedroom. One of the boys, Stan, came into the room a few minutes later.

"You get in trouble for fighting here," he commented.

"Yeah. I guess so."

"But they don't do anything about it. After a while you might get moved to another home."

Michelle shrugged. "I'm going to be back with my brother again soon anyway."

Stan chuckled. "Hah. Don't count on it. You'll probably not end up in the same foster home again."

"What do you mean?"

"You're really new at this, aren't you?" Stan grinned, shaking his head. "Once they split a family up, they don't put it back together again."

"They said it was temporary."

"Guess what? They lie to you 'cause it's easier than telling the truth."

Michelle stared down at her feet, her face getting hot. She looked for a book to read, ignoring Stan, and sat down to read it.

Mrs. Antonio tried everything she could think of to get Kenny to talk to her about the problems he was having at school. He wouldn't talk about anything, he wouldn't go to bed, and he wouldn't eat. He *would* tell her he wanted Michelle to come back, but that was about it.

Mr. Antonio thought he would give it a try. He didn't bring up Kenny's problems, didn't even ask him any questions; he just told Kenny they were going out together. Marsden couldn't tell him what any of Kenny's interests were. So Mr. Antonio just had to guess at what Kenny might like to do. He took Kenny to the theater for a movie, and then they went for a walk in the park and Mr. Antonio bought Kenny a hot dog.

"You like hot dogs?"

"Uh-huh."

"What else do you want to do today?"

Kenny glanced sideways at him. "Go to the zoo."

"Okay. Sure, we can do that."

"With Michelle," Kenny added, looking at him again.

"Well, we can't get Michelle to go with us. But you'll see her at school on Monday. Let's go to the zoo."

Kenny didn't eat more than a few bites of the hot dog. At the zoo, he watched the animals in silence. Mr. Antonio didn't try to talk to him. He just let Kenny think things through on his own. Kenny was somber and silent.

∽

Michelle tried several times to call Marsden before she was finally able to get through Sunday night.

"When am I going to go back with Kenny?" she demanded.

Marsden sighed. "Kenny isn't ready for you to go back there yet, Michelle."

"Kenny wants to be with me."

"He may want you, but he isn't settled in with the Antonios yet."

Michelle raised her voice. "You said it would just be for a few days, just the weekend!"

"Well, he needs more time than we thought he would." Marsden's voice was calm and measured.

"It's been more than a week."

"I know, Michelle. I'll get you back there as soon as possible. But that's not yet."

"You're never going to put me back, are you?"

"I promise we'll get you guys back together, Michelle. For now, at least you still see each other at school."

"It's not fair."

"You'll have to get used to life not being fair, honey. I'll do everything I can for you, but that won't always be enough."

"I used to have a family. Now I don't have anyone."

"You still have a family. You just can't all be together right now."

Michelle rolled her eyes, shaking her head. "Is my mom going to come visit me, like you said?"

"Your mom isn't feeling well right now. Maybe in a while."

Michelle considered this news. "Is she at home?"

"No... she's at the hospital." Marsden's reluctance to impart this information was clear. Michelle wondered how long she had known and not let Michelle know.

Michelle felt her stomach tie in knots. She hadn't felt sorry about June being sick. She had wondered if getting Social Services to take them away had been the right thing to do. But she hadn't worried about her mother. She was worried about herself and Kenny. June was the one who had wrecked their family. But if June was really sick—hospital sick—that wasn't like when she locked herself away in her room, refusing to talk to anyone.

"Is she really sick? She's going to get better, right?"

"Don't you worry, Michelle. You have yourself to worry about. Your mom will be fine." Marsden's words were intended to be soothing, but sounded flat and fake.

"When will I see my daddy again?"

"I don't know. How long is he usually out of town?"

Michelle thought about it. "A week or two... He should be home soon."

"Well, he should call me when he gets home. I'll tell him you want to talk to him."

Monday after school, Michelle tried to avoid Tanner but was unsuccessful. He placed himself in front of her, smiling. "Hi, Michelle."

"Leave me alone," she snapped.

"Come on, Michelle," he wheedled, "you got no other friends, why won't you talk to me?"

"I have other friends."

"I'm not talking about your brother."

Michelle glared at him. "I don't want to be your friend."

"You'll change your mind," Tanner assured.

"No, I won't."

But at recess the next day, instead of being by himself as usual, Kenny was with Tanner. Tanner grinned in satisfaction at Michelle's dismay.

"Kenny and me are best friends now, Michelle. So I guess you'll be hanging out on your own."

Michelle looked at Kenny. "Come on, Kenny. Let's go somewhere else."

"No."

Michelle looked at him, surprised. "Kenny, I don't want to hang around with this guy."

"I do."

Tanner looked smug. Michelle looked for something to say. She could go off and not be with them, but she didn't have anyone else to hang out with. Tanner just stood there grinning. Michelle looked at him.

"I'm hanging out with Kenny, not you."

He grinned and nodded. "You'll come around," he assured her, "I know women."

Michelle just glowered at him. He was eleven years old and he was already pretending he knew everything. When he got to be a teenager, he was going to be insufferable.

Tanner accompanied Kenny home after school. Mrs. Antonio looked them over. "Are you guys in the same grade?"

"No, I'm ahead of him," Tanner explained.

"Well," Mrs. Antonio said, not liking Kenny running with an older crowd, "maybe you could help Kenny work on his homework."

Tanner agreed. "Sure."

Mrs. Antonio nodded and left them alone. Tanner grinned at Kenny. "It's not going to happen," he said with a laugh, pushing the books to the side. "But if you tell them what they want to hear, they leave you alone a lot quicker."

Kenny looked at the books. "I'm going to fail," he worried.

Tanner waved this away, unconcerned. "Nah, they won't fail you here. They pass everyone."

"Yeah?"

"Yeah, don't worry about it."

Kenny nodded, still looking at the books with a frown.

MICHELLE

"Don't sweat it man," Tanner repeated. "Listen, I need your help. Will you give me a hand?"

"Uh-huh."

"I want to know more about your sister. What she likes and all."

Kenny shrugged.

"What's she like to do?" Tanner persisted.

"Read."

"She likes to read?"

"Yeah."

"She's a real smart chick, isn't she?"

Kenny nodded.

"Yeah. I know girls like that." Tanner said meditatively. "I got a few ideas for your sister. What do you think, you think me and Michelle will make a good couple?"

"Sure," Kenny said.

Michelle kept looking for Kenny, but he didn't come into the classroom. She couldn't sit still the rest of the morning, wondering where he was and what had happened. Kenny couldn't afford to miss any school. Michelle was already worried about whether he would be kept back again. With him in the same grade, she could help him keep up. But if he were held back again, he might even get put in a special school. Then she would never see him.

At recess, she convinced one of the teachers to find the Antonios' phone number so she could find out what had happened. Mrs. Antonio answered the phone.

"It's Michelle. Where's Kenny? Is he sick?"

"Oh, hi Michelle. Kenny got hurt and had to come back home."

Michelle got a stabbing pain in her chest. "Hurt? How'd he get hurt?"

"Don't you worry about it. He'll be just fine. He's just lying down."

Michelle hung up the phone. She went outside for recess, her eyes burning and her thoughts whirling.

Tanner sought her out. "Hey, Michelle. How's it going?"

"Kenny's foster mom says he got hurt and had to go home."

"Yeah," he nodded. "I heard about it."

"You did? How'd you hear about it?"

"I heard from my boys."

"Your boys?"

"Like I told you before. In my gang."

"How did they know?"

"I know any time anyone in this school gets beat up."

"He got beaten up?" Michelle repeated. She had assumed he had fallen or cut himself or something like that.

"Sure, what did you expect? He's the kind of kid that gets beat up all the time."

"No. Kenny's strong, he's a good fighter."

"Not against a crowd, he's not." Tanner watched Michelle's expression. "If you want to fight a crowd, you got to have a crowd on your side. Like my gang."

"Then why didn't you help him?"

Tanner shrugged. "I like Kenny... But I got to have a better reason for getting into a fight with one of the other gangs than just liking a guy."

"Like what?"

Tanner shrugged and grinned, and walked away. Michelle watched him go, confused. She left the playground and caught the city bus to the Antonios' house. Mrs. Antonio answered the door.

"Michelle! What are you doing here? You're supposed to be at school."

"I want to see Kenny."

"Well, you can come in for a minute, but you have to go right back to school."

"I have to take care of Kenny."

Michelle went into the house and to Kenny's bedroom. He was lying in bed and turned towards her when she opened the door.

"Misselle."

He used to lisp when they were little. Michelle sat down on the edge of the bed and touched his cheek, looking at his swollen face. One of his front teeth had been knocked out.

"Are you okay, Kenny?"

He nodded. Michelle held his hand. "Why did they hurt you?"

He didn't say anything. Michelle just looked at him. Mrs. Antonio came into the room. "Say bye, Michelle, you have to get back to school."

"I want to stay with Kenny."

"Kenny should rest. Come on."

Michelle went reluctantly. Mrs. Antonio drove her back to school.

At lunch, Michelle ate by herself because she didn't have any friends at school other than Kenny. Part way through the lunch hour, Tanner came over with his arms full of schoolbooks.

"Hey Michelle, how's it going?"

Michelle gave a small shrug and looked down.

"Hey listen, you're good at school, right? Kenny said you're real smart."

"I do okay."

"You think you could help me with my homework? I'm gonna get kicked out if I don't hand something in."

Michelle looked at his books. "What are you doing?"

"Whatever you're good at. I'm behind in everything."

"Okay. English."

Tanner dumped his books on the table. "I got a book report to do. You wanna help me?"

"Okay."

"Great," Tanner enthused. "I owe you one."

Michelle took Kenny's books home to him after school. Mrs. Antonio called Mrs. Loller to tell her Michelle was going to stay there for supper and help Kenny with the day's schoolwork. Michelle went up to Kenny's room and went through the homework with him, telling him the answers. She had been there for a while when Tanner showed up.

"Hey, Michelle. How's it going, Kenny?" He saw Kenny's face and whistled. "They did a real number on your face, didn't they?"

Kenny nodded, fingering the bruises on his face. Tanner sat down on the bed, like Michelle. "Thanks for helpin' with my homework today, Michelle."

Michelle nodded. "Yeah, whatever."

"Say, tell ya what. You keep doin' my homework with me and I'll bring Kenny into my gang. We'll make sure this doesn't happen again."

Michelle hesitated. She looked at Kenny and the bruises on his face. "I—I guess."

"I knew you would. You're a smart chick."

Michelle scowled. She didn't like agreeing to spend any more time with Tanner, but she did want to protect Kenny. He was her responsibility and she couldn't protect him from schoolyard gangs. Only another gang could do that.

"You and me will get to know each other," Tanner said. "Pretty soon, we'll be real good friends."

"Don't count on it."

Tanner grinned. "I like a challenge."

Michelle stayed until Mrs. Loller came to the house to get her.

CHAPTER Six

Marsden opened the door and looked around the apartment to see if anything had been disturbed. Nothing looked like it had been touched since they had taken June away from there when she had gone back for Kenny's teddy. Justin had not returned from his last run. Marsden went to the school and pulled Michelle out of her class.

"I need some help from you, Michelle."

Michelle shifted nervously. "Okay."

"I need to know how I can get in touch with your Daddy. Where would he go if he was not at home and not at work?"

Michelle looked at her, biting her lip. "Do you think something happened to him? Do you think he got hurt?"

"I think he's just gone somewhere other than home. Do you know where he might go?"

Michelle thought about it for a long time. "He has a friend," she said finally.

"It would be really helpful if you could tell me something about him."

"Her," Michelle corrected, "it's a girlfriend."

Somehow, Marsden had expected this. "Can you tell me where this girlfriend lives?"

"No. I've only been there a couple times. I don't know how to get there."

"What's her name?"

"Sondra."

"Do you know her last name?"

"No." Michelle shook her head.

"Do you know anything about Sondra? Where she works?"

"No."

"I'm hoping that's where your dad would go if your mom wasn't home. You'd like to talk to him, wouldn't you?"

"Yeah. I have her phone number," Michelle said finally.

"You have Sondra's phone number? Why didn't you tell me that right away?"

"Daddy said I can't give it to anyone."

"I think it be okay in an emergency, don't you? Your mom is sick and we need to talk to your dad about you and Kenny."

"I guess... but you can't tell Mama."

"I won't," Marsden promised.

"I have her number in my book. I don't have it memorized."

"Okay. You give me a call when you get home and give it to me, okay?" Michelle nodded. "You have my number, right?"

"I have it in my book."

"Okay. Call me as soon as you get home and I will see if I can track your daddy down."

Rather than calling Sondra and tipping her off they were looking for Justin, Marsden looked up the address in a reverse directory and went to her apartment.

There was no answer. She went back downstairs and eventually tracked down the manager.

"I'm with Social Services. I'm looking for Sondra Goering in three-oh-one."

He looked Marsden over. "Is she in trouble?"

"No. I'm just trying to track down a friend of hers."

"Who, the boyfriend?"

"Yes."

"Well, you're out of luck. Miss Goering moved out two days ago."

"Forwarding address?"

"Didn't give me one. Sorry."

"Well, I guess I don't need anything else from you."

"The boyfriend was with her. Him and the one kid. The handicapped one."

"He helped her move?"

"Yup."

"Did they leave anything behind? Anything at all?"

"No. Cleaned out really well. Nothing left."

Marsden nodded. "They didn't mention where they were going? In the city? Another city?"

"They didn't say anything. Sorry."

"Okay. Thanks for your help."

She shook hands and turned to go. But he wasn't ready to end the conversation. "Are you here about the other kids?"

"You know the other kids?"

"Sure. Kenny and Michelle. They were here all the time when Justin was in town."

"All the time?" Marsden repeated.

He considered. "Once every two weeks or so. Not every time Justin was here, but still pretty regularly."

Marsden nodded. "How did he behave around the kids? Were they happy to be with him?"

"I didn't usually talk to them. I just saw them occasionally. They didn't seem to mind being with him."

"He was never rough with them?"

"No, not that I ever saw. Never had any complaints from anyone in the other apartments."

"Did they ever talk to you about their mother?"

"No."

"And you never saw her."

"Oh, no. Never."

~

Michelle sat down when Marsden told her to sit, wondering what was going on. Marsden usually smiled at her reassuringly and asked her how she was, but today she looked serious, a frown line between her eyebrows.

"I think you lied to me, Michelle."

"No, I never—"

"You told me you didn't know where Sondra lived because you'd only been there a couple times."

"Uh-huh."

"But you've been to Sondra's apartment plenty of times."

"No!"

"The building manager says you were there every couple of weeks for the last few years."

Michelle swallowed. She hadn't thought about there being anyone to disprove her story.

"So you lied to me, didn't you Michelle?"

She stared at her shoes. "I guess so."

"I want you to tell me the truth now."

"I've been there before."

"Have you talked to Sondra since you've been in foster care?"

"No."

"I want the truth, Michelle. I'll find out if you lie to me."

Michelle tried to figure out what to tell her. "I called her to see if my Daddy was there."

"And what did you find out?"

"She said if Daddy got there, she would tell him to call me."

"And have you talked to your dad?"

"No."

"Are you telling me the truth?"

"Yes."

"Michelle, I want you to look at me."

Michelle looked up, having difficulty meeting her eyes.

"Did Sondra tell you she was moving?"

"No."

"I think she did."

"No, she didn't."

"Did she give you her new address or phone number?"

"No."

"Where were they moving to?"

"I don't know."

"Don't you want to talk to your daddy?"

MICHELLE

"Yes." Tears sparkled in Michelle's eyes. "But I don't know how to call him."

"Do you have his work number?"

"He drives a truck; he doesn't have a work number."

"No cell phone? I don't want you to lie to me anymore, Michelle."

Michelle nodded. "I know."

"I don't want to find out you've been lying to me when I'm trying to help you."

"I'm sorry."

"Okay."

∼

Even less pleasant for Marsden than confronting Michelle about her lies was the job of talking to June at the hospital.

"I want to see my kids again," June insisted.

"I know you do, June, but I don't think you want the kids to see you in this kind of shape."

"I want my babies."

"I want to talk to you about Justin, June," Marsden tried to redirect her.

"I want to see Justin."

"Do you know where I could find Justin?"

"He said he wasn't going to come back again." June started to cry.

"Justin told you he wasn't going to come back?" Marsden repeated.

"He said—he wouldn't need me to tell him where I moved to. He wouldn't see me again."

"You were going to move?"

"We always move if there might be trouble."

"So Justin never intended to contact the kids again?"

"I don't know. Where are my babies?"

June dissolved once more into tears and Marsden took her leave.

CHAPTER Seven

Kenny sat in class watching the teacher write on the board. He rubbed his bruised cheek, thinking about Tanner's gang. He knew Michelle didn't like Tanner, but Kenny didn't make friends easily. Someone treating him like he was important was not a common occurrence.

The teacher looked over the class to find someone to answer her question. She looked at him. "Kenny?"

Kenny slid further down in his seat. "I dunno," he said, almost too quiet to hear.

"Have you been listening?"

"Yeah."

"What are we talking about?"

Kenny looked away, unable to answer. He looked at the board, but couldn't read it. He shook his head. The teacher sighed. "If you want to keep up, you have to listen. Stay after school."

Kenny put his head down. Michelle turned around and looked at him. Kenny looked away from her.

∼

"You ready to go?" Tanner asked Michelle, waiting for her after school let out.

Michelle shook her head. "I have to wait for Kenny."

"He'll catch up to us."

"He won't know where we went."

"You're not his mama. Come on."

"He'll probably just be a few minutes. I gotta wait."

Tanner shook his head. "Would you wait for me if I was staying after?"

Michelle shook her head definitely. "No."

He laughed. "Well, let me tell the other guys I'll be a few minutes."

"You're going to wait?"

"You can tutor me while we're waiting." Tanner grinned and left to talk to his boys. When he got back, he sat on the pavement next to Michelle to study.

Michelle had been worried about the 'gang,' but the first day they just talked and watched TV. She had worried they would be getting into trouble. They talked tough, but she didn't think they would actually do anything.

Tanner kept sitting down next to her and moving up close. Michelle kept moving away from him. He just laughed and would do it again a few minutes later.

It occurred to Michelle as the evening wore on that she should call the Lollers so they wouldn't wonder where she was. She found the phone and called them. "I forgot to tell you I was coming to a friend's house," Michelle apologized. "It's okay, though, right?"

"We've been worried about you, Michelle. You should have called us sooner."

"Yeah, I forgot."

"Is Kenny with you? The Antonios were looking for him too."

"Yeah. Do you want to call them back? I don't know their number."

"Okay, but Kenny should call them too to make sure."

"I'll be home in a little while. We already did our homework."

"Okay. Don't be long."

Mrs. Antonio looked out the window, watching for Kenny. He was out later and later now. They hadn't given him a curfew because they liked to think they could be reasonable and help him set his own limits. But Kenny wasn't catching on. Or maybe he had determined that as long as he kept a good attitude, he could get away with pretty much anything.

Pretty soon something was going to have to change. They were going to have to put their feet down on what rules Kenny had to operate under. He never argued with them. And if they told him to come home earlier, he would come home earlier for a few days, and then slip back again gradually. He rarely called to say he was going somewhere after school. Occasionally Michelle called.

At least Michelle was more mature than Kenny, and would, Mrs. Antonio hoped, look out for him. Although she wished Kenny would develop his own friendships separately from Michelle, she couldn't see how their closeness could be a bad thing. As long as Michelle wasn't in the same home to interfere with his discipline.

Kenny got home long after dark and Mrs. Antonio sent her husband to talk to him this time.

"You're pretty late getting in, aren't you buddy?" Mr. Antonio asked.

Kenny shrugged, pulling off his jacket and hanging it up. "I guess."

"Do you know what time it is?"

"No."

"It's after ten."

"Oh. Sorry," Kenny said automatically, his voice flat.

"Where were you?"

"With Michelle."

"Both of you should be in bed before now, especially on a school night."

He nodded. "Okay."

"You'll be home earlier tomorrow?"

"Yeah."

"Good. You'd better scoot off to bed."

Kenny nodded and went to his room. Mr. Antonio went back to his wife.

"Did you tell him he was out too late?"

"Yes."

"And...?"

"He did everything right, except for convincing me he was sincere."

Mrs. Antonio sighed. "Maybe we would get further if we talked to Michelle."

~

The gang gathered at Tanner's house, noisy and restless after a long day at school. Michelle looked for a place to sit down where Tanner couldn't squeeze in beside her.

"Hey, look what I got," Tanner said, brandishing a bottle.

Some of the boys were impressed, but Michelle shrugged. "So what?"

"It's booze, stupid. You can't exactly just buy it at the corner store."

"I know what it is."

Tanner glared at her. "So you want some, Miss Sophistication?"

Michelle shrugged. "I don't like the taste."

"You've never drank it before."

"Sure I have. Mama was always drinking. Ask Kenny."

Tanner looked at Kenny, who nodded. Tanner swaggered. "Well, I've had it before too. I just didn't think you two goody-two-shoes would have."

"Are you going to open it?" Reggie demanded. "Or just stand around talking about it?"

Without further bravado, Tanner opened the bottle and took a swig. He tried to keep from grimacing and passed it on. Everybody tried to act like it wasn't the first time they'd tasted alcohol, but most of them didn't pull it off like Kenny and Michelle did. The first time the bottle went around; everyone had a taste to see what it was like. The second time Tanner got it, he tried to take a longer drag on the bottle but put it back down sputtering and coughing.

"Hey, show him how it's done, Kenny," one of the boys suggested, laughing.

Kenny took the bottle and tipped it up, swallowing a few mouthfuls.

"Slow down, Kenny," Michelle warned.

He put it down and grinned at her. The bottle was passed on to someone else.

"It just went down the wrong way," Tanner protested, not wanting them to think he couldn't handle the alcohol. "Give it here."

This time, he took it slowly and managed to suppress his natural reaction. He smiled triumphantly. "See, what did I tell you?" No-one seemed particularly impressed. Tanner tried to distract their attention. "So are you as good a drinker as your brother?" he asked Michelle.

"I told you I don't like the taste that much."

"Well, it isn't the *taste* you drink it for."

Michelle shrugged. Tanner passed her the bottle again.

Michelle knew after the first few months that Justin wasn't going to come back. But she still hoped he would. Marsden said June didn't want to see them yet. She was still sick and had to 'sort things out.' Michelle didn't particularly want to see June again. She knew she should love her mother and want to see her again, but she didn't. Even when they were tiny, she couldn't remember loving June. She loved her daddy, even though he was home so rarely, but she didn't know why June had gone and had three babies she never cared for. June hit, yelled at, and ignored them, and Michelle felt no attachment whatever to her. If she'd been a good mom, Justin wouldn't be gone. And Kenny and Michelle wouldn't be separated.

All the same, she knew she was supposed to love her mother even if June was mean to her.

She also knew, after the first few weeks of separation, that what Stan told her was true; Marsden never had any intention of putting her back with Kenny again. They would never again be a real family.

Stan had been in foster care since he was younger than Michelle, so he really knew the ropes and could tell her a lot of things. If she were home after school or on a weekend—which was seldom—he would come into her room and talk to her, telling her how it was. It was good to have someone who would be honest with her and show her the ropes. She couldn't trust adults.

MICHELLE

∼

Michelle and Kenny had each celebrated a birthday in foster care. Then it was summer vacation, and they got a break from the daily grind of school. Until the Antonios decided that Kenny might be helped by summer school. Michelle was horrified.

"They can't make him go to school in the summer!" she protested to Marsden.

"They can and I think it's a good idea. It will help him to get ahead, improve his marks."

"Kenny's not good at school. Summer school's just going to make him feel stupid."

"It was go to summer school or fail the grade. How do you think *that* would make him feel?"

"They wouldn't keep him back again. He's too old."

"Kenny could still end up in a special school if summer school doesn't help him. I am hoping that this will work. But if it doesn't, then there is no reason to keep him in a system where he cannot succeed."

"That's stupid," Michelle snapped. "You don't know what you're talking about."

"Michelle, you watch your mouth. I'm talking to you like another adult because you are a bright girl and I know you want what is best for your brother. I want you to feel like you are part of Kenny's life, but you cannot control his life."

Michelle hated having someone else in control. She took care of Kenny and didn't like anyone else making decisions for them. And Kenny didn't like school and shouldn't have to be subjected to it during the summer when he was supposed to have a break.

"You don't know what's best for Kenny. I do," Michelle asserted.

"Well, you can tell me your opinion, but I don't have to follow it. I am responsible for you. I have to answer for what happens to you."

"You don't know anything."

∼

"When's Kenny get back from school?" Tanner questioned, flashing his brand new watch.

"Four o'clock."

"Well, let's go walk to his place. He'll be back pretty soon. You can do his homework so he can come out with us."

Michelle shrugged. They caught the bus a block from Tanner's house and rode it there. After school started up again, Tanner would be in a different school, in middle school. Michelle hoped that meant they wouldn't see him anymore, or at least not as much.

"You could be in middle school if you wanted to, you know," Tanner commented.

Michelle stared at him. "What?"

"You don't have any trouble with the work that I do. You could skip ahead to seventh grade no trouble."

He had to be crazy. "Why would I skip three grades?"

"Well, no reason to. I'm just saying you could. You know more than I do."

"That isn't hard. I know more than the teachers, too."

Tanner laughed. "Well, you're modest!"

Michelle didn't laugh. Tanner looked at her with an odd expression. "You serious?"

"Yeah."

"How do you know that?"

Michelle shrugged. "They take a long time to answer questions. They don't know how to do stuff."

"That's just 'cause they're trying to explain things to the rest of us morons."

"I know more," Michelle repeated.

"Well, I ain't gonna argue with you. You're smarter than I'll ever be."

"Yeah."

Kenny threw his books down on the bed angrily.

"What's the matter?" Michelle asked, sorting through them to see what he had to do.

"School's dumb."

"Yeah, I know."

"I want a break."

"Why don't you fake sick tomorrow?"

"I want more than just a day."

Michelle started scribbling down answers in his books. "Well, they're not going to give it to you."

Kenny rifled through his drawers and pulled out the camping canteen Justin gave him for his sixth birthday. He took a drink.

"Give me a swig," Tanner commanded. Kenny gave it to him. Michelle looked at them disapprovingly.

"Don't drink here. You'll get caught."

"How long are you going to be with that stuff?" Tanner asked, drinking anyway.

"I don't know. Half an hour."

Tanner screwed the cap back onto the canteen. "All right. Just don't be long."

Michelle scowled. "You bug me and you're going to be doing it."

"Okay, okay. Let the genius work."

He and Kenny sat down at the other side of the room to talk while Michelle worked on the homework.

CHAPTER
Eight

The Lollers were out and Michelle went to talk to Stan. He was watching TV. Michelle sat down beside him.

"Hey, how's it going?" Stan questioned.

"Okay."

"Wish the summer lasted forever, huh?"

They'd been back at school for a couple weeks. Michelle and Kenny weren't in the same class again, so the only time they saw each other was after school and on weekends. And then Tanner was usually there, if not the whole gang.

"Yeah," Michelle agreed, "I hate school."

"Don't know why. You get A's without even trying."

Michelle shrugged.

"I like school okay," Stan said, grinning. He was always getting in trouble for bad marks or not getting along with his teachers. "But it isn't 'cause I get good marks."

"What do you like?" Michelle asked.

"I like the social aspect." Stan smiled at Michelle like he'd told her a joke.

"Your friends you mean?"

"I mean the girls."

"Oh."

He looked at her out of the corner of his eye. "Although I got a pretty good-looking chick right here in the house," he said.

"Who?" Michelle asked, thinking about the younger girls. She and Stan, and Joey, who was between them in age, were the oldest. The twins were six and the Lollers' own kids were just small.

"You. You think nobody noticed?"

Michelle had been watching the changes in her body with interest. She wore bigger clothes to hide her developing figure because none of the other girls in her class were changing yet. She felt awkward, but pleased too. Stan was so much older than she was that she hadn't expected him to notice.

"I'm not that good-looking," she protested.

"Sure you are. You telling me the boys at school haven't noticed yet?"

Michelle shook her head. "They haven't said."

"Well, they will before long." He put his arm around her shoulders. "You're going to have them swarming around you."

"You think I'm good-looking?" she repeated.

Stan studied her. He held her face in his hands and kissed her wetly on the lips. "Does that answer your question?"

Michelle's heart was racing. She looked at Stan in a new light. She hadn't expected that sort of attention from anyone. She and Stan sat there looking at each other, trying to determine their next move.

Neither said anything. Stan leaned forward and kissed her again. Michelle kissed back tentatively. Stan wrapped his arms around her and pulled her close. A moment later, Michelle was flat on her back on the couch, his weight on her. Michelle breathed harder, curious and enjoying the encounter.

Then Stan's manner changed. His hands grew rough as he clawed at her, his movements tense and jerky. Michelle stopped kissing him back, scared, but Stan went on. One hand went under her shirt and his clumsy groping hurt her. Michelle squirmed and pushed his hand away. Stan used both hands to swiftly undo her jeans.

"Don't," Michelle protested, pushing his hands away. She saw, with surprise, that he already had his fly undone. Stan tried to get his hand into her panties and Michelle wasn't strong enough to pry it away. She turned her hips and flipped him off the couch.

Stan crashed onto the floor and Michelle zipped up her pants. Before he could protest, she ran to her room and shut the door.

Michelle wasn't sure what to do after that. She still didn't want to go out with the Lollers and the younger kids when they had to go places. But she wasn't so comfortable staying alone with Stan. She went to be with Kenny more often, even though it meant that she had to be with Tanner and the rest of the gang. Kenny was getting into fights at school again, even though some of the gang was still in the school and hadn't moved up to middle school with Tanner. It was well known around the school that Kenny was a little bit slow and easily provoked into a fight.

He didn't always lose, though. Kenny was a naturally good fighter and Tanner spent time teaching him some dirty moves to defend himself.

"It ain't like you're boxing and gotta follow some set of rules," Tanner instructed. "There isn't any referee who's going to penalize you for hitting below the belt or pokin' someone in the eye. You get in a street fight or rumble and the other guy can expect dirty fighting."

Kenny nodded, shifting from one foot to the other, hands ready for when Tanner decided to stop talking and start sparring.

"Okay," he agreed.

"You hit him where you know it's gonna hurt. Privates, knees, eyes, whatever you can. He can't guard or cover them all at the same time."

Kenny feinted a kick at Tanner's knee and when Tanner turned to guard it, shoved his shoulder. Tanner laughed. "Less talk and more fight, Kenny?"

Kenny nodded. Tanner stopped talking and focused on Kenny's attack.

It was a while before Michelle and Stan were alone in the house again. Michelle stayed in her room to read, something she could not do while the younger kids were at home and liked to play there. She looked up from her book and saw Stan in the doorway.

"What do you want?"

"I'm sorry about before, Michelle. I got carried away."

"Uh-huh."

He came into the room and Michelle didn't tell him to stay out.

"Can we still be friends?"

"I guess."

He sat down on the bed with her. "I went too fast," he said.

"Yeah."

"You did sort of like the making out though, didn't you? You were kissing back."

He sounded embarrassed. Michelle looked at him. "Yeah," she admitted. It made her feel older and sophisticated. That was something teenagers and adults did and Michelle was flattered that he saw her as mature enough to be interested in. It felt good. The kissing hadn't scared her.

"So it's okay if we do that again," Stan deduced.

Michelle shook her head. As much as she had liked it, she was nervous about what would come after.

"Oh, come on, you want to do it some more, don't you?" he wheedled.

"No."

He moved closer. "Come on, Michelle, let's do it."

"No."

"She said no," Tanner said from the door. Neither of them had heard his approach and they both jumped. "So leave her be." Stan was older than Tanner, but Tanner was just as big and looked tough. "And if you bug her," Tanner warned, "I'll beat the crap out of you. Let's go, Michelle."

Michelle went, but that wasn't the end of it. Tanner gave Michelle a lecture about standing up for herself and not getting involved with guys like Stan because she was still 'just a baby.' Which only made Michelle resentful of Tanner and rebellious enough to try something.

Michelle thought everything would be fine because Joey was home too. When Stan came into her room, she didn't think anything of it. He pulled the door shut behind him.

"Don't want Joey walking in on us," he said, locking it.

Michelle didn't say anything.

"Does that mean yes?" Stan ventured.

"Just making out," Michelle clarified.

"Yeah, sure."

He came over to her and Michelle put down her book. After a few moments of self-consciousness, they had picked up where they had left off. Michelle was enjoying herself, thinking about Tanner and how wrong he was about her being a baby. They were both sweaty and out of breath when Stan's hands started roving again, but more gently than last time. Michelle ignored it, not wanting to stop. But when he had both of them mostly undressed, Michelle squirmed and tried to throw him off. Stan was ready for it and not taken by surprise this time.

"Hold still," he snapped.

"Don't. Come on, stop it."

He reached over and grabbed a pillow. He put it over her face and Michelle pushed it away.

"You make a peep and it's lights out," he threatened.

Michelle didn't know what to do. She just lay still and tried to think her way out. He was stronger than she was and had her pinned down.

At last she couldn't just lie there anymore. After fighting with him for a moment with all her strength, she tried to scream for help. Instantly, the pillow was over her face, clamped down hard so she couldn't escape it. Michelle stopped trying to scream, just trying to breathe again, but she couldn't.

And as Stan had promised, the lights went out.

It was like waking up from a nightmare. Michelle wasn't sure as she drifted back to consciousness what had really happened. She lay there on the bed trying to sort out the images and trying to pinpoint the messages her body was sending her. Her ears were pounding and she couldn't figure out if she hurt all over or if it was just her head. She isolated a sound like a door opening, and turned her head, opening her eyes a slit. Tanner stepped into the room. That was good. Tanner would tell her what was wrong.

"Michelle? Michelle, are you okay?" His voice sounded unreal and far away.

Michelle tried to form the words to ask him what was wrong, but she seemed to be caught in a nightmare, the scream still paralyzed in her throat.

Tanner shut the door again and walked closer. "Michelle?"

He swore and Michelle wondered if he was angry with her for not going to meet him and Kenny as planned. He was right beside her. He pushed her hair out of her face.

"Are you awake?"

Michelle still couldn't find her voice, but she nodded, pretty sure she *was* awake now.

"You wouldn't listen, would you? You think you know everything, but you don't know guys."

She wasn't sure what he was talking about. Tanner knelt on the bed by her, clumsily threading her legs through her clothes. They felt rough and abrasive, like clothes that had been hung up wet and dried all stiff. Michelle decided it was more than her head that hurt. It was her whole body.

"It hurts," someone said. It sounded like Michelle's own voice, but like she was listening to it on a tape recording, not from inside her head.

"Yeah, I bet it does," Tanner agreed. He did up the buttons on her shirt and left it untucked.

"Let's go to my place," Tanner suggested. "It's safe there and I don't want your folks thinking I did this."

He moved around the room for a few minutes. Michelle knew he was cleaning up after the disaster, but she wasn't quite sure what the disaster was. He came back over to her and slid her feet off the edge of the bed.

"Stand up, Michelle." He was up and across the room again, opening the window. "It stinks in here," he told her. He came back to her again and pulled her hands to make her sit up. He laid the pillows out.

"Stand up, Michelle. Please."

With a little bit of help, Michelle was standing. She still couldn't seem to concentrate on what was going on. She felt like she was in a bubble, separated from the rest of the world. Tanner let go of her to fix the blankets on the bed. Then he took her by the arm and led her away.

They went to Tanner's house. Tanner's parents were rarely home, so it was a good place for the gang to meet. Most of them, including Kenny, were already there. Tanner hustled Michelle past them to the bathroom.

"Why don't you have a shower?" he suggested. Then he left and went back out to the others.

"What's wrong with her?" someone asked.

Michelle listened for his response, but if Tanner answered, it was too quietly for her to hear. Michelle sat down on the toilet and stared into space for a long time before moving to obey Tanner's instructions. She started to undress.

Suddenly she found her voice. "Kenny!"

Kenny cracked the door open a moment later.

"I'm bleeding," Michelle said, staring at her underpants.

Kenny looked uncomfortable. He didn't know what to say or do. He stood there, his face getting red. Tanner pushed past Kenny. "What's wrong?"

"I'm bleeding," Michelle told him.

"That happens sometimes. It won't last long."

Michelle stared at her panties, her senses rushing back to her too fast to understand the signals. "They're on backward."

"Are they? Sorry, that's my fault."

Michelle stared at the blood without comprehension. "But I haven't ever had my period before."

"That's good," Tanner said, sounding relieved.

Why was it good?

"It hurts," Michelle cleared her throat. "Why does it hurt?"

"Sometimes it does. It looks like he was pretty rough."

There were bruises on her thighs. Michelle unbuttoned her shirt and looked at herself. Kenny watched with wide eyes, his face deep red. They had shared a room for years, seen each other change countless times, but that was before Michelle had started to develop. She had scratches and bruises underneath her shirt too. Michelle stared at them.

"What happened?" Michelle asked, trying to put it all together.

"Don't you remember?"

"No."

She thought back, but the last thing she could remember was her and Stan making out. Then she suddenly understood. She swore, feeling nauseated.

"Did he drug you or something?" Tanner asked. "I thought you were just in shock."

"He put the pillow over my face," Michelle said. "He smothered me."

Tanner shook his head.

"I'll kill him."

She thought at first it was Tanner who said it, but it was Kenny.

"I'll help," Tanner said, not to be outdone.

"No," Michelle told them both. "I'll do it."

The three of them looked at each other. A pact was formed among them. However it was done, it would be done. Tanner was the first one to move.

"You having a shower or bath?"

"A bath."

He started the water running, sitting on the edge of the tub to test the temperature. He was staring at her and slowly Michelle regained her modesty, feeling her cheeks warm and turning away from him. She pulled her shirt shut.

"Let's go, Kenny," Tanner ordered. He paused at the door and looked back at her. "I wasn't looking at you," he explained, "I was looking at the bruises."

Michelle nodded. Tanner left, shutting the door. Michelle slipped off the rest of her clothes and stepped into the hot water.

CHAPTER Nine

Wesson and Denver responded to the nine-one-one call. The young female on the phone said she thought she killed her brother. She had also said something incoherent about an intruder in the house. They killed the siren and lights before they pulled up to the house and circled before going in. The back door was hanging open, and it was through that door they entered. There was a TV, a video machine, and a stereo on the floor of the kitchen. The young man who must have been the brother was lying on the floor between the kitchen and living room. Wesson dropped to one knee to look at him. His shirt was drenched with blood and he had no pulse. They went by him and checked out the rest of the house. The girl who had made the call was still curled up around the phone in the master bedroom. Her shirt was also wet with blood and she was holding a knife in her hand.

"Hi there, honey," Denver whispered. "Are you hurt?"

She shook her head.

"Do you want to give me that knife?"

She held it out to him, her hand shaking. Denver took it from her. "Attagirl." He handed it off to Wesson, who handled it carefully and put it in an evidence bag. "Great, now stand up and let's go downstairs, okay?"

She got up slowly and Denver looked her over to make sure she wasn't hurt. He nodded to Wesson. Wesson went down to the kitchen

MICHELLE

ahead of them and called for the homicide team. Denver sat in the bedroom with the girl.

"What's your name, honey?" Denver questioned.

"Michelle."

"Do you think you can tell me what happened, Michelle?"

"Stan and me were upstairs." Her voice was small and tentative.

"Stan's your brother?"

"He's my foster brother."

"Okay. Then what happened?"

"There were noises downstairs. Stan said to wait upstairs and he'd see what it was."

"Did you stay upstairs?"

"For a while."

"Did you hear anything after he went downstairs?"

"No."

"So what did you do?"

"I went downstairs. Stan was there—bleeding."

"So you weren't the one that stabbed him."

"He was still alive. I pulled the knife out and he died."

She said it shakily with a bit of a sob. Denver took her hand and didn't have the heart to tell her it probably was her pulling out the knife that had finished him off. You were never supposed to pull a knife from the wound.

"Do you know how we can reach your parents, Michelle?"

"They'll be home soon."

"Okay. I want you to just stay here while I go check on how things are going downstairs. Okay?"

Michelle nodded. Denver went down to talk to the homicide boys he heard arriving.

Kay looked around the main floor and spoke with Denver.

"Looks like a burglar thought everybody was gone, but there were two kids left upstairs," Denver outlined. "One of them came down to check on things. The intruder stabbed him and ran."

"I heard on the radio the girl stabbed him."

"No, she pulled the knife out."

"I see. Where's the rest of the family?"

"She thought they'd be back soon."

Kay looked over her notes and nodded to Erickson, her partner. "Looks pretty straightforward. The burglar was wearing gloves, left smudge marks but no fingerprints. Only fingerprints on the knife are Michelle's. A neighbor saw a blue van stopped in the lane shortly before we were called. The boy bled out. Since nobody else saw the burglar—"

"Just one thing bothers me."

"What's that?"

"The wound. It's so low."

"It might have been a sheath knife and was pulled from an ankle or boot—and administered from a crouch."

"Then it should have been underhand rather than overhand."

"Not necessarily."

"Still…"

"What are you thinking?"

"Michelle said initially that she killed him. She's about the right height."

Kay chuckled and shook her head. "And then she made it look like a burglary gone wrong? What about the van?"

"It's just a thought, something to look into."

"If she was thirty instead of ten, I would consider it. But she's just a kid. There's nothing to indicate she was the one who killed the boy."

Erickson shrugged. "It's time to make inquiries anyway."

"Are Michelle and Stan often left alone in the house?" Kay asked Mrs. Loller.

"Yes. I don't like to leave Michelle alone, but Stan is old enough to look after things."

She said it and then realized how wrong they had been. She looked apologetic, giving a little shrug.

"Michelle likes to be left alone?"

"Yes, she's quite a loner, unless she's with her brother."

"Stan?"

"No, her natural brother. Kenny. He's at another foster home."

"And Stan likes to be home too?"

"Yes. Usually, he offered to stay with Michelle and we didn't have to ask him."

"They got along well together?"

"Yes, they never fought."

"Did Stan get along with the rest of the kids?"

"Yes, he was easy to get along with."

"How did he do at school?"

Mrs. Loller sighed. "School wasn't Stan's strong suit. He was always getting into trouble."

"What for?"

"Bad marks. Talking back to teachers. Harassing other students."

Kay raised her eyebrows. "How was he harassing other students?"

"Stan had a troubled past. He didn't relate well to the other students." Kay didn't point out that she had just said Stan got along with the other foster children. "He sometimes got… too familiar with the girls."

"I see. How old are the other kids here?"

"Joey is twelve, between Stan and Michelle. The twins are six. My kids are two and four."

"Maybe we could talk to Joey before we see Michelle again."

"I suppose. He's watching TV downstairs."

They pulled Joey away from his program to question him. He seemed excited to be questioned by the police. "I wish I had been here," he blustered. "I wouldn't have gotten hurt."

"Did you usually stay here with Stan and Michelle?"

"Sometimes."

"Did you spend much time with Stan?"

"Well… when he'd let me."

"Was everything okay between Stan and Michelle?"

"Yes…" There was something more behind his answer.

"Are you sure?"

He nodded, looking sly. "Stan and Michelle were—you know—making time."

There were a few seconds while they looked at each other. "How do you know?"

"Stan told me. Said she was ga-ga over him."

"Really. Interesting. You believed him?"

Joey shrugged. "I dunno. He exaggerates sometimes. I figured she liked him, even if they weren't—you know."

"Hmm. Did you ever ask Michelle about it?"

"Michelle? No, she doesn't talk to me. She's a snob."

"Why didn't you stay home with them yesterday?"

"I don't like to stay home as much as that. I don't like to be alone."

Michelle sat down nervously with the officers. Kay questioned her, figuring that as a woman she would have a better rapport with kids. She gave Michelle a reassuring smile. "How are you feeling today, Michelle?"

"Okay."

"Sleep good?"

It was a moment before Michelle answered. "I had nightmares all night."

"Yeah. What you went through yesterday was pretty traumatic."

"Uh-huh." Michelle nodded.

"How did you feel about Stan, Michelle?"

"He was okay."

"You liked him?"

Michelle lifted her shoulders in a shrug. "I dunno."

"Did the two of you spend time together?"

"Some."

"Joey said you and Stan got along pretty good."

Michelle shook her head, her lips pressed together. "Not that good."

"Michelle, I know you're only ten, right?" she nodded. "But Mrs. Loller said you're a very smart girl. Do you know what I mean when I talk about intimacy? Do you know what that means?"

Michelle's eyes slid away from Kay. "Yeah…"

"Can you tell me… if you and Stan were intimate?"

Michelle got red and Kay knew she understood the question. "No."

"It's important you don't lie to me, Michelle. If you guys were intimate, you can tell me. I won't tell Mrs. Loller. Okay?"

"We didn't do anything!"

"Stan told Joey you did."

"He lied."

"I'll bet that makes you mad. Did you know about it before this?"

"No."

"Was it you who stabbed Stan, Michelle?"

Michelle's eyes widened in surprise. "I didn't mean to kill him. I just wanted to stop it."

"Wanted to stop what, Michelle?"

There were a few minutes of silence while Michelle looked at them. "I wanted to stop the bleeding," she said as if it were obvious.

"Did you ever see the burglar?"

"No. I was upstairs."

"Did you hear any voices downstairs?"

"No."

"What were the noises you heard downstairs?"

"Noises, footsteps, moving around..." Michelle trailed off and gave a little shrug.

"What did you hear when Stan went downstairs?"

"Nothing."

Kay considered. "What was the first thing you saw when you went downstairs?"

"Nothing. Just Stan... and all the blood."

"You didn't see anyone else?"

"No."

"Or hear anyone?"

"No."

"Okay. You let me know if you remember anything, all right?"

"Uh-huh."

∼

"How'd it go?" Tanner questioned.

"Okay."

"Did the cops take you downtown?"

"No," Michelle shook her head irritably. "They just talked to me at the house."

"Do they think you did it?"

"No."

"You're one smart chick, Michelle. You know that?"

"Yeah. Well, it was pretty easy."

"I should have done it," Kenny said.

If Kenny had done it, he would have botched it up. But Michelle didn't tell him that. "It was something I had to do myself," she said firmly.

"This is cool," Tanner said, leaning back in his dad's easy chair comfortably. "We're gonna get away with this. Do you think they'll come question me?"

"Why would they question you?"

"Because I'm your best friend. Won't they want to talk to me to find out what kind of person you are?"

"You're not my best friend. Kenny's my best friend."

"Kenny's your brother."

"I don't want to talk to the police," Kenny protested.

"The police aren't going to ask you anything," Michelle told him. She glared at Tanner for suggesting it. Tanner shrugged.

"No, the cops ain't going to question anybody," Tanner agreed. "I'm just joking around. The cops are gonna put this to bed without any trouble."

"I won't talk to any cops."

"You won't have to. I'm just being dumb, Kenny."

"Okay."

"Let's go find the gang."

CHAPTER Ten

If Michelle had any thoughts of being able to make a split from Tanner and the gang, she could forget about it after the incident with Stan. The gang was just trying to establish themselves and figure out who they were, and to have someone among them take her revenge and foil the cops like that was just what they needed. Confidence increased, and although Michelle was not the leader of the gang, she was definitely central to it. And Tanner considered himself to be Michelle's guardian since she had regained consciousness after the attack. He was more possessive than ever and was always with her.

Michelle was surprised the Lollers let her stay with them after Stan was gone. She expected them to ask for her to be moved somewhere else. But they didn't. They said it wasn't her fault. Other than Joey, that made her the oldest child in the house, so she could boss around the younger children without being bossed around herself. Joey didn't bother her. He never said anything to her, but he looked at her funny sometimes and Michelle wondered if he suspected the truth. The cops had said Joey told them she and Stan were intimate. So Stan had told Joey that much. Whether Stan had told him the rest of the story or not, Michelle didn't know. And she didn't ask. As long as he left her alone, she would leave him alone.

Michelle was the first one in the gang to start carrying a weapon. She got a small sheath knife similar to the one that had killed Stan.

For the first little while she wore it on her ankle, but it made her nervous because she could always see the bulge under her jeans. Michelle didn't want a pocketknife that she had to worry about opening . Since she was wearing big shirts to hide her figure anyway, she switched the sheath to her belt underneath her extra large t-shirt. Nobody could tell.

The guys in the gang couldn't get away with carrying artillery because they were searched regularly. Nobody suspected Michelle of being armed, so she got away with it.

~

Michelle walked into the house to find Kenny and the others. The air was blue with smoke. "It stinks in here," Michelle said. "What are you guys smoking?"

Tanner stared at her as if he hadn't understood her. Michelle shook her head. "You're stinking up the house," Michelle told him.

Tanner swore. "My folks'll kill me if they come back to the house smelling like pot!" He went to the window and opened it.

"Is that what it is?" Michelle questioned. "Marijuana?"

"Yeah, sweet Mary Jane. You never tried it?"

Michelle wrinkled her nose and shook her head. "No. It stinks."

Tanner grinned. "Well, you gotta at least try it. Come on," he handed her his joint, "take a toke."

Michelle hesitated, then tried it. She shook her head. "I don't know why you'd want to inhale this stuff."

"You get used to it." He took it back and Michelle sat down to watch TV with them. She got up a few minutes later to call the Lollers and swayed on her feet.

"Whoa."

Tanner looked at her. "What's the matter?"

"I feel weird. My head is all... floaty."

Tanner snickered. "It's the grass."

"It is?" Michelle considered for a minute. "This is weird."

"Michelle's gettin' stoned," Harris announced, delighted.

"I am not!" Michelle retorted. She looked at Tanner. "Am I?"

"Well, maybe not yet, but you will be."

Michelle went out to the kitchen and opened the window. She

took deep breaths of fresh air, trying to clear the fuzziness in her head. Tanner came out to see her after a while. "Hey, Simpson. What's the matter?"

"Just trying to clear my head."

He studied her face. His eyes looked strange, distant. "Whatcha got against getting high? It'll make you feel good, help you relax."

Michelle shook her head. "I don't want to."

"Why not?" Tanner persisted.

Michelle tried to find the words. "I don't want to... lose control."

"It's exactly what you need."

One of the guys started calling for Tanner. He caught Michelle by the arm. "Let's go outside."

She jumped when he grabbed her and jerked away.

"You need *something*," Tanner snapped. He motioned her outside.

They sat on the steps outside in silence for a few minutes. Tanner held a joint out to her. Michelle didn't move.

"Take it," Tanner insisted. "You need it."

"No."

He lit it and held it out to her again. "Come on. Do it."

Michelle finally gave in and took it. She smoked it, trying not to inhale much of the smoke. When she was finally finished the joint, Tanner took her back into the house.

Kenny was coming out of the bathroom and saw them. "Where did you go?"

"We were just outside," it was Tanner who answered. "Nowhere far."

"Doin' what?"

"Smokin'. You guys want to go out somewhere? Man, I want to go somewhere."

"My head hurts," Michelle protested.

"It'll go away. Let's go somewhere."

"Where?" Kenny asked.

"I don't know yet. Let's get the guys."

In a few minutes, the gang was gathered up and they went out.

Hartley and Boulder approached the group of preteens.

"You kids are out a bit late, aren't you?" Hartley asked, looking them over. They were all young, lower middle school or upper elementary school. Not real tough-looking, but even little kids could make trouble if they put their minds to it.

"We're not doing anything," a dark haired boy retorted.

"I didn't say you were. But now that you mention it, what are you up to?"

"Just out walking. Getting some air."

"Anything wrong with that?" another chimed in.

"Your parents know you're out this late?"

"Who are you kidding? They don't care."

"I think you guys should be heading for home."

"We're not ready to go home yet."

Hartley looked at their faces, lingering on each one. There was a girl in the back, and she was obviously younger than the others. "Somebody's sister?" Hartley questioned.

They followed his eyes to Michelle.

"She's Kenny's sister," one of them admitted, gesturing to one of the boys.

"Pretty late for you, sweetheart. I think we should take you home."

Michelle looked at the others. She hadn't called the Lollers to say she'd be late. And she wasn't feeling very good. But Kenny and Tanner and the others would not be happy if she just left them.

"I don't want to go home."

"How old are you, honey?"

"Ten."

Hartley shook his head. "Come on. You can't be out on the streets this late. Do you want me to book you as a runaway or just drive you home?"

"Leave her alone," Tanner protested. "She's with us, nothing's gonna happen to her."

"Stay out of it, or I'll be taking you home too. Your parents going to like you going home in a squad car?"

Michelle looked at the others. "I guess I gotta go."

There were shrugs and nods. Tanner glared at the cops but didn't argue any further. Hartley nodded. "Good. I'll take you and your brother home, shall I?"

MICHELLE

Kenny shook his head.

"We don't live together," Michelle explained. "We're in different homes."

"Okay. Well, we'll take you. The rest of you, get home on your own so I don't have to come back and bother you some more."

Michelle went with the officers back to their car, staring at the ground.

"So what's your address?" Hartley questioned, opening the door for her.

Michelle gave it to him.

"What are you doing hanging around with those guys? Don't you think they're a little bit old to be hanging out with?"

Michelle shrugged. "I want to be with Kenny."

"What's your name, honey?"

"Michelle."

"Michelle what?"

"Michelle Simpson."

"I don't want to have to pick you up this late again, Michelle."

Michelle didn't say anything.

~

Mrs. Loller opened the door. "Michelle! Are you okay?"

Michelle nodded and stood there, looking down at her feet.

"What happened? What did she do?" Mrs. Loller questioned Hartley.

"I didn't do anything," Michelle protested.

"She was out with her brother and some other friends. I figured it was a little late for her to be out, so I brought her home."

"Thank you so much. What were you doing?" Mrs. Loller demanded, looking at Michelle again, "Where were you guys?"

"We were just outside."

"Where's Kenny? Did you take him back home too? The Antonios have been looking for him."

"No, we only brought Michelle home. She was the youngest."

"Well, Kenny is—" Mrs. Loller hesitated, looking at Michelle. "Kenny is pretty young too," she said meaningfully.

Hartley nodded. "We'll keep our eyes open for him. And

Michelle..." Michelle met his eyes reluctantly. "I don't want to pick you up this late again."

Michelle looked back down at her shoes.

"You'd better go to your room," Mrs. Loller told her.

Michelle obediently went to her room. She moved slowly in the dark, not turning on the light because the Lollers' baby was asleep. She undressed and put on her PJ's and got into bed. She had a headache and was glad to be in bed. Mrs. Loller came in a few minutes. She turned on the lamp. The baby didn't wake up. Mrs. Loller picked up the clothes Michelle had left on the floor. She held them up to her face.

"Have you been smoking?" she demanded.

Michelle shook her head.

"Then who was smoking?"

Michelle thought quickly. "We went to the indoor skate park," she explained. "It's really smoky there."

Mrs. Loller frowned and nodded. "You know better than to start smoking, don't you Michelle? It's very bad for you and you don't want to get addicted to something like that at your age."

"I know. I don't like cigarettes anyway."

"Good. You make sure you stay away from anyone who tries to get you to smoke or drink."

Michelle thought of Tanner, who not only tried to get her to smoke and drink, but also to try pot and who she knew very well would like to get her into bed.

Mrs. Loller started to get ready to go. Michelle sat up in bed. "How old were you when you first got a boyfriend?"

"A boyfriend." Mrs. Loller bit her lip and looked at Michelle. "I had friends who were boys all through school. Do you mean a really serious boyfriend?"

Michelle nodded.

"Well, I don't know. I guess I started dating when I was fifteen, which was really pretty young. I didn't have a steady boyfriend, though, not until I was about seventeen."

"But you kissed before."

"Yes, a little. But not... seriously. Goodnight kisses, a little experimenting." Michelle could tell Mrs. Loller wasn't very comfortable with this. "You're too young to be thinking about relationships now,

Michelle. You need to have some time just being a kid. All the complications of boyfriends will come soon enough."

"I know... I just wondered."

"Are kids in your grade starting to pair off already? Is that why you're asking? Sometimes a small group of kids starts experimenting before the rest and putting pressure on the others. But it is normal not to have a serious relationship until you're older."

"Okay."

"If something like that ever happened, you could talk to me about it. Some things you need to talk about to work through."

"Sex, you mean?"

Mrs. Loller looked startled and tried not to look like it. "Well, yes. Sex and other things. You can talk to me if you're having problems." They were both quiet for a while. Mrs. Loller finally moved. "I need to get to bed. Is there anything you need to talk to me about?"

"No."

"Okay. You go to sleep. It's way past your bedtime."

Mrs. Loller tried to get all the kids dressed and fed, and Joey and Michelle helped out as usual. Joey complained about having to do it, but Michelle always did her chores without complaint. She was so good with the younger children.

Michelle helped the twins finish getting dressed and picked up the baby, who was starting to fuss at being left alone. Joey went downstairs with the twins to get breakfast going. Mrs. Loller watched Michelle with the baby while she tried to get four-year-old Sylvan dressed. Michelle was looking a little pale after her late night. She pulled the fussy toddler against herself, murmuring to her. Mrs. Loller frowned, noticing Michelle's developing figure for the first time. Michelle wore a lot of baggy clothes, which was the fashion. It was only because of Michelle's questions of the night before that Mrs. Loller realized Michelle was starting to grow up. When Michelle put Teeny down to take her downstairs to breakfast, she straightened her shirt to hide her figure and headed for the door.

"Michelle." Michelle turned around and looked at Mrs. Loller.

"Why don't you come home after school's out and we'll go shopping for some things for you?"

Michelle followed the direction of Mrs. Loller's eyes and blushed. She folded her arms in front of her chest.

"Okay? You come home after school and we'll go out."

Michelle nodded. "Okay."

CHAPTER Eleven

Kenny wasn't at school when Michelle got there. She looked for one of the boys in the gang and confronted Jamie. "Where's Kenny?"

"I don't know. I ain't seen him."

"Did he get in trouble? Did he go home?"

"I don't know."

"The police didn't come back?"

"Nope."

"Did he get in a fight today? Already?"

"I ain't seen him, Michelle. Honest!"

Michelle was pulled out of her first-period class and sent to the office without explanation. Marsden met her there and took her to an empty office. "There's something we need to talk about, Michelle."

"Is it Kenny?" Michelle's stomach was cramping as she worried about him. "Is he okay? Where is he?"

"Kenny's in his class now. I had to talk to him too."

"Oh. Are you going to put us back together again?" Michelle asked, but didn't expect a positive answer.

"Well, yes."

Michelle blinked in surprise. "Am I going to the Antonios?"

"No."

"Kenny is coming to the Lollers?"

"No."

"Then where are we going?"

"To your mother."

Michelle stared at Marsden. "You can't send us back to Mama. She can't take care of us."

"Your mom has been going through a lot of counseling and training since you lived with her last. We think she's ready to handle it now."

"She hasn't even come to see us since we've been here. She didn't even send us birthday cards!"

"We're not going to just drop you into this, Michelle. Your mom will visit each of you at your foster homes a few times. Then you will each stay with her for a weekend, supervised by a social worker. Then you'll both spend a weekend together with her, unsupervised. Then you'll move in after that. We're not going to just send you home."

"What if we don't want to live with her?"

"Let's just try it out before you make any judgments," Marsden cautioned. "You need to give your mom a chance to make things up to you."

"I don't want her to make up with us. I want her to leave us alone."

"It is better for you to live with your mom than with a foster family if she's able to take care of you."

"She couldn't take care of us before and she can't now!"

"We'll see. It isn't up to you."

Michelle sat sullenly. She stared at Marsden. "You told Kenny?"

"Yes, he got here before you did."

"What did he say?"

"Kenny had as little to say about it as he does about anything else. He just sat there and didn't say a word."

Michelle nodded. Kenny wouldn't tell Marsden how he felt about her news. He would wait until he could talk to Michelle. If he talked to anyone about it.

Marsden let her go back to her class, but Michelle couldn't pay any attention to the lesson.

∼

Tanner argued when Michelle said she had to go straight home after school and Michelle hesitated.

"What's more important than coming with us?" Tanner demanded.

"None of your business," Michelle snapped. But she looked at Kenny, wanting to talk with him. As much as she wanted to go home to go out and buy necessities with Mrs. Loller, she knew she and Kenny had to talk.

"Kenny... Would you come with me?" she suggested.

Kenny shook his head. Tanner blustered. "Come on, Michelle, whatever it is can wait. We need you here."

"I can't go home one day?" Michelle demanded.

"Not today."

"Stay here, Michelle," Kenny agreed.

"Okay. I guess. I gotta call the Lollers," Michelle conceded.

"You can call from my place," Tanner told her.

When Michelle called the Lollers, Mrs. Loller didn't sound surprised. "Miss Marsden told me about your mom. I can understand you and Kenny want to talk about it."

"Thanks. So we can go to... we can go to the store later?"

"Sure Michelle, no problem."

"Okay," Michelle agreed in relief. "Can we go Saturday?"

"We'll plan on it."

"Okay."

Michelle hung up. She nodded at Tanner, who was watching her from the doorway. "I can stay around," she told him.

"Good. I don't like you trying to mess with our routine."

"It's not a big deal. Where's Kenny? I gotta talk to him."

"In my room."

"Leave me alone with him, okay?"

"Whatever. What's up with you guys today? What are you so twisted up about?"

"None of your business."

Tanner shook his head. "Don't take a long time with him, okay? I wanna go out and do something tonight."

"We just have to talk."

Michelle went to Tanner's bedroom and opened the door. Kenny was sitting on the floor with his back against the bed, a bottle in one hand and a joint in the other. Michelle shut the door behind her.

"You okay, Kenny?"

He shrugged. Michelle sat down beside him. Kenny offered her a drink and Michelle took a sip just to join him. She got up for a minute to open the window and air out some of the smoke and then sat down beside him again.

"I don't want to go back to Mama either," Michelle said, although Kenny hadn't said anything about it.

Kenny shrugged.

"Don't block me out, Kenny. I remember what it was like."

He looked at her for a minute. "I don't remember much," he said.

She knew he remembered more than he let on. It hadn't been that long ago. "Dad's not going to be there to help this time," Michelle said.

Kenny took another drink and Michelle saw tears glistening in his eyes. Michelle put her arm around his shoulders. "I'll still be there," she promised. "I'll look after you. And maybe Mama will be better now like Mrs. Marsden said."

"We'll be together now," Kenny said, sounding like he was repeating something someone else had said.

"Yeah, that's right."

A tear rolled down Kenny's cheek, and he brushed it away. Michelle ruffled his hair and stroked it like he was a hurt puppy. "It's going to be okay, Kenny."

He shook his head. He put down the bottle and cigarette and put his face in his hands. Michelle held him close, rocking back and forth.

When Tanner came in, Kenny was asleep. Tanner scowled and bent over him and shook him. "Kenny. Come on, time to get some action. Wake up."

Kenny didn't stir. Tanner picked up the wine bottle and looked at the level. "How much of this crap did he drink?"

"I don't know. He was drinking before I came in."

"Well, this is just great. We were gonna go out. Kenny's out for the count. What'd you let him do that?"

"You're the one who thinks everybody should drink all the time. You know I don't like all the booze."

Tanner scowled at her. He walked out of the room. Michelle tried

MICHELLE

to make Kenny comfortable on the floor where he'd fallen asleep and followed Tanner.

They didn't go out together, but instead Tanner and a couple of the boys went out for a while and came back with some videos. Michelle looked at the jackets and found they were pornographic. She turned up her nose.

"I'm not watching this stuff."

"Oh, come on, Michelle," Tanner protested. "How do you know whether you like it until you see them?"

The others were excited to see the videos and quickly overruled Michelle's protests. Michelle tried to decide whether to just leave. Tanner tried to convince her otherwise. "Look, Michelle, just kick back with us and enjoy yourself. Just take a few tokes and watch."

"I don't want to."

He lit a joint and gave it to her. "Just enjoy it, Michelle."

"Why do you always want me to do things like this?"

He grinned. Michelle took a couple of drags on the joint and it didn't taste as bad this time as before. Tanner made her sit beside him to watch the movies. A few minutes into the video, he was putting his arm around her. Michelle tried to shake him off.

"Just leave me alone, Tanner."

"Relax, I'm not doing anything to hurt you."

"Just leave me alone."

He didn't move. Michelle put up with it and smoked the pot, waiting for that sense of well-being to come over her. Sitting there in the dark, watching the weird flashing of the flick on the other side of the room, with Tanner's arm tightening around her, the haze of the grass gave her a feeling of unreality. Like she was watching someone else, separate from herself. It was almost as if she was watching herself on TV.

She watched Tanner groping her in the dark and for a while she didn't do anything about it. Eventually, she pulled herself together and pushed Tanner's hands away from her. She stood up and went to the bathroom. Tanner was waiting for her in the hallway when she walked back out, having decided it was time to go home. He startled her by kissing her, first on the cheek and then his lips brushed hers. Michelle backed away from him. Tanner stopped, seeing the tears in her eyes.

"What's the matter, Michelle?"

"I'm going home," Michelle told him, voice shaking. "Just leave me alone."

"What, because I kissed you?"

Neither of them said anything for a moment.

"Look, Michelle," he said in a conciliatory tone. "You know I like you. I have ever since I first saw you. I get impatient sometimes. I might push too hard, but I'm not Stan. I'm not going to do what he did. I'm not going to hurt you like that."

Michelle took a deep breath, trying to block out the memories he brought back. Then, whether it was the pot or the tension or Tanner's words, it all came pouring out. She started sobbing and Tanner pulled her close. Michelle cried into his shoulder. At that moment, Kenny staggered out of the bedroom. He glared at Tanner.

"What'd you do to Michelle?" he demanded.

"I didn't do anything to Michelle. She's just high."

Kenny transferred Michelle's grip from Tanner to himself. "Just leave her alone," he growled.

Tanner shrugged and walked away.

∽

Michelle really didn't want to go home after school, but Marsden must have anticipated that and picked her up after school so she couldn't go anywhere else. Michelle got into the car and watched out the window, her stomach getting more and more queasy.

"Looking forward to seeing your mom again? It's been quite a while."

"I don't want to see her," Michelle muttered. "She doesn't care about us."

"Give her a chance."

Michelle didn't say anything more. There was no point arguing over how she was supposed to feel about the visit. She was quiet until they got to the house. Marsden came into the house with her to supervise.

June held out her arms to Michelle. "There's my baby. Hi Michelle, how are you doing?"

Michelle submitted to being hugged, then pulled away and sat down in the easy chair in the far corner of the room. Marsden nodded to June. "I'll be in the kitchen. Let me know if either of you need anything."

"Okay."

Marsden left the room. June sat down as close as she could to Michelle.

"Boy, you've sure grown up, Michelle."

"Yeah, that happens."

June looked at Michelle unhappily. "I didn't want them to put you guys in foster care. I was in foster homes when I was a kid like you. It was Justin who did this to you, not me. I never wanted them to take you away."

"I did. We asked Daddy not to leave us with you."

"You were too young to know what you wanted. If Justin hadn't told you the system would be better, you wouldn't have asked."

Michelle stared at June. There were so many things Michelle had wanted to tell June when they saw each other again. But now she found herself unable to say anything at all. June wasn't going to listen to anything Michelle said. She had never listened to anything Michelle said before, why start now?

"So has it been okay? You've been in a good family?"

Michelle nodded. "The Lollers are nice," she said neutrally.

"They seem like good folks. Some of the families I was with... weren't so good."

"Uh-huh."

"You take care of Kenny?"

"Yeah, I look after him."

"Pretty soon we'll all be back together again. All together in a family."

Michelle was surprised. "Daddy too? Will Daddy be coming home?"

June's face fell. "I don't know where your daddy is. I haven't been able to find him."

Michelle nodded. They weren't going to be a family again. No Daddy, no Marcie. Only June, Kenny, and Michelle.

All in all, Marsden was pleased with the initial visits between June and the kids. There had been no shouts and accusations between June and Michelle, even though each felt wronged by the other. The reunion between June and Kenny had been painfully awkward and Marsden had not left them alone together as she had with Michelle. Kenny had said hello to June, but nothing else. He nodded or shook his head at a few of June's questions, but mostly he just sat there, looking at her with wide eyes as she tried to connect.

Marsden drove June home after the visits and went up with her to the new apartment. June watched her as she looked around, checking out the cupboards, fridge, closets, and bathroom.

"Don't you trust me?" June questioned resentfully, sounding like one of the kids.

"I'm just doing my job, making sure everything will be safe for the kids when they come."

"You're not going to find any booze."

"That's good. If you can stay dry, you've at least got a chance of keeping them."

"I'm going to keep them."

Marsden nodded. "We'll do what we can to help you out."

CHAPTER Twelve

Mrs. Antonio looked at Kenny, who was sitting at the kitchen table with his face in his hands.

"Are you okay, Kenny?"

He shook his head, not looking up.

"What is it? What's wrong?"

He didn't answer.

"Are you sick?"

Kenny shook his head. He looked miserable.

"Is something wrong at school? Is someone getting on your case?"

Kenny shook his head again. He glanced up at her but quickly looked away again. He seemed as if he wanted to talk to her, but he was too shy to tell her what was the matter.

"Are you upset about your mom? Going back there?"

He didn't move. He sat with his head in his hand, pink with embarrassment and thoroughly unhappy. Mrs. Antonio put his cereal bowl and a box of cereal on the table and didn't say anything.

He went to school without protest and Mrs. Antonio frowned as she vacuumed, trying to figure out what was bothering him so much. She vacuumed the master bedroom and then went into his room. Kenny's bed was unmade, which was unusual. He knew the house rules, which listed making his bed in the morning as one of his daily chores. She went over to pull the sheets up and finally understood. The sheets were soaked. Kenny had never wet the bed before. He was twelve, way too old for this 'babyish' problem. No wonder he hadn't been able to tell her when he wanted to.

Mrs. Antonio stripped the bed, found Kenny's wet clothes in the laundry hamper, and started the washer. Then she went to call Marsden.

Michelle barely slept all weekend. As Kenny was the oldest, he was the one who spent the first weekend with June. Kenny, never one to say much, had grown quieter and quieter as the day approached. He'd had to stay after school a lot for not paying attention in class. Michelle spent the weekend on pins and needles, wondering how he was doing. She stayed in her room most of the time, avoiding Tanner and the gang. She and Mrs. Loller went out on Saturday to buy Michelle some clothes, but Michelle didn't enjoy it like she thought she would. She went back home and went to her bedroom and didn't even put them on. She just didn't feel like doing anything, thinking about Kenny alone with June.

If anything happened at the apartment with June, Kenny wasn't telling anyone. The first thing Michelle looked for was bruises, but there were none visible. Mrs. Antonio hoped that actually having spent the weekend with June would help release the tension, but he was still wetting the bed. Mrs. Antonio wondered if he'd wet the bed at his mom's and he was regressing to earlier behavior from when he'd lived with her before. At least after Mrs. Loller showed him how a few times, Kenny could wash the sheets himself.

"Michelle, are you listening?"

Michelle dragged herself from her contemplations and looked at the teacher. "What?"

"Are you paying any attention?"

"No."

The teacher looked startled at her flat answer. "You need to pay attention, this is important. If you don't understand these equations, you'll fall behind in the next unit."

MICHELLE

Michelle shrugged.

"Pay attention," the teacher warned, not liking her response.

"I don't have to," Michelle snapped. She hated being singled out in front of the whole class. Especially when she already understood what the teacher was lecturing on and had more important things to think about.

"Go to the office."

Michelle stood up and walked out. She went to the office and sat down in the waiting chairs. The vice principal saw her and went over to see her, one eyebrow raised. "Michelle? What are you doing here?"

"Teacher sent me down."

"What for?"

She sighed. "Not paying attention in class."

"Come into my office."

Michelle followed him. He pointed her to the chair in front of his desk and shut the door. He sat on the corner of his desk, looking puzzled. "Usually it's Kenny we see down here. Not you."

Michelle shrugged.

"Do you have something on your mind, Michelle? Something you want to talk about?"

"No."

"Why weren't you paying attention in class?"

"I don't care about math. I was thinking about something else."

"What were you thinking about?"

"I have to stay with my mom this weekend," Michelle explained. "I don't want to."

He nodded, arms folded as he studied her. "Why not?"

"We asked to be put in foster care because she couldn't take care of us. Now they're sending us back. I just don't want to go."

"Do you think it's possible your mom has changed? That she could take care of you now?"

"No."

"You guys are getting pretty big. It isn't like you need a lot of babysitting anymore. You can probably do most things for yourselves."

"You don't get it."

"Then explain to me."

Michelle shook her head. She didn't tell people about how their mom hit them. Things like that didn't happen to normal kids. And talking about it just made more problems. "I can't."

"You need to be able to concentrate while you're in class. Maybe if you could talk about what's bothering you, you could get it off your mind."

"I don't want to talk about it."

"You know how important school is."

"Not that important."

He looked astounded by her response. "Michelle! How do you expect to get a job or function in the real world if you don't get an education?"

"I get along fine without school."

"Now, maybe. But when you get older, you're going to need this."

Michelle was silent and didn't bother to tell him how stupid he was. People who had to go to school to learn were stupid. Michelle was so bored with what they were teaching that it almost put her to sleep. Even Tanner's work was too easy.

"I expect you to pay attention in class. Whether you think you need it or not. Okay?"

Michelle shrugged. "I don't have to."

"If you don't want to get suspended, you'd better. Okay?"

Michelle stared at his disturbed expression and shook her head. "I get A's," she pointed out, "I don't have to pay attention. I don't care if you do suspend me."

There was a long period of silence while the vice principal thought this over.

Tanner thought the whole thing was hilarious.

"You got suspended?" he repeated incredulously. He laughed. "You?"

"Yeah. So?" Michelle stared at him.

"Well, I always expect it of Kenny and the rest of my boys, but never you. You're so straight."

"I hate school."

"Yeah, but I never thought you would dare get in trouble over it."

Michelle shrugged. She was dreading what the Lollers were going to say when they found out. And Marsden. But she just couldn't bear sitting in the stifling classroom trying to slow down to the speed of the other eleven-year-olds anymore. It was too hard to do with everything else she had to worry about.

∼

Michelle got up as usual the next morning and tried to figure out how she was going to tell Mrs. Loller she had been kicked out. She helped with the chores, as always, and when they were in the kitchen getting everything ready, Michelle stood watching Mrs. Loller.

"I got in trouble yesterday," she said finally.

"So I hear," Mrs. Loller commented without looking up.

"You heard?" Michelle repeated.

"I got a call after school yesterday."

Michelle breathed out, trying to relax. "Did they tell you I…"

"Got suspended? Yes."

"Why didn't you say anything?" Michelle demanded, her voice getting higher.

"I figured you needed some time to think it through."

"Did you tell Marsden?"

"No. I think you'd better tell her."

Michelle sat down with a thump. "Do I have to?"

"I think so."

"Are you mad?"

"I'm pretty disappointed. You do so well in school. But I'd like to hear your side of the story."

Michelle stared out the window. "I wasn't listening in class. I couldn't."

"You know you need to pay attention if you want to keep out of trouble."

"I'd rather just be suspended and not go."

Mrs. Loller raised an eyebrow and apparently couldn't think of an adequate response.

∼

Marsden walked Michelle up to June's new place. Michelle looked around the tiny apartment. She had thought their old apartment was small, particularly once she'd lived with the Lollers. But the new place was much worse. There was a kitchen just big enough to house a small fridge and a stove. There was barely any counter space around the single sink, but it was obvious from the three stools crammed in there that June was expecting them to eat there in the absence of a proper table.

The mottled carpet had holes in it. There was a musty, moldy smell. One bedroom. Michelle looked around, trying to figure out where they were all going to sleep. The couch in the living room must be a hide-a-bed. But that still only gave them two beds and three people. Michelle dropped her bag on the floor and went to look at the bathroom. A grimy shower stall, no tub. She walked back out to the living room and sat down on the couch in front of the TV.

"This is a dump."

"Michelle..." Marsden warned.

"I can't afford anything better since your daddy dumped us all and took off," June whined. "You think I can get a good job after taking care of babies all these years? I've never had a job before."

Michelle slumped in the couch and didn't say anything.

"I had to work real hard to get this place," June said sullenly.

"That's not my fault."

June's look answered the comment without words. As far as she was concerned, it was all Michelle's fault.

Marsden excused herself after a few minutes and left the two of them alone for the weekend.

"Michelle, why don't you help me with supper?" June said.

Michelle looked up. "I'm not hungry."

"Don't try that on me. I don't know what you're pouting about, but you better quit it and help."

Michelle remembered this. She got up and went into the tiny kitchen. "What do you want me to make?"

"There's some hamburger mix in the cupboard."

Michelle found it and turned the stove on. There was barely enough room to turn around in the kitchen. Michelle read the instructions on the back of the box.

After dinner, June turned on the TV and watched it the rest of the evening. Michelle had forgotten to bring any books with her so there was nothing for her to do but sit and stare at the screen.

~

Marsden tried to make the transition as easy as possible for everyone. But the kids were so opposed to going back with their mother, it was a difficult job. She kept them at the same school and got them bus passes so they didn't have to deal with a school change on top of everything else.

Mrs. Antonio was worried about how Kenny was going to handle it. His reactions seemed to indicate he was already struggling. Michelle seemed to be dealing with it, aside from the brief school suspension. She had little to say about it to anyone.

~

The first evening they all spent together was pretty subdued. June was polite to the children, maybe a little overwhelmed by having them both back. Michelle and Kenny were falling asleep before June decided it was bedtime.

"You guys better go to bed now," she decided, turning the TV off and going into her bedroom.

Michelle looked at Kenny. "Get up, sleepyhead," she urged, "so I can get the bed out."

Kenny got up, yawning and rubbing his eyes. Michelle pulled the bed out and pulled the blankets back. Without really thinking about it, Michelle started changing for bed. Kenny flushed red and turned away from her. Michelle looked down at her bared chest. She and Kenny used to sleep in the same room before, but that was before they had started to grow up. It was going to be harder now. Michelle quickly finished changing into her nightgown.

"Okay," she told Kenny, climbing into bed to cover the skimpy nighty. She closed her eyes. A few minutes later, Kenny slipped into bed. Michelle opened her eyes to make sure he had shut off the lamp. He had. Michelle closed her eyes again and lay very still.

CHAPTER
Thirteen

Somehow they made it through the weekend. Michelle was relieved to be back at school on Monday and away from June and the ugly apartment. Although things were not yet the way they were before they went into foster care, she knew it was only a matter of time. June wouldn't be able to keep up the facade of being nice for long. Then she would show her true colors. And there would be no Daddy to calm her down this time. Michelle felt powerless to stop what she knew was going to happen.

After school let out, they didn't take the bus back home like they were supposed to. They went to find Tanner and the gang instead.

"We gotta get some dough," Tanner said. "I wanna order pizza and get some booze."

"Where are we going to get money?" Michelle said reasonably.

Tanner thought about it. "There's that pawn shop down the street."

"What are we going to pawn?"

Tanner left the room. He returned with a bag in his hand. He showed it to Michelle. "My mom's jewelry. I don't think much of it is real, but he doesn't have to know that."

"Your mom's? Isn't she going to notice?"

"Yeah, well, a guy's got to sacrifice for his friends sometimes. Next time you got to find something to pawn."

"We don't have anything," Michelle protested. "Mama lives in this dump with hardly even anything to eat! She doesn't have anything to pawn."

"Then you'll have to find something else to contribute," Tanner told her.

"Come on," Michelle protested.

"Come with me to the pawnshop. Kenny can stay here with the rest of the guys."

Michelle acquiesced. She and Tanner went together to the pawnshop. Michelle didn't like the looks of the place. It was crowded and dim and the man behind the counter stank. He pawed through the jewelry with fat yellow fingers.

"Where'd you steal this stuff?" he questioned.

"It's my mom's," Tanner said innocently. "She told me to see what I could get for it to buy medicine for my little brother."

The man's smile was a sneer. "Are you going to be bringing stuff to me regularly?" he asked. "Because I sometimes give my regulars special deals."

Tanner brightened. "Sure. I mean, who knows how long little Timmy's going to be sick."

"Yeah," the man agreed, "who knows? If you and your girlfriend can get me some merchandise in like-new condition, I can give you good prices."

Tanner nodded thoughtfully. "I'll get you some new stuff," he agreed, looking around the shop at the jewelry, watches and stereo equipment. "So what can you give me for this?"

The man pushed the jewelry around. "It's all just cheap stuff," he commented and gave him a price. Tanner was pleased.

"Great. I'll bring you some more stuff soon."

Tanner eagerly took the money and he and Michelle left. Tanner was very pleased with himself. "That stuff was just junk. Imagine what I can get for new stuff."

"Where are you going to get new stuff?"

"Where are *we* gonna get new stuff," Tanner corrected. "You're in this with me. I told you it's your turn next time."

"Where, Tanner?"

He shrugged. "I'll help you. Right now, let's go home and get something to eat."

Michelle woke up fuzzily, disoriented. It was dark and she didn't know where she was. Her head hurt. Probably from drinking. Michelle lifted her head and looked around. She was sleeping across someone else, Michelle could feel his leg. She assumed it was Kenny and they'd fallen asleep together in front of the TV. He stirred when she lifted her head from his lap.

Michelle started to pick objects out of the darkness. They weren't at June's apartment, they were still at Tanner's. Michelle shook his leg. "Kenny, Kenny wake up."

"I'm not Kenny," Tanner's dry voice informed her.

Michelle started and pulled away from him. "What happened?"

"Nothing happened, precious. You fell asleep."

"Is Kenny here?"

"Sure, you think he'd leave without you?"

"We gotta go home," Michelle said, starting to get up.

"It's late, Michelle. How are you going to get there?"

"The bus."

"The last bus has gone."

Michelle swore. "I'm going to be in trouble."

She got up and went to the phone. She dialed June's new number with uncertain fingers. June answered the phone after four or five rings.

"Yeah?"

"It's me, Mama."

"Michelle? Where are you?" June demanded.

"I'm at a friend's. I—I forgot to tell you I was sleeping over."

"Is your dimwitted brother there too?"

Michelle swallowed and bit her lip. "Kenny's here."

June sighed. "I thought something had happened to you guys. What's the matter with you? You can't just go running off without telling me."

"I forgot."

"I might believe that of Kenny, but not you, Michelle. You're doing this because you're trying to get back at me for something. Well, it's not going to work. Stay wherever you like. I don't care."

Michelle was confused. She hung onto the phone for a minute longer. "So, it's okay if I stay here?"

"Yeah. Next time don't even bother to call."

June hung up. Michelle stood there, her mind whirling. "Okay," she said finally, and slowly hung up the receiver.

"What's up?" Tanner asked from the darkness of the hallway. "What'd she say?"

"I don't know," Michelle mumbled, and she looked around, disoriented. "Where's Kenny?"

"He's asleep, don't bother him. You can stay? She's not gonna come get you?"

"Yeah."

"Good. Come on, then."

He took her by the hand and led her to his bedroom. Michelle resisted. "No."

"Shut up and go back to sleep. I'm not going to do anything."

Michelle lay down. As soon as she closed her eyes, she started drifting. She was aware of Tanner lying down beside her, and then she was asleep again.

She woke up in the morning to Kenny shaking her. "Michelle. Wake up."

Michelle rolled over to avoid his grasp and rolled into Tanner.

"We got school," Kenny insisted.

Michelle rubbed her eyes, looking at Tanner sleeping next to her. "What day is it?"

Kenny shrugged.

Michelle tried to clear her head but was too fuzzy. "Tanner," she shook him, "Tanner, what day is it?"

Tanner grumbled and pushed her hand away. "What is it?"

"What day is it?"

"Friday."

"We gotta go to school."

"So we'll be late."

Michelle sat up and slid out of bed. Tanner's older sister stopped in the doorway, sweeping her greasy blond hair back from her face.

"Tanner, you better get your butt out of bed and get your friends out of here before Dad gets off of night."

Tanner propped himself up on one elbow and swore at her. "Dad won't care if anyone's here, Emma. Just mind your own business."

"He ain't going to like you sleeping with your girlfriend, is he? You're not even supposed to have a girl in your bedroom."

Tanner grunted. "Like you ain't supposed to spend the night away from home? Don't you think Dad's going to want to know how come you let a girl stay over with me? Maybe I'll tell him it's because you were sleepin' at your boyfriend's house."

"You know I don't have a boyfriend," she snapped.

"Well, he ain't gonna believe me if I tell him you got a girlfriend."

She flushed and swore at Tanner. She looked Michelle up and down, scowling. "You're too young to be sleeping with my brother. He's trouble. You just stay away from him."

Tanner got up. "Leave her alone and get out of here," he said threateningly.

Emma backed off. She walked away, and Tanner shook his head. "Man, she is so screwed up."

"What do you mean?" Michelle asked, squinting at him and rubbing her throbbing head.

Tanner grinned. "She likes girls, not guys. Don't you get it? She's mad at me for letting you stay here because she's jealous."

Michelle felt sick. "Jealous?" she repeated. "You mean…?"

Tanner laughed at her expression. "Yeah, she thinks you're cute. Poor Michelle; not only are the guys starting to notice you, but now you got girls wanting favors too!"

Michelle shook her head. "You're lying."

"Think whatever you want," Tanner said with a laugh and a shrug. He stretched sleepily. "Well, I guess I'm awake now. We may as well go."

Michelle nodded, happy to have him thinking about something else instead of making up stories to bug her. Tanner got out of bed and nodded at Kenny.

"Hey, Kenny. Are any of the others still around?"

Kenny nodded.

Tanner went into the bathroom and shut the door. Michelle went out to the front room to see who was still there. There was garbage from the night before all over the carpet. A couple of guys were still sleeping. A couple were awake, smoking or just looking around tiredly.

"Well, it's little Michelle," Anderson commented. "You and Tanner have a nice sleep?"

Michelle scowled. "Get lost."

"Oh, come on. You two go off together and we're not supposed to notice?"

Michelle bit her lip. "We were just sleeping," she snapped, "not doing anything."

She knew there was no point in telling them, but she said it anyway. She couldn't convince them, but she couldn't just let it go without protest. Anderson nodded knowingly. "Well, next time, come sleep with *me*, huh?"

Michelle walked out of the house. The door slammed behind her, and a few minutes later Kenny ran up behind her and caught up.

"Slow down, Michelle."

She slowed down slightly for him. "I hate those guys."

Kenny didn't say anything for a moment. "They're just joshing," he said.

"Well, it isn't something to joke about."

He walked beside her.

"Do you know what time it is?" Michelle asked.

He shook his head. "Must be late."

They didn't say anything until they got to the school. Kenny waved at Michelle and hurried to his class. Michelle entered her class quietly. The teacher looked at her as she crept to her desk and sat down and said nothing as she finished her lesson. After she finished talking, she motioned Michelle to come up to her desk. Michelle approached and stood nervously.

"Do you have a note?" the teacher questioned.

"No."

"Why are you late?"

"Slept in."

"It's half-way through the morning."

"I was up late."

"You'll have to stay in at recess and lunch to go over what you missed. And a detention after school."

Michelle nodded. Kenny would have detention too. And Tanner, if he went to school. She turned to go back to her seat.

"And Michelle..." Michelle turned back. "Don't make a habit of this, or you'll go to the office."

~

Michelle was serving her detention alone in the classroom when Marsden walked in. Michelle looked at her uncertainly, biting her lip.

"Hi, Michelle."

"Hi."

Marsden sat down on top of one of the other desks, facing Michelle. "I talked to your mom this morning."

"Uh-huh."

"She says you and Kenny never went home last night."

"We fell asleep at a friend's house. I called Mama last night. She said she didn't mind."

"Well, I am responsible to keep track of you and I say you can't stay away from home on a school night. If you want to sleep over somewhere, I need to talk to a chaperone who will be there. Understand?"

Michelle nodded.

"You know what expectations I have of you, Michelle. Don't pull stunts like this."

"It wasn't a stunt."

Marsden frowned. "Do you understand what I just told you about being chaperoned?"

"Yeah."

"Then I don't want any argument on what's appropriate."

"I just said it wasn't a stunt. It was an accident."

"Was Kenny with you?"

"Yes."

"You know he follows your example."

"I was tired. We both fell asleep."

"I don't want it to happen again."

Michelle shrugged. Arguing was only good up to a point. Marsden wasn't listening.

"How did things go on the weekend?" Marsden questioned after a moment.

"Okay, I guess."

"So you feel a little bit better about being back with your mom now? Now you know everything will be okay?"

"I don't know that."

"Nothing happened this weekend I should know about?"

"No."

"Would you tell me if there was?"

Marsden made a point of meeting Michelle's eyes. Michelle looked away. Would there be any point in telling Marsden if something was wrong? She and Kenny could probably take care of themselves just as well as any foster family could. At least with June, they had the freedom to come and go as they pleased. There was no curfew. As long as June didn't tell Marsden the hours they were keeping. But if June started hitting Kenny again? Would Michelle go to Marsden with that?

"I don't know," she said finally.

"You can trust me, Michelle. I don't want you to think I'm out to get you. I'm trying to keep you safe."

Safe like she'd been at the Lollers', with Stan? That wouldn't have happened if they had just stayed with June. And maybe June was right. Maybe Justin wouldn't have taken off if he hadn't known the kids would be away from June in foster care. Maybe he would have stuck around to help out. Maybe Michelle *had* made the wrong decision.

"I know."

"Good. You and Kenny need to come to me if there are things going on that shouldn't. Your mom may still need some extra help keeping things together."

Michelle nodded. "Okay."

Although Kenny didn't want to, Michelle insisted they go home after school. She wanted to talk to June.

"Oh, you're home," June commented when they walked in.

Kenny sat down on the pulled-out bed to watch the TV June already had on. Michelle stayed standing. "Mama?"

"What?"

"How come you told Mrs. Marsden about us not coming home last night?"

June didn't even look at her. "I don't know. I was mad."

"So you want me to call Marsden whenever I'm mad at you?"

June looked at her. "What?" Michelle didn't say anything. "You're not going to tell her any lies about me."

"I won't have to tell lies," Michelle pointed out.

June scowled. She turned back to the TV and didn't say anything until the show was almost over. Then she spoke without looking up.

"I won't tell her if you don't come home," she said, "but only if you don't tell her things about me."

Kenny turned and looked at Michelle, eyebrows raised, impressed. Michelle went into the kitchen to make something to eat.

CHAPTER
Fourteen

Michelle looked over the watches on the display rack idly, looking to see if they had the style Kenny wanted. She wished they could have the money welfare gave to June for them. Where it went to, Michelle wasn't sure. The rent on that dump in the slums couldn't be that much. But Michelle didn't know what June spent it on. She couldn't even do what Tanner had done because she didn't have anything to pawn.

Michelle looked at the rack of watches with new eyes. She glanced around to see if anyone was looking at her.

~

Tanner was impressed by Michelle's take. "Man, what did you do? Knock over a convenience store?"

Michelle shrugged. "It's not much," she said, even though it was the most money she had ever held in her hand. Tanner counted it out again.

"We should elect a treasurer for the gang," he said thoughtfully, "to look after dough like this. I mean me and the guys; we'll just spend it all at once."

Michelle nodded. Tanner handed it back to her. "You hold the bag, Michelle. I trust you."

Michelle was surprised. "I thought you wanted money for the gang."

"I do. I'm going to make sure the others start contributing too. But when they do, you're taking care of the cash. I'm no good with money. I can never keep it."

"Okay," Michelle said doubtfully. "You want me to put it in the bank?"

"If you want," Tanner said, "I guess no one could steal it that way."

"Okay."

∼

Michelle and Kenny went home for a few minutes to change clothes, since it had been a few days since they had been home. Michelle glanced around the quiet apartment for June. The bedroom door was shut, and she couldn't tell if June was home or not. Kenny changed in the bathroom while Michelle changed in the front room. As they were getting ready to go, Michelle tapped on the door.

"Mama? Are you home?" There was no response. Michelle turned the doorknob and pushed the door open. June was lying on the bed. "Mama? Are you asleep?"

June didn't move. Michelle glanced over her shoulder at Kenny, who was standing at the door to the outside hall, ready to leave.

"Just wait a minute," Michelle said. She went up to June and touched her arm.

"Mama?"

She looked around the room. Watching June carefully, Michelle could discern June's shallow breathing. The air in the room was hot, like the door had been shut for a long time. Michelle tried to decide what to do, not wanting to get involved in June's problems. She stood there for a minute, and Kenny came into the bedroom.

"Is she dead?" he asked flatly, as if he wouldn't care if she was.

"No. Passed out."

"Let's go."

"We should call an ambulance."

"Let's just go."

"What if she doesn't wake up?"

Kenny shrugged. Michelle shook her head. "People would figure it out sooner or later. Marsden would come by. Who knows where we'd end up? It's better here. No one watches us."

Michelle talked herself into it. She picked up the phone and there was a dial tone. Somebody had paid the phone bill. Maybe Social Services. Michelle dialed nine-one-one.

"Do you kids want to ride to the hospital with us?" one of the medics asked, after loading the gurney with June on it into the ambulance.

Michelle shook her head. "We'd better stay here until Dad gets home. Then we'll all go together."

"When will he be home?"

"Soon. Half an hour."

"Okay. He can fill out the admitting paperwork when he gets there. As long as it's not too long. Okay?"

Michelle nodded. "Sure."

As they drove off, she tried to figure out who they were going to get to fill out the admitting papers for June. She didn't want to call Marsden. Justin was not going to come home and do it. If no one filled them out, someone would call Marsden for sure.

"Come on, Kenny, we gotta go."

Kenny didn't question it, he just went with her. They went to Tanner's house, and Michelle explained the problem.

"I need to get someone to pretend to be my dad on the phone," she explained, "someone who sounds older. He can say he got tied up out of town and give them all the information they need. And he can tell them a neighbor is looking after me and Kenny so they don't call Social Services."

Tanner nodded. "We could get Andrew's brother. He's cool and he has a really deep voice."

The gang had been out for a while and they were bored.

"Let's do something," Tanner said tightly, all wound up. "I mean let's really *do* something. Not this baby stuff. I mean—if we're a real gang, let's do something."

"Just one problem," Michelle said dryly.

"What?"

"We're not a real gang."

"What are you talking about?"

"You really think you're a real gang? Where's your turf? Does anyone even know who you are?"

Tanner looked uncomfortable. "Well, we're not one of the main gangs," he admitted grudgingly.

"You're not a gang at all. You just think you are."

The other boys were agreeing with Michelle, which wasn't good for Tanner. He looked around at them. "You all think that? That we aren't really a gang?"

"We just hang around together," Templeton pointed out. "We never really do anything. And Simpson's right—no one knows who we are."

"Well... so what do we do about it?"

No one said anything. Eventually, they all looked back at Michelle, who shrugged widely.

"We could join a gang," Kenny suggested.

There was silence. A few of the boys shook their heads automatically, pride kicking in. Tanner just stared at Kenny, who hung his head in shame for saying something dumb in front of the boys he respected. Tanner slapped Kenny on the shoulder and didn't say anything. The silence was eventually broken by tentative conversations among the gang. Tanner, Michelle and Kenny all remained quiet and contemplative the rest of the night.

"You know, Kenny's not so dumb," Tanner said to Michelle.

"I know he's not," Michelle snapped back.

"Don't get all huffy. You know I got nothing against Kenny. He's a good guy. I'm talking about last night when he said we oughta join a real gang. He's right."

"I know."

"Most of the guys aren't going to want to do it."

"Uh-huh.."

"So what are you going to do? Stay with the boys or come with me?"

Michelle shrugged.

"Is that a yes or a no?" Tanner persisted.

"Depends what Kenny does. Just stay with the guys, I hope. You're the only one who wants a real gang."

"Kenny will come with me. It was his idea."

"I hope not."

"He will," Tanner assured her.

Michelle went back to the apartment to check on things. Kenny had refused to go back with her, so she had left him with Tanner. Michelle went into the apartment and looked around.

"Mama?"

"What is it?" June demanded from behind the closed bedroom door.

"Are you okay, Mama?" Michelle asked, going into the kitchen to check out the fridge and cupboards.

"Of course I'm okay."

The fridge was empty. The cupboards were nearly empty. The bedroom door opened and Michelle turned around. A man stood in the doorway. He was tall, rough-looking, and wore lots of leather and jewelry. Michelle swallowed.

"Who are you?"

"Jason," he enlightened her. He walked into the kitchen entryway, studying Michelle. June stood in the doorway of the bedroom for a moment, looking pale and disoriented. She dragged herself into the bathroom and shut the door.

"So you're her kid?" Jason questioned.

"Yeah. Is she okay?"

"She's pretty strung out. But she'll be all right."

"Are you her boyfriend?"

He grimaced. "Her? You have to get that one pretty doped up to get anywhere with her. Mostly I'm just her supplier."

"Oh. A pusher."

He shrugged. "I prefer supplier, but whatever you want."

Michelle tried to inch toward the doorway to get out of the kitchen, staying as far from him as possible.

"You gave her too much before," Michelle informed him. "She just about died."

He didn't appear to care. "She owes me some dough. I came by to see if I could get anything out of her. But she doesn't seem to have anything around here worth crap."

Michelle got as close as she dared to him and then made a dash to try to get by him. But he was waiting for it, and he caught her before she could get past.

"Until *you* got here," Jason added. "I'd write off some of her bill for you."

Michelle squirmed to escape his grasp, but he was strong. He forced her into the bedroom and tossed her onto the bed. Michelle grasped under her shirt for her knife. Her hand closed around the hilt as June came back into the room.

"Leave her alone," June warned. "If you lay a finger on her I'm never buying from you again."

He laughed. "You'll come back to me, baby. You can't go without."

"I can find another dealer."

"Now why would you want to go and do that? Not everybody would be willing to give you a line of credit just to be with her." He indicated Michelle with a casual gesture.

"Keep away from my baby girl."

Jason studied her for a moment, then shrugged. "You'll change your mind after a while. I'll be back tomorrow and I expect to see some cash."

June nodded. "I'll get you some."

He walked out. Michelle heard the hallway door shut after him, and breathed out, relieved.

"You okay, baby?" June asked, moving toward Michelle.

"He didn't hurt me," Michelle said, letting go of her knife and trying to calm her shaking muscles.

"You stay away from guys like that. Don't you know better?"

"I didn't know he was here. You never told me."

"Well, I thought you had some sense."

Michelle decided to let it go.

"Do you need anything, Mama? I came to make sure you were okay."

"I don't need anything from you."

"Money?" Michelle suggested.

June looked at her sharply. "Where would you get money?"

"How much do you need?"

"Couple hundred more than I got."

Michelle got up. "I'll get you some if I can," she promised. She walked by June and left.

She was still shaking when she left the building. She tried to calm herself down, tried to block the experience from her mind. She went to the bank.

When Michelle got back to Tanner's house, Kenny was waiting for her outside. "You took forever," Kenny complained.

"I know. Mama needed some help."

"Tanner and me are joining the other gang."

"You don't want to do that, Kenny. You don't know what it's going to be like."

"I want to go with Tanner."

"We don't want to do that. The new gang will be involved in all kinds of things—"

"I don't care," Kenny maintained stubbornly.

"Why? What did Tanner tell you?"

"Nothing. I just want to go with Tanner."

Michelle shook her head. "You don't know what it's going to be like."

Kenny shrugged.

CHAPTER
Fifteen

"This is Dan Thompson," Tanner introduced the boy to Michelle. "He's one of the guys in the gang we're gonna join up with. He says he can get us in without a problem."

He was older and taller than Tanner. Dark, shaggy hair.

"I said I could get *you* in," Dan corrected, studying Michelle and Kenny while chewing on an unlit cigarette. "I don't know about them."

"Kenny and Michelle have been good members of my gang," Tanner defended them. "They'd be good for any gang."

"Maybe. She's pretty young. And we don't really have girls in the gang. Kenny, I can probably get in with you. But her... I don't know."

"If I can't get in, Kenny doesn't get in either," Michelle said.

Kenny scowled at her but didn't argue. Dan considered this new information for a moment.

"I don't know. You Tanner's girlfriend?"

Michelle glanced at Tanner. "Would that get me in?"

"Mmm. Maybe. No guarantee. I don't know what the guys are going to think about it."

"You said anything you said would go," Tanner reminded Dan, prodding his ego.

"Yeah. If I tell them, they'll let you in. And Kenny. But her? Girls are a different story."

"Do you have any other girls in the gang?" Michelle asked.

"Well, a couple. They just sort of hung out with us for a while. Everybody sort of forgot they were girls. You're different, though."

"Different how?"

"Too young... not tough enough."

Tanner grinned suddenly. "Don't let her looks fool you. She's a lot tougher than she looks. Eh, Michelle?"

She knew he was thinking about Stan, wanting her permission to tell Dan about it. She shook her head. She raised the hem of her shirt a few inches to show Dan her knife, without saying anything. He raised his brows.

"Nice. Where'd you get that?"

"Bought it."

"Anyone can buy a knife. Can you use it?"

"If I have to."

Dan nodded. "Well, maybe. We'll see."

Tanner nodded, satisfied. "You'll see. She's a credit to any gang."

Dan shrugged. "I know what it's like to have to look after a younger sibling," he told Kenny sympathetically.

Michelle's anger rose. Kenny take care of her? She took care of Kenny, and her mother, and even the gang. She didn't need anyone to look after *her*.

"Nobody takes care of me," she snapped at Dan. "I don't need to be babysat."

He looked at her and didn't say anything. It was obvious he simply didn't think it was worth the argument. He didn't believe it.

When they both got unsatisfactory report cards that had to be signed by a parent, Kenny stayed with Tanner and Michelle braved the lion's den with both cards. She wouldn't have actually had June sign them if the teacher hadn't warned her they would be placing a follow-up call to June. It was not the first time they had received unsatisfactory report cards.

June was alone in the apartment. Michelle wondered briefly what had happened to the job June was supposed to have. Michelle threw the report cards down on the couch next to June and went into the kitchen. June glanced at the papers.

"Did you bring any money?" June asked.

"Maybe." Michelle looked in the fridge. "You didn't buy any groceries again, Mama."

"I don't eat much."

Michelle picked up the phone and got a dial tone. She called the grocery store to deliver to the apartment.

"What are these?" June asked, looking at the report cards.

"Marks. You have to sign them."

June looked at them. "I never had to sign them before."

"Well, this time you do."

"What do they say? I can't read this small print and handwriting."

Michelle took them from her. "You can't read a thing, can you?"

"I can read fine. I just need glasses or something."

"Uh-huh. They say Kenny's marks aren't doing so great and my teachers think I'm uncooperative."

"Kenny always was stupid."

Michelle turned on her. "You leave Kenny alone! What'd he ever do to you?"

"Where is he, anyway? He get in trouble?"

"He's scared to come here."

June shook her head. "What're you getting in trouble at school for? I thought you were the smart one."

"I don't like school. Just sign them, okay?"

June scrawled her name on both reports. She had a signature like a ten-year-old. She tossed them aside. "You're quite the little boss, aren't you?"

"Shut up," Michelle told her tiredly.

"What?" June stood up and shoved Michelle. "You show me some respect! I'm your mama!"

"Keep your hands off of me! You can't push me around anymore."

June raised her hand to strike and Michelle moved out of the way. "I'm not a baby anymore. You can't hurt me."

June lashed out, but Michelle blocked the blow and hit June with a closed fist. Her knuckles stung but she felt exhilarated. All these years, she'd been afraid of June. But she could hit back. She could get the upper hand. June couldn't control Michelle.

June cried out at the blow. "You hit me! What'd you do that for?" She covered her face, crying. "Don't hit me."

"You hit me and Kenny plenty more than that," Michelle pointed out. "You hurt him real bad sometimes."

"You don't know what it's like to try to raise two kids like you," June wept. She collapsed in a storm of tears.

Michelle went back to the kitchen and got the bottle she had seen there earlier. She handed it to June. "Here. Drink that."

"You're just like my daddy!" June muttered.

Michelle was surprised. June had never mentioned any family before. She had always assumed June grew up with foster families or in an orphanage.

"Do you want it or not?"

June took it from her. Michelle watched TV until the delivery man got there with the groceries. She paid him out of the money she had brought for June. She unloaded the groceries into the fridge and handed June the rest of the money.

"Don't spend it all on drugs," she said. June took the money without answering and tucked it into her jeans pocket. Michelle shrugged. "Well, I guess I'll see you around."

Michelle saw Jason outside the apartment building. She tried not to be seen by him, but he spotted her and approached her rapidly on his long, gangly legs. "Simpson. I want to talk to you."

Michelle couldn't outrun him, so she waited until he caught up to her, although she kept her hand under her shirt on her knife and kept her distance.

"You give her money?" Jason demanded.

"What's it to you?"

"If you gave her money, she can pay her tab. So did you?"

"I don't want her buying drugs. They're bad for her."

"Well, it doesn't stop her from buying them. So?"

Michelle sighed. "Yeah, she's got money. But you watch how much you give her. Or I won't bring any more money."

He laughed. "Fiery gal, ain't ya? Look, you want to make some easy money?"

Michelle frowned. "What're you talking about?"

"I need someone to make a few deliveries for me. I'll pay you good."

Michelle considered, then shook her head. "I can get money."

"Well, don't work too hard for it. 'cause you can get it easy from me."

Michelle shook her head again. "No."

"Well, think about it anyway. And I'll tell you what. You ever want to start distributing for me, I'll give you discount prices. Got me?"

"I don't do drugs."

"Maybe not. But I'll bet your friends do."

Michelle walked away from him.

~

"We're going shopping," Tanner announced.

"Shopping? Where?"

"I want to get you some things," he said obliquely.

"What things?" Michelle demanded.

Tanner grinned at her. "I been thinking about what Dan said the other day."

"About what?"

"About you looking too young. And not tough enough. We're gonna get you fixed up so you'll fit in."

Michelle tried to protest, but Tanner wouldn't listen. Kenny waited for them, his eyes bright with anticipation.

She agreed to the bright red lipstick and the blush Tanner picked out at the drugstore, but refused the blue eye shadow and goopy mascara. Kenny liked the black lipstick for some reason and Michelle eventually agreed to buy it.

The next place Tanner took her to, Michelle hung back at the door. "No way, Tanner."

"Come on, what are you scared of?"

Michelle stared at all the brightly colored tattoo patterns plastered all over the walls and the full-color nude poster showing body piercing sites. "Everything," she said, wide-eyed.

Tanner laughed. "You got your ears pierced, didn't you?"

"That's different. I was just a baby."

"It doesn't hurt," Tanner showed off his earring. "Really, it's nothing. Kenny's going to get an earring, ain't ya, Kenny?"

Kenny nodded. A girl popping gum, who had rings in her ears, nose, and eyebrows, came up to them. "Help ya?"

Tanner took over, not giving Michelle a chance to decline. "We want a row of studs here," he said, drawing an imaginary line along Michelle's ear, "and a ring here," he pointed to the top of her ear. And..." he considered, "Maybe a nose-ring..."

"No," Michelle said, "I don't want a nose-ring."

"Well, what about belly-button then?" he suggested.

"No one would see it, what's the point?"

"We'll buy you a couple of those short shirts that show it off."

"I can't wear a midi," Michelle argued, and lifted up her shirt to show him her knife.

"Well, not at school, but you just wear a big shirt over top at school. Then when you get out, you take it off. I think the navel ring and knife together would look cool."

The older girl waiting on them nodded. "Very cool," she agreed. She studied Michelle, making her squirm. "Look at some of the tattoos too, okay? I'll get ready while you do."

"*You're* doing it?"

"Why not? It doesn't take a brain surgeon. I can even do it to myself."

"I don't want you doing it."

The girl shrugged. "I'll see if Wade is free. But usually he just does the artwork."

Tanner glared at Michelle when the girl walked away. "Why are you being so hard to get along with? It's like a little gun, they just hold it up to your ear and pull the trigger. It's not like they could slip."

"She's not hygienic. I could get an infection."

"They keep the tools clean."

"I don't want her doing it. I don't want an infection."

Wade was walking out from behind the curtain in the back, and he grinned when he heard her. He was a big, blond man. He wore leather and had all kinds of tattoos on his arms, but his manner was calming and professional.

"You wouldn't be the first one Carrie had scared off. Come on over here and sit down and let me show you what we do."

He gestured to a chair and Michelle reluctantly went over. He showed her his tools and the earrings and indicated the bottle of alcohol on the table.

"Everything should be sterile when we take it out of the sealed packages. But I like to rinse them off just to be sure. I'll also wipe your ear with alcohol before we start, so no bacteria on your skin gets into it. If you notice redness or swelling, you come back and see me right away and I'll take a look. Okay?"

Michelle nodded mutely.

"Okay. Carrie told me what you want. You want to pick out the earrings you like?"

Michelle did. While he was washing up, she watched Carrie come back into the room and go up to Tanner and Kenny again. Kenny had his new earring done before Michelle's first one even went in. Wade talked to her soothingly while he worked, and Tanner was right, the earrings didn't really hurt.

Wade had her lie down for the navel piercing. Michelle lay with her shirt held partway up while he swabbed her down and inserted the ring. Then he sat her back up again.

"That's all there is to it. That wasn't so bad, was it?"

Michelle shook her head.

"How about a tattoo?" he suggested. "You've got fantastic skin."

"No, I don't think so."

"Come here, let me show you some of them. We have some pretty artwork you might like."

He walked her over to the wall with the tattoo patterns taped to it and showed her a small grouping.

"These are some of the favorites among the young ladies. Flowers, hearts, butterflies, birds, all very small and very discreet. You put them here," he touched the sleeve over her right bicep, "or here," he turned her and touched her back over her shoulder blade, "or here," he touched her breast fleetingly, "where they don't show when you're dressed conservatively. You want to put on a strapless gown, halter-top, something with a wide v-neck or sleeveless, and you don't even have to think about jewelry. It's already there. And guys find tattoos on ladies very attractive."

Michelle hesitated. "I don't know."

"Look at them and I'll go talk to your friends and see if they need anything else."

He went over to Tanner and Kenny to see what they were interested in. There was a big, intricate dragon Tanner wanted across his chest and a skull and crossbones Kenny wanted on his hand. Wade was tactful.

"Neither of you has had one done before?"

"No."

"We usually like to start with something smaller. Some people react to the dyes, so we like to start slow. Say, this other dragon on your bicep. More visible than your chest. What do you think?"

"You're the expert," Tanner acquiesced.

"And you," Wade turned his attention to Kenny, "the back of the hand isn't a bad place for someone experienced. But it's more sensitive than biceps or some other areas. You might like to try another site for your first one."

Kenny shook his head adamantly. "No, I want it here."

Wade shrugged. "All right. Let's see if Michelle has made up her mind."

They went over to Michelle. "So what are you getting?" Tanner demanded.

"I don't know if I want to."

"Sure you do. Which one do you like?"

Michelle pointed to a rose with thorns.

"Don't pick a girly one," Tanner protested. "Come on, get something tough."

"If I'm getting a tattoo, that's the one I'm getting."

"Okay. Fine. That's the one Michelle's getting."

The tattoos took a long time, but Tanner wasn't ready to call it quits. They went to buy new clothes. Michelle wouldn't buy most of what Tanner pointed out to her. She agreed to some shirts and tops that showed off her new navel ring and tattoo, but refused to consider the short skirts he liked.

"I don't wear dresses."

"You'd look good in one."

"I thought you didn't want me to look feminine."

"Yeah, I guess." Tanner frowned, looking at her critically. "You still don't look that different. Blue jeans are okay, but you need something else." His expression brightened after a moment. "I know."

Michelle felt really out of place at the motorcycle shop. She wasn't even old enough to drive. But when Tanner showed her the black leather pants, she knew they were in the right place. She loved their look and feel, and also fell in love with a black leather jacket on display nearby. Tanner grinned at her.

"So am I right? You want them?"

"Yeah."

"Good. Now we just need one more thing."

"What?"

Tanner grasped one of her long locks of hair. "This cutesy hair. You gotta get something done with it."

Michelle touched her hair, frowning. "My hair? It's not bad. It's not much longer than yours."

"Yeah, well, long hair on a guy is tough. On a girl, it's just girlie. What did you call it? Feminine."

"So you think I should cut it?"

"Cut it, dye it, something."

Michelle sighed. She'd never been particularly proud of her straight, drab hair. But she'd always worn it long. If Justin came back, he'd never recognize her. A streak of rebellion rippled through her. Justin was never going to come back. It was stupid to keep wishing he would.

"Both," she said recklessly, "bleach it and get it cut short."

Tanner raised his brows. "Okay. Then, I think we'll be done."

Michelle nodded.

She changed at Tanner's house after her hair was done.

"Boy, you look butch," Tanner exclaimed. "You'd better stay away from my sister!"

"That's what you wanted, isn't it?" Michelle snapped.

"Yeah, but I never thought you would look quite so different. Have you looked in the mirror?"

"No."

There was no mirror in Tanner's room where she had changed into her new get-up.

"Come on," Tanner said, steering her towards his parents' room.

MICHELLE

Michelle stared at the mirror, not believing what she saw. She looked nothing like herself. She wasn't sure who she looked like. Some biker chick. She looked at least a couple years older, like she was a teenager instead of a kid. The halter top showed off her figure, the navel ring, and the tattoo. And her knife. The leather pants made her legs look long and slim.

"Didn't believe me, did you?" Tanner questioned, laughing. "Put on your makeup."

Michelle got out the lipstick and blush they had talked her into and put it on carefully, trying not to make it too obvious. Tanner nodded in satisfaction.

"I can't believe how different you look. Dan's going to flip. He's going to have to take you now."

Michelle dressed more conservatively for school. Although she was wearing the halter top underneath, she wore one of her big shirts as usual. She didn't wear any makeup. But she still looked different. She still had her "butch" haircut and dye job and her new earrings. The teacher opened her mouth as if to speak, upon seeing Michelle, but then closed it and didn't say anything. Michelle went to her desk and sat down. She could hear whispered comments around her, but no one dared say anything to her face. Michelle sat and stared at the blackboard, feeling self-conscious and alone.

CHAPTER Sixteen

Dan laughed when he saw Michelle.

"What did you do to the poor kid? It's not Halloween!"

Michelle's face got hot. She looked at Tanner.

"You don't think she looks better?" Tanner asked, surprised.

"Better than what? Maybe when she grows into the look. Man, she looks like something out of some kiddie porn!"

He was bigger than she was. Older by six or seven years. But that didn't mean he could make fun of her. "I'm no kid," Michelle snapped. "I'm smarter than you are and I've seen plenty."

"Yeah, you been around the block, I can tell. Come on, when I was your age—"

Tanner held up his hand warningly, but it was too late. Michelle went off like a firecracker. "When you were my age, what? You were looking after your junkie mom? And your brother? And your dad took off? Had you been in foster homes? Had your whole family taken away from you? Had you killed someone yet? I bet you ain't been through all that yet!"

Dan was floored by her outburst. He didn't say anything for a few minutes. Michelle waited furiously for him to respond, glaring at him.

"You mind if I take your girlfriend for a walk?" Dan asked Tanner.

"Uh, sure," Tanner said, startled, motioning for him to go ahead. "If she wants to go."

Michelle shrugged. Dan struck off down the street and Michelle followed him. They were both silent for a while, then Dan spoke. "One day I came home after bein' out with some of the boys. My li'l' brother George was sitting on the steps outside the house. The house was empty and our folks had just cleared out." Michelle listened, hearing in Dan's voice a familiar emotion. Abandonment. She waited for him to go on. "Georgie ain't right anymore. He was in an accident after that. I gotta look after him."

"Like Kenny," Michelle murmured.

"I wish he was like Kenny," Dan said sadly.

They walked in silence.

"I wasn't your age, though," Dan admitted. "I don't think I could have handled it then. I was just out on the town at your age. My folks taking care of things."

"So don't get on my case about being a kid. We had to go into foster care when I was eight 'cause of my mama beatin' up on us all the time. And that was no picnic." Michelle didn't know why she was telling him everything. She'd been holding it all in and it just came spilling out. "They ended up splitting me and Kenny up and my daddy took off for good."

"I didn't mean nothin' personal." He didn't say anything for a while. "You say your mom's a junkie?" he questioned.

"Yeah."

"That's tough."

Again the pain, the understanding in his voice. Michelle glanced at him. "Your folks?"

"No."

"Your brother?"

Dan shook his head silently. He wasn't offering any explanation. Michelle didn't pursue it. There was another long silence and Dan led her into an ice cream shop. He bought a couple of plain cones and they sat down.

"Who'd you kill?"

Michelle startled. "What?"

"You said you bet I hadn't killed anyone. When I was your age. So who did a kid like you ice?"

She was surprised he had taken in everything she had said. She should have been more careful. She didn't know whether to tell him the truth or not.

"A guy. Foster brother. Cops don't know, though. They think it was a burglary."

"I'm not gonna go running to the cops with the news. So what for? Why'd you do it?"

"Personal reasons," Michelle said finally, choosing not to reveal more than that. Dan considered this and shrugged.

"So don't get in your way, is that what you're telling me?" he teased.

Michelle gave him a small smile and nodded. "Yeah. That's right."

"I can get you in. I think. But, umm… you may have to fight for your rep. It ain't gonna be easy."

Dan introduced Tanner, Kenny, and Michelle to the members of the gang who were there. He did it too quickly for Michelle to remember them all later. She would remember the one Dan introduced as 'Wheels,' though. He was thin and pale with sunken eyes so dark they looked bruised. And he was in a wheelchair.

"Well, why don't we go to the arcade?" Dan suggested.

There were murmurs of assent from around the gang. Dan motioned casually to Wheels. "Why don't you bring Wheels?"

Michelle was surprised, she thought he would want to take care of himself. She went over to the boy.

"Take off the brakes," Dan advised.

"I know," Michelle snapped, already with her hand on the wheel brake. Dan looked surprised. He shrugged. Wheels' head swiveled to look at Michelle. She couldn't read his expression. He turned back away from her again. Michelle followed the rest of the gang to the flashing, beeping, noise-filled arcade. Michelle looked at Wheels.

"Where do you want me to put you?"

"Anywhere," he said uncaringly.

"Um, okay." Michelle parked him where he had a good vantage point and stood around for a few minutes, awkward. Then she left him alone.

Later, they were back at the gang headquarters and Michelle took the bottle being passed around but didn't drink from it. She started to hand it off to Dan, but the boy next to her poked her, making her jump.

"Don't give it to Dan!" he hissed.

"Why not?"

"He's a twelve-stepper."

"A what?"

"AA. He don't drink since what happened to Wheels."

"Oh." Michelle handed it off to another boy instead.

CHAPTER Seventeen

Michelle was headed home to check on June, but she stopped when she saw the police car and watched to see what was going on.

A couple of cops led June out of the building. Michelle watched in disbelief. Another car pulled up beside the cop car and Marsden got out, immediately questioning the officers. They stood talking for a minute, and Marsden talked to June. It was obvious from her body language she was frustrated and June was not helping her. The cop put June in the car and drove off. Marsden looked around and saw Michelle watching her. For a moment, she didn't recognize Michelle. Then her head jerked up in recognition. Her mouth opened.

"Michelle?" she called finally, in astonishment.

She hadn't seen Michelle's new get-up before. And Michelle was in the full gang get-up, not her school clothes. Michelle stood rooted to the spot for an instant while the reality of the situation flashed through her mind. June had been arrested. Who knew what for. Social Services was not going to leave Michelle and Kenny with her anymore. Maybe June was going to jail. But even if they released her, Social Services was not going to let Kenny and Michelle stay with her. They would be split up again and sent somewhere else.

Michelle turned and ran. She didn't know where she was going, only that she wasn't going to stay and let Marsden catch her and take her somewhere else. Marsden didn't even follow. She just stood there and watched Michelle run.

Kenny took the news about June being arrested in stride. He didn't care. He hadn't gone home since that first day or two anyway. He'd stayed with Tanner or someone else in the gang. Even Michelle wasn't sleeping at home, she never knew what might happen at June's apartment at night. Just because nothing serious had happened yet, that didn't mean it eventually wouldn't.

"We can't go to school," he pointed out.

Michelle thought about it. He was right. If they went to school, Marsden would already have told the staff she had to talk to them. If they showed up, they would get taken to a foster home or a facility right away. She nodded.

"Yeah, I guess you're right."

Kenny nodded, satisfied. "I don't want to go to school anymore."

"Well, I guess we'll have to lie low, so you don't have to go. Nobody knows we're with the gang now. No one at school. They won't know where to look for us."

"So you're free," Tanner said enviously. "Social Services won't look very hard. They won't even put up posters. If I took off, my parents would be looking all over for me. And Emma would tell them where to look."

Michelle laughed. "Yeah, it's nice coming from a broken family, huh?"

Tanner shrugged. "So where are you guys going to live now?"

"Same as usual. Your place sometimes. Wherever works out."

"Zeke's looking for roommates, you know," contributed Dan, who'd been listening in on the conversation.

"You think he'd want us?" Michelle said skeptically.

"He wants someone to help pay the rent. Why should he care who it is?"

Marsden was very worried about Michelle and Kenny. She had been so shocked by Michelle's appearance at first that she hadn't had time to wonder what was going on. But the more she thought about it and talked to people in the building or at the school, the more worried she became.

Michelle had obviously changed. Fallen in with a bad crowd or was trying to get attention by rebelling. Those in the building who had paid any attention said most of the time she was around, she wore a halter-top on its own, or when cooler, wore a leather jacket over top. Marsden had been able to see her stark makeup and bleached hair from across the street, and they told her about the earrings and tattoo. But Michelle hadn't been around much, and no one realized she had a brother.

June had always told her things were going okay—the kids were settling in, the job was going well, they were finally getting a chance to be a family again. It had been a good snow job. Marsden should have realized something was wrong. But she had too many families with obvious trouble to be spending her time on families who seemed okay.

If she had followed up with June's boss, she would have found out June hadn't lasted there more than a few days. To neglect the family to the point that June was captured on a closed-circuit camera holding up a convenience store—there was just no excuse good enough.

June said the money Michelle brought her just wasn't enough to live on. Marsden shuddered to think of what Michelle was doing to bring in any money at all. She wasn't babysitting or working in a burger joint dressed like that. And why was Kenny never at the apartment? What had happened to him?

The school's reports only put her at ease on one point.

"Oh yes, Kenny's still around. Although why he hasn't been put in a special school, I don't know. He cannot keep up with the kids in his own grade, let alone those his age."

"We should pursue that option a little more vigorously. His schoolwork hasn't improved?"

"I don't think the boy can even read, to be honest. But someone looks after his homework."

"Michelle, I guess. How is she keeping up?"

The principal stretched his legs out under his desk and folded his arms. "Michelle is so completely opposite to Kenny in ability. He tries but can only spin his wheels. Michelle could head her class if she tried. But she just doesn't care. Well—you remember when she got suspended. Nothing could convince her she needed to listen in class. She doesn't do any of her homework and hands in nearly-perfect tests."

"Have there been any... changes in her behavior lately?"

"Her behavior? No, not lately. That is—she hasn't changed much since she went back to her mother. Her behavior took a downturn then, but settled into a plateau. She really hasn't been the same since she went back. If you want to look at other indicators, though... her changes in appearance the past few weeks... there has been some speculation about substance abuse... but she won't talk to teachers or counselors..."

"How about her marks?"

"Still good. Because of her test marks, not her homework."

"And Kenny? Any changes in his behavior?"

The man considered. "Hard to put a finger on. They've both had a considerable number of tardies since they went back to their mom. Kenny is still getting into fights. Neither of them has any particular friends here. They stick together."

"What made you think Michelle might have a drug problem?"

"Just general indications—possible depression, inattention, even combativeness in class. Her clothing and image changes."

"When they get in tomorrow, I want to see them both. And I should talk to anyone who might spend time with them too. Going back to their mom was a difficult adjustment. This may be even harder on them."

"Surely you'll see them tonight, before they come back to school tomorrow."

"Well, I hope to. I'll spend the night at the apartment in case they come back there. But it sounds like they may have found alternate arrangements lately."

Zeke wasn't sure about taking on Michelle and Kenny as his roommates. He surveyed Michelle. "I wasn't planning on a girl roomie, you know. It might sort of cramp my style if I want to bring a chick back to the place to mess around."

"I wouldn't care. You got a separate bedroom, don't you?"

"Well, I got two bedrooms. You guys would have to share. You wouldn't want that, I guess."

Michelle wasn't letting him off that easy. "We've shared rooms plenty. We could put up a blanket or room divider."

Zeke thought about it. "You ain't gonna freak or nothing if I bring a girl home?"

"As long as you don't freak if I bring home a guy."

Zeke pictured it and laughed. "Okay, you got a deal."

It was Tanner who suggested Michelle and Kenny throw a party for their move-in. Michelle wasn't sure. "Where am I going to get anything for a party?"

"Be creative, Michelle. You can do anything you put your mind to—you'll prob'ly throw the best party anyone's ever seen."

"I dunno, Tanner."

"Let's do it," Kenny agreed. "It'd make us part of the gang."

"We're already part of the gang," Michelle pointed out.

"Not really. Not yet."

She couldn't argue about it. She knew it was true. They weren't really accepted yet. Michelle tried to figure out how she was going to get what she would need for a party for the gang. She was so much underage, no one was going to sell her anything.

Marsden filed a report with the police when Kenny and Michelle didn't show up at their mother's apartment. She had hoped they would come back, but she hadn't expected them to. Michelle had run, but the expression on her face hadn't been one of fear. She hadn't wanted to be caught, but not because she was afraid.

CHAPTER Eighteen

Michelle figured if she hung around Jason's corner for long enough, he'd show up again. He was probably in the apartment building, or one close by, collecting on a debt. She was aware people were watching her and tried to ignore them. A couple of boys pulled over in a fancy sports car.

"Hey, baby. You wanna come to a party?" one of them shouted.

"Get lost." She turned away from them.

Their tires screeched as they pulled away. Michelle bit her lip, put her hand on her knife and waited. It was an hour before Jason showed up. "Hey Simpson, someone told me you were hanging around here. Looking for me?"

"Yeah. I need—"

"Come on. We'll go somewhere safer. Someone will see you here."

"So?"

"So the cops watch this corner and your social worker's been hanging around looking for you. You want her to find you?"

"No."

"Then let's go for a walk."

Michelle walked with him.

"Sorry to hear about your mom," Jason said.

"What did she do?"

"Knocked off a convenience store. Stupid."

"Mama never was smart."

Jason chuckled. "So what do you want, kid?"

"I'm supposed to be having a party."

"Good for you. You bring me new customers and I'll supply your parties free."

"It's going to be a big party."

"Even better. More people, more potential customers."

Michelle thought about it. "So how do I get them to change to you as their dealer? Will you give them a discount?"

"Your party supplies will be top quality. They'll notice. They'll ask you where to get it."

"And do you have a business card or what?"

He laughed. "You take their orders. I'll contact you. You can distribute for me."

Michelle was hesitant. "I don't know..."

"What are you worried about? That you're going to get caught? Come on. Who's going to be watching you? And even if you got caught, you're not going to the pokey on a first offense."

Michelle shrugged. She scowled at him. "I don't want to be in the middle of this."

"If you don't get in the middle, you don't get the dough. Look, Simpson, you've got to just take the plunge. Am I asking you to dope up yourself? I know you're straight. We're just talking about a business deal. You came to me, remember."

"Okay," Michelle said. She held out her hand to shake his. "A business deal, then. But just for this once."

"We'll start with this once," Jason maintained, the corners of his mouth twitching up.

Michelle added another set of initials to her list, with a set of numbers and code words in the column opposite. The list was getting long. She was astonished by the number of guys who had come up to her to ask about her source. The party was loud, rowdy and wild.

"Michelle, this is the best party I've ever been to," Waters told her, standing too close. Michelle backed up.

"Yeah, thanks."

He leaned on her shoulder, his smoking cigarette in her face. Michelle tried to squirm away. "Yeah, help yourself."

"Mmm," he slid his arms around her, "don't mind if I do."

Michelle struck out, struggling to free herself from his grasp. "Let me go."

"You know, the stuff is good, but the entertainment is lacking."

Michelle pulled her knife from its sheath and put the point against his stomach. "I told you to back off."

Dan approached and tugged Waters back by the elbow. "Waters. Come on. What are you bugging Michelle for?"

Waters looked at the knife before him and Dan behind, and backed off.

"Go watch TV. They're putting on a skin," Dan ordered.

"Would rather have had some skin here," Waters grumbled, but he went over to the other boys in front of the TV.

"You want me to stay with you?" Dan asked. "The boys might get a little out of hand."

Michelle nodded. "I don't want to get ganged up on."

"Yeah. Parties like this are a blast, but guys get high and things can happen."

Michelle watched the boys. Her head hurt from the smoke in the air. She'd had a couple swallows of beer, but no more than she could help.

"You don't drink or anything?" she said to Dan.

"I smoke. But just cigarettes, no pot. Not since Georgie."

"How come I've never met your brother?"

Dan looked at her quizzically. "What are you talking about? You've met George."

Michelle shook her head. Dan stared at her. "Wheels," Dan said, and pointed to the boy on the other side of the room. "George is Wheels."

Everything suddenly became clear. Michelle didn't know why she hadn't realized it before. But no one had ever referred to Wheels as George around her before. She had assumed he had always been that way. But he hadn't. Dan had said George was in an accident after their parents took off, that he hadn't been the same since. He had said he wished George was like Kenny, and Michelle couldn't understand why until then.

"Was he hit by a drunk driver?" she asked, remembering what Sheldon had said about how Dan stopped drinking after Wheels' accident.

Dan looked at her, pained. "Do we have to talk about it?"

"No. Sorry. I never know when to shut up."

They stood in silence for a while, watching the rest of the gang. They were the only two who were not drinking or shooting up, smoking or popping pills.

"*I* was the drunk driver," Dan said quietly.

Michelle glanced at him, and looked away. "Sorry."

"He wouldn't be like that if I wasn't an alcoholic."

Michelle nodded. There was no point in her denying it, saying it wasn't his fault. It was his fault, and he knew it.

Dan looked guiltily across the room at Wheels. "He used to be so different. Now... it's not just the wheelchair. He's different inside. His personality."

"What was he like before?"

Dan thought back. "Innocent. Just a kid. Real naive and all. He didn't like to drink, but I took him out with me. You know. After our folks left. He was scared of the gang, but he had to hang out with them because I did. I was the only one looking after him. He was happy most of the time." They both gazed at the bitter expression on his lined face. "He worried about everything, but he was still happy. He was a good kid."

"Is he ever happy now?" Michelle asked tentatively.

"I don't know. He doesn't talk to anyone. I think he's... satisfied sometimes; but not really happy. Mmm..." he searched for a word, "contented. I think he's contented when things are quiet and going okay for him and he ain't in a lot of pain."

They both fell into an uncomfortable silence for a while. "I have a sister in a wheelchair," Michelle offered eventually.

Dan turned to her with interest. "Really? How old?"

"A year younger than me. I haven't seen her for years, though."

"Why is she in a wheelchair? Was she in an accident?"

"No. She has cerebral palsy," Michelle scratched her arm, missing Marcie's big, open-mouthed smiles. "They never told me much about it. I guess mama had trouble when Marcie was born and she didn't get oxygen right away. That causes brain damage."

Dan nodded. "Yeah. Georgie wasn't breathing after the accident. Not for a long time. He gets kind of queer sometimes, doesn't remember things or gets mixed up."

One of the other gang members walked up to Wheels, talking to him for a minute. Michelle was alarmed when he made a movement to plunge a needle into George's arm. She took a step forward. Dan put his hand on her arm and shook his head.

"It's okay. He's in pain a lot of the time. The dope makes him feel better for a while."

"He shouldn't be taking that. He should be taking a prescription painkiller. It could hurt him."

"It doesn't matter. He doesn't care. It couldn't make things any worse. He has pain pills from the doctor. They're narcotics anyway."

"What if he overdosed?"

Dan shrugged. "He doesn't care anymore."

Michelle watched Wheels pityingly across the room of rambunctious gang members.

Michelle had fallen asleep on the couch sometime in the middle of the party. She sat up, stiff from her awkward position. She looked around. The apartment was a mess. Cans and needles and garbage all over the place. A number of the revelers had slept over, sprawled around the room. She got up and stepped over a couple of sleeping bodies. There were guys in the bedroom too, on her bed. Michelle saw Wheels asleep in his chair. She went over to him and put her hand on his shoulder.

"Hey, Wheels," she whispered.

He lifted his head slowly, his eyes cloudy with sleep. He focused in on Michelle. "Huh? What is it?"

"You must be sore sleeping like that. Do you want to lie down?"

"What do you care?"

Michelle was taken aback. "Do you want to lie down?" she repeated, not knowing what else to say to him.

Wheels turned his head back and forth, working out a stiff neck. "Who's going to move me? You?"

"Yeah."

"I'm too heavy for you."

"I could try."

"And drop me on the floor? No, thanks."

He was still moving his neck around stiffly. Michelle went around behind him and without asking, started massaging his neck.

"Don't do that," Wheels protested. But he didn't squirm and didn't protest after the first. He sighed after a minute. "Oh, that's better."

Michelle rubbed his shoulders, and his thin muscles relaxed under her fingers. After a while, Michelle stopped. Wheels looked around at her.

"You got good hands," he said.

Michelle grinned. "Yeah. I'm starving. What do you want to eat?"

"I'm not hungry."

"You're too thin. You gotta eat something."

"The painkillers take away my appetite. I don't want to eat."

She ignored his protests and released the brakes on his chair. She pushed him into the kitchenette and took a look through the cupboards. It was almost as bad as June's apartment. She put instant coffee in a couple of cups and put the water on to boil. Wheels watched her with dark, sunken eyes. Michelle found some dry bread and put it in the toaster. There was nothing but peanut butter to put on it.

Wheels accepted the toast when she handed it to him. Michelle poured boiling water into the mugs.

"That's too heavy," Wheels said. Michelle looked at the wasted muscles of his arms and found a lighter cup for him. They ate without speaking. Michelle looked out the dusty window at the brightening sky.

"Next time there'll be more to eat," she promised. "I haven't gone shopping yet."

"It's okay."

Wheels' hands shook when he raised the coffee cup to his mouth.

"Do you do arm exercises?" Michelle asked.

"No. They wanted me to do physio, but it was too hard."

"I bet you could really get strong arms if you tried."

He shook his head. "I'm a quad. They'd never be strong."

"I thought quadriplegics couldn't move their arms."

"Depends where the spinal damage is. But they can never be strong."

"Why not?"

He shook his head and didn't explain.

"You should still go to physio. Maybe you could at least move your wheelchair around on your own."

He scowled. "I can move it some. Just not far."

"Don't you want to be independent?"

"No."

Michelle was surprised. "Why not? Dan won't take care of you forever."

"Yes, he will," Wheels maintained. "He promised."

Michelle could well imagine Dan promising that in a guilt-stricken moment. "Well, sometime he'll change his mind," she said logically. "He'll want to do things on his own."

"If he goes away, I'll kill myself."

"Is that what you told him to make him promise?"

"I didn't have to. But he knows."

Michelle shook her head. "Great relationship you've got with your brother."

Michelle remembered the list of orders in her pocket and decided she wanted to see Jason as soon as she could. She didn't want to be carrying around evidence of her crime all day long.

"I gotta go. You need anything?" she asked George.

"I don't need anything from you."

Michelle shrugged and left the apartment to see if she could find her dealer.

Jason wasn't there. Michelle went into a coffee shop and waited for him to show up. It must have been obvious she was watching the corner because the woman behind the counter spoke to her.

"You're not going to find him out this early, honey."

"Who?"

"Mr. Sleaze out there. He's up most of the night. You won't see him until this afternoon."

"Oh." Michelle looked down. "I just wanted to ask him something."

"Uh-huh. You're much better off staying away from him."

"I'm not a junkie. I don't do drugs."

The woman gazed at her for a minute. "You know, I believe you, honey. The addicts are still sleeping. So what do you want *him* for?"

Michelle shrugged uncomfortably. "I just have to talk to him."

The waitress looked at Michelle's outfit and make-up. "Why do you want to get yourself in trouble? You're a nice-looking girl. Go to school and stay out of trouble."

Michelle finished her coffee and pushed the mug away. "Yeah." She got up.

"You don't have to run away."

Michelle shook her head and left. If Jason wasn't going to be around until the afternoon, there was no point in staying around waiting for hours. She went back to the apartment.

∼

Marsden went to the school again on her way back from another appointment.

"Have Kenny or Michelle Simpson been around yet?" she asked, hoping the school had just forgotten to call her.

"No. We haven't seen them since you were by."

Marsden shook her head. "Where have those kids gone? Where would they go?"

"Have you talked to the police?"

"Yeah. They'll start an investigation. But I don't know how thorough they'll be. There are so many missing kids. They won't do anything more than the proper preliminaries."

"Well, I'll let you know if they show up here. They might after a while."

"I hope so."

∼

Dan looked up when Michelle came in. "Where've you been? Wheels said you left real early before anyone was up."

"Yeah."

"Well? Where were you?"

"I just went out. So what?"

Dan looked for something to say.

"Are you going to help me clean up?" Michelle demanded.

Dan looked around the room and wrinkled his nose. "I suppose someone's gotta clean the place up."

Michelle took a package of garbage bags out of her grocery bag and handed one to him. "Fill it up," she told him. "And anyone else who's still around can help."

Dan laughed. "You've got nerve," he said.

But it was Dan, not Michelle, who kicked awake the guys who were still there sleeping or lounging around and armed them all with garbage bags. There were complaints from the boys, but they must have had to clean up after parties before. Michelle unloaded the groceries she had purchased while the others dragged around, complaining about their hangovers. A couple more placed orders with Michelle. She dutifully wrote them down on her list and put it back in her pocket.

"That was some party," Tanner commented, stopping for a smoke when he should have been cleaning up. Michelle glared at him and he spread his hands questioningly.

"What?"

"Get to work. You suggested the party, you can clean up."

"I told you you'd throw a good party if you put your mind to it. Didn't I?"

"Yeah, you did."

"So?"

"So what?"

"Aren't you going to thank me?"

"Thanks. Now clean."

"Slave driver," Tanner teased and went back to work.

Tanner hadn't talked to her much during the party like he usually would have. He was too busy getting to know the other guys. And it might have had something to do with Dan hanging around with Michelle too. Although Dan had introduced them into the gang, there was no love lost between Dan and Tanner. Michelle suspected Tanner had delusions of taking over the leadership of the gang. It wasn't like there was a formal leadership structure. Michelle supposed Dan was the leader, since everybody focused on him and usually did what he told them. But it wasn't like he had been elected President or Commander or whatever you called a formal leader in a gang.

But most of the gang was older than Tanner. Dan was probably twenty and Tanner was only fourteen or fifteen. He wasn't going to be taking over the gang any time soon. Someone younger than Dan might eventually take over when he got tired of the gang. Dan was one of the oldest. At eleven, Michelle was the youngest, though she tried hard not to look it.

∼

It turned out Michelle didn't have to go looking for Jason. He showed up at the apartment in the early afternoon. He looked around, an eyebrow raised.

"Well, this doesn't look too bad. How did the party go?"

"We spent an hour cleaning up afterward. And I don't know how many garbage bags we used."

"Uh-huh. Everybody satisfied with the quality of the goods?"

"Yeah. I got some orders for you."

She handed him the list and he unfolded it and read through it. "Good. You did a great job. I'll get this stuff for you and bring it by in a day or so." He took out a pen and removed the cap with his mouth while he put the paper against a wall to write. "You're new, so I'm going to write down prices here for you. Don't give anybody the goods without money up front. It's bad for business. My cut will be seventy percent of what you take to begin with. After a while, I'll start lowering the purity," he looked around to make sure no one would overhear him, "and then you can take fifty percent."

He handed the paper back to Michelle and she looked at the column of numbers, adding it up in her head. She bit her tongue before telling him the total in astonishment. Instead, she kept her mouth shut and folded the paper again.

"Don't you need this?"

"I'll estimate what you need. If there's any extra, you can do what you want with it. Sell it, use it, give it away. Whatever you want."

Michelle felt her stomach tightening again. She was apprehensive of having him bring drugs by the apartment. They hadn't been caught at the party, but sooner or later, whatever police were watching Jason would figure out which apartment he was going to and bust them.

"Don't bring it by here. Let's meet somewhere else."

He shrugged. "If you want."

"Yeah. So the cops aren't watching my place."

He nodded. "You're a smart kid. You'll keep out of trouble."

Michelle wasn't so sure.

Kenny and a couple of the guys were out together and went to the pool hall they hung out at sometimes. A couple of boys from his school class were there fooling around. When they saw Kenny come in, they watched him, talking to each other quietly. After a while, they came up to the table where Kenny was playing.

"Hey, Kenny."

Kenny nodded to them and didn't say anything.

"The cops were at school looking for you and your sister."

"Uh-huh."

"How come you haven't been at school lately?"

Kenny shrugged, concentrating on lining up his shot.

"Are you going to go back?"

"No." Kenny lined up his next shot. The boys exchanged glances. Kenny took the shot and moved to the other side of the table.

"Why not?"

Kenny glanced up at them and didn't say anything.

"What do you guys care about what he does?" Gerard questioned, irritated with the other boys hanging around, "just quit pestering."

The boys were hesitant to let it drop. They hung around watching Kenny's slick shooting. "Hey, you're good," one of them said in amazement.

"Why wouldn't he be?" Gerard asked. "Kenny's cool."

"But he's dumb," the other blurted.

Kenny whipped around with the cue in his hand and jabbed it towards the boy's stomach. Gerard grabbed at Kenny. "Hey, cool it, Kenny. Not in here." He looked at the other boy. "You want to take it outside?"

"No. I didn't mean that. I just meant at school, you don't do so good. I didn't mean to say that."

Kenny jabbed him in the gut once with the pool cue and then turned his back to continue with his game. Gerard motioned for the other boys to leave, and they did.

∼

Michelle met Jason and he gave her a ratty knapsack.

"You know what this is worth," he commented. "I don't trust just anyone with these kinds of goods, but I'm relying on you to give me good value, all right?"

Michelle nodded. "I won't give anything away without payment."

"You got it, kid."

Michelle looked around nervously. "Someone's going to see me with this."

"If I'd given you an attaché case, you'd have a reason to be nervous. But all kids have knapsacks. No one is going to think it's out of place."

"Are you sure no one followed you? The cops aren't watching?"

"Now you're sounding like an accomplished dealer. Don't trust anyone."

"No one followed you? You're sure?" Michelle persisted.

"No one followed me. But we've been here long enough. See me when you've got my dough. Okay?"

"Okay."

Jason walked away.

∼

Everything went smoothly, better than Michelle had imagined. Everybody paid like they were supposed to without much pushing. Michelle checked everybody off the list as they paid. Kenny hung around as she went through what was left in the bag.

"You got extra?" he questioned.

"Yeah. Jason said I could do what I wanted with it."

"Can I have it?"

Michelle hesitated.

"You gonna sell it?" Kenny asked.

"No."

"Then give it to me."

"You take too much. It's not good for you."

Kenny said nothing. Michelle eventually handed the bag to him. Kenny took it, nodding. He walked away and Michelle didn't ask him what he was going to do with it.

∽

Michelle handed Jason the wad of bills and watched him thumb through it. He glanced up at Michelle. "You're not compulsive, are you?" he said with a snicker.

"What do you mean?"

"I mean most of my guys don't arrange the bills smallest to largest, right-side-up, serials forward. And I don't need an itemized receipt."

Michelle felt her face flush. "I thought you'd want the list."

"I keep it in my head. Put nothing on paper you can keep in your head, kid."

Michelle nodded. "Okay. Well, that's it, I guess."

Jason shook his head. "I brought another load for you."

"I didn't take any more orders."

"You only need to take one. They'll be stopping by regularly now. Keep track of your inventory and let me know when you get low on something. Square up with me every week, and we'll be in good shape."

Michelle didn't take the bag he held out to her. "No one has asked me for anything else."

"They will."

"I didn't want to do this."

"Well, guess what, cookie? You're doing it."

Michelle looked at him. "I'm not a drug dealer."

"You can call yourself whatever you like."

"I'm not doing it."

He put the bag in her hand and walked away.

CHAPTER Nineteen

Dirkson watched Jason and the girl talk for a moment and then the money passed hands.

"That's the second time we've seen them together. I think we'd better bust her."

Perrot, his partner, nodded. "Yup."

They waited until the two separated and followed the girl down the street. Once they were a safe distance away from Jason Corker, they closed in on her. They each took one of her arms and she struggled to get away, went for the dagger she kept displayed prominently. They twisted her arms back behind her back to restrain her. She swore and struggled desperately.

"Cool it, kid, just take it easy."

"Let me go! Get your hands off of me!"

"You're under arrest. Now just settle down."

She stopped squirming and looked at him. "You're not cops."

"Yeah, we are."

He clipped a pair of handcuffs over her wrists and let go of her to pull out his shield for her. Perrot kept a tight grip on her. She looked at his ID. "Is that real?"

"You're a cynical one, aren't you? Yeah, it's real."

She looked at him in dismay. Dirkson picked up her dropped bag and unzipped it. Pale, she watched him pull a handful of drugs out of it. Dirkson shoved them back into the bag, shaking his head.

MICHELLE

"Well, I guess you and I are going to get acquainted. Come on, kid. We'll go to the station."

The girl walked with them back to their car. Perrot opened the door for her and guided her into the back seat. She sat there looking sick.

∼

They waited for booking to call their number and then took her up to the counter.

"What's your name, kid?" Perrot demanded.

"Michelle Simpson," Michelle said, in hardly more than a whisper.

"Michelle? You got a prior record?"

"No."

"With this amount of dope? Uh-huh. Check it anyway." The booking officer nodded and punched it in.

"No priors." He scrolled through the information on the screen. "But there's a missing persons on her."

"Runaway?"

He nodded.

"Figures. Call her guardians for me."

After booking her through, they took her into the small interrogation room. She sat down in the chair he indicated. "How long have you been dealing, Michelle?"

"I don't know what you're talking about."

"How old are you?"

"Twelve."

"How long have you known Corker?"

"Who?"

"Your pusher. Jason Corker."

"I don't know any Corker."

"Don't be hard to get along with. If you cooperate, things will be much easier for you."

"I don't know what you are talking about."

"Why did you run away from home?"

"I didn't."

Perrot studied her. "You must be very scared. This is the first time you've been picked up. You're in a scary place, with no one you know around. Don't make it any harder on yourself. Just help us out."

Michelle rubbed her arms and looked down.

∼

Dirkson motioned Perrot out of the room.

"Her social worker is on the way. She says Corker is Michelle's mom's pusher. They didn't know Michelle had any involvement with him."

"Well, now they know. I'm going to see if I can get anything out of her before the social worker gets here."

"Okay."

Perrot went back in. Michelle glanced up at him.

"So are you using too, Michelle? Stupid question. You've got that much stuff, of course you're using too. How much?"

"I don't do drugs."

"Uh-huh."

"I don't. I'm clean."

"You're probably high as a kite right now. Now come on. Give me a hand. I think you're a smart kid. If you can help me out with Corker, I can get you off. I can help you."

"Help me what?"

"Help you stay out of jail."

"I'm not going to jail," Michelle said blankly.

"You've just been arrested for drug dealing. What do you *think* is going to happen to you?"

"You can't put me in jail "

Perrot shook his head. "You've got a lot to learn."

∼

Marsden and Dirkson walked in. Michelle grew even more tense at her social worker's presence.

"Michelle," Marsden exclaimed. "Are you okay? We've been worried sick about you!"

Michelle looked away. "Nothing's wrong with me."

"Where's Kenny? Is he okay?"

She nodded.

"Who's Kenny?" Perrot questioned.

"Michelle's brother. Where have you two been staying, Michelle? With a friend?"

"None of your business."

"It certainly *is* my business. You know Kenny's..." She fished for a word. "Kenny needs some supervision."

"Kenny's taken care of."

Marsden studied Michelle. She walked around the table to get a better look at her costume. Michelle squirmed under Marsden's critical eye.

"Can I talk to Michelle alone?" Marsden requested.

Dirkson nodded and motioned for Perrot to follow. "Yeah. For a few minutes. But we still have more questions for Michelle to answer."

The door shut behind the two cops. Marsden continued to stare at Michelle.

"Leave me alone," Michelle grumbled, folding her arms protectively.

"What have you gotten yourself into?" Marsden questioned.

"Nothing."

"Look at you. Bleached hair..." She tousled Michelle's hair and Michelle jerked back from her. "Body piercing, a mile of bare skin. What for?"

"That's the way I like to look."

"You look like a little tramp. Are you walking the strip?"

Michelle was shocked. "No! I wouldn't do that."

"Oh, you wouldn't. But you'd sell drugs."

Michelle looked uncomfortable. "They weren't my drugs."

"How stupid do you think I am? I haven't ever had one of my kids turn to dealing before?"

"I'm not dealing."

"How did you get the money to pay for your mom's drugs?"

Michelle was startled. "I never dealt to get the money I gave mama. And I didn't pay for her drugs, I bought her groceries."

"With what money?"

Michelle didn't answer. Marsden paced across the room and sat down on the other chair. "This guy your mom was involved with is bad news. Whatever he's doing, you can bet he's not trying to help you out. Corker's got a long list of convictions for drugs and other crimes. And he's not getting you involved because he feels sorry for you. Or likes you. Or whatever he says. He's doing it to make money and to get someone else doing the dirty work."

"I didn't know there were drugs in that bag. I was holding it for a friend."

"What friend?"

"I don't want to get anyone in trouble."

"You need to cooperate, Michelle. Do you know what happens to kids who get mixed up with drugs like this?"

"Nothing's going to happen."

Marsden shook her head in disgust and knocked on the door to be let out.

"I can't get anything out of Michelle," she told Dirkson. "Who knows how deeply she's mixed up with this Corker character. Michelle and I have never developed a rapport. She's too stubborn."

"Well, she's probably pretty deeply involved if he's her mom's dealer. You'd be well-advised to get her out of the city."

"Before I can do that, we have to find her brother. I'm not going to take Michelle out of the city before she takes us to Kenny."

"Well, you're going to have to do something. Court won't release her if you don't have a plan to keep her out of trouble."

"When will they hear it?"

"Tomorrow. Until then she'll be detained at the youth center."

"It'll do her good. Might take that pride down a notch. You can talk to her, but I doubt if she'll be cooperative with you."

"We'll give it another go."

It was Dirkson who came in to question Michelle the second time. He sat down across from her.

"Hi, Michelle."

"Hi."

"Your first time doing this gig, huh?" he said sympathetically.

"I haven't been arrested before," she confirmed.

"Yeah. It can be pretty overwhelming the first time. But you get used to it. Once or twice more and you'll be a real pro."

Michelle scowled at the assumption she'd be dumb enough to get caught again.

"But you probably know what to expect just from talking with friends. It helps, knowing what to expect." Dirkson chuckled. "Don't look at me like I've just insulted you. Of course you've got friends that have been in trouble. Why else would you be dressed up like that? You're trying to look tough so you won't stand out."

"I like dressing like this," Michelle protested, surprised to have him guess her motives so dead-on.

"Sure you do. It makes you feel more secure. More like one of the gang."

"I like the way it looks."

"Yeah. So tell me what's going on here. What happened to your mom? And your brother?"

"My mom's a stupid junkie. She's in jail."

"And you never thought you'd be following in her footsteps."

"I'm not."

"And your brother?"

"What about him?"

"Your social worker seems pretty concerned about him."

"Kenny's fine."

"Why did the two of you run away?"

"We didn't run away... we just stopped going home."

Dirkson smiled slightly. "Uh-huh. So things weren't going so good at home, huh?"

Michelle shook her head. "Mama was always high, didn't care where we were. So we stopped going home."

"How long has this been going on?"

"Since we were sent back there."

"Before that?"

"We were in foster homes."

"Do you want to go back to foster care, then?"

"No. I like being on our own."

"No adults?"

"No nothing. Just us."

"Just you and a pusher and some junkie friends."

Michelle looked at him. He wasn't accusing. He wasn't asking. He was just stating a fact. Speculating, Michelle corrected herself. He didn't know. He was just guessing.

"Can I go?" she asked.

"No. You're not going anywhere. You and I still have plenty of talking to do. Do you want a smoke?"

"I don't smoke."

"Coffee?"

"Yeah."

"All right. Hang tight."

"I'm not going anywhere," Michelle said sarcastically.

Dirkson grinned and walked out.

It was a long day for Michelle. She didn't mind talking to Dirkson as much as Marsden or the other cop. He didn't accuse her of being a drug dealer. He just talked to her. But even so, it was wearing. At the end of the day, he put handcuffs back on her and took her to the youth center. After she was checked in, a woman hustled her into a room in the back.

"Take off all the jewelry," she instructed briskly.

Michelle slowly started to remove her earrings. The woman pulled a uniform off of the shelves on the wall and watched her.

"Belly ring too."

Michelle awkwardly unfastened it. She hadn't taken it out since she had first had it pierced.

"Is that it?"

Michelle nodded, rolling her eyes.

"Oh, don't give me that look, missy. You wouldn't believe some of the body parts I've seen pierced."

Michelle remembered the posters at Wade's tattoo place and shuddered. "That's it," she confirmed.

"Good. Change into this."

Michelle took the uniform and waited for the woman to leave her alone.

"I'm not going anywhere. You were arrested for drug dealing, right?"

Michelle nodded.

"My job is to help ensure no drugs come into this facility. They may have frisked you at the police station, but that's not going to do it for me."

Michelle flushed and took off her jacket and pants.

"How old are you?"

"Twelve."

"Is this your first charge?"

"Yes."

"Are you smuggling anything in your body?"

Michelle shook her head.

"Look at me and answer."

Michelle looked at her. "No."

"I'm authorized to do a body cavity search."

Michelle swallowed. "You don't need to."

"Okay. You're young and I don't think you've got the experience yet. But if you prove me wrong, I won't treat you so well next time."

Michelle nodded.

"All right. Finish changing."

Michelle looked away and took off her remaining clothing, her face hot with embarrassment under the woman's watchful eye. Once stripped, Michelle quickly pulled on the uniform. She was escorted out of the room straight to a cell. It wasn't a cell like she would have expected. There were no bars, they were just small rooms with steel doors and tiny windows for observation. She thought there would only be one person per cell, they were so small, but there was a bunk bed inside and another girl already there. The door was shut behind Michelle.

"Hi," the girl on the bunk said.

"Hi."

"Sara Kilmoore. You?"

"Michelle."

"First time?"

Michelle shook her head. "No."

"Liar. I can spot a greenie a mile away."

Michelle didn't argue. Sara grinned. "Yeah, I thought so. Nice try, though. So what for?"

"Drugs."

"Uh-huh. Lotsa that going around. Just don't buy from narcs, ya know? It's not hard. Check out your sources."

"I didn't buy from a cop."

"Sure."

Michelle boosted herself up onto the top bunk.

"Top bunk's mine," Sara told her.

"You're already on the bottom."

"So? That means I can't have the top if I want it?"

Michelle looked over the edge of the bunk at Sara. She was probably sixteen, and a husky girl. Michelle would be no match for her in a physical confrontation. Michelle swung down from the bunk. Sara smiled.

"Well, you got some sense anyway."

Michelle sat on the floor opposite the bunks and waited for the lights-out bell to ring. Sara watched her for a while before choosing to ignore her. It seemed like forever before the lights in their cell and all down the corridor went out. Michelle waited for Sara to move from the bottom to the top bunk. Then she crawled into the bottom. She lay wide awake, listening to the sounds of the building and the hall and the rooms around them. She was tense and couldn't even close her eyes, she was so wired.

They had been in bed for an hour or two when Sara suddenly sat up with a gasp.

"Are you okay?" Michelle questioned.

Sara jumped out of the top bunk. "Where are you?" she demanded in a husky voice.

"Right here. What's wrong? Did you have a nightmare?"

Sara climbed into the lower bunk, feeling for her. Michelle grasped her hand. "I'm right here. It's okay."

Sara pulled her off of the bed suddenly. Michelle was too surprised to fight back. She was on her back on the floor and Sara's fist hit her square in the mouth.

"If you ever touch me again, I'll kill you," Sara hissed.

Michelle tried to protest, tasting blood. "I didn't—"

Another blow smashed across her face. Michelle struggled, but Sara was straddling her and was too heavy to throw off. Michelle's mind went back to being assaulted by Stan. Before Sara could attempt to silence Michelle like Stan had, she screamed. Sara hit her again and again, not even trying to cover Michelle's mouth to quiet her.

Michelle waited for the footsteps to pound down the hallway, a key to turn in the lock of the door, but nothing came. Only her own screams, eventually followed by crushed whimpers.

Finally, Sara's punishment ended and she got up. She said nothing. She climbed back into the top bunk and was quiet. Michelle drifted into oblivion.

CHAPTER Twenty

She awoke to blinding light and someone shaking her. She pulled away and tried to get up.

"Come on, time to get up," a male voice ordered. Michelle tried to force her eyes open and look around. The man who had awakened her pulled her to her feet. Michelle rubbed her eyes, but they were so tender she could hardly touch them.

"Hit the shower quick and you can still get to breakfast," the guard told her. He hustled her down the hall to the steaming shower room, where someone else handed her a towel and another uniform. In a daze, Michelle let them guide her into a shower stall, where she mechanically lathered up and rinsed off. She dried off and dressed again. The memories of Sara's beating filtered into her memory. She looked around at the various guards and workers who did not appear to see anything out of the ordinary. Was it possible there were no visible bruises? She walked past a mirror and looked at herself. There were definitely visible bruises. A black eye, a lump on her head, a split lip. One of the guards noticed her dawdling and caught her by the arm.

"Come on. Never been here before? Cafeteria's this way."

Michelle looked at him. "I got beat up," she told him incredulously.

He didn't even glance at her face. "Don't be a troublemaker," he warned.

"But my bunkmate—"

"Didn't you hear me? I said don't make trouble."

"It wasn't me."

"Keep your mouth shut and you won't get in trouble."

Michelle could see there was no point in reasoning with him and gave up. He took her to the cafeteria and Michelle lined up with the others. She raised her eyes and looked around. Sara was on the other side of the cafeteria. Their eyes met, and Sara's expression didn't change. Michelle looked away. Did Sara not remember what had happened? Or did she really think Michelle had *touched* her? Or did she just not care who she hurt? Michelle looked away and didn't look back at her. She ate her breakfast quietly, not looking at anybody. Afterward, a guard handcuffed her and put her on a bus with several other kids going to the courthouse.

Marsden waited for the bus to get there from the youth center. Michelle was the first hearing, and Marsden wanted a chance to talk to her before it started.

They escorted all the juveniles into the courthouse. Marsden motioned to Michelle to come over to her. Looking down, Michelle approached her and sat. She waited for them to unlock her handcuffs.

"What happened to you?" Marsden questioned, seeing the bump on Michelle's head even before she looked up. Michelle lifted her head. She had a black eye so bad her eye was swollen almost all the way shut. Her lip was split and swollen and she had numerous other scrapes and bruises on her face as well.

"I got beat up," Michelle said.

"Are you okay? Who beat you up?"

"The other girl in my cell."

"What did the guards say? Did they know she was dangerous?"

"I don't know."

"Well, what did they say when you told them?"

"They told me not to make trouble."

"What did you do to provoke her?"

Michelle looked at her quizzically. "Nothing."

"Nothing at all? What happened?"

"You let them put me in that dump and I got beat up for nothing at all! I didn't do anything."

"You must have—"

"I didn't do anything!"

"Well… we have to get ready for the hearing. Are you ready?"

"I guess."

"Are you going to agree to help the police?"

"No."

"How do you think I'm going to keep you out of jail, then?"

Michelle shrugged. "It's my first time."

"That helps, but I'm not going to recommend you for foster care if you won't give me some sort of indication this won't happen again."

"You want me to look like this the next few years?" Michelle demanded, indicating her face.

Marsden looked at her and didn't answer.

The judge saw Michelle's bruises and felt sorry for her. When Marsden explained Michelle had gotten mixed up with her mother's dealer, he saw a reason to go easy on her.

"This isn't like a seventeen-year-old selling drugs to buy a car or support his own addiction," he said. "This is a child who needs to be protected from her mother's addiction and her connections. I'll convict on the charges since she's obviously guilty, but I'm suspending the sentence."

He went on to explain that as long as Michelle wasn't convicted of anything else while she was a juvenile, the conviction could be wiped from her record. He looked at Marsden, his brows drawn down like he was angry.

"You need to find somewhere safe for Miss Simpson. Somewhere secure."

Marsden nodded quickly. "Yes, your Honor. I'm already looking into it."

"She may technically be a criminal as a result of this conviction, but I don't want her treated like one. She needs supervision, not prison."

Marsden tried to figure out where to put Michelle. She took Michelle back to the Social Services office with her while she looked for a home.

The home Marsden decided on was a halfway house for juveniles, a home with supervision and strict rules.

Michelle didn't say anything as Marsden drove her there. She wondered what the gang was doing, and if they had heard what happened. Marsden stopped and Michelle got out of the car. She went up to the house before Marsden and rang the bell. The door was opened as Marsden caught up with Michelle. The girl who answered the door looked them over.

"New girl?" She cracked her gum.

"Yes," Marsden confirmed. "Is Mrs. Craig around?"

"Yeah. Come in."

Michelle and Marsden stepped in. Michelle looked around. "Where's my room?"

"Oh, little Miss Perfect thinks she's going to get her own room," the girl sneered.

Michelle glared. "I've never had my own room in my life. Where'm I supposed to sleep?"

The other girl shrugged unhelpfully. She popped her gum again and, looking at Marsden, turned to get Mrs. Craig.

"I want you to try to get along here," Marsden warned Michelle, "behave yourself and try to fit in."

"I don't fit in anywhere."

"Well, try. The judge is going to want to hear you're getting along."

Michelle shrugged.

∼

"You want to come to the drop-in center with me?" Rebecca, one of the other girls, asked.

Michelle looked at her. "What's that?"

"The drop-in center? You've never been there? It's great. If you need a place to sleep or shower, or get something to eat, you can go there."

"Like the Y."

"Sorta like the Y, but it's better. If you need some extra cash, you can go there to get casual labor for a day or two, they'll set you up. Or if you want psych or confession or something."

At Michelle's blank look, Rebecca enlarged. "If you want counseling, you know, if things are going rough. You can tell them what's going on, and they aren't allowed to call the police or nothing because it's confidential. Same with confession. If you want to talk to a priest."

"Oh. I don't do that."

"Yeah, well, they got lots of good stuff over there. Rec center too, if you just want to hang out and play some games or ball. I go there a lot."

Michelle shrugged. "Yeah, I guess I'll go with you."

"Okay. I just gotta tell Mrs. Craig where we're going. Just wait for me for a minute, okay?"

Michelle nodded and waited for her to get back.

They spent most of the afternoon at the drop-in center, hanging out with other kids and playing the rec room games. Rebecca looked at her watch and motioned to Michelle.

"We have to get back to the house."

"Go ahead."

"I told Mrs. Craig I'd keep an eye on you. We have to be back for supper."

"I'm not going back."

"Come on. You don't want to get into trouble on your first day."

"I'm not getting in trouble."

"You mean you're not going back at all?" Rebecca said incredulously.

"Yeah."

"You have to!"

Michelle shrugged. "What can they do?"

"Put you in juvie, that's what they can do. Are you crazy? Do you know what juvie's like?"

Michelle motioned to her bruised face. "Yeah, I do. Now get off my back. I'll do what I like."

"Mrs. Craig is gonna be all over my back. Thanks a lot! You coulda told me instead of getting me in trouble."

"You didn't ask what I was going to do."

"Yeah. My mistake."

She walked away. Michelle hung out at the drop-in center for a while longer, then went home.

CHAPTER
Twenty-One

"Michelle! Are you okay?" Kenny was the first one to see her approach. Michelle hugged him briefly.

"Got busted," she explained.

"I know."

"I didn't know if you would hear."

Kenny nodded.

"Who hit you?" Dan asked.

"Girl in juvie."

"Those chicks can be pretty tough."

"She was psychotic."

Dan nodded. "Uh-huh. Don't doubt it. Nasty looking."

Michelle sighed. "I gotta go change," she said, indicating her plain clothes with disgust. "I'll meet you guys in a while."

"I'll come up with you," Dan offered. "We can talk."

Michelle shrugged. "Okay."

Dan walked up the stairs with her to the apartment. He watched Michelle check through her clothes for an outfit to wear.

"We knew because your dealer stopped by to see what happened to you," he commented.

"What? Oh, yeah. I wondered." Michelle pulled off the reputable shirt Marsden had dressed her in. She was wearing a bra underneath and Dan had seen her in halter tops plenty of times before. She pulled a short midi on over top. Her jewelry was in a bag they had given her and Michelle put the earrings back in carefully. Dan watched her try to put the navel ring back in.

"Tanner said he'd distribute the stuff while you were in lockup."

"Yeah, that's great. I'd rather he did it."

"He'll rip you off."

"I don't care. I don't want to do it."

"You're just nervy 'cause you got caught once. You'll get back into it."

Michelle scowled. "I dunno. I never liked doing it."

"Do you need a hand?" Dan grinned as he watched her try to re-fasten the navel ring.

"It's really tender. I can't hold still to put it back."

"Hang on a minute. I can do it for you."

He left the bedroom. Michelle heard him open the fridge and he was back a moment later. He showed her an ice cube.

"Brace yourself," he warned.

Michelle took a deep breath and held her stomach muscles tight. Dan put the ice cube against her skin. Michelle broke out in goose bumps. "Oooh, that's cold," she murmured, putting her hand over his.

"It's an ice cube."

"It's melting," Michelle complained after a few minutes.

"Is it numbing up?"

"Yeah."

"Okay," he took it off of her. "Give me the ring. I'll put it in."

Michelle handed it to him and he threaded it in. Michelle breathed out. "Thanks."

Dan grinned. "No problem. Make sure you put alcohol on it too. Don't want to let it get infected."

Michelle nodded. "Yeah, I will."

She stretched and looked herself over. She decided the blue jeans would do for the day and buckled on her knife sheath.

"I guess that's it."

"You're not going to do your face?"

Michelle shook her head. "No. I'll get infected if I put gunk on top of this mess." She gestured to the cuts on her face.

"Yeah, I guess that makes sense. You gonna come out with us tonight?"

"Sure. What's up?"

"Oh, nothing special. Just out to do some damage."

Michelle nodded. "Okay. Where's Wheels today?"

"Hospital."

"What happened?"

"Happened? Nothing. He just has to go in for a bunch of tests every now and then."

"Oh. So nothing's wrong?"

"There's plenty wrong. Nothing new, though."

"Good. I worry about him not being able to take care of himself."

"I take care of him."

"Yeah, but you can't forever. He's gotta learn how sooner or later."

"He can't, Michelle. He ain't never going to be able to take care of himself."

"Well, you gotta make some kind of alternate arrangements. What if something happened to you? Or you decided you don't want to look after him anymore?"

"That ain't never gonna happen."

"Never's a long time."

"Georgie ain't gonna live a long time. Quads don't have a long life expectancy."

Michelle thought about that for a few minutes in silence. What was the point in worrying about Wheels if he wasn't going to be around for long? Best to just keep him reasonably happy until he died. Why mess with it?

Tanner was with the others when Michelle and Dan got back down from the apartment. He brightened when he saw her.

"Hey, Michelle. Long time no see. How's it going?"

"Okay," Michelle shrugged.

"Nice shiner."

Michelle said nothing. Tanner's gaze shifted to Dan and he scowled. Michelle caught the look and wondered what his beef was. She pretended not to notice.

"I got to take Georgie back to the apartment," Dan said. "You want to come along?"

"Yeah, I guess."

"We gotta get the car first."

"What's he do when we're all out?"

"Watches TV. Sleeps. He can't do much."

"I know."

Dan walked her to his car, a big old junker parked in an alley near his place. Michelle climbed in and stretched out her feet. They were quiet all the way to the hospital. It was a comfortable silence, and Michelle didn't feel any need to fill it. Dan turned up the radio and didn't push for conversation.

They got to the hospital and Dan led the way to the wing where George was waiting. The nurses greeted Dan by name and called a doctor to come talk to him.

"Hey, Wheels," Michelle greeted him.

He just frowned self-absorbedly and didn't answer.

"How're you doing, bro'?" Dan asked.

"How'd you feel after being poked and prodded all day?" George grumbled.

The doctor got there and greeted Dan familiarly. "You have a minute to go over these test results?"

"Yeah, sure."

They went off to the side and conferred. They were only a few minutes and then Dan was back to get Wheels.

"Have you had someone look at that?" the doctor asked, studying Michelle's face.

"No. It's not that bad."

The doctor looked at his watch. "Well... let me take a quick look. Come down to one of the exam rooms."

Michelle trailed along behind the doctor and he led her to an examination room. He sat her down and shone a light on her face. He wiped the cuts with antiseptic, studying her face from several angles.

"So, who beat you up?" he asked.

Michelle considered it. If she told him it happened in juvie, he might file a report of some kind. And he might tell Social Services she was hanging out with Dan. They would track her down and put her away again.

"You're not going to tell me?" he asked, prodding and pulling on a couple of cuts.

"No."

"Well, this is pretty nasty." He put a piece of suture tape across a split in her skin to pull it together. "I want to look at your head. How's it feel?"

Michelle touched the worst of the bumps on her head. "Kinda sore."

"Yeah?" he examined her head, his fingers firm and gentle, parting her hair for a better look. "Have you been feeling dizzy? Headache, nausea?"

"I got a headache."

"Mm-hmm. How about the rest? Are you okay?" he left her head alone and stepped back around her, his eyes going clinically over the bare skin under her midi. Michelle ran her hand over her ribs. They were tender, as was her stomach, but there were no visible bruises.

"Yeah, I'm okay."

He shone a light in her eyes, one at a time, and made her follow his finger with her eyes. He also made her close her eyes and touch her nose. "I want you to take it easy for a while. You may have a slight concussion. If you start feeling sick or that headache gets worse, you come back here and get checked out. Okay?"

Michelle nodded.

"Good. Well, I have rounds to do, so I'll let you guys take George home."

Michelle joined Dan and George again and the doctor repeated his warning to Dan. "You look after her and make sure she takes it easy. She's been beaten up pretty good and needs to be careful for a few days."

"Sure, doc."

Then they were left alone again. Dan bent over and released the brake on George's wheelchair and pushed him out to the car. Michelle watched while Dan lifted George into the car and folded up the chair to throw into the trunk. He buckled George into the front seat and Michelle got into the back.

There was no conversation on the way back, either, but with George's heavy breathing, sighing, and moaning, it was not the comfortable silence of an hour earlier. Dan unfolded the wheelchair and put George into it at the apartment. They went upstairs. Dan looked at Michelle.

MICHELLE

"Why don't you turn on the TV for a few minutes? I got to take care of... some things."

Michelle did as she was asked. Dan talked to Wheels in the other room while he took care of 'things.' Michelle listened to them, but couldn't make anything out. Only George's bitter complaining voice, Dan's low, forcefully cheerful one, and the noises of crackling plastic wrappers, water running, and unhurried movement. After a while, Dan brought George in, carrying him in his arms, and deposited him on the couch.

"There. Now you can watch TV."

Wheels didn't respond to this, watching the TV indifferently.

"Let's go," Dan told Michelle.

"Okay."

"How come you're always hanging out with Dan?" Tanner complained as they walked along with the gang.

Michelle glanced at him. "I don't spend much time with him. Just with the gang."

"You're off alone with him all the time. Are you sleeping with him too?"

"No. I'm not sleeping with anyone."

He eyed her. "Huh. 'Cause you know you're my girl."

"I'm not anyone's girl, and you know it. Certainly not yours."

"I'm the one that got you into the gang."

"So? Leave me alone, Tanner. I'm never going to be your girl."

Tanner shook his head. "You'll change your mind. You know I'll wear you down one of these days."

"No, you won't," Michelle said with equal certainty.

CHAPTER
Twenty-Two

Tanner took over Michelle's drug route, and Michelle was happy to have it out of her hands. She didn't know how much Kenny was also involved in it, or she might not have been so happy. But Kenny wasn't as much her responsibility as he used to be. He might not be book-smart, but he had a way with the gang and held his own.

Michelle and Kenny both enjoyed life without school. School hadn't been much fun for either of them. Hanging out full time with the gang was a pretty good life.

Without the drug money, Michelle went back to shoplifting to support herself.

She was good but all of her success made her sloppy. It wasn't long before a store detective stopped her as she left his department store.

"Not so fast," he said, grabbing her by the arm.

Michelle tried to shake his grip. "Let me go!"

He laughed. "Oh yeah, I'm just going to let you walk away."

Michelle knew she was caught, but tried to bluff her way out. "Let me go. What do you want?"

He pulled back his jacket lapel to show her his security badge. He was heavy. She could see the sweat-rings under his armpits. "And I've seen you here all too often. This time, you got caught."

"What are you talking about?"

"Come with me."

He marched her to an 'employees only' hallway and to an elevator that went down to the basement. He didn't look strong, but his grip on her was tight. Michelle looked around nervously at the dim, unfinished basement. He took her to a small storage room with boxes on shelves and shut the door. Michelle swallowed, her stomach tightening. She got a cold, sick feeling like she was being squeezed around the middle.

"Show me what you took," he said.

"I didn't take anything."

"Empty your pockets."

Michelle looked for a way out of the situation. "I'll give the stuff back," she offered. "And I won't come back here again."

"Empty your pockets."

Michelle put the goods on the table and waited for him to react. The guard's eyes moved over them.

"Well, kid, do you know what this means?" He pointed to an 'all shoplifters will be prosecuted' sign. "Or maybe you can't even read it."

"I can read it. Come on, I've never taken anything before…"

"Yeah, right. You're no amateur."

"I'll do whatever you want. If you call the cops, I'll get taken away from my brother. I'll get put in juvie. Come on…"

He shook his head. "Strip."

"What?"

"I want to see if that's everything you took. Show me."

Michelle took off her jacket. "Where am I going to hide anything?" she demanded, gesturing to her skimpy shirt and tight pants. He approached her.

"Do you think guys like this whole punk thing?" he asked, looking at the earrings, the navel ring, and the new red streak in her bleached hair.

Michelle was humiliated.

The guard put his hand on her midi. "Take it off," he repeated.

∼

Michelle walked by Kenny without saying anything and went into her room. Kenny, frowning, got up and followed her. He went through the sheet hung on a rope separating the two sides of the room to where Michelle was lying down on her bed.

"Michelle?"

"Just leave me alone, Kenny."

"What's wrong?"

"Nothing. Go watch TV."

He sat down on the edge of the bed and touched her hair. "Come on, Michelle. What's wrong?"

"I don't want to talk about it. Just leave me alone."

He sat beside her for a few minutes, not saying anything. Finally, he stood up. "You could tell me," he said sadly and walked away.

Tanner confronted Michelle holding up a pill bottle.

"So if you're not sleeping with Dan, what are these for, huh?"

Michelle realized what pills he had and grabbed at them, getting red. "Where did you get those?"

"You told me you weren't sleeping with anyone."

"Give them to me!"

Tanner handed them over. "What do you need birth control pills for?" he persisted angrily, as if she had done something to hurt him.

Michelle was surprised he knew what they were. She wouldn't have expected him to even stop to puzzle through the label on the bottle, much less actually know what the prescription was for.

"Lay off, Tanner. It's none of your business."

"What, you start fooling around behind my back and it's none of my business?"

Michelle nodded her head emphatically. "That's right. Why would it be any of your business?"

"Because..."

Because in spite of her repeated refusals, he still refused to give up the idea that she was his girlfriend. Michelle felt rebellion rise within her, overcoming the hurt and confusion of the past few weeks.

"Why should you care about who I sleep with? Do I ask you who you've been with every night? Why should I tell you?"

Tanner tried to approach it with more tact. "Look, Michelle. I know you. Ever since what happened with Stan, you've been shy of guys. So seeing this... tell me what's going on?"

"None of your business."

"You know you can talk to me."

"I don't want to talk to you about it."

"What about Kenny? Will you talk to him about it? I just want to make sure everything's okay, Michelle."

Michelle knew what he wanted. She shook her head and refused to tell him anything. Even if she wanted to, how could she tell him about Joshua, the security guard at the store? That he had agreed not to call the police if she kept going back there to see him. She was scared it wouldn't last and scared it would. She was sure there were people at the store, other employees, who would figure out what was going on sooner or later. But if he were turned in, would he turn on her too? She hated his clumsy hands, his fat body. But she knew if she were charged with anything again, they'd put her straight in juvie.

Even if they didn't charge her, she'd fled custody and they wouldn't put her back into a home she could just walk away from again.

"I'm okay," Michelle told Tanner firmly. She pocketed the pills and walked away.

"What's with Michelle lately?" Dan asked Kenny and Tanner or anyone who happened to care, "Seems like she's worried about something all the time."

"Who cares about Michelle?" George growled.

Dan looked at him sideways. "You don't fool me, man. I seen the way you watch her. You've got a crush on her."

George's jaw dropped in astonishment, making the others laugh.

"She's got some new guy," Tanner informed Dan. "She won't say who." He paused. "She says it's not you."

Dan looked surprised. "Me? No way. She'd go for Wheels before she'd go for me."

Kenny was listening to the discussion without contributing.

"You know who she's seeing?" Dan asked him.

"No. She's scared to tell anyone."

"Scared? How come?"

"I dunno."

"So how come she's so tense? A boyfriend should mellow her out," one of the others said.

"He's not a boyfriend."

"How do you know, Kenny?"

"I dunno. I just do."

"What do you mean, he's not her boyfriend?"

Kenny shrugged. "She has nightmares."

"Like she used to?" Tanner asked sharply.

Kenny looked at him for a moment, frowning. "Yeah... like she did before."

Tanner scowled at this. The others didn't comprehend.

"What are you talking about?" Dan asked. "Before when?"

"None of your business," Tanner told him. "It's between us and Michelle."

"Come on, fill us in. What are you talking about?"

Tanner shook his head smugly. It was his, Kenny's, and Michelle's secret. Dan was an outsider. But he looked at Kenny and nodded. They would have to find out what was going on and help Michelle out.

The police arrived and tried to make sense of the confusion. There were a couple of hysterical young clerks, a guard who looked pale and stunned, and numerous thrill-seekers who were hoping to catch a glimpse or get involved. An older employee with a name tag that said 'Carol' tried to take charge.

"It's downstairs. I'll take you. I don't know who's been down there and what's been touched."

"Great," Greenan said, "we have a contaminated scene. Well, take us down."

Carol led them down the service elevator to the storage rooms under the building. There was a small room with its door shut. She gestured to it and stood back. Greenan and Rogers went through the door. A large, bloody body in plain clothes sprawled on the floor.

There were boxes that had been swept off of the shelves. Greenan had expected the guard to be in a uniform, but he was in plain clothes. His clothing was saturated with blood, now dry and stiff. Greenan could see a few stab wounds, his clothing puckered around them.

"Okay. The team should be here in a few minutes. How long has he been here?"

"I don't know the last time someone was in here. We don't really use this room. HR says he didn't show up for work two days ago."

"I'll need a list of everyone with access to this room."

Some time later, Greenan and Rogers addressed the assembled group of employees to try to sort out who knew what.

"When was the last time anyone saw Joshua?"

They looked around at each other, exchanging frowns of consideration and murmuring thoughts to each other. It was interesting to watch the crowd consciousness as they identified who had probably seen him last. One of the male employees became the focus and Greenan raised a questioning eyebrow at him.

"I don't know... Couple-three days ago."

"What was he doing?"

"He'd just apprehended a shoplifter."

"Where did you see him?"

"In back somewhere."

Rogers sensed the employee was holding back, and exchanged a look with Greenan. "Where in back?"

"I don't know."

"Did he go downstairs?"

"I don't know."

"Did he often take shoplifters downstairs?"

"No... sometimes, though."

"So did you think he was taking the shoplifter downstairs?"

"Maybe. I don't know."

"Can you describe the shoplifter?"

"No-o-o... I don't remember."

"Did anyone see the shoplifter Joshua arrested?" Greenan asked the group. There was no telling if the shoplifter had anything to do with Joshua's murder. But it was a good lead.

"I think it was this young kid—punk girl," someone contributed.

"Oh, her," another said. "I know the one you mean."

"She's comes here often?" Greenan questioned.

"Yeah, She must live in the neighborhood. I'm sure everyone's seen her around. Young, probably fourteen, earrings, tattoo, bleached hair—with a red streak in it last I saw."

"The one who carries a knife in a sheath?" another employee said suddenly. "That sheath on her belt?"

There were nods of agreement. A dagger in a sheath was a good lead. "Does anyone know her name or where she lives?" Rogers asked.

"She's probably with one of the gangs. She's pretty hard to miss."

"Had she been arrested here before? We might be able to find her name if she was."

There were looks exchanged around the room, but no one answered. Greenan waited.

"I've seen him with her before," one of the employees admitted at last. Everyone seemed reluctant to say more.

"How long ago?"

"In the last few weeks."

"We'll see if we can find her name in his records."

"Why would she come back if he'd arrested her here before?" someone asked.

Others gave him dirty looks, scowls intended to silence him. Greenan tried to figure out what was up. "I think that's enough hinting around," he said sternly. "Why don't you just tell me what's up?"

Everyone was awkward and quiet. "We've seen Joshua with her a few times lately. We figured he wasn't arresting her, but... maybe he was seeing her."

"Seeing her? Having a relationship with her?" A few reluctant nods. "And she's only fourteen?"

"She could be older... but she looks pretty young."

MICHELLE

Greenan and Rogers worked opposite sides of the street with a description of Joshua's young punk girlfriend. A few people paused, with a flicker of recognition in their eyes, but they refused to help. Others looked hurriedly at the description and shook their heads.

They eventually ran into a beat cop who was happy to help out. He read the description thoughtfully and nodded after a minute.

"Yeah, I think I've seen her with the fifth street gang. I'll point you to a couple of their hangouts."

They didn't recognize the girl at first, they weren't sure until they were close enough to see her tattoo clearly. Her hair was no longer blond with a red streak, but mostly black with a thin white streak along one side. Greenan's practiced eye told him she was nowhere near fourteen like the witnesses thought.

Rogers approached her from the side and closed his hand over her arm firmly. "Excuse me. I need you to come with me."

She turned her head and looked at him, her expression blank. "Who are you?"

"Homicide."

"What do you want?"

"I told you. I want you to come with me."

She didn't move. The boys in the gang were watching but made no protest. Rogers tugged on her arm and she went with him. Rogers was pleased with her compliance and pleased the gang hadn't put up a fight. Greenan opened the door to the squad car for them.

"What's your name?" Greenan demanded.

"I'm not telling."

"Come on. We can fingerprint you and find out anyway. Save us some time."

She considered this for a few minutes. Greenan wondered what she was on. Her reactions were a little too slow, her expression a little too slack. He eased the knife out of her sheath and she didn't even look at it. Rogers handcuffed her.

"If I tell you..." she started.

"Yes?"

"You can't call Social Services."

"You a runaway?"

She nodded. "They'll put me in lockup."

"Okay. So we won't turn you in to Social Services. Now, what's your name?"

She studied him. "Michelle."

"Michelle what?"

"You won't call Social Services?"

"I told you I won't."

"Simpson."

"Michelle Simpson?"

"Yeah."

Greenan nodded. "And are you wanted for anything other than being a runaway?"

Michelle shook her head.

"Good. So what can you tell me about Scott Joshua's murder?"

Michelle shook her head. Her eyes were distant and cloudy. "I don't know anything about any murder."

"What can you tell me about Joshua?"

"Don't know him."

"I'm told you do."

"Who told you that?"

"Some of the people he worked with."

"They're wrong."

"I don't think so. They described you pretty well," Greenan said, although he wasn't sure the description would hold up under scrutiny.

Michelle shrugged.

"Do you know what will happen if you're convicted of this?" Greenan questioned.

"I've been in juvie."

"What for?"

"Trafficking."

"So you know what it's like. You want to go back there?"

"I'm not going back. You don't have anything on me."

"We have your knife."

She looked down at her empty sheath. "So?"

"You can't wipe off the most minute drops of blood. If we find even one cell, we can find out if it's Joshua's and we'll have you cold.

That's all we need. We already have witnesses who put you at the scene."

"If there's any blood on my knife, it's not his. I don't even know the guy."

"I think we'll find out differently."

She just stared at him and admitted nothing.

"So was Joshua one of your customers? Maybe you gave him some stuff that wasn't so good and he got upset. Or he owed you money, maybe."

Michelle shook her head. "I'm not dealing."

"Okay," Rogers said, putting down his papers, "we've got some interesting developments. One, she's broken her bond. She was supposed to be doing time at a supervised facility while awaiting trial. I also pulled records from the past couple of years on similar cases—short, double-edged dagger, unknown assailant. Her name shows up on one of them."

"She killed someone else?" Greenan raised his brows.

"She was questioned as a witness. She was in the house when it happened. It was a burglary gone sour."

Greenan shook his head. "So was she involved or is she copycatting this time?"

"This was a couple years ago, she was only ten or eleven."

"So it just gave her the idea."

"Looks that way. Forensics has the knife, so they'll tell us if it's the murder weapon."

"I think we'd better arrest her."

"Yeah. Talk to her a bit longer, see if she'll identify a motive."

"I'll give it another go. But so far she won't even admit to knowing him."

When Michelle refused to say anything about Joshua, Greenan approached it from another angle. "Where were you a couple of nights ago?"

"I dunno."

"So you don't have an alibi for the night of the murder?"

"I was probably with my friends."

"Who?"

"One of them. I don't remember."

"We'll need to verify your alibi. If you really have one."

"I'm not usually alone."

"So who were you with?"

Michelle shrugged. "Dan maybe. Other guys."

"Who's Dan? Where would I find him?"

"Dan Thompson."

"Is he in the gang?" Greenan prompted.

"Yeah."

"Who else was with you?"

"I don't remember. Different guys were coming and going."

They put Michelle under arrest so they could hold her while they checked out her alibi. Dan Thompson was actually not too difficult to find. They already knew a few of the gang's hangouts from looking for Michelle. They went back to a couple and he identified himself when they asked for him.

"What do you want?" he asked.

"We want you to answer a few questions."

"Go ahead. Shoot."

"Why don't you come down to the station with us?"

Dan looked them over. "Why should I? I told you I'd talk to you."

"Where were you a couple of nights ago?"

"Hanging out. I don't know. When?"

"Two days ago. Late afternoon or early evening."

Dan considered, rubbing his forehead. "You want to give me a clue? I don't keep a real schedule."

"Who would you have been with?"

"With? The gang. I don't think I would've had a girl with me or nothing."

"You weren't with a girl?"

"No. Only Michelle, but it's not like that's romantic or nothing."

"You're sure Michelle was with you?"

"Yeah. She's been around most of the time."

"How long was she with you?"

"I dunno." Dan looked up, contemplating. "Like, mid-afternoon until late. One, two in the morning."

"You weren't separated from Michelle at any time?"

"Doubt it. I woulda noticed if she'd wandered off. We've been keeping an eye on her."

"Why?"

Dan shrugged. "She's just been kind of moody lately. Kind of... off..."

"Drugs?"

"No, Michelle's clean."

"You sure? She was sure acting stoned today."

"Michelle doesn't do drugs."

"She has a conviction for trafficking."

"She's not doing that anymore. And she was never taking them herself."

"So who else was out with you two that can corroborate Michelle was around all night?"

"Um, Tanner. Michelle's brother, but I dunno if you want to talk to him. Some of the other guys."

"Why don't I want to talk to her brother?"

"Kenny's a little slow. He doesn't ever have much to say. And he has been pretty stoned lately."

"I want to talk to anyone else who was there—and Kenny too. Understand?"

"You won't get anything out of Kenny, but you're welcome to try."

"I will. I want to know exactly where she was at all times over the past two days. And I'd better not find out anyone is lying to me, or there'll be trouble."

"Aw, why would we lie to you, officer?" Dan said with a grin that was too much of a smirk. Greenan didn't trust him.

"We'll see about that."

The boys weren't quite as helpful as Dan had promised, but they all gave similar details, giving Michelle an alibi. Worse yet were the results of the forensic tests on Michelle's knife. There was not any of Joshua's blood on it. It was not the murder weapon. They were forced to let Michelle go. If she had killed him, she'd had the foresight to buy herself another dagger and ditch the murder weapon. And that would be unusual behavior for such a young suspect.

∼

Michelle walked back into her bedroom, undressing slowly to go to sleep.

"Are you okay?" Kenny asked from the other side of the room divider.

Michelle stopped and looked in Kenny's direction. "Yeah, I'm okay."

"I mean—everything is okay now, right?"

Michelle didn't answer right away, thinking about the question. "Everything is okay now, Kenny."

"Good," Kenny said, "I don't like it when things are wrong."

Michelle got into bed and pulled up her blankets to vanquish the cold. "Everything will be okay now," Michelle repeated to herself.

CHAPTER Twenty-Three

Michelle rubbed George's neck and shoulders while she waited for Dan to finish talking to the doctor. George didn't complain. He relaxed as soon as she touched him. He asked for the massages now, instead of protesting them. Dan and the doctor walked in.

"Hello George, Michelle," the doctor greeted. "How are you doing, pal?" he asked, tousling George's hair.

"You know better than I do," George muttered.

"Well, you're going to be with us for a while longer. Take it easy, okay?"

George made no response. The doctor looked at Michelle, frowning. "Are you okay? You're pretty pale."

Michelle shrugged. "I've had the flu for a while."

"Yeah?" He studied her. "How long?"

"A few weeks."

"Come to the clinic tomorrow and have someone look at you. Okay? Shouldn't be flu after so long."

"Yeah, maybe."

"Is that a new tattoo?"

Michelle brushed her fingers over the long, skinny wolf on her shoulder. "Yeah. Just a few days ago. Still scabby."

He took a closer look at the tattoo. "I've told you before to stay away from those places. You'll pick up an infection or hepatitis or worse."

"I only go one place and he always uses a clean needle."

"You're still taking a risk. When you go to the clinic tomorrow, make sure they clean it up."

Michelle shrugged. "Whatever."

"Make sure she does," the doctor told Dan firmly.

"Hey, I don't control Michelle. She'll do whatever she feels like. Doesn't matter what I tell her."

"Make sure you go to the clinic," the doctor told Michelle again and left.

It wasn't the next day, but a few days later that Michelle did break down and go to the clinic. She sat in the waiting room for a few hours and started to get impatient with the lack of reading material. She was finally called into one of the examining rooms and sat and waited some more. The doctor came in and smiled at her cheerfully.

"Got a bit of a bug, have you?"

"Yeah. Stomach flu."

"Nauseated? Throwing up?"

"Yeah."

"How long?"

"A few weeks."

"That's a long time. Why don't you lie down and let me feel your tummy, huh?" Michelle obeyed. "Any food allergies? More stress than usual lately?" he questioned as he palpitated her stomach.

"No."

"Have you been losing weight with this flu?"

"No."

"Any patterns to your nausea? Mornings? Nights?"

"No. Most of the time."

"Are you drinking... smoking... taking any drugs...? Confidentially."

"No. Just a bit."

"Okay. We'll get back to that. Are you dieting? Taking laxatives or other kinds of over-the-counter drugs? Do you make yourself throw up?"

"No." Michelle gave an impatient snort. "I don't have any eating disorders."

"Good. How's your appetite? Still good?"

"Yeah, fine. I keep eating and I keep throwing up."

"Okay. Why don't you sit up again?"

Michelle did so.

"I'm going to need a urine sample from you and we'll go from there."

"Okay."

When she had waited for another half hour, the doctor came in to talk to her again. He pulled up a stool and sat down. "Michelle, you've got some choices ahead of you. You're pregnant."

"Pregnant?" Michelle repeated. "No, look," she reached into the pocket of her jacket and pulled out her pills. "Look, you guys gave me birth control."

"Sometimes pills alone are not enough. Your best bet is a barrier method plus pills."

"But you're wrong! I haven't been with anyone."

"In how long? You must have been active or you wouldn't have gotten the prescription."

"Not for a few months, though. So I couldn't be."

"When was your last period?"

"I haven't had it."

"Well, your uterus is enlarged. I suspect you're a ways along. You figure out how long ago it was since you were having sex, and we'll schedule you for an ultrasound to see how big the baby is. Then you'll have to decide what you're going to do."

"I want an abortion. Can you do one here?"

"No. You're going to need money and parental consent if that's the route you're going. And depending on how far you are along, you may have to go to the hospital rather than just a family planning center. Okay?"

"I don't have any parents."

"Well, whoever your guardians are. You're too young to have the procedure without consent."

"I'm old enough."

"Personally, I agree that if you're old enough to get yourself into this position, you're old enough to get an abortion. But that's me, not the law. You'll have to get consent before any doctor will do the procedure."

"You can give yourself an abortion, can't you? I've heard of girls..."

"Don't try it. It's dangerous. You'll end up with permanent damage. Don't try to do it yourself."

"Okay."

"Promise me you won't."

Michelle shrugged, looking away. "I won't."

"The clinics can give you counseling without your parents. So if you aren't sure or need to talk it over, they'll help."

"Thanks."

"No problem. There are better methods of birth control than abortion, so next time I want you to talk to me before you get yourself into this kind of trouble."

"I got the pills before."

"Pills aren't enough. You talk to me after this is all over and we'll make sure you understand your options."

"Okay."

Michelle went to a few abortion clinics, but couldn't find one that would look the other way and give her an abortion without parental permission. And she wasn't about to go to Social Services and turn herself in.

She wished for the first time she had a girlfriend to talk to, someone who knew her way around and could give Michelle advice. Surely there was somewhere underaged girls could go to have things taken care of.

At a loss as to what to do, she finally approached Dan about it. He was older and more experienced. He had to have run into it before.

She explained the dilemma and Dan considered it. "Well, this isn't exactly the kind of problem I deal with every day," he said with a self-conscious chuckle.

"You must know a girl who..."

"Yeah, you'd think so, wouldn't you? But I don't really have... extended relationships with girls. And they don't exactly talk to me about that kind of thing."

Michelle turned away, shaking her head. "So you can't help?"

"I'll help you out, Michelle. I promise. I might just need a while to get you any information. I'll have to figure out who to talk to."

Michelle nodded. "There's gotta be somewhere I can go."

∼

"You're in the same gang as Dan Thompson, aren't you?" the girl asked Tanner, pulling back from him and taking a minute to catch her breath.

"Yeah, I am," Tanner agreed, puffing up with pride at being associated with the older boy.

"I thought so. I guess his girlfriend's in trouble, huh?"

"Girlfriend? He doesn't exactly have a steady girl."

"Steady enough he's trying to get her a black market abortion." She laughed, always pleased to see someone else in such a position. Tanner laughed too.

"Sounds like ol' Dan got himself in a bind," he agreed. "I'll have to have a word with him, explain about the birds and the bees."

She giggled. "Believe me, Dan knows more about them birds and bees than you do! You'd better talk to her first. She's the one who's too young to give consent for her own abortion. Cradle robber."

"I thought you only had to be fourteen or sixteen to get an abortion without consent."

She nodded. "Exactly."

Tanner shook his head. "What's he doing chasing twelve-year-olds? I didn't think Dan even knew any twelve-year-olds." After he had said it, his mind went to Michelle and he swore. "Except Michelle."

The girl giggled again. "Well, I guess she's the one."

"Michelle isn't Dan's girlfriend. She's mine."

The girl was silent for a moment, then chuckled uncomfortably. "Sounds like Dan's been pickin' apples off of your tree, huh? No wonder he was so worried about getting an abortion."

"Shut up," Tanner said sharply. "You don't know anything about it."

She shrugged and tried to distract his attention and attract his interest back to other things. But Tanner was no longer interested in what she had to offer.

"I'm gonna kill him," he growled. "They both lied to me. They both lied and said they weren't sleepin' together. And I believed her. I swear I'll kill him."

"You're going to kill Dan? I doubt it. He's twice your size," she pointed out.

"I will. I'll kill him."

"In ten years, maybe, not yet," she muttered, angry at Tanner for his sudden lack of interest in her.

Tanner went barreling into the apartment and ran into Kenny. "Where's Michelle?" he demanded.

Kenny looked at Tanner and was slow to reply. "Out."

"With Dan?"

"Maybe."

"Well, is she or not?"

Kenny shrugged.

"Where are they?"

"None of your business."

"Kenny, it's Tanner you're talking to. Your old pal. I want to know where they are."

"I'm not going to tell you."

"Kenny," Tanner grabbed him roughly by the arm and pulled him close. "You tell me what I'm asking."

Kenny favored him with a glare and pulled away. Tanner tried to keep ahold of him but was surprised at Kenny's strength. There were a couple of years between them and Tanner had not noticed how Kenny had bulked up lately. Tanner let his fingers slide off, rather than to risk challenging Kenny and losing.

"Come on, Kenny," he wheedled. "Between buds. Where'd your sister go?"

Kenny turned away from him. "Leave her alone."

"I'm not going to do anything to Michelle. It's Dan I'm gonna kill."

"Dan didn't do anything."

"You don't know anything about it."

Kenny shook his head. "Leave Michelle alone. Just stay out of it."

"Do you know where they went?"

"Yeah."

"Is she getting an abortion?"

Kenny shook his head. "Went to talk to a doctor. He has to see her first."

"So you know all about it."

Kenny didn't answer.

"How come you never told me Dan got her pregnant?"

"It wasn't him."

"Is that what he told you?"

"Nobody told me."

"How do you know it wasn't Dan, then?"

"She wouldn't let anyone touch her."

"She let *someone* touch her."

Kenny shrugged. "You already know that."

Tanner shook his head. "That store cop? No, man. That was ages ago."

Kenny shrugged. "There hasn't been anyone else."

"Yeah, sure. No one but Dan."

The doctor put the transducer on Michelle's stomach and watched the monitor, which was turned away so she couldn't see it. He moved it around a couple of times and then removed it. His expression was blank.

"I'm afraid I can't help you."

"Why not? They told me you do sometimes," Dan protested.

Michelle was used to hearing this by now and didn't say anything. The doctor cleaned up his instruments.

"I sometimes help young girls who can't get consent," he agreed. "But I can only do first trimester at the clinic. Second trimester has to be done at the hospital. It's a different procedure and there's more risk of complications. You," he told Michelle, "are definitely second trimester. I might even guess third trimester. I'm afraid you've simply waited too long."

He removed his surgical gloves with a snap. "I'm sorry," he said.

Michelle nodded.

"What can we do?" Dan asked. "Do you know anyone who will do it?"

"No. Like I said, it has to be done at the hospital. You can't do that without involving a lot of people. Too risky."

"Well, don't you have any suggestions?"

"All I can say is, you're going to have this baby. If you want me to get you the name of some adoptions people, I can do that. We can hand the baby directly off for adoption, you don't ever have to see it. But you are going to have to have it."

Michelle didn't say anything.

Tanner saw Dan's car pull into the parking lot and saw Dan and Michelle get out. Even the distance he was from her, Michelle looked tired and pale. He watched them talk for a moment before separating. Dan gave Michelle a quick peck on the cheek and patted her on the back. Michelle went up to her apartment alone. Tanner approached Dan before he could start the car again and leave.

"Hey, Dan," he said casually. "Where ya been?"

"Tanner. Just hanging out. How's it going?"

"Going just fine from your view, huh?" Tanner said, bringing his gun out to zero in on Dan's chest before Dan could guess anything was up.

Dan looked at the gun coolly, his expression not changing, then he looked at Tanner's face, raising an eyebrow. "What's this about?"

"It's about you and Michelle. Always lying to me, saying there's nothing going on. And then this."

"What are you talking about?"

"You don't fool me. I know what's going on!"

"Tanner, what are you high on? You're off your gourd!"

Tanner jabbed the gun forward sharply. "You got her pregnant and now you're getting her an abortion."

Dan laughed shortly. "Who told you that?"

"I got my sources. You can't tell me it's not true."

"She's pregnant, sure. But I didn't get her that way. You know there's nothing between me and Michelle."

Tanner felt a hard point digging into his back. He looked over his shoulder, startled. Michelle held her knife against his back. "Drop the piece," Michelle ordered.

"Yeah, I knew what was going on here. You two can try to keep it from me, but—"

"Drop it, Tanner!" Tanner lowered the gun. "Get out of here," Michelle told him, "and stay out of my life."

"You're supposed to be my girl—"

"I'm not your girl or anyone else's. Not yours, not Dan's, not anyone's!" Her face was red with anger. "Just stay out of my life!"

Tanner didn't move.

"I said get lost," Michelle said through her teeth.

"If it isn't Dan's baby, whose is it?"

"None of your business. Now leave me alone."

Tanner finally beat a retreat. Dan watched him go. "That guy is so psycho," Dan said, rolling his eyes.

Michelle shook her head disgustedly. "He's been after me since I was a kid. And he's getting worse."

"Who told him you were pregnant?"

"I haven't told anyone but you. Who'd you tell?"

"No one."

"Do you think I'm showing?" Michelle asked, looking down at herself in concern.

"No. I can't tell. He must have overheard us."

"I gotta find a way to get rid of this pregnancy."

Dan nodded thoughtfully. "I could get you some stuff. There's some pills you can use—I don't know if it works this late."

"I'll try."

"Okay. I'll see what I can get."

CHAPTER Twenty-Four

Rogers and Greenan watched Dan's apartment building casually, not expecting to see anything. Michelle was no longer under constant surveillance, but they watched her occasionally in the hopes that she might get careless and do something that would help them in the Joshua case. If she were the killer, she might eventually lead them to the murder weapon. If she weren't, she might lead them to the real killer. People got careless after some time had passed.

They had watched Michelle go into the building with Dan an hour or so before, hanging on his arm, bent over like she had a stomachache or bruised ribs.

Dan came out of the building without Michelle. He was carrying a paper grocery bag with the top half rolled down. Rogers jumped out of the car and followed him into the alleyway, where Dan shoved the bag into a garbage bin and pulled some other debris over it. Dan turned around and headed back to the apartment building. He jumped when he saw Rogers watching him. Scowling, he tried to walk by.

"Where are you going in such a hurry?" Rogers asked amiably.

"What's it to you?" Dan snapped, trying to push past.

"Hold on. I want to see what you just put in there."

Dan saw Greenan approaching and tried to pull away from Rogers before Greenan got there, but Rogers already had his cuffs out and snapped them over Dan's wrists.

Dan didn't try to fight it. He stood and watched as Greenan went to the garbage bin and pawed through it to find the package.

"This it?" he asked.

Rogers nodded. Greenan unrolled the top. "Let's see what's inside, shall we?"

He pulled out a mass of bloody towels. The first thing he thought of was Joshua's murder and the missing murder weapon. It was wrapped up in the towels. But the instant he thought about it, he instantly discounted it. The blood was fresh, bright red. The Joshua murder was months before. He unfolded the towels and felt sick. Among the blood and mess was a tiny body.

Greenan folded the towel over again and swallowed. "Where did this come from?" he questioned Dan.

"I don't know what that is. Never saw it before."

"We both saw you put it in the garbage. You can't deny it."

"You saw me take out the trash. You pulled out the wrong bag."

"Take him to the car," Greenan told Rogers. "Hang onto this. Call it in. I'll go upstairs."

Greenan went up to Dan's apartment and stopped at the door. He hesitated, trying to decide whether to knock or whether to kick the door in. He tried the handle and found it unlocked. He opened the door quietly and slipped in, his hand on his gun.

George was in the front room and his eyes widened when he saw Greenan. Greenan saw George feeling for something beside himself and moved in quickly and picked up the small gun before George's weak hands could grasp it.

"Michelle!" George called out a warning. His wobbly glance over his shoulder told Greenan where to find her. Greenan went to the bedroom. Michelle was sitting on the bed trying to put on her shoes. She was very pale and tired-looking. She looked at Greenan with his gun.

"What's going on?"

"You're under arrest."

Michelle blew out her breath. "For what?"

"For murder."

"I didn't kill anyone."

"We caught Thompson downstairs with the baby."

"There was no baby," she said blankly. "I only had an a— miscarriage."

"I saw the baby. That was no miscarriage. Come on."

She stared at him. "You're just out to get me. You tried to get me for murder before."

"I think you should be quiet until you talk to a lawyer."

Michelle looked down at her shoes and tried to reach them again. She couldn't bend over far enough to reach them. Greenan watched her for a minute and put his gun away. He knelt down and put her feet into her shoes and tied them up. Michelle sighed and nodded.

"Thanks."

He stood up and pulled her gently to her feet. Then he escorted her to the front room. Michelle gestured to George. "You can't leave Wheels all alone."

Greenan looked at George. "Someone will look after him. There will be police all over here in a few minutes."

He walked her down to the car. Dan was already sitting in the police car. Greenan opened the door and helped Michelle in.

"Are you okay?" Dan asked.

"Yeah."

"You look pretty rough."

"I'm okay."

Dan watched her and didn't say anything further.

The medical examiner looked dispassionately at the bloody bundle.

"Infant female. Newborn, no more than an hour or two old. Premature. By two-three months."

"Can you tell whether it was born dead or died after?"

"At this point, no. Maybe after a more thorough examination. Color is poor. If it wasn't born dead, it might never have breathed."

"Smothered?"

He shrugged unemotionally. "Possibly."

"Could have been saved if they called the medics?"

"Impossible to know. Doctors lose babies too."

Rogers sat with Dan Thompson in the cool interrogation room, sitting close to him.

"Why don't you just tell us what happened," Rogers told Dan, "so we can get this whole thing cleared up?"

"I don't have anything to tell you. So Michelle miscarried. Since when is that a police matter?"

"If that's what happened, why don't you just describe it for me? Tell me how it happened."

Dan looked at his watch. "I gotta go home and take care of George. He can't be on his own long."

"Someone is taking care of him."

"Maybe, but they don't know all of his medications and everything, do they? They know he had a kidney infection last week and has to take antibiotics four times a day? You have to let me go so I can look after him."

"We'll see. Tell me about Michelle and the baby."

"There's no baby," Dan maintained.

"Did she induce the abortion?"

"This ain't a police matter. You go to the hospital to question all of the girls who lose their babies? You got no real criminals to chase?"

"I know Michelle has killed before and now you or she has done it again. If she really did miscarry, you shouldn't have any problem telling me about it."

"Why should I? It's private. It ain't any of your business." Dan folded his arms across his chest.

"Thompson, I can stay here asking you questions all night. You're the one who wants to get out of here."

"Michelle losing her baby is none of your business. I don't care what you say."

While Rogers questioned Dan, Greenan was trying to get somewhere with Michelle.

"What happened, Michelle?" he asked gently. "Why don't you tell me about it?"

"I don't want to talk about it."

"I know. But we need to know what happened. Then you can go home and rest."

"Nothing happened. I was having really bad cramps. So I called Dan. He took me to his place. I passed a bunch of blood and stuff and we cleaned up. Then you came in."

"Was the baby alive?"

"There was no baby," Michelle insisted. "Just a miscarriage."

"I saw the baby. You may think that was just a mass of cells, but it was a baby. Now tell me what happened when it was born."

"It wasn't born, it was miscarried."

"Tell me what happened."

"I just did."

"Was Dan the one who cleaned up?"

"Yeah. I wasn't really in any shape to."

She was still very pale. They probably shouldn't even be questioning her in that condition.

"So it was Dan who smothered the baby."

"Nobody smothered anyone. It just happened like I said."

"I don't think it did."

"Well, you weren't there." Michelle leaned her elbows on the table, face in her hands.

"How far along were you?"

"I don't know."

"Do you know the baby probably would have been just fine if you'd called a doctor? It probably could have survived if it had been taken care of."

"You don't know what you're talking about."

"Do you know it's murder if you could have saved the baby and didn't do anything? Or if Dan smothered it, you would be an accomplice?"

"I told you what happened."

Greenan looked at his watch. "You think about it. Because this is a life we're talking about. An innocent baby's life."

He walked out and left her there to stew. His superior was waiting outside for him, having watched the interview.

"She may be telling the truth," Orlando pointed out. "It may just have been a spontaneous miscarriage and the baby was already dead."

"I would be willing to accept that if she didn't have a history. But this is one cold little girl. She's our prime suspect in one murder and implicated in another. She's murdered two men and now she's murdered her baby."

"The medical examiner hasn't confirmed murder. And there is no evidence or proof in the other two."

"If she simply miscarried, why didn't they take her to the hospital or call an ambulance? Why hide the body? The medical examiner can't even tell the difference between a baby that died of SIDS and one that was smothered. How is he going to tell if the baby never drew a breath because it was too premature or because someone manually smothered it?"

"Do you think she's in good enough shape to be questioned?"

"I'll give her a break for a while. It's more than she deserves. I'm going to go talk to Thompson's brother."

George had not been put in an interrogation room, but was in the waiting area. He was slumped in his wheelchair staring into space. An officer at a desk nearby was keeping an eye on him. Greenan pulled a chair up close to George and sat down.

"Hi there, George."

George tilted his head to the side and looked at him dully. "Yeah?"

"I wonder if you could help me out."

"No."

"Come on, George. You haven't heard the question yet. Don't you want to help your brother?"

"I don't wanna talk to you."

"Well, I'm sorry to hear that. Because I think you could help."

George's head tipped the other direction and he ended up looking at the ceiling.

"Why don't you tell me what happened today?"

"When?" George asked distantly.

"When Michelle came over."

"She wasn't feeling good," George observed.

"No, she wasn't, was she?"

"She had a stomachache. Dan took her into the bedroom to lie down." George's description was naive, as if he didn't understand what had happened.

"What happened when she went into the bedroom? Could you see or hear anything?"

"No," George said flatly, but then he proved his answer wrong with his next words. "She was crying. I couldn't tell what Dan was saying. Michelle was swearing and crying. I didn't know what was wrong."

"You didn't know she was pregnant?"

His head lolled to the side. "No. Is she?"

"She was," Greenan agreed.

George frowned. "That's strange. How'd she get pregnant?" he said to himself.

"Dan wasn't the father?"

"No. They're not sleepin' together."

"This morning when Michelle was there, did you hear the baby cry?"

He blinked and shook his head. "I didn't hear any baby."

"Michelle's baby. Did you hear Michelle's baby this morning?"

"Michelle doesn't have a baby."

"She had a baby this morning."

"No, she didn't."

"So you didn't hear anything. You heard Michelle crying and Dan talking, but you didn't hear a baby cry."

"Yeah, that's right."

"Did you hear Michelle and Dan fighting at all? Arguing?"

"No."

"After Michelle stopped crying, what happened?"

"Nothing. Dan went downstairs."

"You've been a really big help, George. I appreciate your help."

"I'm not going to help you."

Greenan studied George. He seemed sincere.

"Okay, George," Greenan agreed and left him alone.

"Your friend George seems to have quite the crush on you," Greenan commented to Michelle when he went back to see her.

"No, George doesn't even like me," Michelle said in surprise.

"Sure he does. But he seems to have a couple of wires crossed upstairs, doesn't he?"

"George isn't all right in his brain since the accident. You shouldn't even be talking to him."

She was probably right on that point. But George was a witness; they had to get corroborating testimony from him.

"Well, he managed to give a pretty lucid account of what happened today, when you went to Dan's. So why don't you give me your explanation again and we'll see if they match up this time."

"I told you what happened. And George wasn't in the room. He couldn't tell you anything unless he made it up."

"Why don't you start at the top again? You and Dan think you're protecting each other, but you're just making things worse."

"I think we'd better make arrangements to put Michelle and Thompson into lockup until we get the medical examiner's report back. I don't want to take the chance of letting them go and not being able to get them again."

Orlando nodded. "Book Michelle in. I'm not so sure about Thompson. His brother needs specialized care. He can't go far."

"Thompson is old enough to know when to run. He knows he's caught. His brother won't keep him from running forever."

"I don't think he'll run. Anyway, it's the girl you want. Let Thompson go."

Greenan shrugged, frustrated. "If you're sure that's what you want."

Orlando walked away and Greenan looked around. He had seen another of Michelle's friends hanging around a minute before. After a few minutes, he saw the boy again. Greenan approached him, trying to remember his name. They had talked before, after the other murder. Kenny. The one Dan had said not to talk to.

"Hello there, Kenny."

The boy looked at him. "Are you in charge?"

"What do you need?"

"I'm looking for Michelle. My sister."

Right, he was Michelle's brother. Greenan had forgotten that part. "Yes, Michelle's here. She's under arrest. I'm afraid you can't see her, though."

"You can't keep her here. She's sick."

"She's just fine."

"She's sick," Kenny insisted.

"Did you know she was pregnant?" Greenan asked curiously.

Kenny shrugged and didn't say.

"Did you know Michelle planned to kill her baby?"

"Are you going to let her go?" Kenny asked impatiently.

"No. Not today."

"You going to take her to the doctor?" Kenny persisted.

Greenan thought back to Michelle's appearance during the interrogation. She had just been through an unattended medical procedure; maybe she should go to the doctor.

"If you're that concerned about her, I'll have Michelle looked at by a doctor."

"Yeah."

"What makes you think Michelle is sick? You must have known what she was planning today."

Kenny shook his head. "I just knew."

"Are you and Michelle twins?"

"No."

Kenny turned and walked away. Greenan watched him go and then returned to the room where Michelle was still sitting.

She was sitting with her head down on the table. She looked up when Greenan entered. "How are you feeling?" Greenan asked.

"I don't feel great," Michelle admitted.

"Do you want something to eat? Or maybe to see a doctor?"

Michelle wiped her forehead. "I'm not hungry. Maybe a doctor."

"Okay. I'll take you over to the station doctor."

"She needs to be in hospital," the doctor advised, glancing at Michelle lying under a sheet on the examination table. "She's not in very good shape."

"What's the matter?"

"She's bleeding pretty heavily. And I don't know how much trauma there has been. I haven't done an internal exam. She should be under medical supervision."

"Okay. I guess we can put her under guard at the hospital. She'll probably be okay tomorrow?"

"I don't know. Leave it to the experts."

"Can you tell if the miscarriage was spontaneous or induced?"

"An abortion? I can't tell you. What difference would it make?"

"At this point, I don't know. Maybe none. But I need to know as much as possible."

"As her doctor, I can't tell you anything anyway."

Greenan called Social Services when Michelle was sent to the hospital. Michelle and Kenny's social worker was not in, but the emergency line worker dutifully took his message. Greenan may have promised Michelle not to call her social worker during the last investigation, but that didn't mean he couldn't this time. He could do the right thing and get Michelle and Kenny off the street.

CHAPTER
Twenty-Five

Marsden had a couple of officers go with her to find Kenny. Now that she knew where to look, it wasn't hard to find him. He tried to run when he saw them coming and the two officers ran after him. It was close, but Kenny hesitated at the end of the street before turning, and one of them tackled him. Kenny was knocked breathless to the pavement and they handcuffed his hands behind his back. Marsden joined them.

"Kenny, are you okay?"

"Leave me alone."

"We can't let you stay on the street like this, Kenny. We'll take care of you."

"I take care of myself."

"You're much too young to take care of yourself. And Michelle won't be back after this either. We'll take you both somewhere you'll be safe."

"Let me go."

Marsden shook her head. "Why don't you take him to juvenile? I have to find out what's happening to Michelle."

~

Michelle woke up feeling stronger. She looked around and saw she was in a hospital room. She tried to roll over, but found she was in restraints. A few minutes later, a policeman walked in. He looked at her in surprise.

"You're awake."

Michelle nodded. He sat down and didn't say anything else to her.

"The medical examiner cannot determine if the baby was born dead, died of natural causes, or was smothered."

"So we can't charge Michelle," Greenan concluded.

"No. We'll have to release her. There's nothing we can hold her on."

"Even though it's the third murder she's been involved with."

Orlando shook his head. "We have no reason to disbelieve her story, no way to disprove it."

"I know she and Thompson killed that baby."

"We can't prove it."

Kenny got up from the bunk and ran in place for a few minutes. Once warmed up, he dropped to his knees and did push-ups until his arms gave in. He turned over and started sit-ups. His routine went on until he finished all of the exercises in his program. He climbed back into the bunk and sat still for a while, catching his breath. After his heart rate had settled back to its regular rate, he got back up and started to run on the spot again. He might not be the smartest guy, but he was in good shape. He was shooting up pretty fast and with his hard work, his muscles were growing and hardening. If he stuck to it and practiced, he would be able to beat Tanner or any of the younger group of boys in the gang. And then... Dan or one of the older boys. He would never be smart like Michelle, but he fully intended to be the toughest guy in the gang.

Marsden picked Michelle up from the hospital.

"Before you get any ideas of taking off on me, keep in mind that

Kenny's already in custody and if you run, the two of you won't be together."

Michelle glanced at Marsden. "Where are we gonna go?"

"I don't know yet," Marsden said.

Michelle didn't believe her. They wouldn't have picked her up if they hadn't known where they were taking her. "I'm not going to juvie," Michelle said. "I didn't do anything."

"Well, you got yourself arrested. That's not exactly nothing. And I understand you were pregnant, too. You want to tell me about that?"

"None of your business."

"As your temporary guardian, it is my business."

"No, it's not."

Marsden looked at Michelle. "I'm not trying to upset you, Michelle. I'm not accusing you of anything. I want to help you."

"I don't want your help."

"Michelle, don't be so antagonistic. I'm not your enemy."

"If you weren't my enemy you wouldn't always be trying to take away my home and my brother."

"You'll never forgive me for separating the two of you, will you?"

"No," Michelle agreed flatly.

"I had to do it. It wasn't my first choice. But things worked out okay. You two were still reunited."

"I still hate you."

Marsden was surprised at her strong choice of words. She decided not to pursue it any further. Michelle was obviously in no mood for conversation.

They went to juvie and Michelle waited with Marsden for them to bring Kenny out. A guard eventually escorted him out. Kenny put his arm around Michelle's shoulders. They both looked at each other to make sure they were okay. Marsden signed the papers to release Kenny. Then the siblings were taken to another room to wait.

"Where do you think they'll put us?" Kenny asked.

"I don't know. I thought juvie, but they're releasing you."

They were silent for a while.

"Are you okay?" Kenny asked.

"I'm fine. You didn't get beat up in here?"

"No."

They sat in silence and waited. Eventually, a guard came in to get them. "Come with me."

"Where are we going?"

"Never mind. Come on."

Kenny and Michelle went with him. He handcuffed them together a few minutes later and put them in a van. They were taken to the bus station and put on a bus. The guard put them in the back seat of the bus.

"You'll be met at the other end," he told them, "and if you try to get off the bus, the driver will call the cops. Just stay put."

"Where are we going?"

"Hopefully somewhere you won't cause trouble. Now you two keep quiet and don't bother anyone. Got it?"

"We're not going to bother anyone," Michelle said impatiently.

He nodded and got off the bus.

They traveled for hours. At last, late into the night, a cop got onto the bus at one stop and walked to the back where they were sitting.

"Kenny and Michelle Simpson?" he demanded.

"Yeah."

They got up stiffly. The cop took Kenny by the arm and escorted them off the bus.

"Where are we going?" Michelle asked.

"Tonight? Detention. After that, we'll have to see. I gather you're both runners."

Michelle didn't say anything else. He was obviously already prejudiced against them. He took them to his car and drove them to juvie. Michelle chewed her lip. Her last trip to juvie hadn't turned out so well.

Kenny read her mind. "I'll look after you," he promised.

She had always been the one to take care of him. "We'll be separated," Michelle pointed out, "they won't keep us together."

"I'll still take care of you," Kenny insisted.

When they got to the juvie center, everything was dark. The cop rang the bell at the door and a security guard eventually opened it.

"Closed," he informed them curtly.

"I've got two new admittees for you. They were scheduled."

"Can't be admitted now. There's no one here."

"Well, I've got nowhere else to put them."

The guard squinted at the kids. "Throw them in county lockup. Bring them back in the morning."

"I'm not couriering them back and forth. I'll leave them with you and they can be admitted once the office opens."

"You can't leave them here."

"I'll leave them in cuffs. They can't cause you any trouble that way."

"I don't think—"

"I'm leaving them here. They can be admitted in the morning."

He maneuvered the two of them through the door and walked away.

The guard looked at Michelle and Kenny. "Well, I guess you're my problem now. Come on." He took them through a dimly-lit hallway to an empty foyer. "Sit down there and don't cause me any grief."

"I have to go to the restroom," Michelle informed him.

"Hold it."

"I've been holding it half the bus trip."

"Then you can hold it a few more hours," he said unsympathetically.

"Just let me go to the bathroom. I'm not going to try anything."

"Sit down and don't bother me."

Kenny sat down on the floor obediently. Michelle stood there shifting her weight back and forth. "Come on, please," she wheedled. "I won't bother you at all, I won't say a peep. Please let me go."

He studied her, grinning. Michelle held her legs tightly together, biting her lip. She was angry, but she couldn't hold out much longer. "I'll do whatever you want. Please!"

"No," Kenny said sharply, "don't say that. You don't have to do anything for him."

"Kenny, I'm gonna wet my pants!"

"So do it. They'll give you fresh clothes."

The guard gave in. "Okay. Come on. I'm not unlocking you, so you'd better not be shy."

Michelle glanced at Kenny. He looked away. The guard took them to the bathroom and kept a close eye on them. Michelle kept up her end of the bargain and didn't bother him again.

―

Michelle hadn't expected to fall asleep sitting on the floor, but in the morning the guard shook them awake. "Okay, you two. Get up. Let's go."

Both of them got to their feet stretching sleepily. Kenny rubbed his eyes, yawning. The guard took them up to the admitting desk. "Two juvies brought in last night," he informed the administrator at the desk. "I'm told they were expected."

The man looked at a clipboard list. "Kenny and Michelle Simpson?"

They nodded.

"Yeah, I have their admitting papers. Temporary detention. Bring them on back."

A few minutes later they were finally unlocked and separated. Michelle tried to breathe deeply and keep her stomach from tying in knots. She wasn't going to get beaten up this time. She would be on her guard; no one would take her unaware. And Michelle planned to make a weapon the first chance she got.

They put her through the showers and then left her in a cell. Michelle sat there shivering for a while, still damp from the shower. She kept waiting for them to come get her back out, or talk to her, or put someone else into the cell. But bells rang, people walked by in the hall, a meal was slid to her under the door, and still no one talked to her.

Kenny also sat in a cell by himself. He wasn't worried like Michelle was. He'd been okay in juvie. He lay on the bunk with his mind blanked out. He got up a few times to exercise, but other than that he was satisfied to just lie there alone.

It went on for a few days. Neither one had contact with anyone else. Then one day—Michelle had lost track of what day of the week it was and Kenny didn't care—they let them both out. Michelle wandered around her section getting a feel for the lay of the land, casing everyone out. She wanted to make sure no one could beat her up. She didn't want anyone to think she was an easy target. She studied people's faces and tried to figure out who was dangerous and who could be trusted.

"Hey little girl," an older girl said, approaching her. "You looking to make some friends?"

Michelle looked her over and folded her arms. "What would it take?" she demanded, as tough as she could sound.

"You'd have to do whatever I told you to."

"What would you tell me?"

The girl studied her. "You seem pretty savvy. Why don't you come to my room?"

Michelle hesitated, but then she swallowed her fear and followed. "What's your name?"

"Thrasher."

"I'm—" Michelle caught herself before using her first name, "Simpson."

"Yeah, I know."

They got to the other girl's cell.

"Siddown."

Michelle looked at the bunk. "Why?"

"I thought you were willing to do whatever I told you."

Michelle sat.

"They're going to put you in a cell with someone else," Thrasher informed her. "I could get you in here."

Michelle looked at Thrasher again.

"Are you going to beat me up?" she asked.

"Not unless I got to. You do what I say and I won't got to."

Michelle shrugged her shoulders. "I guess it would be okay if I got moved in here."

"Good," Thrasher approved, "I'll get you put here, then."

Michelle nodded, her stomach tense, worried she'd made the wrong choice and might still get beaten up. Or Thrasher might have something else in mind.

"Sometimes we share time slots with the girls in section B," Brian informed Kenny. "Weight room, library, out on the compound. If your sister got put in that section, you might get a chance to see her."

Kenny nodded. "Good."

"Usually they try to spread members of the same gang across several sections so they can't conspire. So they probably made sure you two won't be able to talk."

"I'll still get messages to her."

"Come with me," Thrasher said, stopping Michelle. "You don't want to go to the library; that's where all the girls go. We can go to the weight room."

"I've never done weightlifting."

"So? That's where the guys go."

"I heard they got internet in the library."

"Yeah, and everything is blocked. Come on, trust me. The weight room is better."

Michelle looked down the hall toward the library. It had been a long time since she'd read a good book. She sighed. "Okay."

Thrasher led the way. Michelle looked around the room. Weight lifting was not her thing. Then across the room of sweating boys, she spotted Kenny. Thrasher turned to talk to her, but Michelle was gone, hurrying across the room to throw her arms around him. Kenny clasped her for a moment.

"Hi, Michelle."

"Are you okay?"

"Yeah."

A guard approached them. "Break it up, you two."

Michelle took a small step back from Kenny. "We're not doing anything."

"No touching, no conversation. You want to be in here, you are working out."

Michelle shrugged. "Fine. We'll work out."

The guard nodded. Kenny went back to his workout. Thrasher

joined Michelle. "So, who's the cute guy?" she whispered. "He your boyfriend?"

Michelle shook her head. "My brother."

"You didn't tell me you had a brother. You're holding out on me."

"I didn't know you would care."

"Care? You're always on the lookout for a good make in here, Simpson."

"Yeah, I guess."

Michelle hadn't thought before about girls being interested in Kenny. She looked at him with new eyes as he was pumping iron. His tanned, lean face and dark hair were tough and handsome. His figure —if guys had figures—was well-proportioned, his muscles hard and well-defined. He was surprisingly good-looking. Not a lot of girls hung around the gang, so Michelle hadn't noticed any girls chasing after him before. Kenny noticed her gaze and looked questioning. Michelle shrugged and looked away again. She followed Thrasher over to one of the weight machines and took instruction from her on how to use it. Thrasher worked out on the machine next to her, leaving Michelle to try it out. Michelle worked her muscles, deep in thought. She was concentrating so hard that for a while she didn't notice she had started to bleed again.

Thrasher motioned to Michelle as she moved on to another station. "Over here, Simpson."

Michelle rested for a moment and then sat up. The movement brought a gush of warm fluid between her legs and she looked down. Her uniform was soaking up the blood. The bench was smeared with it. Michelle motioned for Thrasher to come over and got slowly to her feet.

"What's wrong?" Thrasher questioned.

"Something's wrong," Michelle said, indicating the blood. She tried to explain further, but couldn't get the words out. Thrasher was staring at the blood. She swore.

"Are you okay? You'd better get to the infirmary."

Michelle nodded. She put her hand on Thrasher's arm to steady herself, but then the dizziness suddenly overcame her and she stumbled to her knees.

"Come on," Thrasher encouraged, trying to help her back up. "You can do it."

A guard noticed them, and grabbing another guard, hurried towards them. "What's going on? Let go of her!"

They pulled Michelle and Thrasher apart and Michelle found herself on the floor, unable to get up. Her head was spinning and everything around her seemed disjointed. Fingers probed her throat for a pulse. "Where are you hurt? What happened here?" a voice demanded.

"Get out of the way," Michelle heard Kenny's voice. "She's my sister!"

There must have been more guards arriving in the weight room. The other inmates were being evacuated from the room. Kenny fought back against being removed. "Michelle's my sister, I'm not going anywhere."

"Did you see what happened?" The guard swore in frustration, probing Michelle's lower abdomen for an injury. "I can't see where she's hurt!"

"She just started bleeding again," Kenny's voice explained

"Again? What do you mean? People don't just start bleeding."

"From inside. She had an abortion."

The guard suddenly understood. He yelled to one of the others. "Where's medical? She's losing a lot of blood!"

Eventually, others were there. Medics. They lifted Michelle onto a stretcher and she drifted off to sleep.

Michelle woke up in a hospital, alone. She lay there unmoving, drifting along, only partially conscious. After some time, a doctor came in and looked at her chart.

"Hi there, honey. How are you feeling now?"

"Okay," Michelle said faintly.

"Good." He took her blood pressure and pulse and checked her IV. "Why don't you tell me what happened?"

"I had a miscarriage a while ago. Then I was lifting weights today and just started bleeding everywhere."

"How long ago was your miscarriage?"

"I don't know—just before they put me in detention."

"You don't know how long ago that was?"

"No... they put me in solitary for a while. I don't know how long, exactly."

"I see." He put the blood pressure cuff on her. "What were you in solitary for?"

"Nothing. Just got there."

He pumped the cuff up. "What are you at the Center for?"

"Nothing. They're just holding us."

"Us?"

"Me and Kenny, my brother."

"What are they holding you for?"

Michelle shook her head. "I told you, nothing. They said it was temporary. While they found a placement for us. But it's been a long time."

CHAPTER
Twenty-Six

The doctor talked to one of the prison officials about Michelle's condition. "We're still giving her blood to get her pressure back up. She's conscious, but seems confused."

"Confused how? Delirious?"

"No. She's coherent, but she says she doesn't know why she's at the Center."

There was silence at the other end for a moment. "I see. But you think she'll be back on her feet before too long?"

"Sure. As long as she waits for a while before lifting weights again. Just out of curiosity, why was she incarcerated?"

"I couldn't tell you off the top of my head. I don't have her file in front of me."

"And you didn't look to see what it was so you would know how much security we would need over here?"

"It wasn't anything serious."

"Then what was it?"

"I'll have to look it up."

"I'd appreciate it. It would help me talk to her and maybe break through the confusion."

"I'll call you back."

The doctor doubted if he would, but politely hung up.

Kenny was taken from his cell and put in handcuffs. He didn't bother to ask what was going on or where they were going. In a place like that, it was better to just go along with the flow. They didn't like explaining things. He was taken out of the detention center to an unmarked car. Kenny looked at the social worker or policeman who got into the driver's seat and neither of them said anything. Kenny sat with his hands cuffed behind his back.

They drove to a big, old building that was obviously some kind of halfway house. There were grilles over the windows. His escort took him up the walk. Kenny stood at the door with him waiting for an answer.

"When will Michelle get here?"

"Couldn't tell you."

Kenny didn't pursue it. The door opened. "Kenny Simpson?" the man who opened it guessed.

Kenny nodded.

"Good. Come in."

Kenny went in. There was an institutional air about the building. The smell of harsh cleaners, warmed over dinners, and stale cigarettes.

"Turn around."

Kenny turned to let them unlock his handcuffs. Before taking them off, another bracelet closed over his wrist. Kenny looked at it when his hands were released.

"It's an electronic tracker," the man informed him. "You will be put back in detention if you go somewhere you are not given permission to go. I have your history and I'm telling you there's not going to be any running around with gangs while you're here. You're going to school, you're living here. Anything else is off-limits until you prove yourself."

Kenny shrugged, looking around.

"No alcohol, no drugs. Random drug testing will be done, so be warned. No weapons or any kind of contraband. We search rooms regularly. Don't try it."

"Anything else?"

"Don't get smart. We run a pretty tight ship here. If you can't take it, you're back in detention in a second. This is the only way out."

"Where's my room?"

"I'll take you up."

Kenny followed him upstairs. "When's Michelle coming?"

"Your sister? Sometime this afternoon. But if we get trouble from either of you, you'll be split up."

The doctor stood over Michelle with her chart. "You're looking pretty good. How do you feel?"

"Good."

"That's what I want to hear. Ready to be out of here?"

Michelle shrugged. "Back to the Center? I suppose."

"Actually, they're transferring you to a half-way house. They're not allowed to hold you at the Center for more than a day without a court order."

Michelle was surprised. "You checked up on them?"

"I've seen them do this before. I just made a short phone call."

Michelle didn't say anything for a moment. "Thanks," she said awkwardly, unsure what to say about it.

"No problem. No weight lifting for a while, okay? And pay attention if you do anything that requires any exertion. You really did a number on yourself with that abortion. I don't know what kind of problems you may have in the future if you try to get pregnant."

Michelle nodded. "Okay."

Kenny looked up when he heard footsteps in the hall. Michelle walked in.

"Kenny!" She hugged him, and after a moment they stepped apart and compared bracelets.

"They tell you the whole spiel too? About the drugs and everything too?"

Kenny nodded.

"It's like juvie, just smaller," Michelle said impatiently.

"We're back together, though."

"Yeah. That's something. All of that solitary in juvie drove me nuts."

Kenny nodded. "What are we going to do?" he asked.

"I don't know. Lie low for a bit. Figure things out."

"Are we going to go home?"

"To the gang? I doubt it. Find somewhere here we like."

"They say we gotta go to school again."

"We'll figure something out. I'll help with the homework."

"I don't like school."

"I know. We just gotta figure out how to get out of here without ending up in juvie."

Lights out at the halfway house meant lock-up. The doors had locks on the outside and leaving at night would mean breaking the door down. Michelle sat down on the bed she had been assigned to.

"What if I get sick again?" she asked Susan, her roommate.

"Unless you're really sick, just live with it. If you make them unlock the door at night, you better be on the way to the hospital," Susan advised,

"I just got out of hospital."

"Do they know that?"

"Yeah."

"Well, maybe they wouldn't give you trouble, then. But don't plan to make waves."

"I'm not. How long have you been here?"

"A few months."

"What's it like?"

"Like prison. Maybe worse."

"How long are you here for?"

"Until they think I'm ready for the outside. Hopefully not for too long."

"How long does it usually take?"

Susan looked at her and shook her head. "I haven't seen anyone get out," she said bleakly. "They all go back to juvie."

In the morning as they got dressed and ready for school, Michelle drilled Susan with the questions that had occurred to her in the night.

"How sensitive are these things?" she gestured to her bracelet.

"They'll set off alarms if you go more than a block or two away from school or here."

"Exactly how far?"

"I don't know. I've gone across the street for a smoke, but that's about it."

"What've the others gone back to juvie for?"

"Drugs, running, being seen with the wrong people. Whatever they can get you on."

Kenny looked around at the other kids, most of them quite a bit younger than he was because he'd been kept back so much. He sat in a desk at the back of the room and slouched over, trying to make himself invisible.

Michelle was looking around her new classroom at the other girls. They all seemed pretty clean-cut and mainstream, a contrast to Michelle's colorful image. She had worn a halter top that showed off her tattoos and navel ring. And she wore tight black leather pants with it. Most of the other girls were in jeans and t-shirts. Michelle knew how much she stood out among the mostly conservative class. She looked for a seat in the back. The other students watched her and made comments to each other.

The teacher came in and looked at the class. "Take your seats," he advised. Everyone quieted down and sat. Reading his lesson plan, the teacher raised his head and scanned his students. "We have a new student today. Michelle, welcome. If you need help keeping up, please talk to me."

Michelle ducked her head, embarrassed. "Can I go to the restroom?"

"Go ahead."

Michelle walked past the rest of her classmates and out the door. She walked by a couple of classrooms and glanced in to see if Kenny was there. She went to the washroom and put more makeup on. She didn't know what she was trying to prove by putting on the black lipstick and other makeup. She knew it would just attract more attention to her, but she felt insecure and it was like putting on a mask. She didn't want them to see her fear.

She had bummed cigarettes off of Kenny, who had bummed them off of someone else, and she smoked for a couple of minutes to relax herself before going back to the class. She headed back to her desk. One of the girls whispered something as Michelle went by, and she heard "freak" at the end of the sentence. Michelle turned back to the girl.

"What did you say?" she demanded. Her voice was loud and the teacher stopped talking and looked at her.

"Is there a problem, Michelle?"

"Yeah. I ain't putting up with any little hussy disrespecting me! You want to say anything about me, you say it to my face!"

"I didn't say anything about you," the girl protested.

"You liar!" Michelle shoved her. "You think I didn't hear you? Come on! You got something to say to me?" Michelle gestured for the girl to stand up and face her.

"Michelle," the teacher said warningly, coming closer to them. "Why don't you take your seat so I don't have to send you to the office?"

"Oooh, I'm scared," Michelle sneered. "I've never been to the office before."

"Come talk to me in the hall," he told her.

Michelle hesitated, looking at the girl who had called her a freak. The teacher motioned and she followed.

"Look, Michelle," he said quietly, when they were out of the room. "I know you're at Trebleck and I don't think you want to get yourself in trouble the first day. They're not too tolerant over there. You're new here. The other students don't know you yet. If you get in a fight with Tracy, I don't have any choice about sending you to the office."

Michelle shrugged, looking at the tile floor. "I guess."

"Don't worry about anyone else. You just sit and listen to the lesson and don't fuss about what's in everyone else's heads. Okay?"

"Okay."

"I understand it's been a while since you were in school last. Let me know if you need some extra help."

"I don't need your help."

He motioned her back in. He put his hand on her back as she entered and Michelle shook it off and went back to her seat. Tracy looked away and didn't say anything this time.

"I heard you beat up some girl today," Kenny commented.

Michelle looked at him in surprise and laughed. "I just shoved her. Yelled at her."

"What for?"

"Because I didn't like the way she was looking at me," Michelle said.

Kenny shrugged. "There's a gang," he commented.

"What gang?"

"Jaguars."

"You're going to try to get in with them?"

"*We* are."

"We're going to stay here?"

"Maybe not here," Kenny twirled his finger to indicate Trebleck House. "But if I can get in the Jags..."

Michelle shrugged. "They aren't going to let us stay here and hang with a gang. They already told us."

"I know."

"Better figure out what we're going to do, then."

"I'm gonna talk to one of the Jags tomorrow."

Michelle nodded. Before, joining a gang had been a big deal. But it hadn't been as bad as she thought it would be. Yes, they got into trouble, sometimes ended up in juvie, but that wasn't the worst thing that could happen. They accepted each other and enjoyed each other's company. If Kenny wanted to get out of the mini-prison and back on the streets, she was agreeable.

They stayed at Trebleck House for a few more days while Kenny negotiated with the Jags. Michelle grew to resent the bracelet, drug testing, and institutional atmosphere of the place more and more. Once Kenny had everything straightened out, they cut each other's bracelets off at school and took off. Kenny introduced Michelle to all of the boys and they went to the apartment they were to share with Butch and Clyde, a couple of the Jags.

"Your sister got a boyfriend?" Butch asked Kenny, with Michelle standing right there.

"No. But you leave her alone."

"Would I bug her?"

Kenny scowled. "How do I know?"

Butch grinned. "I think you got me made," he admitted.

"You try anything and I'll use this," Michelle warned, lifting her dagger slightly and sliding it back into the sheath again.

"Yeah? You as tough as you pretend to be?"

"You wanna find out?" Michelle challenged.

He acted like it was a big joke. "No, I wouldn't want to do that," he laughed.

Michelle looked around the apartment critically. She'd seen worse places. It didn't smell like rats, at least. She didn't know where the gang spent their time, but it was probably not there. It was just a place to crash on the mattresses on the floor after a long night out.

Some of the Jags went to school sporadically when they felt like it, but Michelle and Kenny were in the majority that had no use for school. Michelle found them to be a little more wild than Dan's gang, but not too bad. The occasional turf war with one of the other gangs kept their fighting skills sharp, but they weren't constant.

CHAPTER
Twenty-Seven

She didn't expect to get caught in a vice bust at the pool hall, but the younger kids—not Jags—liked to hang around and deal their drugs there, so maybe it shouldn't have been such a surprise. A couple of cops walked in at a leisurely pace and raised their voices to announce the bust. More cops came in. Everyone scrambled to get rid of their drugs before they were caught, but the cops knew what they were doing and were ready for everything.

Michelle didn't fight them. She let one of the cops grab her and quickly frisk and cuff her. She looked around for Kenny. She was clean, but Kenny probably had drugs on him.

At the police station, Michelle was left alone for a while before someone came in to talk to her. An older cop came in and sat down across from her.

"Have I picked you up before?" he questioned with a frown.

"No."

"You look familiar."

Michelle shook her head. "I've never been here before."

"Don't bother trying to lie to me about something like that."

"I'm not. I just moved here."

"Huh. You look really familiar to me. Oh, well. What were you doing at the pool hall?"

"Playing pool."

"Right. You in Scott's gang?"

That was the younger gang. "No. The Jags."

"You're too young for the Jags."

"No, I'm not. I'm in the Jags."

"I've been on vice since before you were born. Don't try to snow me. Where's your jacket?"

"I'm brand new, don't have one yet."

"You have any drugs on you?"

"No."

"In your system?"

"No."

"Nothing? Hard, soft, prescription?"

Michelle hesitated. "A little beer. Not much."

"We do blood tests, you know. Is that all we're going to find?"

"Yeah, that's it."

"Any priors?"

"Convictions?"

"Yeah. Prior convictions," he said dryly.

Michelle rolled her eyes. "Trafficking."

"Ah, now we're getting somewhere. So you *do* deal."

"Not since then."

"That's what you were doing at the pool hall, right?"

"No. I was just hanging out with the Jags."

"Dealers don't just stop dealing. My boys find anything on you?"

"No."

"You're lucky. What's your name, sweetheart? And where are you living?"

"Michelle Simpson."

He wrote it down. "My wife's name used to be Simpson," he commented.

"Yeah?"

"Yeah. You wouldn't be related, would you? You look a little like her."

"I don't have any family. Just my brother."

"Huh." He shrugged it off. "Where are you living?"

"With some other Jags."

"Which ones?"

"I don't know their real names. Butch and Clyde. And Kenny."

"Kenny? Is he new?"

"Yeah. My brother."

"Okay. Kenny Simpson—he also goes by Simpson, does he?"

"Yeah."

The cop wrote the names down, frowning like there was something he was supposed to remember. "Your brother, any convictions?"

"No."

"Is he older or younger than you?"

"Older."

"Why aren't you living at home?"

"We were in foster care."

"Is your mom's name June?"

Michelle stared at him, astounded. "What? How did you know that?"

He stared back at her. "And your uncle is Justin?"

"Justin's my daddy! Do you know where he is?"

"Sweetie... you're my wife's niece. You stayed at our house once when you were just a little tyke. June was expecting again at the time."

"Marcie! That's my little sister."

They both stared at each other.

"I don't come from here, though," Michelle protested.

"No, June and Justin were in trouble and left town. June just came back for a visit one time."

"Mama never said anything about her family."

Charlie nodded. "They cut themselves off."

Michelle shook her head. "You're making it up! You're trying to confuse me."

"Where's Kenny? I'd like to see him too."

"He got arrested too; he was at the pool hall."

"I'm going to go see him, and then call Ruby and tell her about it. She'll want to see you guys."

"Ruby?" Michelle repeated.

"My wife. Your aunt."

At the back of Michelle's mind, she could remember June and Justin arguing about someone named Ruby. But it was so deep in her memory she could have been inventing it. The cop got up and left the room to go see Kenny.

~

Charlie studied Kenny, remembering the little boy who had stayed at their house so many years ago. A little dark-haired, silent child, withdrawn and slow. Michelle had been different; she was loud, precocious and grating, demanding attention. Charlie could see very little of that child in Michelle now, it was too long ago and she had learned to modify her behavior. But Kenny—Charlie could still see the cautious, distant look of that little boy.

"Kenny?"

"Yeah?"

"I've just been talking to Michelle. There's sort of a funny coincidence we've run into." Kenny waited silently for further explanation. "My wife is also a Simpson. She's your mother's sister."

There was a long pause and then Kenny spoke. "So?"

"My wife is your aunt."

"Yeah?"

Charlie was stumped by Kenny's apathy towards the announcement. "Did you ever hear your mom talk about Ruby?"

"No."

"You're not interested in meeting her? A relative?"

"You want us to come live with you?"

"Well, no I hadn't thought about that."

Kenny shrugged.

Ruby couldn't believe it when Charlie told her the news over the phone. "June's kids? They're here in town?"

"Yeah," Charlie chuckled. "I just busted the both of them. They're in the Jags."

"That's my old gang!"

Charlie was surprised. "That's right. I'd forgotten! Well, they're following in your footsteps."

"Where's June?"

"I don't know. I didn't ask. I was so stunned to find them here I didn't know what to say."

"Can I come down and talk to them?"

"Sure."

"What's going to happen to them?"

"I don't know. I'll have to talk to the Captain. See if I can get them off. I'm not sure if either of them had possession or not. Might need to have a hearing."

"I'll see you down there."

∽

"Michelle has a prior conviction, but she didn't have any drugs on her. Kenny has no priors, but we have enough to get him on simple possession," Charlie summarized.

"And these kids are related to you," the captain said.

"To Ruby. They're pretty young and don't have long records. I think it's possible that with a little attention, we could turn them around."

"Let's see their rap sheets."

Charlie handed over the computer printouts and the captain looked them over.

"The girl has two murder suspicions."

"No evidence to charge."

"Well, Charlie, you've been doing this as long as I have. If you want to try taking these kids under your wing, give it a try. We don't have to charge them."

∽

Michelle looked up when the door opened and a woman walked in. She had shoulder-length blond hair and was pretty, though she had some lines around her eyes.

"Michelle?"

"Yeah."

"I'm Ruby—your aunt."

Michelle looked her over. She was surprised she could see similarities between Ruby and June. Especially around the eyes and mouth. "Are you really mama's sister?"

"Yeah, June's my little sister."

"How come she never talked about you?"

Ruby sighed. "June and Justin ran away. From what I gather, Justin was afraid the police or Social Services would catch up with them. So they never contacted us."

"How come you never looked for us?"

"Well... I told June I wouldn't."

Michelle looked away. "You should've anyway."

"I'm sorry. I thought it would be better."

Michelle didn't say anything.

"Do you feel like telling me what happened?" Ruby asked.

Michelle shook her head. "We got taken away when I was eight."

"I went into foster care when I was eight too. So did June."

Michelle shrugged. She was curious about Ruby, but so surprised by suddenly meeting up with a relative and so angry to find out she had relatives, she refused to try to connect with Ruby. Ruby didn't seem put out by this.

"This is so weird, running into you guys like this. I never thought I would see you again after this long."

Kenny was more inclined than Michelle to like Ruby. She could see it in his eyes. But he didn't say anything. Michelle didn't think he could quite follow all of what was happening. He was rubbing his temples and getting that tight look around his eyes that told her he was getting a headache as he came off his high. Charlie had brought them both into a conference room and Ruby joined them. She supposed it was meant to be less formal than the interrogation rooms, but she didn't feel comfortable.

"We're wondering if the two of you would like to stay with us for a few days," Charlie suggested.

"Why would we want to do that?" Michelle demanded. "We got our own place."

"I suppose I could call your social worker instead."

Kenny looked at Michelle with a worried frown.

"I would think you would like to stay with us and get to know your aunt," Charlie continued.

"She never did anything for us."

"I'd like to now," Ruby said.

Michelle shook her head. But she caught Kenny's worried look and sighed. "Whatever. If you want. I don't care."

Charlie nodded. "Okay. We'll get everything arranged."

"We didn't have to come here, you know," Michelle said, as they were finally left to themselves at Ruby and Charlie's house in the small hours of the morning, in the spare room that Ruby said had belonged to Sheree, her daughter.

"They woulda sent us back to juvie," Kenny pointed out.

"They didn't."

Kenny rubbed his eyes with his palms. "We can split anytime. My head is killing me..."

"I'll get you something."

Michelle peeked out into the hallway before stepping out. She didn't want to talk anymore to Ruby or Charlie. But they appeared to have gone to bed. Michelle went into the bathroom and pushed the door just shut, without letting it click into place and make a noise. She started to go through the medicine cabinet, holding up each bottle in the dim light of the streetlight shining through the window. There were cough medicines, a couple of prescriptions, some herbal pills... The door flew open suddenly and Michelle jumped, dropping a bottle with a clatter into the sink. Charlie turned the light on and squinted at her.

"What's going on?"

Michelle picked up the bottle of pills. "I was looking for aspirin," she said.

"In the dark?"

"Didn't want to wake you guys up. I could see well enough."

Charlie glanced over the contents of the medicine cabinet. He selected a bottle and held it out to her. Michelle took the bottle from him.

"This is supposed to be good for headaches too," Charlie said, indicating one of the herbs. "Ruby takes them."

"Yeah, thanks. We don't do that junk."

Charlie had the sense not to point out what kind of junk she had been involved with. He watched her take a couple of aspirin from the bottle and head back to the bedroom.

"Was Michelle up?" Ruby asked when Charlie got back into bed.

"Yeah. Going through the medicine cabinet."

"There's nothing in there to worry about."

"You can get a good buzz from a bottle of cough medicine."

"If she wants it that bad, she can go to the bar down the street too."

"I know. I just wonder if bringing them here is going to make any impact on them."

CHAPTER
Twenty-Eight

Michelle woke up to the smell of coffee. She opened her eyes and looked around, disoriented at first. She thought she was back home with June and Justin. Then she remembered she was at Ruby's but wasn't sure why it reminded her of home. It was much nicer than any of their apartments had ever been. She listened to Ruby's voice in the kitchen for a while. Somehow Ruby sounded a bit like June. June when she was happy, which was rarely. Like June when Justin was home. Michelle got up, stretching. She pulled on her clothes and nudged Kenny as she walked by him.

"Get up, lazybones."

Kenny grunted. "I'm too wasted. Leave me alone."

"I smell coffee."

"Go away."

Michelle shrugged and left him alone. She went out to the kitchen. Ruby looked around at her. "Hi, Michelle."

"Hi." There were already cups out, so Michelle helped herself to the coffee and sat down to drink it.

"Did you guys sleep okay?"

"Yeah. We ain't used to a nice place like this, so we just crashed."

Ruby nodded. "Yeah. Sleeping on the streets isn't exactly comfortable."

Michelle rolled her eyes at Ruby for pretending she knew what it was like. "We got our own place. We don't sleep in a ditch."

"You have a place with some of the other Jags?"

"Yeah."

"Good. Better than depending on friends to put you up."

"Yeah. We've done that before. It wasn't so bad, but having your own place is better."

Michelle had been staring at the picture on the wall calendar and she glanced back at Ruby. Ruby's eyes were on Michelle's dagger. Michelle didn't know if Ruby had seen it the night before or not. She felt her face get hot.

"You gotta have some way to protect yourself. Plenty of guys carry heat—guns."

"I know. I always preferred a switch myself. Can I see?"

Michelle hesitated, then pulled it from its sheath and handed it to Ruby. Ruby looked it over, feeling the balance and looking at the well-maintained edge.

"Nice," Ruby said and handed it back. "I always preferred something I could put in my pocket. But you're more showy than me."

"Who are you?" Michelle demanded, trying to figure Ruby out.

"Charlie didn't tell you?"

"About you being June's sister, yeah."

"No, about me being a Jag."

Michelle studied her. "No way."

"Well, it was a few years ago now. But yeah, I was when I met Charlie, when your mom was about eight."

"You were a Jaguar."

"Here, I'll show you."

Ruby went into her room and came back with a jacket. A leather Jags jacket. Michelle took it from Ruby to examine.

"Wow. I don't believe it."

The leather was worn soft, smooth, and water stained. But the emblazon was still bright. The picture of the big cat in mid-pounce was slightly different from the one on the jackets the Jags wore now, but similar. Michelle ran her fingers over the smooth leather.

"Can I wear it?" she asked. "This is so cool!"

"Uh, yeah I guess you could."

"I don't got my own yet."

"I got mine from a guy leaving the gang."

"I can't wait to show the Jags. I gotta show Kenny."

She hurried back to the bedroom, pulling it on. "Kenny—take a look," she shook him and turned to show him the emblazon. Kenny rolled over and stared.

"Where'd you get that?"

"Ruby—she used to be a Jag!"

"Ruby?"

"Yeah. Weird, huh? She says I can wear it."

Kenny nodded. "You'll get a good rep, for sure."

June went back out to the kitchen. "I'm gonna see if I can get a tattoo of this," Michelle told Ruby, indicating the picture of the Jaguar on the jacket.

"You like tattoos, huh?" Ruby's eyes traveled over Michelle's ink.

"Yeah. They're cool."

"I never could see the point."

"You never got one?"

"No."

"I never liked them until I got my first one."

"How many do you have?"

"Five. I don't know where I'll put this one."

"I never even wore makeup when I was in the Jags."

"Yeah, but you were probably older. I look like a little kid without it."

Ruby nodded. She laughed. "I remember June wearing makeup when she was little. I guess we thought it looked good."

Michelle was silent.

"Sorry," Ruby apologized. "I guess you don't want to hear about your mom."

"How come she never told us about her family? Are there more of you?"

"Our family was pretty messed up. Chloe has been off my radar for a long time. I don't know where she is. And Ronnie doesn't talk to us. She was adopted by her foster family."

"Were you guys orphans or something?"

"Our dad is dead. Last I heard... our mom is still alive."

"Mama never mentioned any family. She mentioned her dad—just once—and I thought it was weird, 'cause I never even knew she had one."

"I don't remember him much."

"She said I was just like him."

Michelle caught the shocked look that flitted across Ruby's face, but it was masked as quickly as it came. "Huh, I wonder what she meant," Ruby said. "But Charlie said you guys at least knew Justin, right?"

"Well, Justin's my daddy," Michelle pointed out. "We didn't see him a lot, but up until we went into foster care, he was around part of the time."

Ruby's forehead creased. "They told you Justin was your daddy?"

"He is."

Ruby shook her head. "Justin is your uncle."

"No, he's not."

"He's our brother. Mine and June's. They may have called him your daddy 'cause there wasn't one around, but he's your uncle."

Michelle considered the bizarre idea and shook her head adamantly. "I've seen them together," she told Ruby, "in bed."

Ruby looked doubtful. "They used to sleep together, when June would have nightmares, to comfort her."

"I'm not talking about sleeping. I'm saying I've seen them..." Michelle's searched for an acceptable euphemism, "be intimate."

Ruby flushed. "No, you didn't! They're twins!"

"Maybe there's two Justins," Kenny suggested from the doorway. Michelle wondered how much of the conversation he had heard or understood.

"That must be it," Ruby agreed, relieved. "We're not talking about the same Justin."

"Justin Simpson," Michelle said, knowing it was no mistake. "Kenny looks a lot like him."

"You both look a lot like him," Ruby said quietly. "What color is your hair normally, Michelle?"

"Brown. Same as Kenny and Justin. June's is the same color."

"Yes, that's right. I remember. Did Charlie tell you we met you once?"

"Yeah. When Mama was expecting Marcie. I don't remember."

"No, I guess you wouldn't. You were pretty young. So she had a girl? Why aren't you together?"

"Marcie's with Daddy—with Justin."

"How long have you been away from each other?"

"Years. Daddy just disappeared when we went into foster care. Never came back to see us."

"That must have been rough."

"Yeah. We liked him."

"But not June?"

"June beat the crap outta us. Why would we like her?"

Ruby had the sense not to be shocked. "I'm sorry. We tried to get June help while she was here. But she just took off."

"Doesn't matter. We got outta there when we were old enough."

Michelle made a big splash with the Jags when she showed up wearing Ruby's jacket.

"Where did you get that?"

Joe pinched the leather between his fingers. "A genuine classic Jags jacket. I don't believe it. Look at that cat—that's a real jaguar."

Michelle showed it off proudly, drinking up the attention.

"Come on, Simpson, where did you get it?" Clyde demanded.

"From our aunt," Michelle said with a shrug. "Turns out we got family here, and Ruby was a Jag."

"No way. When?"

"I dunno. Years ago. She's like forty now. Musta been twenty years ago."

"Look at the commander stripes," Butch pointed out, gesturing to the rank stripes on her shoulders. "Looks like you're in charge now, Simpson."

Michelle laughed. "You gonna do what you're told, Butch?"

"Never."

"Yeah, that's what I thought."

"So how'd you find out about this aunt?" Clyde asked.

"That bust at the pool hall? Her husband was one of the cops that pulled us in."

"She was a Jag and got married to a cop?"

"I guess so, yeah."

"That's just too weird," Joe said.

~

"Are Michelle and Kenny coming back?" Charlie questioned.

"I don't know. They didn't say. They won't be living here. They have a place with the Jags."

"Do you think we should call Social Services?"

"No. They're okay."

"Did I tell you Michelle has two suspicion of murders?"

Ruby shrugged. "So? I did too."

Charlie thought about it. "I guess it's been a while, hasn't it? I forget what you were like back then."

"I'm not that different now."

"You're not on the street anymore."

"I'm still the same person."

"What do you think we should do, then? What about June and Justin? Should we try to find them and let them know what's going on?"

"I don't think it would be the best thing for them. I guess from what Michelle said—June got pretty abusive."

"What about Justin?"

Ruby considered. "I wish I knew what went on. I don't know what to say. They'd like to see Justin and Marcie again. But I don't know what's up with Justin."

"What do you mean?"

"He pulled out on them. But the thing is—Michelle said Justin was their dad."

"Yeah, she said that to me too. I didn't pursue it. We know June and Justin were still living together when June visited."

"But we didn't know they were sleeping together."

"As in…?" Charlie trailed off, frowning.

"As in Kenny and Michelle are Justin and June's biological children."

"No! Are you sure?"

"Michelle's pretty sure about it."

"No wonder they took off."

"Yeah. Maybe we should try to find Justin. He shouldn't be hard to find if he's still trucking."

"I'll see if I can get a line on him. You think the kids would go back to living with him if he came back?"

"No. Besides, I doubt he has much more than a room to sleep in now and then between hauls."

"Then why are we looking for him?"

"Because they haven't seen him or their sister in years. I think it would be good for them to have some kind of connection."

CHAPTER
Twenty-Nine

Michelle had been keeping an eye on Kenny from across the room as the night drew on. Kenny's solution to hangovers was to start drinking again as soon as he crawled out of bed. She wasn't sure how much he'd had to drink or what else he had taken, but he was obviously high, horsing around with the other Jags in high spirits. Kenny was rarely so gregarious, so she knew he must be pretty plastered.

She didn't talk to Kenny about the conversation with Ruby and didn't know if he understood what it meant to them. The thought of June and Justin being siblings blew her away. And they were twins. Somehow she felt like that made it even worse. No wonder Kenny was like he was. It was their fault. And they had still gone and produced two more babies. It made her sick just to think about it.

Kenny was horsing around with the guys and fell down. Michelle watched for him to get up again, but instead the Jags drew back from him, looking at each other anxiously. Michelle pushed across the room to Kenny and found him convulsing on the floor.

"Kenny! What happened?"

"OD'd," one of the Jags guessed.

"Call an ambulance."

"Are you kidding? They won't come to this street. It's got a bad rep."

"We can't just let him die!"

"I could drive him to the hospital," one offered.

Michelle bit her lip. "Yeah. Let's go."

"It's probably nothing," Clyde comforted Michelle, as the others did their best to drag Kenny down to the car. "He'll probably be just fine when it stops."

"He could die."

"Well, that's one of the risks of doping. Kenny knows that."

The cops came to the hospital when the doctor reported Kenny's drug overdose. The other Jags knew they would show up and had already left. Michelle wasn't sure how to get rid of the cops but thought she would try using her newfound family.

"We're staying with a cop," she offered when they started grilling her. "You should talk to him."

"Who? What cop?"

"Charlie."

"Charlie who?"

"I don't know his last name. Charlie. In vice."

The cops exchanged glances and went a little ways away to talk. They didn't come back to talk to Michelle right away, so she leaned her head back and closed her eyes. Her head was pounding from the smoke and loud music at the party. She tried to relax her muscles and just drift away.

"Michelle."

Michelle opened her eyes and looked around foggily. She was at the hospital and Charlie was standing over her. The present rushed back to her. "You came. Kenny's sick."

"So I hear. Did he OD?"

"Maybe. That's what everyone thought."

"How are *you* feeling?"

"I haven't had anything."

"Good. What did the doctor say?"

"No one's talked to me."

"I'll see what I can find out."

He walked away and talked to the administration. In a few minutes, a doctor with a clipboard came to see him. Charlie motioned Michelle to come over.

"The doctor says they've got Kenny stabilized," he advised. "He's going to be okay."

"Is he going to have brain damage?" Michelle demanded.

The doctor hesitated. "It's hard to tell at this point what the permanent damage may be..."

"Will this cause brain damage?" Michelle persisted.

"Every time you take a drink or shoot up, you're killing brain cells. An event like this... he could sustain severe damage."

"How bad?"

"Impossible to predict. You may hardly notice a difference. Or he could be severely disabled."

Michelle thought about George and felt sick. She couldn't bear it if Kenny were like that. She just couldn't deal with it like Dan had.

Charlie put his hand on Michelle's arm. "Kenny's not going to wake up tonight. I think you should come home with us."

"Okay," Michelle agreed. She wondered if that docile voice she heard was actually her own. She felt like screaming. Felt as if she were going to burst. But her voice was faint and far away and she didn't pull away from Charlie when he escorted her out to the car with one hand on her back.

He spoke to her a couple of times in the car, but Michelle could barely hear him and couldn't concentrate on what he said. She was silent and Charlie didn't persist in trying to carry on a conversation.

Michelle was relieved not to be going back to their Jag apartment. Not without Kenny there. She stumbled up the steps at Ruby's house and went to the guest room. She sat on the edge of the bed, and could hear Ruby and Charlie talking somewhere far removed from where she was.

"I think Kenny will be okay," Charlie said. "Young kids tend to bounce back pretty quickly."

"I hope so. How's Michelle?"

"You should check in on her. I think she's sort of in shock. She didn't want to talk to me, but maybe she'll open up to you."

A few minutes later, Ruby came into the room. "Hey, Michelle. You okay?"

Michelle nodded. "I don't want to talk about it."

"Okay. You need anything?"

"No."

"Try to get some sleep. I'll take you to the hospital in the morning."

Michelle nodded. Ruby left, shutting the door behind her. Michelle just sat on the edge of the bed, staring at the wall. She couldn't move, couldn't make herself do anything. It was as if she'd been switched off.

Michelle sat beside Kenny's bed, staring at his face and waiting for him to stir. She didn't know how long she had been there. She leaned back and closed her eyes.

"Hey, Simpson."

Michelle opened her eyes and stared at the figure before her. "Tanner? What—? What are you doing here?"

"Looking for you. Took a while to track you down."

"How did you find us?"

"Wasn't easy. You coulda called to say where you were."

"How would I know you were going to come here? It's a long way to come for a visit."

"I didn't come to visit. I came to be with you."

"What about your family? And the gang?"

"Ditched 'em. I'd rather be with you."

Michelle shook her head, rubbing her temples as she tried to process this. "You're crazy. I don't want you here."

"Well, you got me. Let's go for a smoke. You look like you could use the fresh air."

Michelle hesitated, looking at Kenny.

"He ain't gonna wake up while you're gone. We won't be long."

"Okay," Michelle conceded. She pushed herself stiffly from the chair.

Tanner took her down to the parking lot and lit up.

"Don't you have any regular cigarettes?" Michelle complained when she saw the joint. "I don't want—"

"Come on. You gotta relax. This'll help."

He handed her the lit joint and Michelle took it, too weary to fight. Tanner left her to her own thoughts as they passed the joint back and forth.

"You think Kenny's gonna be okay?" he asked after a while.

"I dunno."

"He's a tough dude. He'll pull through."

"Maybe."

"You think you could get me into the Jags?"

Michelle rolled her eyes. "Why don't you go home, Tanner?"

"I'm gonna find a place here. I'm sick of living with my folks and Emma. I'd rather live close to you."

"Just go back to the gang. I don't need you hanging around here."

"You're not getting rid of me that easily."

"You don't belong here."

"And you do?"

"Yeah." Michelle showed him her jacket. "You see this?"

"Cool."

"I got family that was in the Jags. I do belong here."

"Family? What family?"

"My mom's sister. This was her jacket."

"You never said nothing about that before."

"I didn't know before."

"That's too weird," Tanner said, baffled.

"Yeah."

Ruby had come to sit with Michelle for a while at the hospital. Michelle's hostility towards her was waning as her curiosity grew.

"How did you and Charlie get together?" she asked.

Ruby laughed. "You'll never guess," she said.

"He busted you."

"Yeah. We got along real well and he kept in touch while I was in juvie."

"And you got married."

"A lot of things happened between getting busted and getting married. But, yeah."

"Did you have kids?"

"Charlie adopted my baby. I had an abortion that messed me up and I couldn't have any more kids."

Michelle reflected. "I had an abortion too."

"Uh-huh? Usually you're okay afterward, but I was messed up. You'll probably still be able to have more kids."

Michelle shrugged. "I don't want any."

"I didn't either. Until Stella, my first baby, died. She had problems because I drank so much when I was pregnant."

"Daddy—Justin didn't let Mama drink when she was pregnant. But Marcie was messed up anyway."

"Oh...?" Ruby didn't ask for details.

"She had cerebral palsy. I don't know exactly what happened. Justin always blamed June for it."

CHAPTER
Thirty

The man was wrapped up in his own thoughts watching the TV behind the counter. Charlie recognized him even without the other trucker pointing him out. Charlie walked up to the counter and took the stool next to him. He ordered a coffee.

"Hello, Justin," he said as he stirred it.

Justin looked at him and studied him with a frown of concentration. "Do I know you?"

"Well, it's been a long time."

"You look familiar but I can't place you."

"I'm only married to your sister."

Recognition dawned. "Charlie. How are you? Imagine running into you after all this time!"

"Well, it's not really such a coincidence. What was a coincidence was me arresting the kids after they joined Ruby's old gang."

"The kids?" Justin echoed.

"June's kids. Kenny and Michelle. You know, the ones who call you Daddy that you abandoned."

Justin didn't look at him. "That's not how it was."

"Well, however it was, I think they need you. At least for a visit."

"I don't think I could, after this long."

"They don't know I'm talking to you. But I really think you should come see them."

Justin shook his head. "They don't need me back in their lives. They're better off without me."

"Ruby and I both think it would help the kids to see you and have some contact with you. They don't have anyone else."

"They have foster families."

"You know what that's like. Besides, they're not with foster families now."

"I don't know, Charlie."

"They've had it pretty rough since you disappeared."

"They had it pretty rough before."

"You don't even want to hear about them?"

Justin sighed. "You're going to tell me anyway, aren't you?"

"Kenny's just out of the hospital after a drug overdose and he's in a bad way. They're both in the Jags, Ruby's old gang. Been in juvie. Michelle has a conviction for drug trafficking and has been suspected in a couple of murders."

"And how can I change any of that?"

"I guess you don't care."

"I do care—but I don't see how I can do anything about it. Besides, I have another family."

"Oh, do you?"

"Yeah." Justin brightened a little. "How'd you like to meet them?"

"You live close by?"

"Sure. I stop here to eat if I know Sondra's already fed the kids. No point in her getting dinner out again."

Charlie agreed to go meet the family, for lack of a better plan. He followed Justin's cab in his car a few minutes' drive to the house. Justin walked with him to the door and into the tiny bungalow.

"Daddy!" a couple of children squealed, launching themselves into his arms. Justin's moody expression dissolved beneath a wide grin as he kissed them and ruffled their hair. A woman came to the door and greeted Justin, looking at Charlie curiously.

"Hi. I'm Sondra."

"Charlie. Pleased to meet you."

"Would you like to come into the living room? Justin...."

Justin agreed. "Where's my other girl?" He kissed Sondra and dragged the other kids along with him to the other room. Charlie followed the happy mob.

There was another girl in the living room, this one in a wheelchair. She had little head control, but she jerked it around as Justin came in. She gave him a wide smile and a gruff greeting, incomprehensible to Charlie.

"This is Marcie," Justin said.

"Oh. Kenny and Michelle's sister."

"Yes. Sondra's and my oldest. She's about a year and a half younger than Michelle."

"But she's not yours—yours and Sondra's, I mean."

"She is now," Justin corrected without further explanation. He turned to his wife. "Charlie is my sister Ruby's husband. We ran into each other at the truck stop."

"Oh, how funny. That's great. So how is Ruby?"

"She's fine," Charlie assured her. "We've got the kids staying with us for a bit."

"The kids?"

"Michelle and Kenny."

"Oh... of course. They must be getting big now."

"You've met them?"

"When Justin was still living with June, we had them sometimes," she explained.

Charlie frowned. "Could I talk to you alone, Justin?"

Justin nodded wearily and led him downstairs to a small shop.

"How much does your wife know about your relationship with June?"

"Our relationship?" Justin repeated hesitantly.

"That you and June were..." Charlie had a hard time even saying it, "...siblings and lovers?"

Justin looked at him for a long time and Charlie was starting to wonder if they had it all wrong.

"No," Justin said finally. "She doesn't."

"And that's why you never contacted the kids? You were afraid she'd find out?"

"The kids didn't know anything about us being brother and sister. They couldn't have tipped her off. But I guess they know now from Ruby."

"Yeah. And it was a big shock on all sides. Then why didn't you ever call them? How could you just take off?"

"The kids wanted out. Or Michelle did, anyway. Wanted to get away from June, because she... was abusive. So I got them into foster care. But I knew the next thing they'd do was to investigate our backgrounds and then they'd figure out we were siblings, not married. Maybe charge us. So I told June to scram and I did too."

"Social Services never figured it out."

"They didn't?"

"And they obviously didn't look for you very hard. You were pretty easy to track down."

Justin stared off into space. "It seemed like the only way at the time."

"I think it's time to face the kids again."

"I can't take care of them. I can barely support our kids, even with Marcie's disability allowance."

"I'm not asking you to. I doubt they would want you to anyway, they're pretty independent. I just want you to come see them now and then."

"Have you found June?"

"We haven't looked. They don't want to even talk about her. I don't know all of what happened."

"I'm surprised they even remember us."

"It's not that long since they lived with June."

"Michelle was only eight."

"They've been back since then."

"What? They went back to June?"

"From what I gather."

"Social Services can't do anything right, can they? I'd come home and they'd be covered with bruises. How could they send them back to her?"

"Well, maybe if you'd been there, it would have happened differently."

"Get off my back, Charlie. Okay, I'll come see them. Just leave me your number and I'll work it out somehow."

CHAPTER
Thirty-One

The doorbell rang and Ruby rolled her eyes at Charlie as she passed him his coffee in the kitchen. "I wonder who that could be. Michelle! Get the door."

Michelle took her time getting there. She opened the door and looked at the caller. "Hi, Tanner."

"Hey, Michelle. What's new?"

"Nothing since I saw you last night. Didn't you used to sleep in?"

"I used to sleep in the same place as you most of the time. We weren't separated and I didn't have to get up early to see you. How come you don't sleep at your own pad? What's the point in coming back here?"

Michelle looked over her shoulder at Kenny, sitting on the floor in front of the TV. "I'm waiting 'til Kenny's better."

Tanner stared into the living room, chewing his lip. "Kenny ain't gonna get much better, Michelle. You know that."

"He might," Michelle disagreed flatly.

She was afraid he was right, though. Kenny had woken up. He could still talk, though was silent most of the time, more like when he'd been little and they were still living at home. He could complete mundane, routine tasks like getting dressed in the morning or putting the coffee on. But in the rest of his life he seemed like he was in a fog, watching TV, sleeping, eating. He showed no interest in Michelle's life, no interest in what the Jags were doing. Michelle went out without him and went back home to him as soon as she could. Their own apartment was neglected; Michelle was afraid to leave Kenny alone there. She was afraid he would wander off or start a fire or something. At least at Ruby's, Ruby or Charlie could keep an eye on Kenny while Michelle was gone.

"Are you coming?" Tanner demanded, bringing her back to earth.

"Coming where?"

"Me and some of the guys thought we'd go to the arcade," Tanner said with a note of exasperation in his voice.

"I dunno." Michelle looked at Kenny, like he might have moved since she checked last. "Let me talk to Ruby first."

She went into the kitchen, where Ruby and Charlie were having their coffee.

"Are you going anywhere this morning?" she asked Ruby.

"Nowhere I can't take Kenny along."

"So it's okay?"

"Go ahead."

"Thanks." Michelle went back out to the living room and tapped Kenny on the shoulder.

"Kenny? I'm going out with the Jags, okay?"

He nodded without looking up at her. Michelle wondered if he even knew what she had said to him. She lingered, watching him.

"Come on," Tanner urged.

"Yeah, okay. I'm coming."

Michelle got her coat and went with him.

Tanner touched Michelle's elbow. "Michelle. You okay?"

Michelle startled out of her daze. They had spent most of the day together and she was starting to crash, feeling the barriers she had put around herself beginning to dissolve. She knew she should go back to Ruby's and help look after Kenny, but she couldn't face him. She couldn't keep going back there, seeing him like that.

"Yeah. I'm fine." Michelle looked around, disoriented. There was a movie on the TV, but she had no idea what it was about. "Where's my drink?"

"You finished it. I think this might be the first time I've seen you actually finish a drink."

"You want to get me another?"

Tanner raised his brows. "A second drink? Wonders never cease."

He fetched a beer from the fridge in the adjoining kitchen and brought it back to her. "Here you go, doll."

Michelle took it from him and drank it all. "I want another tattoo."

"Don't you know you're not supposed to get tattooed when you're drunk?"

"I was going to get it before Kenny got sick. I want to get it now."

Tanner nodded his approval.

"About time you moved on with your life. There someplace around here you been to before?"

"No. Some of the others have. We'll ask them where to go."

Michelle awoke in a haze and tried to remember what had happened the night before. She sat up and looked around, squinting in the sunlight. They were at her apartment and Tanner was tangled in the sheets beside her, deep in sleep with his mouth hanging open. Michelle scratched at the bandage across her belly and it burned. She was familiar with the sensation—a new tattoo. She didn't even remember getting it.

Michelle just lay there for a while without moving, her mind wandering. She knew she must have gotten pretty drunk. Not surprising after all she'd been through the last few months. What was surprising was that it hadn't happened sooner.

Feeling sick, Michelle got up and hurried to the bathroom. After her stomach had stopped heaving, she washed her face and mouth and pulled the top of the bandage on her belly away to have a look at the tattoo. The scabby dried blood stuck to the bandage and stung when she pulled it back. It was the Jaguar from her jacket. It looked, on initial examination, as if they had done a passable job of it. Whoever she had gone to.

She went back to the bedroom to change and glanced around at the other mattresses to see who else was there. She dressed and went to the kitchen to get some coffee. She sat with it at the counter on one of the bar stools she and the others had 'found.'

Tanner wandered in, stretching and yawning. "Hey, Michelle. You're up early."

Michelle looked at Tanner, groaned and swore. "At least put on some shorts, Tanner."

He poured some warm water into a cup and added some coffee crystals, grinning. "I think you oughta be able to see what assets I'm bringing to this relationship," he chuckled.

"We don't have a relationship."

"We do now," he corrected. His eyes met hers and didn't waver. Michelle's heart sank.

"No," she protested.

"Afraid so, sweetheart. Are you still taking those birth control pills? You couldn't tell me last night."

Michelle shook her head.

"Well, maybe you should get some more."

She nodded, stunned by this development. She had denied it to herself when she woke up in bed with him. Even with the tenderness and cramping she felt. But Tanner wouldn't tell her so if it weren't true.

"Don't look so shocked, Simpson. You knew it would happen sooner or later. I told you you'd be my girl eventually." He had a smug, self-satisfied smile.

"Go get dressed," Michelle told him disgustedly.

"Whatever you say, sweetheart."

Michelle gingerly sponged off the new tattoo on her stomach and then dabbed at it with a little alcohol.

"Where did I get it done?" she asked Tanner as he stood next to her, shaving with a dull razor.

"Little place down the street."

"Did they use a clean needle?"

"You insisted. Even drunk, you're still uptight. Kept going on about it being sanitary."

"Good."
"It's gonna look pretty good."
"Once it's all healed up."
"He liked the picture."
Michelle nodded.

CHAPTER
Thirty-Two

Ruby shifted next to Charlie and cuddled up to him. "Charlie."

"Mm-hmm?"

"What are we going to do about Kenny?"

He blinked and turned toward her. "What do you mean?"

"It's one thing if Michelle's here helping keep an eye on him. But she hasn't been back in days. I don't want another baby, especially one that's never going to grow up."

"I hadn't thought about it. Is it really that bad? I thought he pretty much looked after himself."

Ruby shook her head. "No. I mean, he's not a bad kid. He doesn't intentionally cause trouble, but he's like a toddler. You even have to remind him to use the bathroom."

Charlie hadn't realized how bad it was. When he was home, he often chummed around with Kenny, having a beer and watching TV with him. It didn't take much effort and Kenny would happily watch TV until he fell asleep. But having to clean up after a toddler who'd had an accident was different from cleaning up after a teenager.

"I didn't realize he was that bad… I'll look around, see what the alternatives are," he promised.

∽

Michelle was hesitant to go back to Ruby's after being gone without a word for a few days. But she wanted to see how Kenny was. She knocked on the door and Ruby opened it a minute later.

"Hi. Come on in."

Michelle obeyed. She found Kenny in front of the TV, as usual. "Hey, Kenny."

Kenny looked away from the TV. "Michelle! Where were you?"

"With the Jags. How's it going?"

"Did you see Daddy?"

"Daddy? I was with the gang, Kenny. Daddy's not there."

"No. Here."

Michelle studied him, trying to figure out if maybe he was calling Charlie 'Daddy' now.

Charlie stepped into the doorway from the hall and Michelle looked up at him. Beside him stood Justin. Michelle's heart skipped a beat and she looked closer. It *was* Justin. A lot more lines on his suntanned face, but it was him. Michelle stared at him, frozen.

"Hi, Michelle," Justin greeted quietly.

Her heart thumped so hard it hurt. "What are you doing here?"

"I came to see you and Kenny."

"Well, you can just take off again. We don't need you anymore."

"We can go live with Daddy," Kenny offered.

"No, we can't."

"We've been talking about whether Justin could help with Kenny's care," Charlie explained.

"He can abandon us for years and then just pick up where he left off?" Michelle looked at Justin. "You're not going to take Kenny anywhere. Just get lost, like you did before."

"Michelle…" Justin took a couple of tentative steps toward her.

"Get away from me! I trusted you when I was little and you screwed up. You don't get to be our Daddy again!"

"Michelle, Ruby and I can't take care of Kenny full-time," Charlie said.

"And you think he can? He's a total failure as a father."

Justin winced. "You don't know what kind of father I am now. I'm not like I was before."

"I don't care what you're like now. You're not getting Kenny."

"Then who is going to take care of him?"

Michelle thought about Dan and George. Dan could look after his brother and run the gang, and George was in a wheelchair, not just slow like Kenny. "I will. Come on, Kenny. Let's go."

"Michelle, I really don't think you realize the responsibility—" Charlie started soothingly.

"I'm not responsible enough? I was more responsible than Justin when I was eight! He left me to look after Kenny then. You're going to give Kenny to the guy who let Mama beat us and didn't even care? To the guy who just ran away from us?"

"I cared!" Justin protested.

"Then how come you didn't do nothing about it?"

"I figured you were better off without me."

"Come on, Kenny."

Kenny got up obediently. Charlie took a step forward. "I can't let you walk out of here with Kenny, Michelle. I don't think he'll be safe."

"Well, he ain't gonna be safe with Justin either. I'm taking Kenny with me."

"Michelle..."

"You gonna arrest me for lookin' after my family?"

"I'm not arresting you. I'm just asking you to look before you leap. How are you going to look after Kenny by yourself?"

"I can do it," Michelle snapped. She tugged on Kenny's sleeve and they walked out.

Charlie and Justin watched them go.

"Well, that worked well," Justin said with heavy sarcasm.

"She's been through a lot. It may take her a while to sort things out."

"She's sure changed."

"She had to grow up."

"You forget time passes for the people you're separated from. I can't believe she's even the same person. Makeup, that hair, the tattoos... I never liked tattoos on a girl..."

"Well, Michelle likes them. Kids like her have to look tough. You know what it's like in a gang."

"Yeah. I know." Justin continued to watch after the kids had disappeared out of sight. "So what are we going to do?"

"Let's wait for a bit and see what happens. She may change her mind after a day or two of looking after Kenny."

~

Michelle paced up and down at the bus station, waiting impatiently. A few buses had pulled up, but not the right one. She watched the people get off another one and finally saw Dan helping to offload George and his wheelchair. She hurried up to them.

"Dan!"

"Hey, Michelle. How's it going?"

He squeezed her briefly around the shoulders.

"Not so great," Michelle admitted.

"Yeah. After George's accident... I was pretty messed up."

Michelle nodded. She busied herself helping Dan to make George comfortable. George whined and fussed, grumpy from the long trip.

"Where's Kenny?" Dan questioned lowly.

Michelle looked around and nodded to Kenny at the other side of the terminal. He was sitting on a bench, watching the monitor with arrival times on it.

"Okay. Let's go."

~

Tanner's jaw dropped when he saw Michelle coming back with Dan and George. "What are you doing here?" he demanded.

"I called them," Michelle informed him.

"What? Why?"

"Hey, don't sound so excited to see us, Tanner," Dan gibed.

"I am, I'm just... surprised."

"Michelle wanted some help getting things worked out with Kenny. So I came."

"You ain't moving here."

Dan shrugged. "We'll see. I don't know what I'm gonna do yet."

"Where are you staying? You can't stay with Michelle, you know, 'cause there's already me and Kenny and the other guys. There ain't any room for you." Tanner's voice was hard and aggressive.

Dan rolled his eyes at Michelle. "I'll find a place for me and Wheels. Don't get worked up about it."

"I just didn't want you thinking you could stay with Michelle when there ain't room."

"I like to have a little privacy to take care of Wheels." Michelle hadn't thought about that. "Wheelchair access is sort of important too," Dan reminded. "Ground floor's even better. Maybe some of us could rent a house."

"I wouldn't mind that," Michelle volunteered.

Tanner opened his mouth to complain, then changed his mind. "Yeah, I guess we could do that, honey," he agreed, putting an arm around Michelle. "You, me, Kenny, Danny, and Wheels playin' house."

"Don't call me Danny," Dan warned, looking Tanner in the eye.

Tanner backed down. "Yeah, whatever," he muttered, looking away. "I'll see you guys around," he said abruptly and walked away from them.

"He still thinks he's your boyfriend, huh?" Dan asked, watching Tanner's retreat.

Michelle shifted uncomfortably. "Well, he sorta is," she admitted.

"You hooked up with him?" Dan's voice rose a few notches. "Are the prospects around here that bad?"

Michelle laughed weakly. "I was drunk, I guess."

"Michelle drunk? No way."

"I don't remember having more than a couple beers, but I guess I'm not used to it…"

"Or he slipped you a mickey."

"No, I didn't pass out. I still went and got a tattoo and everything. Couldn't have done that if he gave me knock-out drops."

"Date rape drug. GHB. Doesn't knock you out, just makes it so you don't fight and don't remember."

Michelle scowled. "How can you tell, then?"

Dan shook his head. "You can't."

Michelle let it sink in. Would Tanner's ego allow him to use drugs to take advantage of her? He could have done that, or could have used physical force, a long time ago. But was there any difference between taking advantage when she was drunk and when she was drugged?

"You know," Dan said, "just because you slept with him once, that doesn't mean you gotta carry on with him. You just say it was a mistake and you don't want to have a relationship."

Michelle sighed. "I know. But it's easier than fighting all the time."

"Easiest ain't always best," Dan said.

Michelle shrugged it off. She didn't need to be told she was making a bad choice. She just didn't have the energy to make the right one anymore. Easier won out.

∽

A pair of cops approached Dan and Michelle while they sat at a cafe, making plans and catching up on the details of each other's lives.

"You kids are loitering. Why don't you move on?" one of the cops suggested.

"We're just having a cup," Dan pointed out, indicating the empty mugs on the table.

"The manager says you been here too long and you're bothering his other customers."

"We're not bothering anyone."

The cop eyed them. Dan, an older, dangerous looking juvie; Michelle, with her punk black hairdo, tattoos, jewelry, and gang jacket. Kenny, though with a distant look, was still muscular from working out and running with the gang. And though George did not look like a threat to anyone, his scrawny, death's-head appearance was not particularly comforting.

"Come on. Don't cause me any grief. Just move on, that's all I'm asking."

"We don't have to."

"You want me to arrest you?"

"What're you going to do with the boys? Because we're their only family and if you try separating us or putting them in jail, you'll regret it."

"I'll arrest you if I have to," the cop maintained.

"What will you do with Kenny and George?" Dan repeated.

"We'd find something."

Dan said nothing, holding his ground. They waited to see what the cops were going to do.

"Why don't you kids just move on," the second cop suggested.

"We don't have to. We're not bothering anyone."

He looked at his partner. "Let's go."

"What?"

"He's right. And we can't do anything with him," he indicated George with a nod. "We don't have the resources."

They walked away and went over to the manager to talk, shrugging and shaking their heads. Michelle grinned. "Nice," she approved.

Dan shrugged. "They shouldn't have been here bugging us in the first place. We got the right to sit here and drink coffee and talk. We're not doing anything to hurt anyone."

"It's still cool they had to leave us alone."

"You'd better watch Kenny with the cops. With Georgie, it's obvious he can't go to jail. But with Kenny... they can't tell if he's maybe just stoned or bluffing."

Michelle nodded. "Yeah, I know."

CHAPTER
Thirty-Three

Michelle opened the door and walked in. Ruby came out a minute later. "Oh, Michelle. How's it going?"

"Okay."

Ruby studied her. "Where's Kenny?"

"At our place."

"You doing okay with him?"

"Yeah, I can handle Kenny," Michelle assured her.

"You leave him by himself?"

"No, Wheels is with him."

"Wheels?"

Michelle bit her lip and decided not to explain about Wheels. So far things were working out okay with Kenny and George staying together without anyone else around. George ordered Kenny around and watched TV with him, and Kenny did anything physical that needed doing without complaint. So far nothing had gone drastically wrong.

"So, why'd you come by?" Ruby questioned.

"I just wanted to see what was going on."

"With your Daddy?"

Michelle shook her head. "He's not my Daddy anymore."

"Okay. So…?"

"Has he been back?"

"No. He took the hint last time. Charlie knows where he lives if you want to talk to him.

"No. I just wondered how come he showed up."

"He wondered how you guys were doing."

"He never wondered in the last five or six years."

"I'm sure he wondered all the time. But he didn't necessarily know where you guys were."

"He coulda found us," Michelle said stubbornly.

Ruby didn't argue the point. "Justin didn't exactly have a great example for a dad, you know."

"Yeah, I know. You said he was dead."

Ruby motioned for Michelle to sit down. "You don't know the history of your own family. It's pretty sick."

"Yeah?"

Ruby took a deep breath. "Justin shot our daddy when he was eight. Protecting June from being molested by him."

Michelle was stunned. She couldn't think of what to say. They were both silent for a long time. Her daddy, the man she'd loved for so long—even if she hated him now—had killed someone. She knew he was rough and tough and she had seen and could picture him committing other crimes—driving hot goods, doing drugs with June, she could even see him beating someone in a bar fight. But killing his own father? She felt sick.

"Not Daddy," she protested, forgetting she wasn't going to call him that anymore.

"He deserved it," Ruby explained. "What he did was pretty awful. Justin and June were inseparable and he defended her."

Michelle knew Justin would go to great lengths to protect June. She'd seen many times. June acted helpless and Justin couldn't turn away. "Did he go to jail?"

"No. The jury hung and they never retried him. So he didn't have to go to jail."

"So we don't know he did it."

"Oh, there was never any doubt he did it. The argument was that it was justified."

"Justifiable," Michelle corrected under her breath.

"Do you want to talk to him?"

"No. I told you that."

"Okay. If you change your mind, just let me know."

"Yeah. Do you know..." Michelle paused, not sure what she wanted to ask.

"What?"

"Did he say anything about Marcie...?"

"Charlie saw Marcie at Justin's house."

"He did? So she's okay?" Michelle blew out her breath in relief. She had been afraid Ruby would tell her Marcie was dead. "I never even got to say goodbye to her."

"Why did Justin take her and leave you guys?" Ruby asked.

"He always had Marcie, since she was tiny. Mama couldn't look after her."

"That must have been tough."

"Marcie's always been special. We understood."

Ruby looked at her. Michelle ducked her head, afraid Ruby had heard the jealousy in Michelle's voice. She couldn't help but envy Marcie in spite of her handicap. Marcie had never been abused. She had been with Justin all these years and hadn't had to deal with all the crap Michelle and Kenny had.

George was watching Michelle's reflection in the TV. She didn't know it. Maybe she wouldn't care if she did know. She was standing in the hall outside her bedroom, changing into clean clothes while she talked to Dan in the bedroom across from hers. They all lived so close together in the small house any sense of propriety went right out the window. But George watched her covertly so she wouldn't notice his stare.

Dan had said George 'had a crush' on Michelle, but it was more than that. He was obsessed with her body and loved to have her near him. It was great living in the same house as she. He requested massages from her as often as he decently could, electrified by her touch.

"Get me something to drink," George told Kenny. Kenny was slow to get up, but he obeyed. He brought George a beer, thoughtfully swigging the top half before handing it to him, so George's wrist wouldn't tire with the weight.

Dan came out of the bedroom and slipped by Michelle, slapping her on the butt as he passed by. "Finish dressing, I want to go out."

"Yeah, I'm ready," Michelle grunted and pulled on a pair of skinny black jeans.

"Is Tanner ready?"

"Tanner's always ready. I'd rather leave him behind."

"Then tell him you're through."

"I can't."

"Can't what?" Tanner asked, coming out of the bathroom into the conversation.

"Can't get rid of you."

"That's right, baby. Don't you forget it."

"Georgie, you and Kenny be okay for a while?" Dan called to him.

"Yeah, I guess."

George watched them get ready to go. He liked living there better than with Dan's gang, who had known him before his accident and knew what he had been like then. They looked at him differently from the way the Jags did. George got a lot of pitying glances and relished them, but the looks of Dan's old gang were different. They knew him when he could walk and run, and they looked at him and Dan with sad eyes, remembering. They felt bad for Dan, too, and George didn't want anyone giving Dan their pity.

Michelle jiggled her knife in its sheath, anxious.

"What're we doing?" she asked.

"Derry's set up a little exercise over at the corner store at Fifth. Little mom and pop shop. They take in some good cash. Derry figures your cat will bring good luck if anything goes wrong," Sean explained, gesturing to the Jag tattoo on Michelle's bare midriff when he said 'cat.'

"Okay. Is my blade enough? Or will I need a piece?"

"Derry's got heat. He just wants you there to back him up and keep a watch out. Your blade's plenty."

Michelle nodded. "When, now?"

"Once it's dark. About an hour."

Michelle jiggled nervously. It was different from shoplifting.

Different from murder, too, done after meticulous planning and calculation. She knew the way the Jags planned things. That's why they ended up in juvie so often. They didn't inspire confidence.

～

Derry was late getting back. He put a six-pack in the fridge. "Oh, hey Simpson. You ready to go?"

"Yeah, I guess."

"Sean tell ya what was going on?"

Michelle nodded. "Yeah."

"Let's do it, then."

Michelle looked at him. "Like this?"

"What do you mean like this? How else?"

"Well, you got masks? What if we're ID'd?"

"They won't dare. They'll be too scared."

"What if they aren't?"

"It's night. It'll be over quick. They won't get a good look."

Michelle stood her ground despite his exasperated tone. "You think they won't ID me? How many chicks you think there are around here with this hair and a cat tattooed on her belly?"

"Well... you might want to put a different shirt on or do up your jacket," he conceded.

"And my hair? And our Jag jackets?"

"She's got a point," Sean said.

Derry knew a loss when he saw it. He didn't want the other Jags thinking he was stupid. "Yeah... Didn't one of the guys used to have a couple of balaclavas? That and a couple regular jackets and no one would know us again."

"That would work," Michelle agreed.

She felt safer behind the ski mask. No one could tell who she was. The only thing they could tell was she was a girl. No earrings, hair, or tattoos were visible. She kept a sharp eye out the front window while Derry did his thing and got the money from the terrified owners. When he had everything, they both went out the back door to avoid being seen on the street in their masks and followed Michelle's carefully laid out escape route.

They stripped off the masks and outer shirts and left them in a trash can a few blocks away. There was a second gym bag in the side pocket of the one the money was put into, and they transferred the bills and left the bag behind too. Everything was untraceable even if they were found and connected up to the robbery. They went a good ways away, following a maze of alleys, then emerged.

"See? Went down smooth as silk," Derry said.

"Yeah. Because I planned it out."

Derry shrugged, not admitting it.

CHAPTER
Thirty-Four

The phone rang and rang. Michelle finally got fed up with it and answered. "Yeah?"

"Is this Michelle?"

It was Ruby's voice. "How did you get this number?"

"I still have contacts."

"What do you want?"

"I'm going to have Marcie here for a while. I thought you might want to come see her."

"Marcie? Yeah, of course I do! When?"

"Tomorrow about noon. Is that too early?"

"No, I can handle it."

"Okay. I'll see you then."

∽

Ruby watched Michelle step up the walk with Kenny in tow. She stopped for a moment on the doorstep as if she didn't know whether to knock or come in. She chose to walk in without notice. Ruby watched through the kitchen doorway as Michelle looked around and spotted Marcie in her wheelchair in front of the TV. Michelle saw Ruby watching and made sure no one else was there.

"Hi Marcie," she said tentatively.

Marcie's head turned and she smiled widely, babbling something

Michelle could no longer understand. Michelle fell on her, putting her arms around Marcie and holding Marcie's head to her breast.

"Oh, Marcie. I missed you so much. I never got to say goodbye to you. I wanted to. But Daddy... Justin didn't want you to see us go. Did he tell you goodbye for us?"

Marcie's answer was incomprehensible, but her grin wide. The floodgates had broken for Michelle. Ruby hadn't seen her cry when Kenny was in hospital, but now tears and words came gushing out, all mixed together. Michelle hugged and kissed Marcie and told her over and over that she had missed Marcie and still loved her.

Michelle's words started to slow and she grabbed silent Kenny by the hand and pulled him closer. "You remember Marcie, right Kenny? Remember when we lived with Mom the first time?"

Kenny shook his head, looking at Marcie. "She's like Wheels," he commented.

"Wheels is a guy we live with," Michelle explained to Ruby, "he's a quad."

An inkling of an idea started to form in Michelle's mind as she talked to Marcie. Ruby stayed and watched them for a few minutes, and then went on with her own activities. When she had been out of their sight for a few minutes, Michelle motioned to Kenny.

"Come on, we're getting out of here." She released the hand brakes on Marcie's chair and pushed her towards the door.

"You're bringing her?"

"Yeah, we are. Get the door. Quietly."

Kenny got the door and then helped get the chair safely off the front steps. Marcie was very light. They moved quickly to get out of the neighborhood without being caught. Michelle's heart thumped hard and fast. She would be able to see Marcie all the time. And it would hurt Justin. He would wonder if she was okay. He would be separated from Marcie, as Michelle and Kenny had been for so long because of Justin.

They went to the apartment of one of the Jags where she knew there was a working elevator. Ruby had Michelle's phone number, so they couldn't go back to the house. If June had Michelle's phone number, she could get the address. They'd have to find somewhere else to live while Marcie was with them.

Dan had been in bed suffering from the flu or maybe food poisoning all day long. When he heard knocking, he ignored it at first and waited for someone else to answer it. When it continued, he curled his hand around the pistol under his pillow as he struggled to rouse himself. The knocking turned to door-breaking crashes and George started to yell for Dan in a panicky squeal. Dan stumbled out of bed and careened down the hall towards the ruckus. His head was spinning. In the grip of nausea he could not formulate a plan of action or even determine exactly what was going on. With one final crash, the door gave way. At the same time as Dan stumbled into the front room, a couple of cops rushed in, weapons drawn.

"Drop the gun!" one of them shouted. One of them covered Dan with his gun, and one of them switched his aim back and forth between George and Dan. Dan didn't move, squinting at the two of them as he tried to get the rusty gears in his brain moving.

"I said drop it or I'll shoot!"

Dan looked at George, who was as white as a sheet.

"Dan..." he croaked.

Dan wavered. He saw the cop shift his grip on the gun and was prodded into action. He raised his hands above his shoulders.

"Take it easy," he said hoarsely. "Don't get jumpy."

"Drop it!"

Dan switched his grip and held it out to the side by the barrel. "I don't want to drop it, it might go off."

The cop stepped forward gingerly and took it from him. He handed it behind him to his partner and grabbed Dan by the hair on the back of his head.

"Belly down," he ordered, yanking hard and twisting Dan's hair to force him prone.

Dan grunted in pain and obediently lay down on the floor.

"Where is she?" the cop demanded, handcuffing Dan and taking a slow, cautious look around with his partner. Dan didn't know what he was talking about and didn't attempt to answer. They checked the rest of the house and came back.

"Where is she?" the cop said again, kicking Dan in the ribs with a jarring thud that made him curl up protectively.

"Where's who?" Dan asked, even though there was only one 'she' they could have expected to find in the house.

"Marcie Simpson."

"Marcie. You mean Michelle?"

Another pair of cops came in through the broken door. They must have been watching the back until they were sure Dan was secured. "No, Marcie," one of them said, "Michelle's sister."

"Michelle doesn't have a sister," Dan said, squirming onto his side for a better look at them.

The cop who had cuffed him drew back his foot to kick Dan again, but the new guy appeared to be in charge and motioned for him to back off. He approached Dan and looped his hand through Dan's arm, helping him to his feet and then depositing him on the couch.

"Michelle does have a sister. In a wheelchair like your friend here."

That sounded oddly familiar. Dan shook his head, unable to remember. "If she does, I've never seen her."

"Have you seen Michelle today?"

"Umm... I don't think so. Think I heard her leave this morning."

"What about him?" the cop nodded to George.

Dan shrugged and let George answer for himself. "Michelle and Kenny both left this morning," George said, wide-eyed. "They haven't been back."

They cop looked at Dan for confirmation. "Are you stoned?" he asked after a second look at Dan.

"No, sir. I got the flu."

"You don't look so hot."

Dan nodded. "Pretty rocky," he agreed. "But honest, I ain't seen Michelle or anyone else. What'd she do?"

"Kidnapping," he said curtly. "And that's a pretty serious charge."

"Kidnapping? That ain't Michelle's style."

"Actually, I think it's quite in keeping with her style. Running away, taking Kenny with her, this time she took Marcie too."

"You know Michelle's record?" Dan asked.

"I should think so. She was staying with us for a while."

"Staying with you?" Dan repeated dumbly.

"Charlie," George reminded him. "Before we got here. With Michelle's aunt."

"That's right," Charlie agreed. "Listen. This is really important. If you even think you may know where Michelle might be—Marcie has cerebral palsy and needs a lot of care. Michelle has never been shown how to take care of her. Marcie's health is very fragile."

"She'll come back here," Dan assured him, "because I know how to do all that stuff."

"Well, if she comes back, would you pass along a message for me? If she brings Marcie straight home, I'll see to it the charges are dropped. But if she doesn't... Michelle looking after Kenny is one thing, I guess she can handle it, and that's where he wants to be. But Marcie has a good home. I've seen it. And I won't let Michelle do this."

Dan nodded. "Yeah, I get it. I'll tell her if she comes home."

"Thanks. I appreciate it. I think you can understand what Marcie's family is going through, with her being in inexperienced hands."

Dan shrugged, looking at George. "Yeah."

Wilcox walked into the apartment and looked around. "Is Michelle here?"

"Yeah, she's in the back."

Wilcox went to the back bedroom. "Michelle, got a message from Dan."

Michelle looked up from her work. "Yeah? What?"

"Cops are lookin' for you. They been by the house and Dan says they're still watching it in case you go back."

Michelle nodded. "Yeah. That's no big surprise."

"Who's that?" Wilcox said, looking at Marcie.

"My sister."

"You got one of them too?"

"What, a sister?" Michelle said, puzzled.

"No, you know, one in a chair."

Michelle stared at him. "Yeah, what of it?"

"Nothing. I just didn't know."

MICHELLE

"Well, I do. And I'm gonna look after her, too."

"Why you and Dan wanna take care of them instead of letting the government do it, I just don't get."

"Marcie doesn't belong in any institution."

"Well, maybe not, I don't know her. But you gotta admit Wheels does. Then Dan wouldn't have to miss out all the time."

"I have my reasons."

Wilcox studied her and nodded slowly. He saw the look of hatred in her eyes and understood the sentiment better than goodwill. "I guess you do," he conceded.

In the morning, Dan was strong enough to crawl out of bed and make himself a coffee while he considered the situation. He had heard from several sources where Michelle was. Around noon, he got George ready and left the house.

"I don't want to go out," George fussed. "Why can't I just stay here?"

"Because I need you. Come on, don't be a baby about it."

George grumbled under his breath and didn't say anything further that was clear. Dan took him over to the apartment where Michelle had spent the night and let himself in.

"Michelle still here?"

"Yeah. In the can."

Dan stopped at the door for a minute. "Michelle?" he called out, after listening to splashing in the tub.

"Dan?"

"Yeah, it's me."

"Come in here."

Dan opened the door tentatively and looked in. Michelle was bathing Marcie, holding her head up awkwardly with one hand, using the washcloth with the other.

"Come in and shut the door before she gets cold," Michelle told him.

"Sponge baths are easier," Dan advised neutrally.

"Yeah, I know. I just made a mess changing her and was worried I might not get it all."

"Uh-huh. You doing okay?"

"Yeah. I'm new at this, that's all. Maybe you can help me get her out of the tub."

"Sure."

Dan moved up beside her and gave her some pointers on moving wet bodies. He helped lift Marcie over the side onto some towels. He continued the lesson with drying and dressing.

"Does she look okay?" Michelle questioned. "She's all flushed and red."

Dan focused on this and felt her face. "She doesn't have a fever. That cop said she's sort of fragile." He studied Marcie's face for some hint of her being sick or uncomfortable. "Oh," he said with sudden understanding, "she's embarrassed. I'm sorry, Marcie," he looked away from her half-dressed body. "You finish up, Michelle. Call me if you need a hand. Otherwise, I'll just wait outside."

He left the bathroom and waited for them in the bedroom, where Marcie's chair was. Michelle came out a few minutes later with Marcie in her arms, now fully dressed, and put her down in the chair.

"You saw Charlie?" Michelle demanded.

"Charlie? Oh, the cop. Yeah. He was one of the ones who broke the door down last night."

"Oh. Came after me."

"Yeah. He says if you bring Marcie home, he won't charge you."

Michelle rolled her eyes. "I'm not taking her back there."

"Okay. But you'd better go into hiding for a bit. Cops followed me here."

Michelle swore. "You led them right to me! Thanks a lot."

"Hey, I know what I'm doing. Here's my plan…"

CHAPTER
Thirty-Five

The surveillance cops watched Dan leave pushing a wheelchair. They had a pretty good idea Michelle was in the building and stayed and watched for her.

Michelle gave Dan plenty of time to get away and lose his tail if he still had one. Then she took the elevator down and left the building. It took about thirty seconds for them to stop her.

"All right, Simpson, hands up!"

Michelle let go of the wheelchair and put her hands up. One of them pushed the wheelchair away and the other frisked her and took away her dagger.

"Uh, Steve—we've got a problem."

The cop turned at his partner's call and dropped his eyes to the figure in the wheelchair. It was not Marcie, but the pale, wasted young man they had seen at the house the day before. George.

George laughed at the cops in satisfaction. "All you saw was the chair," he accused. "Maybe next time you'll pay attention to the person in it."

"Where's Marcie?"

"Marcie?" Michelle repeated.

"Your sister."

"You mean she's not at home?"

"You know she's not."

Michelle shrugged widely. "Last I saw, she was at my Aunt Ruby's house."

"You're under arrest."

"Oh, yeah? You going to take care of George while I'm under arrest?"

"We'll work that out later."

Michelle didn't fight them. There wasn't anything they could do. Not with George on their hands. And they had no proof she had kidnapped Marcie.

Michelle's stomach knotted when she saw Charlie's clenched fists and the fury in his eyes. She had to concentrate to look uncaring and unaffected.

"Where is Marcie?" Charlie demanded, slamming his hand down on the table. "You think you can kidnap a helpless child from my house and get away with it?"

"I don't know where she is," Michelle responded calmly, as if she really didn't know.

"Don't give me that. And Justin's on his way down now. You think he's going to believe that load?"

Michelle shrugged.

"Why would you do this, Michelle? Explain your reasoning to me. I don't know what you think you get out of this."

Michelle looked at her watch. "George needs to eat. And Kenny's all by himself. I can't stay here much longer."

"Tell me where Marcie is and this will all go away."

"Or else?"

"Or else you're going to jail."

"And who's going to take care of Marcie and Kenny then? Besides, Justin ain't gonna prosecute."

"What makes you think that?"

"Because if he did, it would all come out about him and June. Marcie would get taken away anyway. Maybe he'd do some time."

It was a good point, Charlie had to admit. "You can be prosecuted without Justin's consent," he threatened.

"Even if he says Marcie's with me by his permission?"

"He's not going to do that. He's already filed a report."

"He will if it means everyone finds out about him and June," Michelle maintained icily. "He'll withdraw his statement."

Charlie stared at Michelle and cussed under his breath. "What do you think gives you the right to do this?"

"Because I can. And you can't stop me. It's time for Justin to pay."

"You want to get revenge for his abandonment of you?"

"We had to suffer. Now he does."

"Even if Marcie gets hurt."

"Nothing is going to happen to Marcie. I do have some experience, you know. And help from Dan. He knows what he's doing."

"You're not even an adult."

"What's that got to do with it?"

Charlie shook his head and left the room to see if Justin had arrived yet.

Charlie had obviously talked to Justin before he was allowed in to talk to her. He was subdued, with a confused, beaten expression.

"Michelle... please don't do this. Where's Marcie?"

"I'm not telling."

"You need to let her come home. She'll be scared."

"She's not scared. She's having fun. Never had a chance to be independent before."

"I know you're just doing this to hurt me. Please think about it. There are other people to consider."

"Yeah, who?"

"Sondra. And our other kids."

"You're still with Sondra?" Michelle couldn't keep the surprise out of her voice.

"Yeah."

"Well, she didn't have any problem taking Marcie away from us. We missed her too, you know."

"I know. But it was the only thing to do."

"Well, now I'm returning the favor. I can take good care of her, you know. And she'll get to know her real siblings."

"We could work something else out so you could see her. You could come visit her at the house."

"I don't want to see you and I sure don't want to see Sondra. Marcie's with me now, and if you cause me any trouble…"

"Charlie already told me."

Michelle sneered. "Good. We understand each other, then."

"I don't understand why you want to hurt us. You're the one who wanted to be put in foster care. I did what you asked."

"What kind of choice did I have? You saw what June was like. And she was being nice when you were home. If you guys were going to mess around, the least you could do is not have kids."

"It wasn't intentional… it just happened."

"Gimme a break! Maybe the first time you can argue it was an accident. But after that? You knew what you were doing."

"You don't understand what it was like. It wasn't my fault. It was June's."

"The way I learned it, you pretty much had to be involved," Michelle sneered.

"You don't know what it was like."

"I don't want to. I don't want to understand. That would mean I was sick like you."

Justin just looked at her.

"Why don't you get lost?" Michelle suggested sweetly. "That's what you're good at."

"I always wanted to take care of you kids. I thought I was doing what was best," Justin said as he turned to leave, trying to get the last word in.

"Well, you and June were never exactly bright, were you?"

Justin turned, stung, and opened his mouth to respond.

"I don't know how the two of you ever had a kid like me," Michelle said.

"You always were too smart for your age," he agreed. "What's that word…?"

"Genius?"

"No… Although June always wondered if you were like Ruby's kid. She's a genius, I guess."

"Must run in the family then. Though it apparently skipped a generation."

"That wasn't the word, though," Justin said, as if he had ceased to hear her jibes. "What's the word you use for little kids who are really advanced for their age..."

"Precocious?"

"Yeah. You were precocious. I could talk to you just like an adult."

"Only you couldn't tell me you weren't coming back."

Justin shook his head. "I couldn't. I wanted to, but how could I?"

"How could you take Marcie and not me? You took Sondra with you—she coulda taken care of us better than Mama."

"I couldn't ask Sondra to do that. I didn't tell her you guys went into the system. I let her think you were still with June."

"She knew we were in foster care."

"No. I never told her."

"I talked to her on the phone."

"When?" Justin said blankly.

"You didn't come back and Mama was in hospital, and they split me and Kenny up. I called to see if she knew where you were. She said if she saw you she would tell you what happened and to call. I guess she was lying. You were with her all along."

"I never knew you called," Justin said. "They told me they'd keep you together if they could."

"We were together like two days. Then they moved me away."

"What was June in hospital for? She wasn't pregnant, was she? She told me she was when I left, but I thought she was lying."

"Pregnant? No. No one told me if she was. She had a breakdown or something. They didn't want to tell me what was going on."

"I'm sorry, Michelle. I thought she'd handle it better. But I had to get out. I took care of June my whole life and I just had to get out."

"Well, you made your choice, didn't you?"

"I made the best one I could. You agreed with it at the time, remember? The whole thing was your idea."

"Except the part about you never coming back."

"I told you that you and Kenny might get separated. You knew." They looked at each other for a moment in silence, knowing they would never agree about what had happened. "Will you call me? Let me talk to Marcie on the phone so I know she's okay?"

Michelle shook her head.

"Come on, Michelle, I at least knew you kids were safe and in good hands. But you don't know anything about taking care of Marcie."

"Yes, I do. And you didn't know we were safe—'cause we never were."

There was another period of silence. Justin got up and walked out.

Michelle kept an eye out for cops trailing her but didn't see anyone. She pushed George's wheelchair to the place where she had agreed to meet Dan and Marcie. Dan was pleased to see her.

"So they let you go, eh?"

"Sure. They couldn't keep me there."

"How're you doing, Georgie?" Dan asked, ruffling his brother's hair.

"I wanna go home now."

"We're gonna find a new place. Cops've been to ours and they might come back lookin' for Marcie."

"I don't want a new house," George whined.

"You want to go back to the house where the cops broke the door down?"

"No."

"Then you want a new house. We'll stay at Devon's tonight, I'll find somewhere new by tomorrow."

"I hate new places."

"Yeah, I know buddy."

"How's Marcie?" Michelle asked.

"She's been just great. How much do you know about her care? I wasn't sure about her food."

"Yeah, I used to feed her. She doesn't need a tube. Just soft foods."

Dan nodded. "Okay."

CHAPTER Thirty-Six

Michelle was approached by a young man as she headed home. He had short cropped hair, a tattoo of a black snake on his neck, and was around Dan's age.

"Hey, you. You got a cigarette?"

Michelle shook her head. "Don't smoke."

He stepped in closer to her. "You're with the Jaguars, right?" he said, nodding to her jacket.

"Yeah, so?"

"You introduce me to some guys? I just got out of juvie and I don't got any connections yet. But I gotta get some dope."

Michelle stepped back from him. "You're a cop," she said, more of an assessment than a question, "aren't you?"

"Me? Do I look like a cop?"

He was pretty young if he was. And the tattoos looked real. But that didn't prove anything. Michelle didn't like the smell of him. He was a bit too clean, stood up too straight, and had a sharp, probing look in his eyes.

"You do to me," she asserted.

"Well, I'm not! So are you going to introduce me?"

Michelle shrugged. "No. But come if you like."

He followed her to the new apartment. Michelle let herself in, ignoring him. He followed her into the front room, where Dan was watching the TV with George.

"Who's your friend?" Dan questioned with a raised brow.

"Some narc," Michelle said, "I don't know him."

"A narc?" Dan repeated with a laugh.

"No," the boy protested, "I just got out of juvie. I'm no narc!"

"What's your name?"

"Joe Carter."

"Well, Joe, I don't know what made you choose Michelle, but you're here now. What do you need?"

"Just a place to get on my feet, clear my head…"

Dan nodded. "I imagine we can work something out."

Before long, Carter had been shown around the apartment and introduced to everyone.

"Is this a halfway house or group home?" he asked with a frown.

"No. Why?"

Carter lifted his hands in a shrug. "Well, just the wheelchairs and everything."

Dan laughed, thinking about how it would look to someone outside—George and Marcie in their wheelchairs, Kenny obviously handicapped; they did look like some halfway house or rehab facility.

"No, it just worked out that way. Wheels is my brother and Kenny is Michelle's. Marcie's Michelle's sister."

"Oh. And are you and Michelle…" he trailed off, raising his eyebrows.

"Just friends. Tanner's her boyfriend, but he's out right now."

Tanner had returned in time for supper. Dan had ordered pizza and beer. Michelle was cutting up small pieces for Marcie, who was grinning widely at the festive atmosphere. Tanner grabbed the piece of the pizza closest to him and looked around.

"Who's he?" Tanner indicated Carter, amidst stuffing the pizza in his mouth.

"A narc," Michelle said, without looking up.

Tanner's jaw dropped. Dan laughed at his expression. "She's

kidding, Tanner. This is Joe Carter. He's thinking of hanging with the Jags for a while."

"Oh," Tanner swallowed and took another bite. "He's not staying here, is he?"

"Maybe. We'll see."

"Well, he'd better keep away from Michelle!"

"Why is that?" Carter said mildly, even though Dan had already told him Michelle and Tanner were a couple.

"Because she's my girl, that's why," Tanner's voice was bullish and sullen. "Just stay away from her."

"Why not let her choose for herself?"

Tanner looked at Michelle. "You don't want anything to do with this jerk anyway, do you?"

Michelle looked up from Marcie's pizza with a sly grin. "You're not afraid of a bit of competition, are you, Tanner?"

"Cut it out Michelle. You're my girl and I know how you are with other guys. You'd never go for someone like that."

Michelle shrugged, even though she felt no attraction toward Carter. "You never know."

Michelle didn't think Carter would stick around for long or show any interest in her and she didn't think Tanner would have the guts to do anything about it if he did. Carter was older, after all, and had been in juvie. Tanner was still a pup by comparison. It was only by chance she happened to be around when word came that Tanner and Carter were gearing up for a fight.

"What for?" Michelle demanded. "What's Tanner's problem with Carter?"

Wilcox looked at Michelle with a quizzical expression. "What do ya think? It's over you."

"Me?" Michelle echoed.

"Carter wants to try his hand and Tanner's being territorial." He shook his head. "No offense, but I never could understand why any guy would want to stick with one chick. It just causes problems."

"And they're gonna fight about it? Right now?"

"Yeah, just heading over there right now. You didn't know?"

"No! Come on, let's get over there."

"You wanna watch them tear each other up over you?"

Michelle nodded. "I gotta be there."

"Who are you pulling for?"

She frowned. "I'm not pulling for anyone."

"Yeah, right. You're pulling for Carter, aren't you?" he snickered.

"Who says I would get together with the winner, anyway?"

Wilcox snorted. "Like you'd get together with the loser."

They got to the playground after the fight had started. Michelle couldn't believe it was over her. That might be what they said, but there had to be more to it. Carter was trying to get in good with the gang and Tanner was trying to prove he was just as good as any of the older boys. It couldn't be just over Michelle.

Michelle bit her lip watching them. She had assumed it would be a fist-fight, but blades flashed in their hands. A knife-fight. It wasn't just a couple of boys pummeling out their frustrations on each other. Knife fights could be deadly. And even Michelle was better at knife-work than Tanner. He wasn't the one that had chosen the type of fight. He must have been the one to pick a fight in the first place. Michelle felt sick watching them circle each other trying to gain the advantage. Tanner was too hotheaded, as usual, rushing in before he should and taking too many chances. Carter was careful and sure-footed, patient enough to wear Tanner down.

Tanner darted in again and drew blood. Carter flushed, and pumped up the pace. Tanner was obviously not an opponent to be trifled with. In a knife fight, even someone with just a little skill could do quite a bit of damage. Carter's expression didn't change, but the fight became noticeably more intense. Carter had the upper hand, but he was also bleeding pretty profusely.

He backed Tanner against the wall and worked in close. There were yells from the gang as Carter pressed Tanner. Then he managed to get his knife under Tanner's throat. Tanner froze and his blade clattered to the pavement. It seemed as if time had slowed down. Michelle saw Carter wasn't going to release Tanner, saw his grip shift infinitesimally to draw the blade across Tanner's throat.

"Carter!"

Of course, it was Carter's right to dispatch Tanner if he pleased. Tanner had picked a fight and Carter beat him fair and square. But Tanner had dropped his knife and was now defenseless. Carter's head went up at Michelle's call and he turned towards her, still holding Tanner hostage.

"When did you get here?"

"A few minutes ago."

"You still got feelings for him?" Carter demanded.

"Good ones?"

Carter grinned and slowly dropped his hand from Tanner's throat. "Yeah, good ones."

"No," Michelle said. Though she wasn't sure it was true. She'd never wanted Tanner as a boyfriend, but he had worn her down. Even so, she still had affection for him. And he was comfortable to be around. She had known him for a long time and he was always willing to help her out or do what she wanted, in spite of his jealousy toward Dan and anyone he suspected of having eyes for her.

"Good," Carter said. "Then quit letting him run you. He doesn't own you."

"So what did Tanner mean," Carter questioned later, "when he said you wouldn't go for a guy like me?"

Michelle grew uncomfortable. "I guess I just don't see narcs," she joked, hoping to get away with not really answering.

"Seriously, Michelle." He held her gaze.

"Tanner just doesn't think I should like anyone other than him. He's always been the jealous type."

"Yeah? It sounded like there was more to it than that."

"Don't worry about Tanner."

"Worry? I already took care of Tanner. I'm wondering what my chances are with you."

Michelle shrugged. "I need to go check on Marcie," she said abruptly and left the room.

When she got back, Carter was grinning.

"What?" Michelle demanded.

"You don't think I know you're avoiding my question?"

"What question?"

"About whether you'd think about getting together with me. Don't worry," he said, waving off her protest. "I can wait and see. You didn't say no."

Michelle shrugged it off. "You're nuts."

"Yeah, well, you gotta be a bit nuts to agree to be a narc."

She laughed at him using her own joke and relaxed a bit as they talked about other things.

CHAPTER
Thirty-Seven

"Rumble still on tonight?" Michelle asked.

"Of course," Tanner snapped.

He had been really short lately. Acting like a spoiled kid. Michelle knew it was because of the fight with Carter, but she thought he was taking it a bit far.

"You going to be there?" she persisted, figuring if he was going to be mad at her, she might as well give him reason to be.

"Why wouldn't I be? You think I'm yellow? I can rumble as well as the next guy."

As long as the next guy wasn't Joey Carter, Michelle thought. She didn't say it, but she didn't have to. Tanner would know she was thinking it anyway, and he would be furious.

"You wanna go over with me?" Michelle asked instead.

"Walk with you? I guess. Where's Mr. Wonderful? Don't tell me he's skipping out on the fight."

"Nah. He went by early to case the place out. I been there before, I didn't feel like standing around."

Tanner didn't have an answer for that, so he changed the subject. "Is Kenny gonna come rumble with us?"

"No."

"How come? He can still fight. There's nothing wrong with his fists."

Michelle hadn't thought about it. "I dunno... I don't want him getting hurt."

"He won't get hurt. He's a good fighter. You don't have to think to protect yourself."

Michelle was still hesitant. "I'll see what he says," she conceded, "but he hasn't been interested in hanging with the gang since... you know."

∼

Kenny didn't look away from the TV when Michelle joined him.

"Kenny." He took his time, but looked at her eventually. "Kenny, there's a rumble. You don't want to come, do you?"

She thought that wording it as a negative, there was a better chance of him refusing. But Kenny's eyes brightened.

"Yeah. I wanna fight."

"Are you sure? You don't have to."

"I want to."

"Okay..."

George turned his head to look at her. "Kenny can't go!"

"Why not?"

"What about me and Marcie? You're going to leave both of us alone?"

"You've been left alone before."

"But not with Marcie."

Michelle looked at her sister. "You'll be okay for a couple hours, right sweetie?"

Marcie made an uncertain noise; but after telling Kenny that he could come, Michelle couldn't back out now and force him to stay home to watch Marcie.

"We won't be gone a long time," she promised. "Just a couple hours. You won't even know we're gone."

"What if I need something?" George fussed.

"You've been alone before. Me or Dan will be back in no time."

∼

MICHELLE

Michelle and Tanner left a little earlier than the rest of the gang to meet up with Carter just before the rumble. Carter greeted Tanner casually as if they had no history. But he put an arm around Michelle and gave her a squeeze and a kiss in front of Tanner, not commenting when she flinched at the physical contact.

"Hey, Michelle. All ready for the party?" He meant the rumble, of course.

"Yeah, I'm ready."

"You got any dope?" Carter asked Michelle, then looked at Tanner when she shook her head.

"Yeah," Tanner admitted, "but I don't know about doping before a rumble."

"You never amped up before a fight? Gives you quicker reflexes, an edge."

Tanner looked uncomfortable, handing Carter a few pills. "You don't want to be messed up for a fight. You'll get in trouble if you're strung out."

Carter popped the pills and shook his head, grinning. "I done it before, man. Nothing's going to happen. Give it a try yourself."

"Yeah?"

"Yeah."

"Doesn't make you make mistakes?"

"Nope."

"You fight better."

"You got it. Come on, pop a couple back. See for yourself."

Tanner wavered under Carter's steady gaze. "I dunno, man…"

"Well, if you're scared…"

"I'm not scared. But none of the other guys do it."

"None of them?" Carter repeated skeptically.

"Well, I don't know. Maybe one of the others does, but I always heard it was dangerous to get high before a rumble."

"If you lose control, sure. Everything's dangerous."

Tanner shrugged, as they walked towards the rendezvous. "I dunno. Maybe I'll try it."

Carter grinned and turned his attention back to Michelle. "What about you? How come you're so straight?"

"Michelle's been convicted of trafficking," Tanner offered with a snicker.

"You're kidding! Michelle?"

Tanner nodded, laughing. "Sure. Got caught red-handed with a bagful of loot. Didn't you, Michelle?"

Michelle shrugged, her face getting hot. "Yeah, I did. So what?"

Carter laughed. "It's just I've never seen you carry an aspirin. I guess you learned the first time, huh?"

"I don't do drugs," Michelle said.

"How come? No offense, but a chick in a gang, most of them are pretty heavy into dope and stuff."

"I just don't like it."

"What was it you told me that one time?" Tanner mused. "She said she didn't like to lose control."

Carter considered this for a moment and shook his head. "Sometimes you gotta lose control."

"That's fine to say," Michelle snapped, "but ask Dan what happens when you lose control one too many times!"

Carter and Tanner were silenced. The remainder of the walk to the rumble was completed without conversation.

Michelle tried to keep an eye on Kenny during the rumble, but it was impossible. The fight took all her attention. When she did catch sight of him once, he was intent on the fight and seemed to be handling himself okay. But the Jags did not do well, and Michelle joined the retreat, scanning for Kenny to make sure he didn't get left behind. He was up ahead with Tanner, appearing uninjured.

There was a tap on her shoulder, and Carter was there. "Good rumble, eh?" he questioned, breathing hard.

Michelle nodded. "Not bad. Would've been better if we won."

"Ah, rumblin's not about winning. It's about the adrenaline."

"I'm surprised if you can feel it through the drugs."

He grinned. "There's no high that can't be made better. By fighting, or by other things…"

Michelle glanced at him to ask what other things and saw his look. "Oh. Yeah."

"I think we gotta celebrate tonight."

"Celebrate losing?"

"Nah, just celebrate a good fight."

Michelle shrugged. "I'm sure we'll hit the clubs," she offered.

"Not that there's anything wrong with that kind of entertainment—we can join up later—but I was thinking about you and me."

"The guys wouldn't like it if we skipped out on them."

"We're not skipping out. We're just havin' a private party first."

Michelle looked down. "I dunno."

"You and Tanner were sleeping together, weren't you?" Carter said abruptly.

"Yeah."

"Then what's the matter with me?"

"There's nothing wrong with you."

"Then what's wrong with you?" he challenged.

"I don't know," Michelle said.

"You don't like guys? What?"

"I don't know what."

"That I could at least understand. But I don't get why you're giving me the cold shoulder."

Michelle just looked at her feet and didn't say anything. She couldn't understand the way she felt; how could she explain it to anyone? She couldn't stand the thought of Carter touching her. Or any guy.

"What's Tanner got that I don't?" Carter persisted.

"I've known Tanner since I was a kid," Michelle explained, "ever since we went to foster care."

"Well, I'm not that patient."

"I know."

"If I thought you hated me, I wouldn't bother. But you've never said to get lost."

"No."

"Do you want me to? Just forget it and leave you alone? Because I never got that impression."

Michelle swallowed and shook her head. "No."

Carter shrugged. "Don't be surprised if I'm persistent, then."

Michelle nodded, her face warm.

Michelle thought they'd better check in on Marcie and George before they spent all night out, so she and Dan popped back to the apartment and went about their usual chores without comment. Dan looked up when Michelle called to him.

"Just a second," he told her.

When he finished up, he went to see her. Michelle was bent over in front of Marcie.

"What's up?"

"Something's wrong."

Dan felt Marcie's forehead. "Better take her to the hospital."

"Do you think it's serious?"

"Probably just a virus. But you gotta be real careful about that kind of thing."

"Okay. Will you come with me?"

"Sure. Get a coat on her. Make sure she's bundled up."

Michelle got Marcie ready to go while Dan finished getting George down for the night. Then they went to the hospital.

CHAPTER
Thirty-Eight

Michelle and Dan had been waiting in an exam room for quite some time. Dan yawned. "You want a coffee? I gotta go get something to keep me awake."

"Sure. Bring me one too."

He got up, stretched, and left the room. Michelle rubbed her eyes and looked at her sister. At least Marcie was sleeping.

The door opened and Michelle looked up, surprised Dan was back so soon. But it wasn't Dan. It was a couple of cops. Michelle swallowed and tried to look cool.

"Why don't you tell me who you are?" one of them said.

Michelle shifted. "Marcie's sister."

"Where are her parents?"

Michelle tried to guess at what they knew. "Is there a problem?"

"We're checking up on a report. Where are Marcie's folks?"

"At home with the other kids."

"Why didn't one of them bring her in?"

"Justin's trucking. I said I'd come. Someone had to look after the younger kids."

"Do you have some kind of ID?"

Michelle pulled out her recently-acquired learner's license and handed it over. One of the cops took it, glanced at her face for verification and took a closer look at the license to make sure it was authentic. He handed it back.

"You've got Marcie's health insurance information?"

"Uh, I forgot to bring it. I'll call and ask for the number over the phone."

He nodded and closed his notepad. "If you don't mind, I think we'll just hang around while you do that, and then we'll leave you alone."

Michelle nodded, biting her lip. Who could she call that would catch on and play along with the bluff?

"What's the number?" one of the cops questioned, motioning to the phone on the wall.

Michelle was tongue tied. They both looked at Michelle steadily, waiting as the seconds ticked by. "Do you even know the phone number?" one of them questioned.

Michelle shook her head. "I don't live there."

"I think maybe we should have them come in."

Michelle had a trapped feeling, but she didn't know how much they suspected. "If you want. I can take care of things myself, though."

"I think we'd better talk to your folks."

Michelle didn't bother to protest. One of the cops left the room while the other stayed with her. It was quite a while before he came back.

"Dad's on his way," he advised.

"So did she have permission?" the other questioned.

"Well," the first looked puzzled, "there seems to be some confusion on that point. I guess we'll get it straightened around when he gets here."

Charlie got there before Justin. He lived and worked closer to the hospital.

"Hi Michelle, how's it going?"

"Fine."

"How's Marcie?"

"Doctor hasn't looked at her yet."

Charlie bent over Marcie, saw she was sleeping peacefully, and straightened again. "She looks okay. Maybe just a virus."

Michelle nodded. "That's what Dan figured too."

"It's probably nothing serious, but I'm glad you brought her in anyway."

"Do I have to wait around for Justin? Or is he coming?"

"He's on his way. And I think you'd better wait until he gets here to make sure everything gets settled."

Michelle sat down and waited. She wasn't in the mood for conversation and Charlie didn't pursue it. He talked casually to the officers while they all waited for Justin.

Justin flew in with a doctor in tow. "The admitting nurse said she hasn't been seen yet. She's very fragile with her CP."

The doctor was nodding soothingly. "I'm sure she's fine. The nurses keep a pretty close eye on things."

Justin spotted Michelle and stopped talking.

"This is Justin," Charlie said to the officers.

Justin went to Marcie and kissed her. "Hi, sweetie. Are you okay?" Marcie opened her eyes and smiled broadly at him. Justin brushed her cheek and took her hand in his. "She's hot. She has a fever."

Michelle watched the tender reunion with some pain. Eventually, Justin turned his attention to the rest of the room.

"Charlie. Thanks for coming by. Officers." He looked at Michelle, his face blank of emotion. "So. What happened?"

"Nothing happened. I was getting her ready for bed and noticed she wasn't feeling well."

"How long before that was she sick?"

"She wasn't. Just tonight, so I brought her here."

"Uh, before we get too much into this," one of the cops interposed, "maybe someone could fill us in on the situation and whether you need us here or not."

Justin, Michelle, and Charlie exchanged looks.

"Michelle has been looking after Marcie," Justin said.

"With your permission?"

There was an awkward moment of silence. Michelle held her breath. "Yes, of course," Justin said finally.

Michelle breathed a sigh of relief. The cops relaxed slightly. "Then we'll be on our way."

They left. Michelle stood.

"What tipped them off?" she asked Justin, pulling her jacket on. "You put out a report on me?"

"One of the emergency room doctors knew Marcie and was concerned to see her here without Sondra or Justin," Charlie explained.

"Oh. Well... bye, Marcie. I guess I won't see you again."

She lingered by Marcie's bed for a minute and then stepped out into the hall. She looked around for Dan, and saw Carter hanging around at the end of the hall instead.

"What are *you* doing here?"

"Dan saw the cops and figured he'd better split, 'cause there'd be no one to look after George if you both got busted. So I thought I'd keep an eye out for you."

Michelle saw from Carter's eyes that someone was approaching behind her. She turned. It was Charlie. He studied Carter for a moment with a guarded expression, then spoke to Michelle.

"I think we could work something out for you to visit Marcie, with supervision, if you want to see her again. She is your sister."

"I don't want any cop looking over my shoulder so I can see my own family."

"You make your own decision. You can see her again if you want to."

"Is that what Justin said?"

"He can see you love Marcie, Michelle. But he needs to protect her."

"That's fine. I don't want to see him anymore anyway."

Charlie didn't try to argue it further. "Stop by the house sometime, Michelle. Ruby would like to see you again. It's been a while."

"Maybe."

"Kenny doing all right?"

"Yeah, he's good."

Charlie nodded. He gave her a little pat on the arm and walked away.

"What's a vice cop doing here?" Carter demanded, his voice strained.

Michelle turned back to him. "How did you know Charlie's a vice cop?"

"Oh—I've run into him before."

"Huh." Michelle eyed him for a moment, then shrugged it off.

∽

"How was Michelle?" Ruby asked when Charlie got home.

"Surprisingly acquiescent. I wasn't sure what Justin was going to say when he got there. But he behaved himself."

Ruby studied Charlie's expression. "What else happened?"

"Nothing. I was just thinking how much Michelle reminds me of you."

"In what way?"

Charlie just smiled.

CHAPTER
Thirty-Nine

"Tanner, man, i been looking for you."

Tanner looked at Carter with a frown. Usually, the two of them pretended there was nothing between them, but they still didn't talk to each other if they didn't have to.

"What do you want me for?"

Carter held out his hand. "To pay you back for the dope you spotted me before the rumble."

Tanner took the pill bottle from Carter, looking at the contents. "I just gave you a couple reds," he reminded Carter.

"I know. But hey, I know you don't like me, Tanner, and you didn't have to do that. I got a good source for candy like this now."

Tanner's opinion of Carter rose considerably. "You're a decent guy, Carter."

Carter smiled. "Why don't you call me Joe?"

Tanner's chest puffed with pride. There was a strict hierarchy in the gang and you simply didn't call a guy by his first name if he was higher up than you. You had to be friends or equals to call someone by their given name. There were few exceptions. Carter was older and better-skilled than Tanner, so he was higher up than Tanner, even though Tanner had been with the Jags for longer. Tanner started to feel quite warmly towards Carter.

"You ever need anything from me, Joe," he said, putting the privilege to immediate use, "you just let me know."

"I will, Tanner." Tanner was about to go his own way, but Carter had something more to say. "There is something, actually."

Tanner had an uncomfortable feeling he'd been set up—but even so, the extra prestige of being the older boy's equal was worth a lot. "Anything I can do," he repeated firmly.

"Yeah. Well, it's to do with Michelle."

"Uh-huh."

"You've known her for a long time, and all."

Tanner nodded, waiting for the other shoe to drop.

"What's the deal with her and guys?"

It took a few moments before Tanner understood what Carter meant. "Oh." Tanner felt himself flush and looked away. "Michelle's had some bad experiences, that's all."

"So have a lot of chicks. It doesn't make nuns of them."

"Michelle's no nun," Tanner laughed.

"So how did you—er... change her mind?"

Tanner hesitated but decided it was worth the prestige in the gang and complied. "If you want to get anywhere with Michelle, you're going to need some help."

"That's why I'm talking to you," Carter reminded him.

"No, help along these lines," Tanner held up the pill bottle Carter had given him and gave it a little shake.

"Not exactly my style," Carter said uncomfortably.

"What do you mean it's not your style? You're popping or pushing all the time."

"What did you do? Slip something in her drink?"

Tanner shrugged. "No. It just sort of happened. She got to drinking pretty heavy one night, we both took a few hits, and one thing led to another."

"I thought she didn't drink."

"Yeah, and while she's been sober, no dice, right?"

Carter raised his brows. "Yeah. No dice. So what sent her on this bender?"

"That was just luck. It was over Kenny. She wanted to forget."

"What else makes her drink?"

"I dunno. When she's upset. When you can talk her into it. Sometimes you can just tell her she needs to relax and take a few drinks. After the first time, though, she's not so uptight. It's that first time she's gotta be smashed."

Carter cleared his throat. "Gotcha," he agreed.

He and Tanner both nodded to each other awkwardly, both a little red. Then they parted ways with relief.

Michelle felt lost without Marcie to take care of. Kenny was full of new-found confidence since the rumble. Something had changed in him. He'd been vague and apathetic since the horrible drug overdose, but now he acted like he had a mind of his own again. She could still tell everything was not normal, but he was suddenly interested in being with the gang again and more careful to not do stupid or childish things in front of them.

Michelle even spent some time with George to try to get past the emptiness of having Marcie gone and Kenny being more independent. But his constant whining and fussing got on her nerves and she thought maybe she'd go for a walk. Except she didn't feel like going anywhere, so she just sat on the broken-down old couch and watched TV.

Carter arrived. "Hey, Michelle, how's it going?"

Michelle shrugged. "I'm bored. Maybe I should get another tattoo."

"Why don't we go together? I wouldn't mind getting another one too."

Michelle considered it. "Sure. What are you going to get?"

"I don't know. Maybe a ship. I always liked some of those fancy boats."

Michelle nodded. "Some of them are pretty cool. I like animals or symbols."

"Your jaguar is known all over town."

"Really? Who says?"

Carter shrugged. "All the gangs know it. And I've seen a copy at one of the tattoo places, too."

"I don't want anyone else using it."

"I don't think you can stop them. What are you going to get this time?"

Michelle thought about it, thinking about her body and the tattoos she already had. "I know what I'm going to get," she decided suddenly, "a snake, going around my fingers and up my arm."

"That's going to take a long time."

"Hours," Michelle agreed. "But it's going to look great."

It wasn't exactly how Carter had planned on spending the day, but he didn't want to turn down the chance of a long conversation with her.

"Yeah, it'll be cool. Let's do it."

"Look at this, Carter," Michelle said, pointing to the stylized picture of a dragon on the wall of tattoos. "Not a snake; I'm going to get a dragon. Put its tail around my fingers, and have it going all the way up my arm. Another time I can get a bunch of flames added across my shoulder and back, right?"

"That's a great idea," the tattoo artist agreed, overhearing. He looked her over. It was a cool day and most of her tattoos were covered up. "Have you had any large tattoos done before?" Michelle lifted her shirt to show him the Jag tattoo. "Oh, that's *your* jaguar. I've heard about it. A beautiful piece of work."

Carter nodded to Michelle. "You see? I told you."

"Huh."

"Do you want to get it done today?" the proprietor questioned. "I've got some time if you do. Rainy days business is bad. No walk-bys."

Michelle nodded. "Yeah, sure. Would you be able to finish it today?"

"We'll see how it goes. If my hands get tired or you get tired of sitting, we'll split it up over a few days."

"Okay."

"Come on over and sit down and we'll get prepped." He nodded to Carter. "Are you getting one too or just here for moral support?"

"I'm thinking of maybe getting this ship on my bicep."

"Sure. Let me call my assistant to help you."

Carter was finished way before Michelle. He went over to where Michelle was being worked on to watch.

"Man, that's going to look good when it's done, huh?"

Michelle nodded. The tattoo artist did not look up to speak. "We'll see if we can rival that jaguar," he said with a smile.

"It will," Carter said, looking at the bright greens and purples of the dragon's scales.

Hours later Michelle was stretching out her stiff arm. "It went to sleep an hour ago," she commented, squeezing her numb fingers.

"It'll burn when it wakes up," Carter warned.

"Yeah, I know," Michelle said, rolling her eyes.

"You wanna go for a drink?"

"I guess."

Carter noticed Michelle seemed a little depressed. He wasn't sure whether he was taking advantage of her by suggesting drinks or not. He wasn't forcing her to drink, not even trying to talk her into it. He was just suggesting drinking to her. Like he might with any of the Jags.

As the evening wore on and Michelle got more tipsy, Carter decided against giving her any pills. He had been considering it, but as the time came, he decided he didn't have the guts. As interested as he was in her, he just couldn't do it that way.

"How drunk am I?" Michelle asked woozily.

Carter was getting pretty wobbly himself. "I dunno. How many drinks have you had?"

"I don't know. But I can't feel my arm again."

Carter laughed. "Maybe we should go home and crash."

"I think I should," Michelle agreed. "Crash."

They walked the few blocks to the apartment. Michelle's legs gave way on the front steps. She grabbed Carter to stop herself from falling but ended up pulling him down on top of her. She giggled. "Whoops. I can't quite make it!"

Carter helped her up and held her steady as they got through the front doorway and then into the apartment.

"Your bed is closer," Michelle suggested.

"Yeah."

"I can't make it to mine."

"Okay, we'll just go to sleep on mine."

The two of them stumbled and swayed to Carter's mattress and promptly collapsed there. Michelle dissolved into loud giggles. Carter grinned and tried to shift Michelle off of him. She resisted and sat up unsteadily, straddling him.

"I like you," she said candidly, "even if you are a narc."

Carter got serious in a hurry. "You like me?" he repeated.

"Uh-huh," she smiled.

"Even if I'm a narc?"

"Uh-huh."

"You're pretty drunk, aren't you?"

"Yeah."

"You aren't going to remember a thing in the morning."

"Nope," Michelle agreed cheerfully and leaned over to kiss him.

Carter decided to live in the moment.

Michelle awoke to the unpleasant sounds of Carter being sick across the hall in the bathroom. She squinted her eyes and looked around, disoriented. It took a few minutes to figure out she was in the boys' room. She sat up, but her stomach was queasy and the toilet was already occupied. Michelle lay back down and closed her eyes.

Carter eventually came back and sat down on the edge of the mattress to consider putting his clothes on. Michelle shifted.

"You awake?" Carter grunted.

"Uh-huh."

"I hope you're feeling better than I am."

"Mmm, not good," Michelle admitted, holding her hand over her eyes.

"Do you remember any of last night?"

"Bits and pieces." She propped herself up on her elbow. "I assume we..." she motioned to the mattress, "you know."

Carter nodded. "That bother you?"

"No..." Michelle hesitated, "I know I'm too uptight. I'm sort of messed up."

"Don't worry about it." Carter brushed it off, though he was pleased she wasn't upset about what had happened.

"I just..." Michelle tried to explain, "I just can't take being touched sometimes, you know."

"It's okay." He tried to make light of it. "If all it takes is a couple of drinks..."

Michelle forced a smile. "You can buy me a drink anytime," she agreed.

CHAPTER Forty

"You're hurt?" Kenny questioned, indicating Michelle's bandaged arm.

Michelle shook her head. "No. I got a new tattoo."

"Big one," Kenny observed.

"Yeah. But it's gonna look really cool."

Kenny nodded absently and drifted away. Michelle watched him for a moment, wondering what was on his mind. But even before, Kenny hadn't been one to put his deepest thoughts into words. He walked away from her and joined Artis, one of the other Jags. Michelle went her own way.

∼

Kenny was delighted to have Artis include him in his plan. Artis had asked him to act as a decoy in a hold-up. Kenny was glad for the action. He watched Artis across the store while the robbery went down. They were about the same height and build. And they were dressed in the usual gang uniform—blue jeans and black jacket. Of course, when Artis made his get-away, he would change into something nondescript and walk calmly away while Kenny ran and looked obvious to divert attention.

Kenny ran just before Artis finished. People noticed him and then alarms started going off and a couple of good citizens shouted halfheartedly for him to stop, but no one chased him. After he was a few blocks away, he stopped running and just walked at a regular pace.

He was surprised at how quickly a police cruiser showed up. As it pulled up beside him with lights flashing, Kenny took off again. He heard the car door slam and tried to put on an extra burst of speed. The cops were right behind him. Kenny ducked into an alley, hoping to lose them. But it was a dead end. Kenny whirled around to retreat the way he had come, but they were too close to him and blocked his retreat. Trapped, Kenny didn't stop to consider his odds, he just headed straight for the cops as hard as he could, trying to break through. They stood their ground and one of them reached for his pistol.

"Freeze!" he shouted.

Kenny hesitated as the pistol jumped out of its holster. He came to a stop as it zeroed in on him.

"Smart kid," the cop snarled as his partner moved in to cuff Kenny. "You don't want to get your head blown off, do you?"

Kenny stood there while they cuffed and frisked him.

"You got anything in your pockets I should know about? You'd better tell me now."

"Knife," Kenny offered.

"Closed?"

"Yeah."

"Anything else? Drugs? Needles?"

"No."

The cop put his hands in Kenny's pockets to find the knife and pulled it out. "What'd you run for?"

Kenny shrugged.

Michelle didn't think much of not having seen Kenny for a while until she heard through the grapevine about Artis's plan. He said everything had gone as planned, which meant he made a clean getaway, and if the cops had gotten anyone, it was Kenny. Overall, he was pleased with himself.

"But what about Kenny?" Michelle demanded.

"What about him?"

"You don't even know if he got caught."

"Kenny can take care of himself."

"No, he can't, you moron!"

Artis shrugged. "They can't do nothing to Kenny. You can't treat a kid like him like you would any old hood like me."

"That doesn't mean they won't. Where've you been? You think all the cops follow the rules?"

"They wouldn't do nothing to Kenny."

"You'd better hope not."

Carter walked into the room as Michelle stormed out. "Where are you going?"

"To call Charlie," she snapped, shoving past him.

Carter grinned at the others. "I wouldn't want to be Charlie, whoever he is."

"I think he's that cop her aunt's married to."

The color drained from Carter's face. "Charlie's a cop?"

"Hey, don't look so worried. If she's going to turn anyone in, it'll be Artis."

"Charlie's married to Michelle's aunt?"

"Yeah."

Carter swore.

"Hey man, what are you so worried about? It's not like Michelle's a narc."

"I know," Carter said dryly and walked away.

Charlie asked around for Kenny. Eventually someone managed to point him in the right direction. Charlie let himself into the room where they were questioning him.

"Hello, Kenny."

Kenny looked surprised to see Charlie and nodded a greeting.

"You know him?" Stace, the cop interrogating him, asked.

"Sure. He's Ruby's nephew."

"Oh," Stace looked a little awkward, "he never said anything."

"You shouldn't be questioning him."

Stace got defensive. "Why, because he's related to you?"

"No, because he's not competent to be questioned."

"He's not under the influence, we checked. He's just being stubborn."

"He's mentally challenged," Charlie snapped, "and it shouldn't have taken you more than a few minutes to figure *that* out."

"All these kids put on a dumb front. I didn't know."

"Well, now you do. I'll take him home."

"You can't take him anywhere. He's still up against a robbery rap, competent or not."

"Kenny couldn't plan something like that. Did he have the loot on him?"

"No. He was spotted at the scene."

"Has he been ID'd by the shopkeeper?"

"He's on his way."

"Why don't you go get a lineup arranged and I'll stay with Kenny?"

Stace glowered and walked off. Charlie turned his attention towards Kenny, frowning. "Do you know what you're here for?" he questioned.

"Uh-huh."

"Did you rob the store?"

There was a long pause before Kenny shook his head.

"You had nothing to do with it? Do you know who did it?"

Kenny gazed at him blankly and didn't answer.

"Who did it, Kenny?"

No answer.

"Do you want to go to jail?"

"I don't care."

He had been in juvie before. The threat of imprisonment didn't work on him. Charlie sat and looked at him, thinking.

"Did Stacey hit you?" he asked, noticing the bruises on Kenny's face.

Kenny was silent.

"Kenny. Did that cop hurt you?" Charlie persisted.

"No."

"I think he did. Your face is a mess."

Kenny was silent.

"You want a coffee?"

"Yeah. Smoke too?"

"Sure, I'll see if I can find you some cigarettes."

When he got back to the interrogation room, Stace had returned. "We're about ready for that lineup," he said.

Charlie motioned Kenny to his feet and looked him over. "Take your jacket off, Kenny."

"No, he can leave it on," Stace protested.

"Take it off," Charlie repeated, not wanting Kenny to be picked out of the lineup because of the gang emblem. Which was why Stace wanted him to leave it on. Kenny looked back and forth at them and obeyed Charlie.

They took him to the lineup. As the boys entered the room and stood in front of the darkened witness room, Charlie scrutinized the group. Stace had not done a bad job. The other boys in the lineup were reasonably close to Kenny in age and build. Kenny did not stand out in any way. The shopkeeper looked at the boys.

"It's not one of them."

"Are you sure?" Stace prodded. Charlie shot a warning glance at him.

"No, he's not there," the man said with certainty. "I looked at his face. He's not there."

"One of these boys was seen running away right outside your store."

"Well, he's not the one who came in."

Stace swore. "We caught a decoy!"

Charlie shrugged and said nothing. The line-up was allowed to exit and Charlie intercepted Kenny. "Why don't you wait around for a bit and come home with me," Charlie suggested.

Kenny shook his head. "Goin' home."

"I think you should stay with us for the night to make sure everything has settled down."

"No, it's okay."

Charlie couldn't force him. "Okay. But stay out of trouble, will you?"

"Got my jacket?"

Charlie retrieved it for him, knowing it was probably not by oversight that Kenny had not answered his question. Kenny nodded his thanks and was escorted out.

Michelle was at the house when Charlie got home. Dinner was on the stove. Ruby and Michelle talked while they waited for Kenny. Michelle looked up expectantly, then looked disappointed.

"Don't worry," Charlie told her, "Kenny's fine. He said he was headed home. He didn't want to come back here."

"He's okay?"

"A little bruised, but just fine. Tell him to keep out of trouble."

"Yeah, right. No one hurt him?"

"He said not. I think he might have been slapped around a bit, but he wasn't badly hurt. Just some bruises."

Michelle nodded and breathed out slowly. "We've both been knocked around before. I was afraid... They'd put him in a cell with older guys or beat him bad."

"Nothing like that. It's been known to happen," Charlie admitted. He looked at Ruby with an eyebrow raised. "But we got to him in plenty of time. I'm glad you came by."

Michelle stood up to leave.

"You may as well stay for dinner," Ruby said. "You're here and it's ready."

Michelle hesitated, looking at Charlie.

"You've got no reason to be worried about me," Charlie said.

"Well... okay. I guess."

"Good. Maybe you can convince Kenny to come over sometime soon."

"I doubt it. He's pretty stubborn."

Charlie stifled the urge to smile and say Kenny was not the only one. Ruby glared at him, sensing his amusement. Charlie shrugged and helped Ruby set the table.

"So how have you been lately?" Charlie asked Michelle.

"Okay."

"Justin was asking the other day if we'd heard from you."

"I don't care."

"He wanted to know how you were."

Michelle shrugged and started dishing up. "I don't care what he says. I don't want anything to do with him."

"What about Marcie?"

"He took her away from us. We did okay not seeing her before. I guess we're not supposed to be together."

Charlie could see Michelle was only covering for her real feelings about being kept from Marcie. But there was no reason to challenge her.

Michelle ate quickly, not wanting to be drawn into any conversation. She pushed her plate away empty.

"That was good," she said shortly and stood up.

"Come join us anytime you like," Ruby invited.

"Sure."

CHAPTER Forty-One

Michelle couldn't figure out what was the matter with Carter. He was acting as jumpy as a schoolgirl. "Are you hopped up?" Michelle demanded.

"No."

"Then what's the matter?"

"I don't know. I'm just distracted."

"By what?"

Carter shrugged widely. "Say, Michelle," he said as if he'd just thought of it, "is it true what the guys said, your aunt married a cop?"

Michelle nodded. "Yeah. A vice cop. Weird, huh?"

"A vice cop," Carter repeated.

"Yeah. You've seen him. At the hospital."

Carter nodded slowly. "Oh, yeah. Him. You never told me he was related."

Michelle shrugged. "I don't like to advertise it. I don't mind tellin' people my aunt was a Jag, but I'd rather leave out that she married a cop."

"She was a Jag when she met him?"

"He was the one who busted her!"

"I could never arrest anyone I was in love with," he declared.

"Well, he didn't know her then. They got together after that."

"If she's anything like you, I can see how he'd fall for her."

Michelle eyed Carter. She had never assumed his feelings towards her were anything other than physical. But suddenly he was looking at her differently. He'd never professed love before.

"Are you sure you're not drunk?" she asked suspiciously.

"No, I got a clear head."

"Then what's up?"

His eyes jumped around the room. "I don't even know how to tell you... I hardly even believe it myself sometimes..."

"Oh. You got another girl." Michelle was relieved by the explanation.

Carter giggled at this. "No, no other girl."

"A guy then?" Michelle asked.

"No! I wasn't supposed to fall for you. Use you to get in with the gang, sure, but not get emotionally attached to you."

Michelle pondered on the phrase *emotionally attached* for a few moments. Not because she didn't understand it, but because it wasn't the way Carter generally talked. It sounded like shrink talk. Michelle didn't know why it made her so uneasy.

"What do you mean you weren't *supposed to?*"

"Do you like me, Michelle? I mean really like me?"

Michelle saw right through his deliberate avoidance of the word love. "I like you," she said cautiously. "But I don't know about more than that."

He gazed at her, disappointed. "So if something happened, and I wasn't here anymore..."

Michelle just looked at him. She knew what Carter wanted her to say, but she couldn't lie to him.

"What do you want to hear, Joe?" she said gently, trying to soften it.

"You wouldn't care if I was gone?"

"Of course I'd care. But none of us are gonna be here forever."

"Would you come with me?"

"Where?"

"If I had to go and you had a choice to come with me, would you come?"

Michelle was baffled. "Where would you have to go? Rehab? Where would I go with you?"

"Michelle..."

"What, Joe? I don't get you."

He tried to settle down and focus on her. He looked her in the eye. "You remember when we first met? How you made me as a narc?"

"Sure." Michelle grinned, remembering.

"Michelle, you were right."

That explained the *emotional attachment* thing.

"What?" Michelle said aloud.

"I'm an undercover cop."

She didn't know what to say to this. Michelle's first reaction was to review her past actions to see what he could arrest her for. But he'd already said he wouldn't arrest her.

"What do you think Charlie's going to think about this?" Carter asked worriedly.

Michelle laughed. "Why should Charlie care? Is he your boss?"

"No, I know him casually through the department... but I'm, well, I'm sleeping with his niece..."

Michelle shrugged. "I hardly even know him. He's got nothing to do with my life. And it's not even him I'm related to, it's Ruby."

Carter was relieved. "Well... then all I got to worry about is what my boss is going to think about this."

"What did you do that you weren't supposed to?"

Carter considered this, looking surprised at her question. "Well, I wasn't supposed to fall for you."

Michelle shrugged that off. "What else? Why would he care about that?"

Carter bit his lip. "Maybe I got worried about nothing..."

Michelle shrugged and nodded. Carter breathed out heavily, finally relaxing. But for Michelle, the worries were just started. It was a while before Carter noticed her tension.

"Are you okay? I shouldn't have said anything, I guess."

Michelle shook her head. "What's going to happen now?"

"Nothing, I guess. I was just panicking."

Michelle had to laugh at his naiveté, even though she wasn't so sure it was funny. "And what am I supposed to do, knowing you're a cop?"

He looked uncertain. "Is that it for us, then?"

"For starters," Michelle agreed coldly.

"I won't arrest you, Michelle. I already said that," he assured her.

"Don't do me any favors. I don't want everyone thinking I'm a snitch."

That stumped Carter. "Oh. What am I going to do, then? I have to give them something. I mean, you can't be undercover in a gang for this long without seeing something."

"Tell them your cover's blown and go home."

"If I do, they'll just—" He didn't say what they would do. Put someone else in his place, she supposed. "I guess that's what I'll have to do," he agreed.

There was silence between them for a while.

"I guess I'd better go," Carter said reluctantly.

Michelle nodded. Carter reached out to touch her cheek. Michelle jerked back.

"No goodbye kiss?" Carter asked, half-joking, half-hurt.

"I don't consort with cops—not knowingly," Michelle said sharply.

Carter looked hurt. Michelle didn't care. She was hurt too. He had betrayed her trust. She got up and left him alone.

Tanner knocked on Michelle's door and tried the handle.

"Michelle? I wanna talk to you. What are you doing?"

There was no answer from behind the door. Tanner paused, thinking.

"Dan? Do you know what Michelle's doing? I gotta ask her if she's seen Joe."

Dan poked his head into the hallway. "She's in her room. Been there all day."

"She won't answer the door."

"Maybe she's sick."

"Carter ain't in with her, is he?"

Dan shook his head. "I ain't seen Carter lately, couple days."

Tanner tried the handle again as if it might be unlocked now. "Hey, Dan…" He gestured to the doorknob. "You think you could…"

Dan grinned and approached. He picked the lock swiftly. "About time you learned to do this, isn't it?"

Tanner shrugged, grinning. Dan pushed the door open and Tanner went in. Michelle was lying in bed, pale and unmoving. Tanner hurried to her side and shook her by the shoulders.

"Michelle, wake up! Are you okay? Dan?"

Dan came in too. He bent over Michelle and put his ear to her chest. He swore. "She's OD'd. We gotta get her to a hospital."

"Michelle overdosed?" Tanner repeated, stunned. He looked around the room, but there was no evidence to show what she might have taken.

"Help me with her," Dan ordered, pulling down the blankets and lifting her up. Tanner helped take her out to Dan's car to take her to the hospital.

Carter was surprised when Charlie walked in. They knew each other on a superficial level, but Charlie really had nothing to do with Carter's undercover activities. Carter tensed up, his stomach knotting.

"Uh—hi, Charlie."

"Carter. How's it going?"

"Okay, I guess. Reintegrating isn't going to be easy."

"I wouldn't expect so. How's Michelle?"

Carter shifted. "I didn't know she was related to a cop. Not until too late."

Charlie grinned. "That must have been quite a shock," he said with a laugh. "It gave me a turn when I saw you with Michelle at the hospital."

"If anyone had told me she was your niece, I wouldn't have had anything to do with her."

"I was a little shocked to find out that she was my niece myself. I really didn't meet her much before you. I'm sure you know her better than I do."

Carter flushed. "I know she's underage, but…"

"You were your cover. I just came to ask you how Michelle and Kenny were doing."

"I didn't see a lot of Kenny. Michelle's fine. She was kind of mad to find out I was a cop."

"I guess. It was different for Ruby and me. She knew I was a cop from the start."

Carter nodded. "It was sort of a shock for Michelle. I'd been undercover for long enough to sort of wonder if it was true myself."

"Well, Michelle will get over it."

Michelle was staring out the window when Dan came in, pushing George's chair in front of him. He gave her a smile of greeting, looking like nothing was out of the ordinary. George looked anxious, his eyes fastening on Michelle as soon as he was in the room.

"Hey, Michelle," Dan said.

"Hi."

"How are you feeling?"

Michelle considered her wrists, attached to the bed to keep her restrained. "I feel great," she said dryly. "Just a bit of a headache."

Dan snorted. He parked George a few feet from the bed and pulled the visitor chair over to sit down. "You gave us a nasty scare."

Michelle looked back out the window. "I already got the whole lecture from Tanner, thanks."

But Dan didn't jump all over her. He just leaned back in the chair, studying her.

"Why did you OD?" George demanded, his voice a querulous whine. "Your life is perfect! You're healthy, you can do whatever you want. Why would you want to kill yourself?"

Michelle opened her mouth, but couldn't find the words to explain it to him.

"And don't try to tell me it was an accident," George sulked. "Because we know you don't take drugs. Don't hardly even drink. Why would you kill yourself?"

"I—I can't explain," Michelle said, trying to find something to say to him. Her heart hurt. She was tired, exhausted with life. She felt like she had a hole in her middle. She was empty, totally drained of all the things she used to care about. There was no light at the end of the tunnel. She wasn't even sure there was a way out of the tunnel she was in.

"Was it Carter?" Dan asked, still looking at Michelle with his dark, intense gaze. "Did he say something to you before he took off? Did you guys have a fight?"

Michelle closed her eyes and breathed out slowly. It hurt to breathe. She tried to relax her throat and chest muscles to ease the pain. She breathed in, and back out again.

"It's not just Carter," she said.

"I didn't think so. Look, Michelle, I've had my tough times too. I get it... but suicide ain't the answer."

"Okay."

She opened her eyes.

Dan raised his brows. "Okay?" he repeated.

"Okay. It didn't solve anything and I won't do it again."

"Better not," George grumbled.

Dan said nothing.

"The doctor gave me a prescription," Michelle offered. "He said it'll make me feel better, I just gotta give it time."

"I hope it does," Dan agreed.

Michelle put her hand over her eyes, blocking out his intense gaze. "Tanner's already chewed me out. And I said I won't do it again. I'm doing everything they tell me to and the doctor says they'll have me all fixed up in no time." Her lip curled as she repeated his words. She tried to smooth it out, to tame the despair and disgust. Her disbelief of the doctor's words.

"We're here for you, Michelle," Dan said softly. "That's all. I'm not here to ream you out. Just... let us know when things are getting too bad. We're your friends. We're here to help."

Michelle nodded and swallowed, her hands still over her face.

"Yeah, okay. Thanks."

Michelle was aware Dan and Tanner were keeping a close eye on her and obligingly left her door open so they wouldn't be pounding on it every five minutes to see if she was okay.

She lay on her mattress with a new paperback, but her mind wasn't on the story. She had told Carter she would miss him, but she hadn't anticipated how much.

Every time she thought about missing him, she got angry about his deception and how she had fallen for it. She had made him as a cop the first day, she should have trusted her instinct and kept clear of him. Instead, she'd grown to trust him and accept him as a friend.

He had preyed on her and betrayed her trust.

～

Michelle watched the new boy with more than a little suspicion. His handle was Red, for his hair, but Michelle thought there was something phony about him. And the timing of his appearance, so soon after Carter's departure, was suspicious. She determined to keep her distance. She wasn't going to be picking things up with someone new in the near future.

Red approached her later on when they were hanging out at one of the bars. "Hey, it's Michelle, right? How's it going?"

She stared at him grimly. "I'll bet you're a friend of Carter's, huh?"

He hesitated, looking at her face, his expression frozen.

"Let me clear something up here," Michelle went on. "Just because I liked Carter, that doesn't mean I'm going to take up with every narc who tries to get in with the gang. Okay?"

He backed way off. "Hey, you've got me pegged all wrong! I'm no narc!"

"Then keep away from me. Because if I find out you are, the only way you're leaving the gang is in a body bag. I'm not a revolving door for cops to get in and out of the gang."

He backed away from her, waving his hands like she was crazy. "Okay, whatever. Sorry I said anything to you."

Michelle watched him go, scowling. She wasn't going to fall for the same trick again.

CHAPTER
Forty-Two

After coming out of the tattoo parlor, Michelle looked at the hair salon next door and decided she may as well get her hair done over too. She walked in.

There was no receptionist. One of the stylists looked over at her. "Can I help you, hon?"

"I need my hair done."

"Got an appointment?"

"No. Do I gotta?"

"I think we can squeeze you in. You mind sitting for a bit?"

Michelle nodded and sat down to look at magazines. She half-listened to the buzz of conversation and looked up a minute later to glance at the woman walking by her with a broom. She was astonished.

"June?" she questioned, not sure if it was.

June turned and looked at her blankly, clearly not recognizing her. They stared at each other.

"Mama," Michelle said.

June's expression changed. "Michelle?" she questioned in disbelief, her eyes getting wide.

"What are you doing here?" Michelle demanded.

"Working. I have a job here."

"You? A job?"

June nodded. "What are you doing here?"

MICHELLE

Michelle gestured at her hair, still unable to believe June was there. "Where are you living?" Michelle asked, already worrying about halfway houses, slum apartments, and drugs.

"With Ruby. For a while, until I get my own place."

"Ruby never told me! How long have you been here?"

June shrugged. "Not that long. I told Ruby not to say anything. I... didn't think you'd want to see me."

Michelle tried to cover her confusion. "Well, I didn't. I just—I thought Ruby would tell me something like that."

The hairdresser came over, smiling tentatively. She had 'JoAnne' stitched on her smock. "Do you two know each other?"

June turned to her. "This is my daughter!"

"Your daughter? Why sure, you're as like as two peas. You look just like sisters."

Michelle looked at June. In her mind, June was still a ragged junkie, too strung out to even leave the house. But looking at June now, she had a hard time believing the changes before her own eyes. June looked young, pretty, and clean.

"How long have you been working here?" she asked June, and then turned to JoAnne. "Do you know she's been in prison?"

"Yes, hon. I know. It's okay."

Michelle shifted uncomfortably.

"Did you want a cut?" JoAnne asked, trying to ease the tension.

"Yeah. Style and color. Something sorta punk."

"Come get sat down."

Michelle obeyed.

JoAnne put a cape around Michelle's neck. "Your mom has been doing real well here. We've all been pretty impressed."

"She's never held down a job in her life."

"Everyone deserves a second chance."

"She's had plenty of chances."

JoAnne combed out Michelle's hair in silence. For the next little while, her only questions were about what Michelle wanted to be done with her hair. Michelle watched June about the store, doing her chores. She couldn't believe June was living so close, working only blocks from Michelle's apartment.

"You should be proud of your mom. I don't know what happened between you two, but you need to forgive her. Let go of the anger."

"I'm not going to forgive her for anything. I never wanted to see her again," Michelle said flatly, hoping her tone would end the conversation.

"The Bible says—"

"What do I care what the Bible says? Did she ever care about what was right or wrong?"

"She does now," JoAnne said, removing the cape.

Michelle got out of the chair. "She doesn't even *know* what's right and what's wrong, do you, Mama?"

June stopped and looked at Michelle. "I know I've done wrong," she admitted.

"You haven't done one thing right for us," Michelle snapped.

"I know…" June swallowed. "But I'm trying to change."

"You could never change."

"The Bible says…"

Michelle was incredulous. "*You're* going to quote the Bible now? Oh, I get it. You found religion. That's why you think you're changed."

June was uncertain. "I'm trying to be a good person. What's wrong with that?"

"Religion is the opiate of the masses. You've just gone from one drug to another." She headed for the door. "How much?" she asked JoAnne crisply.

"Oh, this one's on me. Come back again."

"Yeah, right."

Michelle walked out.

~

JoAnne watched the girl go. "Well, I don't know what you two fought about, but it must have been a doozy."

"We didn't fight," June bowed her head. "She was taken away from me because of abuse. Then after I'd got her back… she ran away when I got arrested again."

JoAnne didn't know what to say. "I'm sorry, honey. I guess that's why she's so mad."

"Yeah. She's got a right to be. I don't know how to make it better."

"Sometimes things need time. See if she comes back again."

"She won't."
"Well, sounds like your sister knows how to get her."
"Yeah. Maybe I'll get her number."

Michelle stood at the bus stop, thinking about what to do. She saw Charlie come out of the house for an afternoon shift. His sharp cop eyes spotted her standing there and he pulled to a stop beside her.

"Hi Michelle," he greeted.
"Hi."
"You going in?" He nodded at the house.
"I don't know. Is she in there?"
"Ruby?"
"June."
"Oh, you know about her, do you?"
"Yeah, I ran into her."
"Well, she's still at work."
"Okay."
Charlie put the car in gear.
"Charlie?"
"Yeah?"
"Do they have another cop in the Jags? After Carter?"
Charlie looked at her in silence for a moment. "I'm sorry about what happened with Carter, Michelle. I didn't have anything to do with putting him in and I couldn't do anything once you two got together."

"And now Carter's blown. So did you send another narc into the Jags? He thought you would."

"You know I can't tell you that, Michelle. It would endanger our man. If we had one there."

Michelle nodded. "Yeah, I know."

Charlie pulled out. Michelle stood there for a moment, thinking about it, and then went up to the house.

Ruby answered the door. "Michelle! Hey, I'm glad to see you. How's it going?"

"I don't know."

"Come on in, sit down. What's up?"

"I ran into June a few days ago."

Ruby's eyebrows went up. "She didn't even mention it to me. How did you get along?"

"I don't want to get along with her."

"Fair enough. Did she... seem the same to you?"

Michelle scowled. "She might look and act differently, but I know she hasn't changed. I don't care if she's cleaned up and got religion. She's still the same."

Ruby nodded. "It takes more than a few weeks to change your life."

"I don't really care what she does. I don't care about anyone anymore."

Ruby studied Michelle, a line forming on her forehead. "You're not really feeling like yourself, are you?"

Michelle was surprised at Ruby's perception. She shook her head. "I OD'd, you know. On purpose. A few weeks ago."

Ruby didn't look shocked like Michelle had expected her to. "Did you see a shrink afterward, before you went back home?"

"Yeah. For a few minutes. He gave me Prozac. But... it doesn't make a difference."

"Prozac didn't work for me either. I slit my wrists while I was on it."

"No, you didn't!" Michelle said, incredulous at the thought of Ruby being suicidal. She seemed so together.

Ruby showed Michelle her scarred wrists to prove it. "I know what it's like, Michelle. If Prozac doesn't work, you gotta try something else. Or you'll be dead in an alley somewhere. I know."

Michelle opened her mouth to deny it, but she couldn't. She knew it was the truth.

Ruby sat down across from her. "Now just tell me everything. I won't tell anyone what you say. Not even Charlie. But you gotta talk about it and get the right medication."

"I don't even know what's wrong, really. I mean, things have been worse before."

"It's the chemicals in your brain. Things bother you more... they stick with you, so you can't stop thinking about them all the time. Can't get out of a funk."

Michelle nodded eagerly. "Yeah, you get it!"

"It must be in our blood. I mean, we're not the most well-balanced family."

"Yeah."

"So tell me what's on your mind. And then I'll see if I can get you in to see my doctor right away."

"Okay." Michelle took a deep breath and tried to explain everything that was bothering her.

∼

Michelle had barely walked into the apartment when everyone descended upon her.

"Where have you been?" Tanner demanded.

Michelle could hear the relief in his voice. They'd been afraid she'd done something again. "Take it easy, Tanner. I went to see Ruby. Saw her doctor, too."

"Are you okay?"

Michelle shrugged. "He gave me a new prescription. To try and shake this mood."

"Oh. Good. I've got some pills if you need something, you know."

"I don't want uppers. These are different."

"Okay... so you're feeling better now?"

"It takes a few weeks to work."

"Uppers would work now," Tanner muttered.

Michelle gave him a warning glance but didn't say anything. Dan and Kenny had both come out to see her as well, but they didn't get on her case. They just faded back when they saw she was okay. Michelle sighed in exasperation. She hated having them all over her all the time. Even though she knew it was just because they cared about her.

CHAPTER Forty-Three

The priest said she was forgiven, but June wasn't sure she felt any better. It didn't change what had happened in the past. It didn't make the kids feel any better or change the fact that they were out on the street. And she hadn't confessed everything. There were still parts she held back. She wasn't as pious as she made out. And she suspected others could tell.

She had to do something else. Something for others. If she couldn't do something for Michelle and Kenny, maybe she could do something for other kids on the street. Sort of make up for what she'd done before. It might make her feel better than the emptiness of the priest's absolution.

∼

"You doing anything for lunch?" June asked Freddie as she got ready to leave.

"No. Where are you going?"

"To help out at the soup kitchen. You want to come help?"

"It's not exactly my scene."

"It's not anyone's *scene*. But they still got to eat. Come on, it'll make you feel good."

"I feel good already." June shrugged and turned to leave. "I'm just joking, June. I'll come."

June waited for him to catch up.

~

Once they reached the soup kitchen, Freddie looked around uncomfortably. Most of the people there were teenagers or young adults. Gangs, homeless kids, hookers, bikers, and all sorts of tough-looking individuals.

"I thought it would mostly be old drunks," he commented to June.

"You see the older folks at the morning and night kitchens. Mostly kids and families at noon."

Freddie noticed a few young families throughout the throng. "Don't you worry about your safety?"

"Sometimes there are fights, but usually they get along. You get thrown out, you go hungry."

"But don't you worry about these guys following you home?"

June looked surprised. "No. They're just kids."

"They're more than just kids. A lot of them are criminals. Dangerous ones."

June looked unconvinced. Freddie was amazed that with her constant anxiety over the littlest things at work, she could look so many hoods in the eye without flinching. June suited up, showed Freddie where the caps and gloves were, and started spooning out slop. The kids generally kept their eyes down. Some of them smiled or nodded, but mostly they looked away, embarrassed.

One of the gang boys looked June over brazenly and didn't move on after he was served, holding up the line. "What?" June demanded.

"Oh. Nothin'. You just looked like a friend of mine for a minute."

June looked at his outfit. "You a Jag?"

"Yeah."

"You talking about Michelle?"

He looked surprised. "Yeah, I am. Oh, you must be that aunt of hers, huh?"

"No. I'm her ma."

The line was pushing and jostling, and he was being pushed away. He gave June a half-smile and moved on. Freddie looked at June and shook his head.

"I know gangs," June said with a shrug. "These kids don't have anything against you and me. They're just hungry."

∼

"Saw your mom at the kitchen again," Bobby told Michelle.

"Yeah?" Michelle said, irritated. "She ain't in prison again yet?"

"What's the problem?" Bobby asked. "I think she's cool."

"Yeah, well, she didn't raise you."

"The other folks there, they don't even look at the bangers. Your mama doesn't got a problem talking to us."

"Well, she used to be one herself, so why would it bother her?"

"What gang was she in?"

"I dunno," Michelle brushed it off. "Some no-name gang that ain't around anymore."

"Was everyone in your family into gangs?"

"No, just Ruby and mama and my—her brother." She laughed, rolling her eyes. "Yeah, I guess all my family that I know!"

∼

Michelle saw Dan's glances toward George, who was watching TV in the living room, as usual. Dan's manner was distracted and his forehead was lined with worry.

"What's up?" Michelle asked.

Dan looked at her, pressing his lips together for a moment.

"I've got to get something nourishing into him. The doctor says he's losing weight, but he's not interested in food. With all the meds he's on, he's got no appetite. So how am I supposed to get anything into him?"

Michelle nodded. "What did he used to like? Isn't there anything he might want?"

"No... I've tried all the tricks. He just eats less and less."

"Maybe something home-cooked instead of fast food."

"Who's going to make it? You?"

Michelle laughed. "No, not me! I dunno..."

"There's the soup kitchen," Dan said. "We went to the one at home now and then. Soup is easy to eat, goes down quick... it's not so much work to eat."

"Yeah. You could do that."

Dan's eyes remained on Michelle. "Would you come?"

"Me? Why would I come?"

"He likes being with you. If you were going, he'd be more likely to come along and eat something. You could tell him how tasty it was. He likes to please you."

Michelle hesitated. Going to the soup kitchen would mean taking the chance of running into June if she were helping out. And Michelle didn't want anything to do with her, not even to see her. June serving at the soup kitchen seemed like such hypocrisy to Michelle. June had barely been able to put food into their mouths when they had lived with her. Whenever she could, she'd pushed the cooking onto Michelle.

Dan looked into the living room at George again. Michelle followed his gaze. George's head tilted to the side as he watched the television. He was looking thinner. And paler.

"Yeah, okay," she agreed. "If you want me to, I'll come along."

"I don't want soup kitchen food," George complained.

"What do you want, then?" Dan countered.

"I don't want anything."

"Well, you gotta eat something, so you're coming to the kitchen," Dan said firmly.

"I don't want to."

"Well, Michelle's going, aren't you Michelle?"

Michelle nodded. "Yeah, I'm going to come."

"Will you feed me?" George questioned.

Michelle and Dan exchanged glances. That was something new. Dan shrugged at her. It was up to Michelle, her decision.

"I guess," Michelle said finally, "if you'll go with us, I'll help you."

George nodded. "Then I'll go," he said smugly.

"You don't have to," Dan told Michelle quietly when they were alone a few minutes later.

"I told him I would." Michelle kept her promises.

"I don't know what's got into him." Dan sighed in exasperation. "He can feed himself."

"What's the doctor say?"

"No significant changes. Maybe not that their tests show, but something has changed. Something is worse."

"Maybe some good food will make him feel better."

Dan nodded. "Yeah. I think he needs to get out of the apartment, too. He was different before the accident... he used to like to go out and have fun. But he changed after that. I gotta fight to get him out now."

Michelle didn't say anything right away. In the car with George and Dan, she changed the direction of the discussion. "If you could see your folks again... would you?"

Dan pursed his lips. "Our folks abandoned us."

"I know. That's why I asked."

Dan glanced in the rear-view mirror at George, then back at Michelle. "Are we talking about your mama?"

"Yeah, I guess."

"I guess I'd ask them why they left."

"What if they left because they just didn't want to take care of you anymore?"

"I don't know. I can't imagine ever seeing them again."

Michelle nodded. "That's why I just can't figure out what to do or say. I never thought I'd see either of them again. I never wanted to see them again."

Dan shook his head. "The other Jags say your mom's cool, but I don't know her."

"She thinks since she got religion, I should forgive her."

"What do you think?"

Michelle took her time, mulling it over. "I think she must've loved us more than Justin did," she said. "At least she always wanted us back. But she was just too messed up to manage."

"Yeah?"

"She can't even take care of herself. She should never have had to take care of anyone else."

"Some people just can't handle it. My folks... I didn't think they were doing so badly, but I guess they hid their real feelings. I knew they weren't happy with the gang and all. I was wild, but they shoulda taken Georgie with 'em. *He* never caused them no trouble."

Michelle looked over her shoulder at George in the back seat and shrugged. She knew Dan's guilt. He wished they had taken George so Dan would never have hurt him. They got to the kitchen and stood in line thinking their own thoughts. Michelle stood behind George, rubbing his neck and shoulders. As they got up to the servers, Michelle saw June before June saw her. She watched June leaning over the steaming pots, capped, gowned, and gloved, her face shining with sweat. She was working hard, concentrating on the job. She talked to some of the people who came through the line. She didn't even see Michelle until Michelle was standing right in front of her.

"Michelle!"

"Hi, Mama."

June rested her spoon for a moment, looking Michelle over. "Are you okay?"

"Yeah. These are a couple of my friends." Michelle gestured to Dan and George, trying to get June's focus off of her.

"Jags?"

"Yeah, so?" Michelle challenged, expecting the lecture.

"I see lotsa them here," June said with a shrug. No accusations.

"Oh. Yeah. I guess I'll see you 'round."

They moved on. Dan looked around for a place to sit, and a couple of people who saw the wheelchair moved down the table a seat so Dan and Michelle could sit on the end with George. Dan nodded and thanked them. He put George's bowl and spoon in front of him. George tilted his head, looking at Michelle.

"Looks good today, huh?" Michelle said, picking up George's spoon and filling it. "Beef and barley."

George didn't say anything as she lifted it to his lips and put the first spoonful in his mouth. She got a lump in her throat that she had never gotten when feeding Marcie. She glanced at Dan. He was eating his soup, staring straight down into the bowl, not looking at Michelle and George.

"It's too hot," George complained.

Michelle took a smaller spoonful and blew on it before putting it in his mouth. "How's that, Georgie?"

"Yeah." He gave a wobbly nod.

Michelle continued to feed him. She took a couple of bites of her own meal between each spoonful she fed George. It was not long before George turned his head aside as Michelle moved the spoon toward him.

"No more."

"Have a bit more. That's not enough to keep you until supper."

"I'm full. Can't eat anymore."

"Just another bite?"

"No."

At least he had something good in his belly.

CHAPTER Forty-Four

It seemed that George asking to be spoon-fed was another symptom of his decline. He stopped feeding himself at all and seemed to be getting weaker by the day. It wasn't long before he was in hospital, with a tube down his throat. Michelle sat with him a lot of the time, sometimes with Dan and sometimes on her own when Dan needed a break.

As he neared the end, they took out the tube and just left him on IV fluids.

George gazed at Michelle, frowning. "I wish you knew me before." His voice was still hoarse from the feeding tube.

"Before what?" She knew even before he answered.

"Before I got like this—crippled and helpless." She thought he would stop there. He never said much other than to fuss about his discomfort. "I wasn't a tough like Dan. I wasn't any great jock… but I never realized what a great body I had…"

"I wish I'd known you then, too."

"You probably wouldn't have looked twice at me. But at least I coulda looked you in the eye." Michelle looked at him sadly. "I still hate Dan for this," George murmured.

"You love your brother."

"I gotta love him, he's my only kin. And he looks after me. But… I still hate him."

Michelle gently brushed his hair back from his face. "You look tired, honey."

A ghost of a smile flitted over George's lined, wan face, long unused to smiling. "I like it when you call me honey," he said. He closed his eyes. Michelle stroked his cheek tenderly until his breathing became long and even. She went out into the hall to breathe.

Dan was there, standing in the hall outside the door, his hollow eyes making him look lost. "Is he gone?"

"Not yet. He just went to sleep."

"I'm glad you're here." Dan hugged her and held tight for a long time. Michelle looked at Dan's face when they separated. He was still dry-eyed.

"Are you okay?" she asked softly, holding his gaze.

"It's killing me. I swear it's killing me, watching him die like this. Why couldn't he just have died the night of the accident? What was the point of him suffering for so long and then going like this?"

Michelle shook her head. "There's no point. It just happened."

"You don't believe in anything? God? Fate?"

"No."

Dan gazed at her, unblinking. "In AA, they teach us to put our lives in the hands of a higher power."

"You believe in God?" Michelle was a bit surprised by this.

"I believe in something. You don't have to call it God. But life doesn't make any sense otherwise."

"It's supposed to make sense?"

Dan smiled faintly and gave her a little squeeze. "Not always, maybe. But the big picture... yeah, it's supposed to make sense."

George groaned and Michelle jerked awake. "Are you okay?" she asked, blinking quickly to clear her eyes.

"I need more morphine."

Michelle punched the button on the IV machine, but it was already at the maximum dosage. "There, that should help," she lied, counting on the power of suggestion to ease his pain.

George stared straight up at the ceiling. Michelle looked for Dan. He was fast asleep in the other chair, his face lined with exhaustion.

"Would you hold my hand?" George requested. Michelle laced her fingers through his bony ones. "I'm glad you're here," George said.

Michelle nodded and squeezed his hand lightly. "Do you want me to wake Dan up?"

"No. Just you and me."

"You should go back to sleep until the pain passes," Michelle encouraged, stroking a lock of his hair.

"If I go to sleep…"

"Yeah?"

"I might not wake up."

She swallowed painfully. "Is that so bad?"

"No… waking up is the worst part."

"So go to sleep. Maybe you won't wake up this time." Tears prickled in her eyes.

He closed his eyes. "You know what?"

"What?"

"I'm glad I didn't die that night."

"You are?" Michelle was surprised.

"Yeah… I didn't use to be."

"What changed it?"

"You did." He squeezed her hand. It was barely a flutter against her palm. "I love you, Michelle."

"I love you too, honey," Michelle said gently, her throat hot and choked.

George's eyes remained shut. Gradually his breathing lengthened and faded away.

Dan woke up a while later. He walked over to the bed and looked down at George. "He's smiling."

Michelle nodded silently. There was just a hint of a smile on George's worn face.

"He went peacefully?"

"Yeah." Michelle swallowed, trying to keep the emotions from overwhelming her.

"Thanks for being here, Michelle."

"Sure. I wanted to be."

"I'll go talk to the doctor."

He was back a few minutes later with a grave-looking doctor, who checked for vital signs and looked at his watch before writing on George's chart. "He's at peace now," he said.

Michelle and Dan both nodded.

"Do you have an AA group that meets here?" Dan asked, his voice hoarse.

"Twice a day," the doctor answered, and looked at his watch, in spite of the fact he had just done so in order to record time of death. "You should be able to catch the afternoon session," he advised. "Room 306, next to the chapel."

"Thanks."

"You're going right now?" Michelle asked in disbelief, gesturing at George's bed.

Dan tried to clear his throat. "If I don't go now, I'm going on a bender I may never come back from."

"Oh."

"Will you come along?"

Michelle shook her head. "No, I'll stay here."

"Okay... I'll see you in a bit." Dan paused looking back. "I just don't understand why he had to suffer."

CHAPTER Forty-Five

Michelle waited impatiently for Dan. He was spending almost all his time since George had died at AA meetings. She knew better than to complain about it, but she was still irritated.

People stopped coming out of the meeting room and Michelle looked in the door to see where Dan was. He was deep in conversation with a huge, bearded, tattooed man who looked like a biker. Eventually, Dan noticed Michelle standing there and motioned for her to join him.

"Michelle, this is Steve. He coordinates speakers at the schools, about drinking and drugs and all."

"Hi."

"Nice to meetcha, Michelle," Steve said politely.

"Yeah."

"Think about it, okay Dan?" Steve said, and left them alone.

"Sorry to be so long," Dan apologized. "I didn't mean to keep you waiting."

"Yeah." Michelle motioned in the direction Steve had gone. "Are you really serious about that?"

"Talking to kids? Yeah, I am. If I can prevent another kid from being hurt like George…? Maybe I can make up for what I did."

"Don't you think you have made up for it already? Taking care of him as long as you did?"

"That's not making it right. That's just taking responsibility for the consequences."

Michelle shrugged. "Whatever."

"Maybe this is why George lived as long as he did. So I could explain it to younger kids. What drinking and driving can do, even if you don't kill yourself or someone else."

"Yeah. Maybe."

∼

Michelle sat in Ruby's kitchen, sitting backward in one of the kitchen chairs with her chin resting on the back. She watched Ruby putter about, making supper.

"Do you believe in God?" Michelle questioned abruptly.

"God? I don't know, Michelle. I think things like that are beyond our comprehension. I don't believe in God the way June does."

"What do you believe in?"

"Umm, order in the universe. Extra strength when we need it. That right and wrong exist outside of law or religion."

"Do you believe in fate? That things are meant to happen?"

"I believe we're allowed to make our own choices; we're not just puppets in some god's play."

"But is there a master plan? Do things happen for a reason?"

Ruby frowned. "Things like what? Like Charlie busting me years ago when we first met? And us getting Sheree back?"

"Yeah. And Justin, June, Kenny, and me all ending up here, together, is that just chance? Coincidence?"

"What do you think?"

Michelle thought about it for a long time. She couldn't face it. She couldn't admit it.

"I think it happened for a reason," she admitted finally. "I think it's a second chance for our family."

"Then what are you going to do about it?" Ruby prodded.

"I don't know. I guess maybe I wait for Mama to get home."

Ruby smiled, turning back to her cooking. "She should be here in a few minutes."

∼

When June got in, she walked unsuspectingly into the kitchen to talk to Ruby. She froze when she saw Michelle sitting there. Her eyes darted around the room, looking at Ruby, looking at her escape routes, and eventually, dragging her gaze back to Michelle.

"Hi," she said in a small voice.

"Hi."

"Um... it's nice to see you. How are you doing?"

Ruby turned back to her cooking, leaving Michelle and June to try to sort out the stilted conversation.

"I'm fine," Michelle said. She studied June's face. June had a smile on her face, but it seemed stiff and unnatural. Her eyes were wide. Michelle had seen this level of anxiety before. The only things that would bring June back down were drugs or Justin getting home from a job. "How are you?"

June wrung her hands, still smiling that broad, false smile. "Things are going really good, Michelle." Michelle's name sounded awkward and unnatural on her lips. Michelle had grown so used to the name-calling and cursing, it was sort of a surprise June even knew what her name was anymore. June's lips returned to the awkward smile. "Work. Work is going well. I like working with JoAnne."

"How'd you get that job?"

June breathed out. She looked around the kitchen and Michelle wondered if she would sit down. Instead, June bounced a little on her toes and rolled her shoulders. "Umm... the job..." She looked at Ruby as if she didn't know what to say, but Ruby didn't chime in. "I... through a priest. He knows people. Helps ex-cons out sometimes."

"That's nice of him."

June shrugged and nodded jerkily. "Yeah. He's a good guy. Like Jesus would have been."

Her words hit Michelle like a fist. The only time she'd ever heard June use His name was when swearing and cursing at the top of her lungs. To hear June use it reverently and in a quiet conversation now only made the situation seem that much more fake and precarious. Like they were standing at the top of a cliff staring down, and one breath would topple Michelle off the edge. June being brainwashed by some street ministry preacher didn't make Michelle feel safe.

Michelle stood up abruptly. June shot backward, her hands going up defensively. Something tightened in her face and Michelle saw the old shadows there. June pushed to the brink, her fists clenching, ready to take it out on Michelle. Michelle found her hand on her dagger, slippery with sweat. They both stared at each other, faces and bodies tense, ready for violence.

"Thanks for stopping by, Michelle," Ruby said cheerily, taking one step toward them. "You'll come back again? We should plan on dinner together one of these days. Just something casual. Pizza and chips."

Michelle took her cue and backed toward the door. The three of them watched each other, analyzing every movement, every shift in gaze.

"Yeah," Michelle agreed. "Sometime." She found the doorknob behind her and twisted it. She stepped out the door, turning as she went and slammed the door shut again behind her. She stood there for a minute on the front steps, her heart pounding wildly. She was no longer sure this was such a good idea. Why would she put herself back in harm's way? Why voluntarily open herself up to further abuse by June?

"You up-to-date on all your meds?" Ruby's forced-casual voice carried out through the open kitchen window as she spoke to June.

"Yeah, of course," June's words were sharp, grating on Michelle's ears. "Why?"

"You seem pretty wound up... Some of those pills you take are for anxiety, right?"

Michelle flashed back to a memory of Justin coming home, carefully counting out pills and dividing them into little sectioned pillboxes to make sure June was taking everything she was supposed to. Getting them renewed if they were going to run out before he got back from his next trip. But somehow, June always messed them up anyway, taking too many pills one day, refusing to take any on others, until her behavior spun out of control.

"I didn't know she was going to be here," June snapped. "I wasn't prepared for it. That's all. I don't know what to say to her. She hates me."

"Michelle has had a pretty tough life. You're going to have to be patient and give her time to get used to the idea of you being around."

"I know I wrecked her life. It wasn't all roses for me, either."

Michelle bristled, even though she knew the words weren't meant for her ears. They both thought she was gone. What right did June have to complain about her life? She was the one who had made all the choices. She was the only one who could be held responsible for whatever kind of a mess she found herself in now. June blaming her sucky life on an eight-year-old girl was absurd.

Michelle fought the urge to storm back into the house and have it out with June. That wouldn't be fair. They hadn't meant Michelle to hear. Michelle forced herself to walk quietly away from the house so they wouldn't hear her footsteps as she left for real.

"You had your own problems to deal with," she heard Ruby say. "You're going to need to work on those if you're going to sort things out with Michelle."

∼

When Charlie got home, everything was quiet. June had gone to bed and Ruby was sitting up in bed, leafing through a magazine and watching a late night talk show on the little TV in their bedroom.

"Hi, sweetie," Charlie greeted, bending down to kiss her before getting changed. "How was your day?"

Ruby shut the magazine and laid it aside. "Well, it was interesting," she said, with a good-humored laugh.

"Oh? What happened? Everything okay with Sheree?"

Ruby nodded. "Everything's fine with her last I heard. But we just about had fireworks here."

"Fireworks with..." Charlie nodded his head toward the spare room June now occupied, "our guest?"

"Yeah. Michelle decided to come by. Which is really good, of course. She's opening up to the idea of maybe working things out with June."

Charlie sat on the edge of the bed while he undressed, nodding for her to go on. "So she and June had a little discussion?"

"June wasn't expecting Michelle to be here, so she was taken off-guard. The tension was so thick you could cut it with a knife."

"June didn't try to hit Michelle, did she?"

"You forget Michelle's not a little girl anymore. They're on equal footing now. In fact, Michelle's probably in better shape physically than any of us." Ruby shook her head, laughing softly, making sure not be loud enough to disturb June. Though June had taken tranquilizers before bed and probably wouldn't be awakened by an earthquake. "You should have seen the three of us gang chicks facing off, Charlie. Oh, my."

Charlie got a funny look on his face.

Ruby laughed at his expression. "I may be retired from gang life, but the old habits are still there, like muscle memory. Someone puts up their fists or goes for a knife, and I'm fighting beside the Jags all over again."

"Michelle went for her dagger?"

"A reflex. She didn't pull it out, just grabbed for it. I thought I was going to have to get between the two of them."

"Mmm. You'd better not if she's holding a knife. Just stay well out of the way."

"I'm not going to put myself in danger."

Charlie nodded. "You make sure you don't... Sounds like maybe we'd better plan any future reunions ahead. Make sure everyone knows what's going on and that I can be here to keep an eye on things."

"I could handle it. But I agree... we should make sure everyone is prepared next time. No more accidental confrontations."

CHAPTER
Forty-Six

Michelle was exhausted when she got home. In spite of the doctor's assurance her new prescription would be starting to kick in to eliminate the depression, she still saw no end to the dark tunnel that stretched out ahead and behind her, offering no escape. The apartment seemed quiet and empty. She looked around. Kenny was slumped in front of the TV, his eyes distant and unfocused. She wasn't sure whether he was actually seeing what was on the television program or was just lost in his own world somewhere else.

Tanner came out of the bathroom. "Hey, Michelle. How's it going?" His voice was casual, but his eyes were sharp and demanding, looking her over. Evaluating her. Michelle looked away.

"Great. Where's Dan?"

"Dunno. Out at one of his do's, I guess," he made a twirling motion with his upraised index finger like it was a dance or party. "Pretty soon he's going to have us calling him Professor."

Michelle rolled her eyes. "Is he gonna be back so we can get out somewhere tonight?"

"Do I look like his social secretary? You would know more than I would. What did he tell you?"

Michelle thought back. Dan went on endlessly about which schools and events he was lecturing at, and on top of that, he attended countless AA meetings to maintain his own sobriety. She didn't even try to keep track of all his engagements. In fact, as soon as he started talking about them, she tuned him out.

"I dunno. I don't really listen." Michelle went to the fridge to look for anything good she could scavenge. "What are the Jags doing tonight? I don't want to be stuck at home."

It was so quiet she could hardly stand it. It wasn't like Carter and George and Dan had made all that much noise. But without them, the apartment felt like a black hole. She closed the fridge without finding anything to eat and leaned her head against the door.

"You and me and Kenny can go out," Tanner assured her. "Just like old times. If any of the Jags want to come, the more, the merrier. But I'm not waiting for Professor Dan to provide the entertainment. What do you want to do?"

Michelle paced across the kitchen and living room of the apartment restlessly. "Kenny, you want to go out?"

Kenny didn't raise his head to look at her. "Yeah, sure."

"What do you want to do?"

"Fight."

Michelle supposed she shouldn't be surprised. Kenny's strengths were all physical. He liked to be out doing something, he liked the action. Physical confrontation. That's what he was good at.

"Well... I guess we can go look for some action," she agreed.

Kenny looked up from the TV. "Now?"

"In a while. I just... need to lie down for a few minutes first."

Kenny grunted and his eyes returned to the television. Michelle looked toward her bedroom. She knew lying down wasn't going to cure the stretched-out weariness she felt. In fact, she probably wouldn't even be able to lie still, much less get any sleep. Even the sleep that eventually took her each morning in the gray light of dawn wouldn't make her feel any better. She walked down to her door anyway. Tanner shadowed her. She looked at him as they stood in her open doorway.

"I'll leave the door open," she promised.

"Why don't I come lay down with you?"

Michelle gave him a faint smile. "Tanner, we're not—"

"I know. I won't try nothin'. I'll just... hold you."

He couldn't know how appealing that sounded. Michelle had no desire for a serious relationship with anyone, including Tanner, but just to be held...

Michelle couldn't find a good excuse to say no. Tanner touched her arm and walked her into the room. They lay down on the mattress, and before Michelle could make herself comfortable on the pillow, Tanner pulled her face into his chest and held her in a close embrace. Michelle felt her body melt into his instead of tensing and resisting. Tanner rubbed her on the back and kissed the hair on the crown of her head.

"Just rest," he murmured. "Don't worry about anything. Just relax. I'll look after you."

Michelle didn't know she had fallen asleep until she woke up. Tanner's arms shifted infinitesimally, and his head lifted from where it had nestled above hers. Michelle forced her eyes open. Tanner's arms were probably asleep. He would be cramped after holding her for so long. There were noises in the apartment. Kenny getting a beer from the fridge, then coming down the hall to see if Michelle and Tanner were ready to go yet.

But it wasn't Kenny, it was Dan. And of course, it wasn't a beer can he held in his hand, but a soft drink. He looked into the bedroom, leaning up against the doorframe and blinking at them. Michelle felt Tanner's body go tense. She stirred, pulling back from him.

"I was just trying to catch a few zees," Michelle told Dan.

"Good. You've been looking tired lately."

Tanner let out a small, pent-up sigh only Michelle was close enough to hear. He got smoothly to his feet. "You thirsty, Michelle? I could use a cold drink myself."

"Uh, yeah. Sure."

He walked past Dan. Michelle was almost surprised Tanner didn't shoulder-check Dan as he moved past him. The tension between Dan and Tanner was thick. Michelle wasn't sure why. She and Dan had never had anything but a casual, friendly relationship. There was no reason she should feel embarrassed by him finding Michelle and Tanner sleeping together.

"You don't have to start up with Tanner again," Dan observed in a low voice when Tanner was in the kitchen. "Just tell him no. Kick him to the curb."

Michelle shook her head. "It's nothing. He was just helping me calm down. Being a friend."

Dan took a sip of his pop, studying her. Tanner returned and handed Michelle a drink as she got to her feet. She realized as she pulled the tab that he had gotten her beer. She looked at Dan awkwardly. She felt like she should apologize for drinking in front of him. They all did it all the time, but she felt uncomfortable. She gave him a little shrug and took a sip.

∼

They congregated in the living room, the tension between the boys still strong.

"We going out?" Kenny asked.

"Yeah," Michelle agreed. At Dan's questioning look, she filled him in. "Looking for some action. You know if any of the Jags are doing anything tonight?"

"Probably. I haven't been able to keep track lately."

"Too busy with your lectures, Professor?" Tanner needled.

Dan turned his eyes to Tanner as if seeing him for the first time. Tanner was catching up with Dan in size, but he still hadn't climbed very far in the ranks of the Jags. He was still too undisciplined; unschooled. But he faced Dan boldly, a smirk on his face.

"You got a problem, Tanner?" Dan demanded.

"I got no problem," Tanner said breezily. "I'm not the one getting too old and respectable to run with the Jags."

Dan snorted in amusement. But even as he did, his hand shot out, landing an open-palmed slap across the side of Tanner's head and face with a crack that echoed through the apartment like a gunshot. Tanner didn't even see it coming. His head snapped to the side and he was thrown back into the wall behind him. Dan grabbed him by the front of the shirt, twisting his hand into it so it strangled Tanner's breathing. He pinned Tanner back against the wall. Michelle blinked, surprised Tanner wasn't even struggling, until she noticed the gun in Dan's other hand, the first few inches of the barrel pressed into Tanner's soft belly.

"There's no danger of *you* getting too old and respectable," Dan said in a low, threatening growl. "You ain't gonna survive long enough, yapping like an untrained pup. Do I need a choke chain to put an end to the yapping?" He twisted the shirt tighter.

Tanner's face was turning purple. Michelle wasn't sure if it was because he was angry or because his breathing was cut off by Dan's grip. Tanner gave his head a couple of quick, tight shakes in response to Dan's question.

Michelle was stunned by the crash when Kenny busted a bottle over Dan's head. Dan released Tanner, crumpling to the floor. Michelle tried to catch Dan. "Kenny!" she gasped in horror.

Tanner grabbed Kenny's sleeve. "Come on."

Kenny hovered over Dan, waiting for him to bounce back up, to fight back. Michelle touched the gash in Dan's head, unsure what to do. She looked at Kenny, bewildered. "What'd you do that for?"

Kenny just stared back at her, his eyes dark and angry. Tanner continued to pull on Kenny's arm. "Kenny, man! We gotta get out of here. Come on."

Dan started to move sluggishly. He moved his head back and forth and brought his hands up to feel the injury.

"Now!" Tanner ordered.

Kenny finally heeded his friend. Michelle didn't watch them leave. "Dan. Are you okay?" She swore under her breath. "I can't believe he did that! Dan!"

Dan groaned. His fingers were bloody as he groped at the gashes and growing lump on his head. "What the hell...?"

"I'm sorry. It was Kenny. I don't know why he did that. Are you okay?"

Dan swore. "Is it deep? Does it need stitches? Scalp wounds always bleed like a—"

"It's deep," Michelle confirmed. "Can you get up? Should I get an ambulance?"

He was wobbly getting to his feet. His hands were shaking. Michelle knew he was getting blood on her as he leaned against her for support. She put her arm around his waist. "Are you okay? Are you going to stay up?"

"Yeah. Just go slow."

Michelle was thankful George's needs had dictated a ground-floor apartment. Stairs would have been impossible to navigate. She took Dan to his car and guided him into the passenger seat. His eyes were rolling back as she tucked his feet into the car. She pulled the seatbelt across him and buckled it to keep him upright.

"Stay with me, Danny," she encouraged. She shut the door and hurried around to the driver's side. Michelle turned the key he always left in the ignition and pulled out.

She had a learner's permit, but she hadn't done a lot of practice driving. They usually either footed it or took the bus. Dan was one of the only Jags with his own car. A couple had motorcycles. Michelle glanced at Dan nervously as she pulled out. While technically she did have the holder of a full driver's license in the car, a passed-out supervisor probably didn't count as far as the law was concerned. She adjusted her seat and mirrors as she drove and ignored the honks and beeps of irritated drivers around her as she cut people off, ran stop signs, and generally drove erratically. She kept glancing at Dan to make sure he was still breathing.

Michelle didn't make it to the hospital before she heard the siren. She looked in her mirror, hoping it was an ambulance she could allow to pass her and then follow in its wake to the emergency room. But she wasn't so lucky. It was a police car. Michelle kept going, hoping he was after someone else. But he dogged her and honked his horn a few times and she finally pulled over.

The squad car pulled in behind her. Michelle waited impatiently while the cop sat there, tapped information into his car computer, and eventually climbed out of the car and approached, checking out the car's tags and lights as he ambled up. He leaned down to talk to her, one hand on his gun at his hip. Michelle kept her hands high up on the steering wheel where he'd be able to see them.

"Are you even old enough to drive?" the cop demanded.

Michelle swallowed. "My friend is hurt," she said. "I'm taking him to the hospital."

He leaned down further, looking across her to Dan. He swore at the sight of all the blood. "What happened?"

"He got jumped. Hit over the head with a bottle."

"Is he conscious?" The officer raised his voice. "Can you hear me, sir?"

"He was, but not since he got in the car. I'm sorry, I'm not a very good driver…"

"No, you're not," he agreed. He looked at the road ahead of him, probably calculating how far the hospital was and how long it would take to get Dan there. "I'm going to call for an ambulance. Sit tight."

He turned his back on her and talked on his phone. Michelle reached for Dan's hand and gave it an encouraging squeeze.

"We'll get you fixed up soon. Hang in there."

It was only a few minutes before the ambulance pulled up, and the paramedics came to the car to evaluate Dan. "Can you tell us what happened?" one of them, a woman with dark blond hair, asked, as she opened the door and leaned over Dan.

"Got hit with a bottle."

"How long ago?"

"Not long, just a few minutes."

"How long has he been unconscious?"

"He was knocked out, but then he came to again, he got into the car, but then he passed out again. Ten minutes maybe."

They made a cursory examination and transferred him from the car to a gurney. Michelle watched them swathe Dan's head with bandages. They prepared to transport him. The cop was back at Michelle's side again.

"Whose car is this?"

"His."

"I obviously can't let you drive it away from here. Is there someone you could call who could come and get it?"

Michelle thought about the Jags, but none of them were going to be excited about having to talk to the police to collect Dan's car. "Maybe… my aunt."

"Does she have a license?"

Michelle nodded. "Yeah, sure."

"You got a phone?"

"No."

"Do you know her number?"

"Yeah."

He handed her his phone and Michelle carefully tapped in Ruby's number. Hopefully, Ruby wouldn't be out doing something she couldn't leave. Ruby answered after a few rings.

"Hello?"

"It's Michelle."

"Oh. What's up, Michelle?"

"I need some help..." Ruby didn't jump in demanding to know the details. Michelle tried to sort it out. "I need someone to come get my friend's car. I was... I was driving him to the hospital, but the cops won't let me drive it home."

Ruby didn't say anything at first. "I'll have to get a ride there, so I might be a bit. Where are you, exactly?"

Michelle looked at the street signs and told her.

"I'll get there as soon as I can. How is your friend?"

"I don't know. The ambulance is here to take him in."

"Good. Is it Tanner? It's not Kenny, right?"

"No. Dan."

"I'm sorry he's hurt. Are *you* okay?"

"I'm fine." Michelle pushed back her hair, and looked at her hand, smeared with blood. She looked at her shoulder, where Dan had been leaning against her while she walked him to the car. She was a mess. "I'm not hurt."

"I'll be there as soon as I can."

"Thanks."

Michelle hung up the call and handed it back to the policeman. "She says she'll come. She has to get someone to drop her off."

He nodded and pulled out a computer tablet. "Why don't you tell me what happened?" he said, tapping a few screens. "Give me your name and address first."

She gave him her information and watched the ambulance pull away with Dan. The cop insisted on seeing her identification. He squinted at her picture, looking back up at her face. "You change your hair color often?"

"Yeah." Michelle felt her face get warm.

"What's your friend's name?"

"Dan Thompson."

"Address?"

"Same as mine."

His eyes lingered on her for a minute and he pursed his lips. "He your boyfriend?"

"No. We just room together."

"He could get in trouble, you being under sixteen."

"We're not. Just friends."

He asked for the insurance and registration papers. Michelle went through the glove box and visor pockets to find everything. She looked out at the street, wishing Ruby would get there so Michelle could get to the hospital to see Dan.

"Why don't you tell me what happened? How did Dan get hurt?"

Michelle swallowed. She knew better than to tell him what had really happened. "We were just out. Grabbing a smoke, you know? And this guy, he must have been drunk, just came at him..."

The cop raised his eyebrows.

"What?" Michelle demanded.

"Describe this drunk guy."

"Uh... tall, kind of skinny. Black. He had on a cap..."

"Yeah? That's the story you're going to go with? Some black dude?"

Michelle squirmed under his gaze. "Well, yeah... that's what happened."

"What gang are you two in?" When Michelle didn't respond immediately, he leaned in closer, putting his weight on the car. "It's obvious you're bangers. So which one?"

"Jags."

"Did you get into an altercation with one of the other gangs? Or maybe just another one of the Jags? What was it?"

"I told you already."

"You got quite a bit of blood on yourself." He shifted back and forth, studying her face. Looking for any other clues. "Maybe you got in an argument and you hit him. Is that what happened?"

"No! I'd never hit Dan! He's my... my friend! It was someone else. Some crazy guy."

"I guess we'd better get you downtown looking at photos, see if you can identify him."

Michelle looked for Ruby. She wanted to get to the hospital to see Dan. And to get away from the questions.

"Why don't you start telling me the truth?" the cop persisted.

"I am. So you don't believe me. What else is new? I just want to get to the hospital to make sure he's okay."

The officer's expression softened. "He didn't look too bad," he said. "Head wounds always bleed a lot. The blood vessels are close to the surface. They'll get him patched up in no time. He might have a concussion from the blow, but he's probably suffered worse injuries in the past. By the time you get there, he'll be sitting up eating his dinner."

Michelle nodded, hoping it was true. "He lectures at the schools for AA," she told him. "He's not just a banger. He's really... he really cares about people." Her throat got hot and her eyes started to prickle. She looked away from the police officer, blinking to clear her misty eyes. He didn't say anything while she got herself composed again.

A cab pulled up and Ruby climbed out. She hurried over to them. "Michelle, are you okay?"

Michelle nodded, unable to use her voice yet.

Ruby looked at the cop. "Simon. How are you? Has she been cooperating?"

He looked startled to recognize Ruby. "Other than the old 'some black dude' story," he said, giving Ruby a knowing smile. "She hasn't given me any attitude."

"Michelle is my niece. My baby sister's daughter. Are you done? Can I take her to the hospital?"

Officer Simon studied Michelle. "It would be better if you told me the real story, instead of this con," he advised. "Things happen, I get it. Especially when you're in a gang or when there's alcohol involved..."

"Alcohol? Who said anything about alcohol?"

"You smell like beer, Michelle," Ruby said. "Did he give you a breathalyzer?"

Michelle shook her head and looked at the policeman. "I'm not drunk! I'll give you a breath sample!"

The officer spoke to Ruby rather than Michelle. "I've been watching her. She doesn't show any signs of being under the influence. The boy got hit over the head with a bottle. If it wasn't empty, the two of them might have gotten it on their clothes."

And Michelle had been holding a full can of beer before the fight. She couldn't remember what had happened to it. She ducked her head closer to her chest and sniffed. A good amount of it had soaked into her clothes.

"I'm not drunk," she repeated. "If you think I am, you can test me."

"I said I don't think you are. If that's the story you're sticking too, sign right here." He turned the tablet around and Michelle read the brief description he had typed in. He gave her a stylus and she signed it. "All right. Next time something like this happens, call nine-one-one. Don't drive. You're lucky I don't feel like writing you up for traffic violations, or you'd have so many demerits you'd never get your license. Understood? Practice on some quiet streets and don't drive when you're upset or your supervisor is unconscious. Got it?"

Michelle nodded throughout his lecture. "Yes, sir."

Ruby took a step closer. Michelle got out of the car and went around to the passenger door. Ruby got in and adjusted the seat and mirrors, then put on her seatbelt. "Buckle up, kiddo."

Michelle did. She looked up to find Ruby watching her closely. "What?"

Ruby shook her head. Michelle followed her gaze to the headrest behind Michelle, drenched in blood. Michelle swallowed, her eyes again hot with tears.

"Let's get you to the hospital," Ruby said quietly. She didn't ask Michelle to explain anything. Ruby gave Officer Simon a little wave, shut her door and pulled out into traffic.

Michelle probably should have guessed they wouldn't let her right in to see Dan. Hospitals were full of rules and bureaucracy and they never seemed to work in her favor. Michelle sat in the waiting room, both bored and anxious. People kept looking at her and Ruby eventually suggested Michelle use the restroom to clean herself up. Michelle did her best, but Dan's blood was all over her.

As she walked back out to the waiting area, she saw Dr. Boniface, one of the doctors she knew from George's care at the hospital.

"Michelle?" He stopped to talk to her, his eyes flicking over her clothes, which she hadn't been able to get the bloodstains out of. "I thought I saw Dan's name up on the board. What happened?"

"He got hit over the head. They won't let me in to see him."

"Why don't we see what we can do about that?" he offered.

He put his hand behind her back and escorted her into the treatment area, expertly navigating the curtains around the clustered units. He pushed one open, and there was Dan. Dan wasn't awake, as the cop had suggested he would be. He'd been changed into hospital garb, had an IV in his arm, and his head was bandaged up. Boniface grabbed the clipboard at the foot of Dan's bed and looked it over.

"He's been unconscious since he was brought in. Since shortly after the attack. You probably already know that. They've sutured the lacerations and have ordered some imaging to check for any brain swelling or intracranial bleeding. That means—"

"Concussion or bleeding inside his skull," Michelle supplied.

He smiled. "You get an A-plus. Dan's going to need to rest up for a while, but he'll probably be fine. He'll wake up with one heck of a headache. You want to sit with him?"

Michelle nodded.

"Of course," he agreed. "Do you know if the police have been informed?"

"I just finished talking to them."

"Good. I'll try to check back in later, but I might not be able to. Take care, okay?"

"Yeah."

"You don't have any injuries, do you? This is all just Dan's blood?"

"Uh-huh."

"Good. See you later, then."

Michelle sat down in the chair beside the bed and watched Dan, waiting for some sign of change.

After a while, Ruby appeared beside Michelle. She looked down at Dan. "He's a good-looking boy," she commented.

Michelle looked at Dan's pale face. Most of his dark hair was covered by the bandages. It was shorter than it had been when they had met, what seemed like ages ago when Tanner's gang had joined up with Dan's. Michelle couldn't believe how young and naive she had been at the time. She couldn't help smiling, remembering the first piercings, tattoo, and pair of leather pants. Talk about a makeover.

MICHELLE

When she looked at Dan, she didn't see a Jag or a banger. Not even a recovering addict. She just saw Dan. Her friend. Michelle was still holding his hand and she gave it another squeeze.

"Yeah. He's a nice guy," she said.

Ruby pulled over a chair from behind another curtain and sat down. "So what happened?"

"Like I told the cop. He got jumped by some crazy guy."

Ruby gazed at Michelle. "The number of times that happened when I was on the street..."

"So maybe it never happened to you, but it does happen," Michelle maintained.

"Okay. So... how's Kenny? I haven't seen him for a while."

Michelle glanced at Ruby, wondering if she had guessed at more than she let on. "Kenny's good."

"You two should come over for supper one day soon. Why don't we set something up?"

Michelle shrugged. "I'll have to talk to him."

"We could try for Friday night. Except I suppose Friday night is probably busy for the Jags. Thursday?"

"I don't know. I'll talk to Kenny."

"June would be there," Ruby warned.

"Yeah, okay... I dunno if I can get Kenny to come if she's gonna be there."

"He was okay with seeing Justin."

"Yeah, and maybe he'd be okay with Mama. I don't know how much he remembers about her since the overdose. But before... when we were supposed to be living with her, he wouldn't go anywhere near there. I went back sometimes to check on Mama, make sure she had food," Michelle swallowed, a lump hurting her throat. "But Kenny..." She shook her head. "Not Kenny. She used to beat him pretty bad, before, when we were little kids."

Ruby's eyes were sad. She shook her head. "I wish I could change the past. But none of us can."

"I know. I said I'd try to be a family again. And I will. But..."

"You can't control Kenny and it's all going to take time. I'm not trying to push you into anything you're not ready for. One day at a time."

Michelle looked at Dan again. "Okay." As she watched him, his head ticked to the side slightly. "Hey, Dan... are you awake? Hey..."

His eyes squinched closed more tightly before he opened them, squinting at her through a tiny slit. "Michelle?"

"Hi. About time you woke up."

Dan groaned and put his hand up to his bandaged head, prodding it tenderly. "They sew me up?"

"Yeah. They still gotta take a look inside. See if you got anything in there other than rocks," she teased.

"Not much," he grunted.

"This is my aunt, Ruby," Michelle said, indicating her. "You know, the one who married the cop. I told her about the guy that jumped you."

Ruby quirked a smile at her. "Smooth, Michelle."

Michelle started to sweat in the overly warm hospital room. She turned her gaze away from Ruby, focusing on Dan's face.

"I don't even remember what happened," Dan said. He closed his eyes again.

Michelle exhaled slowly, relieved. Not only would he not be able to give anything away to Ruby or the police to contradict Michelle's story, but he wouldn't know it was Kenny who had hurt him. She could still get Kenny to come back home... once she'd sorted out where he and Tanner had gone.

CHAPTER
Forty-Seven

Dan was still in and out of consciousness, so the hospital didn't want to release him. But they also informed Michelle that visiting hours were over. She wasn't allowed to stay with him overnight since she wasn't family. No amount of arguing that Dan didn't have any family to stay with him made any difference. They didn't care if there was no one to sit with him. He would just be sleeping anyway.

Ruby offered that Michelle could go back home with her and stay at her house, but Michelle shook her head. She didn't want to have to see June again so soon, and she needed to sort out what was happening with Tanner and Kenny. The whole thing just baffled her. Ruby offered to drop her somewhere and Michelle finally selected a street corner that was by the old apartment with Butch and Clyde.

When they got there, Ruby cast a quick look around before nodding. "Better get inside, you don't want to be out here alone this time of the day."

Michelle studied Ruby before getting out. This wasn't a social worker or cop telling her to stay off the streets, it was a former Jag. "Was this in Jags territory when you were with them?"

"Sometimes. But too close to the boundary to be safe. More of a no-man's-land because it changed sides so often." Ruby took another glance down the street and Michelle could see the muscles in her jaw clenching, even though she kept her voice casual. "Some bad stuff happened around here. Stay with others. Don't be alone."

"Yeah, I will."

Michelle got out of the car and readjusted her dagger at her side. Just talking about how this had once been a dangerous area made her anxious. Ruby stayed where she was, watching Michelle, until Michelle was through the lobby doors of the building. Then she pulled out. Michelle went up to Clyde's apartment.

∽

"What is this, Grand Central?" Clyde complained when Michelle walked in and joined the group. "You know you don't live here anymore, right?"

Michelle looked at him with half-lowered lids. "I thought maybe I'd move back," she dead-panned.

Clyde had to look at her twice before he was sure she was joking. He grinned and shook his head. Michelle looked around to see who else was there. A few of the older Jags were, along with Tanner and Kenny.

"Michelle!" it was Tanner who noticed her first. "Hey!" He got up and walked over to her, giving her a rough hug. He smelled strongly of not just beer, but something stronger and sharper too. Maybe whiskey. "How are you? Are you okay?"

"I'm fine," Michelle said, pulling away from him. He had a black eye and a split on his cheek where Dan had hit him. "What the hell was all that about? You pick a fight with Dan, and Kenny hits him with a bottle?" She looked at Tanner and over at Kenny suspiciously. "Was that all a set-up, or what?"

The other conversations around them ceased as everyone listened in on the conversation, exchanging covert glances.

"A set-up?" Tanner repeated. He snorted. "What are you talking about? Dan was gettin' on my case for no reason. Kenny was just helpin' out a friend. Maybe got a bit carried away. Is Danny okay?"

Michelle didn't believe the innocent act one bit. She shot him a look. "He's still in hospital," she said.

"Is Dan gonna be all right?" Clyde asked, butting in.

Michelle glanced at him and nodded. "Yeah. He'll be okay." She turned back toward Tanner. "And you'd better get your story straight before he gets out."

"I didn't touch him, he came after me."

"How much have you had to drink?" she asked, wrinkling her nose and taking a step back from him. "Are you *that* scared of him coming after you?"

Tanner didn't take the bait. Instead, he leaned in closer to her, dropping his voice to a confidential tone, still loud enough for everyone in the place to hear him. "You know why he attacked me, don't you? It's because he's so jealous about you."

Michelle laughed. "Dan? Jealous? He barely even knows I exist these days."

"Why do you think he came for me after we were sleeping together?"

This garnered some interest from the other Jags. "Wait, are you guys back together again?"

Michelle waved off their inquiries, flapping her hand and shaking her head. "No, no. We just laid down for a nap, so we'd be fresh to go out tonight. You know that," she directed this at Tanner. "And Dan knew that. He could tell there'd been nothing going on! He wasn't jealous. You were just mouthing off. Disrespecting him. That's why he went after you."

Tanner raised an eyebrow, telegraphing his disbelief to the other boys. "Yeah, that's right. He just tried to throttle me because he thought I was being mouthy."

Michelle looked at Kenny, trying to get him into the conversation. "You tell them, Kenny. It wasn't anything to do with me! And what did you clobber him for, anyway? You coulda killed him, smashed in his skull!"

Kenny returned a self-satisfied smile. He liked to be thought of as tough. It was good for his rep.

"Tell them Dan wasn't jealous," Michelle insisted.

Kenny's eyes turned slowly to her. "Dan's always had eyes for you."

Michelle swore. "Don't say that! It's not true! Do you even remember when we met Dan?"

She saw his close, guarded look. "He's always liked you," he repeated firmly.

"You don't remember. Is that what Tanner's telling you? Are you trying to put things in his head?" Michelle looked back and forth between Tanner and Kenny. Neither one was going to give anything away. But Michelle knew those weren't Kenny's words. 'Always had eyes for you?' Kenny didn't talk that way.

Tanner could be exasperating. *He* was the one who had always had his eye on Michelle. Even having gotten together and broken up, he still wouldn't leave her alone. But in spite of it all, in spite of his animosity toward Dan, Tanner was Michelle's protector and she couldn't just write him off. He'd helped her through tough times. Held her when she just needed to be held.

"Let's go home," Michelle said to Kenny, suddenly drained.

Kenny shook his head. He turned and looked at Tanner for validation. Tanner folded his arms across his chest. "We ain't goin' back. Neither of us."

"Because of Dan? He'll just come here."

"We won't be here either."

"Where, then?"

"I tell you and you send Dan after me? I don't think so."

"I'm not going to send anyone after you. Kenny's my brother. I gotta know where he is. I look after him!"

Tanner raised his brows. "Do you? I don't think so. Not anymore. You've forgotten all about Kenny. I been looking after him while you've been mooning after Carter and spending all your time with Dan and Wheels, before Wheels kicked it."

Michelle turned her face away from him, guilt tying a knot in her stomach. She knew it was true. She'd been so caught up in all her own emotional stuff she'd hardly paid any attention to Kenny. It had been a relief to have someone else dealing with that. She hadn't even seen what was going on under her own nose. That was her fault. She was responsible.

"Kenny, please? Come on. Come home with me."

Kenny shook his head stubbornly.

"You have to tell me where you're going to be," Michelle insisted, looking back at Tanner.

"You were lucky to find us here. Gives you a chance to say goodbye."

"But you're going to stay with the Jags, right?"

Tanner gave Michelle a long, assessing look. "Do you want to come with us? This is the only time I'm gonna ask."

Michelle realized she was wringing her hands and made an effort to stop. She wanted to go back to the apartment to sleep. She wanted to be at the hospital when Dan woke up again. To help him as he recovered. But Kenny was her responsibility. She couldn't just let him go off with Tanner. Who knew where they were going to end up. They weren't going to wait around for Dan to come after them. And Michelle was too much of a liability to them if she didn't go with them.

"Well?" Tanner raised his brows.

"Yeah, okay. I'll come. You can't just take Kenny away!"

He smirked, giving a little nod.

"Where are you guys going to go?" Butch demanded. "You're Jags. You can't just leave us short-handed."

Tanner considered. "You want us or you want Dan? Because you ain't gonna get both."

The other Jags who were there exchanged looks, considering. The trouble between Tanner and Dan had been brewing for a long time and they'd surely thought about it before. But only in terms of losing one or the other, and Tanner was bound to be the loser in a fight between the two of them. Losing Tanner, Michelle, and Kenny all at once was another story. Michelle was smart, a good planner and problem-solver. Kenny was stronger and getting better with his fists every day. Good to have in a fight. Good muscle whenever you needed him. Tanner was not smart or strong. In skills, he was still in the lower echelons of the gang. But he had leadership ability. When he decided on a thing, he got people on his side.

They clumped together at the far side of the room, then withdrew to one of the bedrooms to talk, closing the door. Michelle didn't have to see or hear them to know what they were going to decide. Tanner had backed them into a corner. Dan might be in the upper ranks of the gang, but he was getting too old and had too many outside interests. In another year, he'd be gone, faded out.

Michelle sat down on one of the bar stools in the kitchen, her legs wobbly. She put her face in her hands, elbows on the counter, and closed her eyes.

"It's okay, Michelle," Tanner said, his voice soft. "It'll all work out.

You'll see. You got nothing to worry about." His hands were on her back. She tensed at first, then relaxed under his kneading, massaging fingers. "You just stick with me and everything will go all right."

"And never see Dan again?"

His fingers stopped moving for a minute, then continued kneading. "That's right. You don't need him for anything. The Jags will look after us. You got no reason to go rushing back to Dan. Right?"

He waited for her confirmation that she didn't need Dan. Michelle was sure Dan had never been jealous of Tanner. But Tanner had been jealous of Dan right from the start, and especially when he started to think Dan and Michelle were getting too close. Michelle knew anything she said now jeopardized her relationship with Kenny. Tanner would use Kenny as a chess piece, taking him away from Michelle if she didn't comply.

But Michelle couldn't let go that quickly, that completely.

"I can't even say good-bye to Dan? Make sure he's okay?" She wiped at her leaky eyes. "He won't even know where to find his car!"

Tanner snickered. "He can steal a better car. I don't know why he kept that old beater after Wheels died. He doesn't need space for a wheelchair anymore." He was silent for a while. Michelle just breathed, trying to keep from sobbing.

The other Jags returned. The verdict was in their downcast eyes before they even said a word. "If it's you three or Dan, then Dan's out," Clyde announced.

Michelle swallowed and nodded. She waited for the other shoe to drop. There was something more. Something being held back.

Tanner sensed it too. "What?" he demanded, no longer rubbing Michelle's back and shoulders.

The other boys looked at each other, no one keen to break the news. But Michelle already knew what it was. "You want me to tell Dan."

"Anyone else, and he's gonna make an example of the messenger," Butch pointed out. "You're the only one he wouldn't kill."

Michelle rubbed her eyes with her fists. She looked at Tanner, waiting for his objection. Tanner's jaw worked and he ground his teeth, considering various options. But there wasn't really any other way, unless he wanted to tell Dan himself. Dan might be injured, but that was no guarantee he wasn't dangerous. Maybe he was even more dangerous, like a wounded bear.

"Fine," Tanner agreed. "Michelle tells Dan tomorrow. Then you come back," he told Michelle in a stern, warning voice. "You get your chance to say goodbye and tell him where to find his car. That's it. You deliver the message he's out of the Jags, and you hoof it back to me. Us. The Jags. Otherwise... Kenny ain't gonna be around by the time you get back."

Michelle scowled. "How do you know he'll be conscious when I get there?" she demanded. "I might have to wait hours for him to wake up. You're staying with the Jags, both of you. Right? That's the deal."

Tanner looked for an argument, a way around it. Then he shrugged and raised his eyebrows. "If you make trouble for me..." He looked in Kenny's direction and then back at Michelle, making sure she got it.

"I'll tell Dan," Michelle said. "And I'll stay in the Jags with Kenny."

She hadn't said she wouldn't see Dan again, and Tanner tried to stare her down. But he'd committed himself to staying with the Jags with Kenny and Michelle, and he couldn't back down from it now. The Jags hadn't let Dan go just to have Tanner change his mind.

She ended up sleeping at Clyde's. There wasn't enough room, but they made do. Michelle was too anxious and too tired to get to sleep. She had a mattress all to herself, a luxury, because she was the only girl there. But she couldn't get to sleep. After she tossed and turned for a couple of hours, Tanner materialized beside her. As angry as Michelle was with Tanner for his scheming and his ongoing obsession with her, she almost sobbed with relief when his arms went around her. She needed someone to hold her close, to quiet the demons. Held firmly in his arms, Michelle was finally able to let her body relax and fall asleep.

When daylight started to creep in through the windows, Michelle prepared to leave.

"There's no rush," Tanner said as she tried to extricate herself from his arms without waking him. "You could stick around a while longer."

"I'd better get to the hospital. See how Dan's doing."

Tanner winced and rubbed his forehead. "I'd offer to come, if I wasn't so hung over. And if he wasn't going to kill me." He grinned.

Michelle shook her head. She couldn't believe she was stuck in the middle of the whole mess. She should never have agreed to hang out with Tanner in the first place. She should have cut him off years ago. But... he'd used Kenny as a pawn back then, too, promising to protect him, to make sure he didn't get beaten up. Michelle wondered who it was that had beaten Kenny up so badly that day back in elementary school. Had Tanner directed that too?

"I'll be back later."

Tanner's grin had disappeared, a serious look replacing it. "You okay, Michelle?"

She opened her mouth to brush him off.

"I mean really all right?" Tanner interrupted before she could speak.

Michelle looked at him. He really did care. It made her crazy, him flip-flopping between jealousy, bravado, and caring. She could never quite get her legs under her. "Yeah, I'm all right."

"Good. I'll see you later. Don't stay there too long."

Michelle double-checked Dan's name was on the plate at the door before poking her head in. She didn't know whether he would be awake, or who the other man in the room was and whether he would be awake. Luckily, Dan was in the bed nearest the door, so she didn't have to walk by someone else to get to him. He looked up when she came into view.

"Michelle! Hey, how are you?"

Michelle pushed her hair back from her face. "I'm okay... you're the one who got hit in the head."

"Well, I know that," he admitted, his hand going to the bandages. "Don't remember much about it, but I can't exactly forget I got hurt."

Michelle walked the rest of the way into the room and squeezed by the bed to get to the visitor's chair. Dan reached out and grabbed her hand as she got closer and gave it a squeeze. He let go again.

"Glad you're here."

She tried to smile. But it was weak and forced and she was sure he would notice and want to know what was going on. "It's good to see you awake," she said. "You kept passing out yesterday…"

"I've been mostly awake today. I think so, anyway."

Michelle shifted in the seat, uncomfortable. "I figured I'd better let you know where your car was, or you'd wonder."

He raised his brows. "My car?"

"Well, I tried to bring you to the hospital, but I got pulled over."

"Did they impound it?"

"No. I got my Aunt Ruby to come and help out. She drove me here in your car and she drove it back to her house. Sorry, I didn't get her to drive it back to your place, but then Charlie or a cab would have had to go there to pick her up…"

"Hey, no worries. At least I don't have to pay impound fees. I can pick it up from her place, once my head is clear enough to drive."

"Yeah, good. I'll write down where it is." Michelle looked around for writing implements and found a thin pad of paper and pencil stub in the little drawer beside Dan's bed. She carefully wrote down the street for Dan. When she looked up, Dan was watching her, his brows drawn down. "What?"

He looked into her eyes. "Why wouldn't I just go with you to get it?"

Michelle shifted in her seat again and looked around the room for a distraction. Dan reached out and touched her face. "Michelle. What's going on?"

"Nothing."

"I know I've got a concussion, but I'm not stupid. Something is up."

Michelle stared down at her hands, at a loss as to how to tell him. Dan sat there looking at her, silent. She wished he would say something. Make a guess. Ask more questions. Something other than just sitting there looking at her.

"It's the Jags," she said finally.

"What about them? We going to have a rumble? You're a good fighter, that won't be a problem."

"No... not a rumble. It's just..." She took a deep breath. "It was all of us or you. And they knew you were drifting away anyway, with all your talks..."

Dan's brows drew down as he tried to process this. "This concussion must be worse than I thought," he said, shaking his head. "All of us or me... what?"

"Tanner said he was taking Kenny. And I had to choose, either stay with you or go with Kenny. And he's my responsibility."

"Yeah...?"

"So I had to say I would go with Kenny and Tanner..."

"Go where?"

"Well, nowhere, it turns out. But they were going to leave, and I have to take care of Kenny."

"They were going to leave... the Jags? Leave town? What?"

"I don't know where. Just that... I wouldn't be able to see Kenny anymore. Tanner wouldn't let me know where they were or see Kenny again..."

"And you said you'd go with them," Dan repeated, though he clearly didn't understand the impact yet.

"Yeah. So then it was all three of us, and the Jags didn't want to lose three bangers all at once..."

"No. Could cause problems."

"So Tanner said we would stay. But only if you were out."

Dan started to tie it together. "So now you and Tanner and Kenny will all stay with the Jags. If I'm gone."

Michelle stared down at her black nail polish. It was chipping around the edges.

"Three or one. It's a logical choice," Dan admitted.

"Yeah."

"And I'm getting too old."

"And lecturing most of the time," Michelle added.

Dan rubbed the spot between his brows. "Okay... they planning to beat me out, or what? It ain't really the best time for me."

"No, just walk away," Michelle said. "They're not planning anything. Just eliminating the conflict." She shifted in the chair. "They wanted me to be the one to tell you. So you wouldn't kill anyone."

He chuckled. "Don't know if I could in this condition. But sending you was a good choice."

Michelle didn't smile. Dan tilted his head. "What's wrong?"

"Tanner doesn't want me to see you anymore."

"Well, he can't very well stop you, can he?"

"With Kenny... he keeps threatening me with Kenny."

"Why don't you tell Kenny to just hang with you and break ties with Tanner?"

"Because he wouldn't. Kenny likes Tanner. Tanner controls him."

Dan closed his eyes. He was silent and still for so long Michelle thought he had passed out again. She leaned back uncomfortably in the chair, closing her own eyes.

"I don't think I ever realized how smart Tanner is," Dan said. Michelle opened her eyes and looked at him. He lay there with his eyes shut, a slight crease between his eyebrows. "I know he ain't book smart. Not many bangers are. But he's... shrewd. Canny. Waiting until I was out of the way, and then pulling this coup... he's not stupid, is he?"

Michelle swallowed. She couldn't tell him Tanner was the one who had engineered putting Dan in the hospital in the first place. She couldn't believe it had all been planned. Either that, or Tanner had been quick to take advantage of the circumstances. But she saw the way he was controlling Kenny. Putting things into his mind. It was no accident Kenny had attacked Dan.

"So what do I do?" she asked.

He opened his eyes. "Look after Kenny."

"But—"

"Just like I had to look after George," Dan said. "He didn't have anyone else. If you'd tried to talk me out of looking after my brother, said I had to choose between taking care of him and being friends with you, you would have been out. Other girls tried to tell me it wasn't my responsibility. That I should just dump Georgie on someone else. And where are they now?"

"Gone."

"Yeah, they're gone. If I had to choose between my responsibility to my brother, and a girl or any other relationship, it was George, every time. If you gotta choose between me and Kenny... you'll choose Kenny. Every time."

A brief shadow of rebellion stirred in Michelle's consciousness. If Dan had tried to talk her out of taking care of Kenny, she would have dropped him, just like he said. But she didn't like being told she had to take care of Kenny. That she couldn't be friends with Dan. It just made her more determined to rebel against Tanner's machinations. Tanner wanted to take care of Kenny? He could take care of Kenny. Michelle would still keep an eye on things. She wouldn't let Kenny get hurt, but if Tanner wanted to take responsibility for Kenny, let him. Michelle wasn't going to stop seeing Dan. Tanner couldn't control who she was friends with.

CHAPTER
Forty-Eight

"Maybe i should come with you," Tanner suggested. Michelle glared at him. "I don't need an escort to my aunt's house."

"Do we have to go?" Kenny complained, twisting his fingers together and scowling at Michelle and Tanner alternately.

"Ruby invited us to dinner. You like going there for dinner. You like hanging with Charlie. We'll be back with the Jags later on." She looked at Tanner. "It's not like we're sleeping over. You guys want to go do something tonight, there's plenty of time. It's just dinner."

"I don't like you sneaking off like this."

"Sneaking off? How are we sneaking off?"

"I don't like it," Tanner repeated.

"I don't care."

"She's going to be there?" Kenny asked.

"Who? Oh, Mama. Yeah. But we're not staying. And Charlie's a cop, he's not going to let her hit you."

"She couldn't hit me, I wouldn't let her," Kenny asserted.

"Yeah, that's right. You're bigger and stronger than her now. You got nothing to worry about."

Kenny rocked back on his heels and looked at Tanner, anxious for his reaction. Michelle leveled a glare at Tanner, letting him know he'd better not try to dissuade Kenny from going to Ruby's.

Tanner gave Michelle a deliberately relaxed, provoking smile. "Would I keep you guys from this little family reunion? After all, it's just dinner, right?"

"That's right." Michelle tapped Kenny on the arm. "Let's go, Kenny."

Kenny looked back at Tanner, waiting for him to say no. When he didn't, Kenny put his head down and followed Michelle. Kenny stayed quiet for most of the journey to Ruby's house. Michelle wondered what he was thinking. Maybe he wasn't thinking about June at all. Maybe, as he had said, he knew June couldn't hurt him anymore and wasn't worried about it.

When they walked up to the house, Kenny's eyes stopped on the car parked out in front. "Is Dan here?"

"No. Ruby just picked up his car after I tried to drive him to the hospital. He hasn't picked it up yet."

"He's out of hospital."

"I know. He just hasn't been by yet."

Kenny looked at the car again and cut a glance back toward Michelle.

"He doesn't remember it was you who hit him," Michelle said. "He isn't going to do anything to hurt you."

"I'm strong."

"Yeah, I know."

Michelle let Kenny lead the way up the sidewalk. They knocked and went in.

"Hey guys," Ruby greeted them with a smile. "Come on in. I'm just finishing up. Dinner will be on the table in about ten minutes. Just relax in the living room for a few minutes..."

Michelle glanced around the room. June was sitting at the end of the couch. Her face was pale like she hadn't been sleeping or was strung out. Her smile looked forced. Fake.

"Hi, Mama."

"Michelle!" June stood up and held her arms out to give Michelle a hug.

Michelle stayed well back from her. "Yeah. Nice to see you, too."

"And Kenny." June turned to the boy.

Michelle had seen June a few times already. It had been a shock to see her at the hairdresser that first time, and uncomfortable seeing her at the soup kitchen and last time at Ruby's house. But she'd gotten a little bit used to the idea of June being around. Kenny had stayed away from the places June went and it was the first time he had seen her since those few days they had gone home after reunification. He stared at June, his mouth turned down. He clenched his fists and moved toward her abruptly. Michelle moved between them, grabbing at Kenny.

"No. Just leave'er alone, Kenny!"

She caught his wrist and kept her body between the two of them as Kenny moved, trying to get closer to June.

"She hit me!" Kenny blurted.

"I know she did. But she's not gonna do that anymore. She can't hurt you anymore. Just look at how big you are."

Kenny glowered at Michelle, still trying to move around her. But he didn't want to hurt Michelle getting her out of the way. He growled, his jaw muscles writhing, tight under his skin.

Charlie hadn't been in the room when they arrived, but he was there now, making himself known.

"Hey, Kenny! It's been a long time, bud. How's it going?" he greeted jovially.

Kenny eyed Charlie, taking a step back from Michelle.

"You following the game?" Charlie questioned. He moved over to the TV and turned it on, changing channels to a football game. Kenny glared at June, then looked at the television screen, distracted. He looked once or twice more at June, each time less focused, and eventually went over and sat down, his eyes on the football game. Charlie sat down next to him, making a comment or two about the action. Ruby withdrew to the kitchen to finish her preparations, and June and Michelle looked at each other.

June's eyes glistened with tears. Conflicting emotions churned around Michelle's stomach. June had brought this on herself. She couldn't deny she had hurt them, especially Kenny. She'd hit them and she'd used drugs and hadn't cared what happened to them. She might be trying to be better now, but she still had to face the consequences of what she had done. Michelle didn't know how long it would take for Kenny to reconcile with her. If he ever would.

"I'm gonna see if Ruby needs some help," Michelle said, moving away from June. June trailed her into the kitchen. Michelle glanced around, and without asking what needed to be done, started to set the table.

June looked at a loss. She just stood there. "What are we having?"

Ruby looked over her shoulder at June and looked amused. "Vegetable stir fry with rice."

Michelle couldn't help laughing at June's look of dismay. June was a very picky eater. She hated vegetables. And rice. She would usually abide a few vegetables on a pizza or in a taco, but sometimes even then she'd pick them out. Kenny and Michelle had grown up being forced to eat the soggy vegetables June prepared for their dinners, but June had not led by example. Sometimes when Justin got home from a trip, he'd bring a bag of fresh produce with him, knowing June wouldn't buy them. Michelle savored the fresh, sweet taste of a nice crisp carrot after a couple of weeks of unpalatable canned peas. It had been better than candy.

Looking at the stove, Michelle could clearly see Ruby was not searing vegetables in a wok, but stirring a thick, red, spicy-smelling meat chili. There were soft white buns arranged on a plate on the counter.

"Relax, June," Ruby giggled. "You like chili, don't you?"

June took a few steps closer to peer into the pot, sniffing cautiously. "Not the kind with beans in it."

"No beans," Ruby confirmed. "Just meat and cheese."

"That looks okay."

Michelle shook her head, laughing silently to herself. June looked at her and Michelle saw a lightning-quick flash of anger. Michelle's heart beat faster, ready for fight or flight. June quickly buried the expression and gave Michelle a shame-faced smile.

"I don't like vegetables."

"Yeah, I noticed."

"It's probably about time your mama grew up and learned how to eat right, huh?"

Michelle raised her brows and didn't answer.

"Justin always used to get after me for not eating healthy stuff. Even eating on the road, he ate better than me."

"Alcoholics and addicts tend to eat poorly," a male voice said from behind Michelle. "Lots of sugar and processed stuff when they do eat, which usually comes second to drinking."

They all turned around. Michelle's grin just about burst out of her. She couldn't help giving him the biggest, most welcoming smile ever. "Dan!" She threw her arms around him and gave him a warm hug.

Loosening her grip, she looked around at June and Ruby, her face getting warm.

"Uh... this is my friend. Dan."

"We've met," Ruby agreed.

June was looking at Dan, scowling. "What do *you* know about addicts?"

Michelle opened her mouth to jump to Dan's defense, but he raised his hand to stop her and answered for himself. "I'm a recovering alcoholic. I didn't sober up until after I caused a motorbike accident that left my brother a quadriplegic. He died not long ago."

"Oh." June lost her defensive attitude. "Sorry. How did you know I'm an addict?" Her eyes drifted over to Michelle. "I guess Michelle told you all about it."

Dan indicated the pendant on June's necklace. A triangle inside a circle. June looked down at it, then clutched it in her hand.

"Oh, yeah. I guess it's pretty obvious."

"To a fellow traveler, yeah," Dan agreed.

"Let's get this stuff on the table," Ruby said. Everybody moved out of the way while she transported the chili over to the table and set it down on a hot pad. Dan was still holding onto Michelle and he gave her a little squeeze, looking down into her face.

"Did Kenny see you?" Michelle murmured.

"He was pretty intent on the TV. I don't think he noticed me."

"Good. Don't want him reporting back to Tanner that you were here."

"Don't let Tanner run your life."

"I'm not."

"Are you staying for supper, Dan?" Ruby asked. "You're welcome to; there's plenty to go around."

"No, ma'am. Thanks. I just came by to get my car. Thanks for helping Michelle out when I got hurt."

"Of course. You're sure, though? You don't want any chili?"

Dan shook his head and rubbed Michelle's shoulders. She leaned back against him comfortably, wishing he could stay. "I gotta go. I got an engagement tonight."

Michelle sighed and turned her head to look up at him. "You're sure you're well enough to start up again?"

"I'm fine. Doctor said I could do anything I felt up to."

"Yeah, I just thought…" she trailed off. "I dunno what I thought. I'll call you later, okay?"

He nodded and withdrew from her. He glanced through the doorway to the living room. "You want me to sneak out the back?"

"You don't have to," Michelle protested. But she looked at the back door and made a little movement toward it.

Dan grinned and walked out the back.

"Is he your boyfriend?" June asked.

Michelle looked at June, pursing her lips. "What business is it of yours?"

"Well… it's not, I know. I saw you with him at the soup kitchen and the two of you seem pretty…" she searched for the words. "I dunno. He just seemed like your boyfriend."

"He's not. We're just friends."

"Okay." June shrugged. "Whatever. I just wondered."

Michelle could see Dan through the kitchen window, climbing into his car and then driving away. Her chest was tight and uncomfortable.

"Time to eat!" Ruby called the boys from the living room.

Michelle turned her attention back to her family. Charlie managed to get Kenny to leave the television for a minute to get something to eat. Charlie led Kenny into the kitchen and stayed between Kenny and June. Kenny looked at June for a minute, his expression vague, and then he turned away, looking at the food on the table. He didn't jump right in to help himself. Charlie took over and dished up for him.

"You want a bun? These ones from the bakery are really nice…"

"Uh-huh."

"How much chili?"

Kenny watched Charlie dish it up. "That's good."

"Some veggies?" Charlie pointed to the raw vegetables Ruby had set out.

Kenny plunged his hand into the vegetables and added a handful to his dish. Charlie handed the plate to him. "You got a fork?"

Kenny picked up a fork and looked back toward the TV. "Can I eat in there?"

Charlie looked at Ruby, who nodded.

"Sure, bud," Charlie told Kenny.

Kenny went back into the living room and sat down in front of the TV. They all breathed a little sigh of relief.

"He got so big," June said. "I thought he'd always be scrawny, smaller than the other boys."

"He works out a lot," Michelle said.

"He was so tiny when he was born."

Michelle watched June carefully layer a spoonful of chili over her bun. She didn't help herself to any of the raw vegetables.

"I thought he was better, though," June said with a frown, taking a fork and stepping back from the table to let others dish up. "He seems..." June chewed on her lip. "He seems worse again, in his brain. Like when he was little. I thought he was doing better. Mrs. Marsden said he wasn't keeping up in school, but he seemed like... he was more normal."

"He was," Michelle agreed. "Then he OD'd."

"He did? When?"

Michelle shrugged. "I dunno... a year ago? More? It messed him up pretty bad."

Ruby and Charlie both nodded. Michelle's stomach felt like it was full of water, heavy and tight.

"He's better than he was, though. He doesn't need anyone to dish up for him. He gets along okay without anyone babying him." She knew her voice was too loud. She had no excuse for being angry over them just agreeing with her. But she felt like they were judging her. Her and Kenny both. Thinking they couldn't take care of themselves.

"It's okay, Michelle," Ruby said.

Michelle watched Charlie and Ruby dish up, making no move to get closer to the table. Charlie hesitated. "Should I eat in here, or do you think I should keep Kenny company?" He directed the question to Ruby but then looked self-consciously over his shoulder at Michelle. "Michelle? What do you think?"

"Go ahead, if you want. He likes someone to watch with."

Charlie nodded and left the kitchen to eat with Kenny. Ruby filled her plate and sat down. June sat in the chair next to her, looking studiously down at her chili and bun.

"Come and eat," Ruby invited.

"My stomach hurts."

June gave Michelle a sharp look. Michelle remembered all the times she had refused to eat supper with June. She preferred to go hungry, sitting in her own room, reading a book. Family dinners were too tense, too dangerous. June trying to control Kenny and Michelle, trying to bend them to her will. The memories brought on a rush of nausea and Michelle steadied herself on the counter. She held her stomach and tried to push through it. This was different. Ruby and Charlie wouldn't let anything happen to her. And Michelle was stronger than June. If June tried to hit her, Michelle could stop her. She wasn't a helpless little kid anymore.

"Come and sit down," June said. "At least come and visit with us. I thought that was why you came."

Michelle shook her head. "I thought I could… but I can't do it." She swallowed hard, trying to keep down the sour bile rising in her throat.

June poked at her food and didn't eat. It set off warning bells for Michelle. June wouldn't eat. She'd start drinking instead. She would go back to the way she had been. Violent. Vitriolic. She would lose the weight that had put a curve back on her cheeks again, become a tired, prematurely-aged junkie. And one day she would die. One day soon, if she kept drinking and doping.

"You've got to eat, Mama."

June looked back at her. "So do you."

It had been a long time since they had eaten together. June had served Michelle at the soup kitchen. Michelle had tried to keep June's cupboards stocked and had cooked meals for her when she was living all alone. But they hadn't eaten together.

Michelle forced herself to sit down at the table, with a safe buffer zone between herself and June. She picked up the last plate and put it in front of her, but didn't fill it. She just looked down at the white plate with a slightly blue sheen, trying to keep her emotions, and her stomach, under control.

MICHELLE

"Can I get you something else?" Ruby asked. "Would you rather have a sandwich or a bit of tea?"

Michelle kept one hand over her stomach. "I don't feel good. I really can't eat anything."

"Well... let's just visit, then." Ruby took a couple of bites of her chili as if she were completely comfortable. June continued to worry her food without eating it.

"I haven't seen you at the soup kitchen lately," June observed, darting a glance at Michelle.

"No, I don't go there. I just went that one time, to try to get George to eat. Dan's brother." Dan had already told her George had died, and Michelle hoped June would understand this without Michelle having to repeat it. She still had a hard time with the fact that Wheels was gone. They hadn't had anything in common, other than Dan, but she had come to love him. Not in a romantic way, of course, but like he was her own brother.

"I never went to soup kitchens or anything when I was with the gangs..." June contributed. "But it seems like a lot of bangers do now, for lunch anyway."

"Just a few of them," Michelle said. "And not every day or anything."

June nodded. "There's so many homeless people now," she mused. "I don't remember there being that many when I was a kid."

"I'm not homeless," Michelle pointed out. "I've... I've got a place."

But she realized as she said it that it wasn't true anymore. She couldn't live with Dan, in the place they had rented together. Hopefully, his speaking engagements were bringing in enough money for him to cover the whole thing by himself. Michelle, Tanner, and Carter were all gone, and he was living on his own. Michelle had been couch surfing with one or another of the Jags, just floating between places with Tanner and Kenny, since Tanner had forced Dan out of the gang.

It hadn't really occurred to Michelle that they were homeless. They were just between places. They'd find someplace to share or squat before long.

She turned her eyes back to her empty plate. She knew she'd be hungry later, but she still couldn't bring herself to eat.

"Justin and I got our own place when we got out of the gang,"

June said. "I don't know how old we were... fourteen?" she looked at Ruby.

Ruby nodded. "Sounds about right. Before Kenny was born."

There was an uncomfortable silence. Eventually, June spoke. "It was good. I liked it there."

Ruby and June ate their chili. Michelle continued to stare at her empty plate, trying to keep the unwelcome thoughts and memories at bay.

CHAPTER Forty-Nine

Michelle felt out of place at the high school. She felt like there was a spotlight on her, like everyone was looking at her. She really didn't stand out that much; she looked old enough to attend the high school, and there were plenty of other kids with piercings or extreme hairstyles. She didn't see a lot of tattoos. But she still felt like she stood out and everyone was wondering what she was doing there.

She followed the signs and arrows down to the gymnasium, where the bleacher seating had been pulled out so students could sit and listen to the lecture. There was a good crowd in attendance. They sat quietly.

Michelle focused on Dan's calm, clear voice as he started to wind up his talk on staying away from drugs and alcohol, or getting help to get sober if you were already addicted. He was a dynamic and powerful speaker. She hadn't actually heard his spiel before and she was impressed. He was young enough the students could relate to his experience; he wasn't just another adult telling them they couldn't have any fun. They couldn't argue with his personal experience. He'd been there and he'd suffered the consequences.

Michelle moved to where she could see the presentation slides that accompanied Dan's speech. As he wound up, he displayed one last slide. It was a collage of three photos. One of two boys, the older one dark, and the younger one blond, standing with their arms over each other's shoulders, smiling at the camera. Michelle recognized Dan's face. A few years younger, but still recognizable. Even though she knew the other boy had to be George, she couldn't recognize him. Full cheeks, sparkling eyes, big smile. Not the George she had known. She tried to swallow the lump in her throat. The middle picture was Dan standing behind George's wheelchair to push it, both of them facing the camera. Michelle could recognize George's face in that one. Drawn, cadaverous, and miserable. Lined with pain and grief. Dan's face was serious. No carefree brotherly smiles in this one. The third picture was of the urn currently in Dan's apartment on a shelf. The plain, brushed-steel urn that held George's ashes.

Michelle didn't hear Dan's final words. She became aware he had closed and the audience was applauding, some of them standing up. She made her way up to the front, elbowing her way through the stream of students now trying to get out of the gym. She felt like she was in a fog. It was the first time she'd seen a picture of George before the accident. Before his life was ruined. Dan had talked about him. Talked about how both of them had been forced to change. But she'd never been able to picture what they were like before. She was shaking.

As she worked her way against the tide of students leaving the gym, she thought back to Kenny's overdose. It had hurt her, seeing how much it set him back, how damaged he was. But at least it wasn't her fault. It wasn't the same as with Dan, who knew his actions and his addiction had directly caused the devastating blow. And George had been changed far more by the accident than Kenny had been by his overdose.

She broke free of the crowd leaving the lecture, only to find another crowd gathered around Dan. People who wanted to shake his hand, compliment him, or ask him a question. A few were teachers or staff. Most of the rest were girls.

Michelle felt unaccountably irritated with the girls crowding around Dan, vying for his attention. They were just stupid little girls. Spoiled and sheltered and going to school every day without a care in the world. They didn't have any kinship with Dan. No connection. They were just cheerleaders flirting with the quarterback.

Dan was smiling and talking, trying to answer their questions and make them all feel good. It was a few minutes before he spotted

Michelle on the fringes of the group and sent a look in her direction. A few of the girls turned to see who he was nodding at. Michelle scowled at them. She just wanted them all to leave so she could talk to Dan and he could get his stuff cleaned up, and they could go somewhere for a while. But he kept talking, smiling and nodding, and the clocked ticked on.

Eventually, there were only a few girls left around Dan, and Michelle stood next to him, tapping her toe impatiently. He continued to schmooze and answer questions. Michelle got the feeling the last girl was trying to out-wait Michelle, hoping Michelle would leave so she could have Dan to herself. Maybe she would offer to help him carry his gear out to the car or ask him out for coffee. Michelle ground her teeth and gave the girl as obvious a dismissing look as she could. Eventually, the girl shrugged and said goodbye, walking away. Dan sighed and gave Michelle a cursory hug around the shoulder.

"How's it going?"

"You know you were supposed to be done an hour ago?"

Dan looked at his watch. "I was done an hour ago."

"Then what are you doing here still?"

He grinned and started picking up his things. "The people who stay to talk afterward are the ones who really need to hear what I have to say. People who are struggling with addiction, or have family members or friends who are, and need to know what to do next. I can't just abandon them."

"Those cheerleaders?" Michelle scoffed, with a look toward the last couple girls who were straggling out of the gym. "They don't have a problem."

Dan stopped and looked at her. "You can't tell by looking at someone, Michelle. It's not like wearing gang colors. Addicts can be found in all walks of life. Even cheerleaders."

Michelle looked away from him, uncomfortable with his intense gaze. "Well, they don't look like they need help. Except to get your phone number."

"Do you know how hard it is to keep your weight down that low?" he challenged. "Girls like that smoke cigarettes, take speed, starve themselves, make themselves throw up. Those are all addictive behaviors. Ones that will kill them, if they can't get straightened out."

Michelle helped to load his gear up, not looking at his face. "I still think they just wanted attention," she grumbled.

Dan was silent as he finished picking his things up. They walked together out the rear gym door into the parking lot where his car sat waiting. He opened the trunk and they loaded it up. Dan stopped and turned to face Michelle, leaning against the bumper.

"Michelle... you've never had an addiction, right?"

Michelle shook her head. "No way," she agreed.

"So I get that you're not very sympathetic toward people who do. Your mom. These kids. Even Kenny. You think it's just a matter of willpower. Choosing to do it or not. But that isn't how it works."

"I know. I get what addiction is."

He turned his back on her to walk up to the driver's door. He climbed in and opened the passenger door for Michelle.

"I don't think you really do," he said. "You might understand the idea of addiction. You might understand how it works physiologically. But you don't understand what it is like to be out of control, at the mercy of a substance or behavior."

"I saw what it did to my mama. I knew I couldn't ever let it happen to me. I couldn't ever let myself get addicted to anything."

"But you can't *choose* not to get addicted, Michelle. You're lucky you're able to have a beer or a smoke now and then and not get addicted, especially with your family history. To be able to just decide you're not going to have another one. But it isn't like that for everyone. For some people, they're addicted the first time they try it. They can't choose to just try it once and decide they don't like it or don't want to ever do it again. One drink, one smoke, one hit... and they're hooked."

He pulled out of the school parking lot. Michelle looked out the window, playing with the stud in her pierced lip with her tongue. "Is that what happened to you?"

Dan drove for a while, focused on the road. Michelle didn't think he was going to answer. Finally, Dan sighed and glanced over at her. "No. I was a lot more stupid than that. I didn't think I could just try it one time and then decide to leave it alone. I thought I could party all the time and still be in control. I thought I was macho, being able to down more than any of the other boys. That I was indestructible. I could drink and take as many drugs as I wanted and not get in an accident, not get arrested, and not have to deal with any of the other consequences of my actions. I don't know when I got addicted, I was never sober long enough to find out."

Michelle thought about the pictures. Dan and George arm-in-arm, happy. And then the tragedy that ruined their lives, ending with that steel urn on Dan's shelf. Preventable. All because he had decided to drink.

"Addiction sucks," she said.

Dan snorted. "No kidding."

~

Charlie had suggested that maybe Michelle could meet with Justin in a setting other than Ruby's house. Michelle was already having to deal with June being at Ruby's house and didn't want to go to Justin's house and also have to see Sondra and their other children. It would just be too much. So they had picked out a setting that Justin would be comfortable in; a truck-stop that he frequented.

Michelle intentionally got there before the time that they had agreed to meet so that she would have time to look around and suss out the place before Justin got there. But when she arrived, she immediately saw Justin up at the counter, there ahead of her. He was keeping an eye on the door and saw her come in. Michelle's heart started to beat harder. The exit was behind her. If she wanted to go, all she had to do was turn around and retreat. But she hadn't gone to the truck stop just to run away. She swallowed and tried to slow her breathing. She made an effort to relax her tense muscles. It was Justin. He had hurt her, but never physically. They'd never fought that way. She knew she was in a public place, there was no way that he would touch her, or let their conversation get loud enough to attract attention. She could just relax and talk to him.

Slowly, Michelle made her way up to the counter, her stomach twisting and cramping. It was Justin. Her daddy. Beloved and longed after for so many years. She had blown any previous chances at reunification, but here they were to give it one more go. To face hurt another time and try to reconcile.

Justin didn't get up or offer to hug her. He didn't even offer his hand. He stayed sitting where he was, staring down at the coffee mug in his hands, as she sat down on the stool next to him.

"Hi," he greeted.

"Hey."

"You're early."

Michelle gave a small, nervous laugh. "So are you."

"I didn't want to miss you."

The waitress behind the counter bustled over to see them. "Coffee?" she suggested.

Michelle nodded. "Yeah. Thanks."

A mug was placed in front of her and filled from the waiting carafe. The coffee was too hot to drink, and Michelle blew on it, trying to figure out what to say.

"So... how are you doing?" Justin asked.

"Okay, I guess. It's all pretty strange, these days."

He took a sip of his coffee. "What do you mean?"

"Being here, where you live. Mama coming here to stay with Ruby. It's just... weird."

"I guess. When Sondra and I came here, we never expected to see any family again. Even though this is where I came from and I knew Ruby still lived here, I never really planned to run into anyone."

Michelle frowned, thinking about it. "What about the rest of your family? Do any of them live here anymore?"

Justin stared toward the pickup window between the dining area and the kitchen. His face was a mask, devoid of any emotion. "I don't know. Our mom still lived around here after the trial, but we haven't had any contact with her since we were eight. Since... our dad died. Chloe stayed with her. Ronnie stayed with her foster family. June was in contact with Ronnie a little bit before we left town. Before Kenny was born. But I don't think she's had any contact since then. I haven't... looked for anyone."

"So it's just you, and Ruby, and Mama."

He nodded. "Only half of us... but that's more than it's been the last few years."

"Ruby told me... about your dad."

"I try not to think about it." His lips pressed together. "He ruined our family. To this day, I can't understand how he could be so twisted... so sick."

Michelle kept her mouth shut, deciding it was best not to point out the parallels.

"And our mom, she helped him," Justin said.

Michelle glanced over at him. "Really? I didn't know that part."

She could see his Adam's apple bob as he swallowed. He raised his coffee cup to his lips and took another drink. He still didn't look at her. "It was years before I understood how much she was involved, how she covered for him and helped him to… prey on them." He took another swallow and gazed down at the coffee in distaste. Probably wishing it was something stronger. "I should have killed her too."

Michelle breathed through her mouth, nauseated. She had talked herself into understanding how he could have shot his father, trying to protect June from harm. And he'd been so young at the time, he couldn't have understood the consequences, how serious what he'd done really was. But this was different. Regret over not having killed both of them.

Justin was looking at her. His eyes were dark and bitter. He looked small. "Charlie told me about *your* record," he said, his mouth twisted into a grimace. "So don't try that 'holier than thou' look on me."

Michelle looked down at the counter, her heart beating faster. Though she wanted to deny it, of course he was right. Twice she had conspired to take someone's life, the same as Justin had. She couldn't even claim the altruistic motive of protecting someone else. It was purely selfish. But it seemed different. Thinking about Justin killing his father and now wishing that he'd killed his mother to punish her for her part in the abuse was different from the pain and fear of being assaulted herself, of fighting to defend her life and her right to be in charge of her own body.

"It feels different," she confessed. "I'm not saying it is. Just that… it's different when you're thinking about what someone else did."

"You weren't there. So you can't judge."

"No… you're right."

For a while, neither of them said anything. Michelle searched for a way to carry on. "So… how's Marcie?"

"Marcie's good. She asks about you."

"Does she?" A sob caught in Michelle's throat and she tried to swallow it, to find a way to speak around it without giving herself away, but she couldn't go on.

Justin nodded, not looking at her. "I'm sorry I kept you kids apart all these years. You had Kenny, and Marcie had the other kids, so I told myself it was all okay. But... you all should have been able to know each other."

"Yeah. I wish we had. And I wish... that you had come back. So we could at least have visited you."

"I couldn't. I assumed that as soon as they started to investigate, they'd find out the truth about June and I, and they'd charge me... put me in jail. Maybe even both of us."

"So you protected yourself and left them to charge Mama?"

"No! I told her to run. I told her that they were going to find out we were siblings and she should disappear before they did. I don't understand why she stayed."

Michelle put her coffee cup down, carefully centering it inside the wet ring it had left on the counter. "Because she loved us. She couldn't abandon us."

"I loved you too, Michelle."

She rotated the cup in a circle. "Not in the same way, I don't think."

"Michelle... you have to understand about June. What happened to her... it changed her. Forever. For years, I tried to help her. Tried to protect her and help her to heal. But she was damaged. Something is..." he searched for the words, his voice getting more hoarse, "... something is broken inside. She's never going to be... my June again. The way she was before. Her brain... her heart... her spirit... they don't work the same way anymore. She's different than you and me. She's sort of... lost."

"Uh-huh."

"She worked with a therapist for years... but it never made her better."

Michelle took another sip of her now-cooling coffee, thinking about her conversations with Dan. "When did she get addicted?"

"Whoa..." Justin gave a low whistle. "That's a tough one. She's tried lots of different meds, prescriptions, over the years. When we were with the gang, that's when she started using heavily... street drugs, mainlining... but before... she started drinking when she was eight or younger. Dad gave her booze," Justin's voice was pained and he turned his face away from her, shaking his head slightly. "To make her forget. To make her easier to handle."

He swallowed and didn't say anything for a long time. He rubbed his eyes with the pads of his fingers. Like he was tired rather than wiping away tears.

"For years... she couldn't sleep without at least a drink. Sometimes tranquilizers too. We tried to wean her off when we were getting out of the gang and then when she found out she was pregnant. She tried. She did really well for a couple years... but when Marcie was born, the bottom kind of dropped out."

"Why? Because of Marcie's CP?"

He nodded. "There was no way she could take care of a baby so seriously handicapped. She had a hard enough time with Kenny. And you were still so young. But things changed after Marcie was born."

Michelle pondered this, thinking about her questions. All the unanswered stuff swirling around in her head. After all, what did she really need to know? She knew June hadn't been able to take care of them. June had been a different person then. Overwhelmed with the children. In the throes of addiction. Now she only had to take care of herself. And she had a job and was clean, or trying to be.

"Why did you blame Mama for Marcie having cerebral palsy?"

"I didn't," Justin protested. But his voice was weak. He must have known he couldn't convince her of the fact.

"Yes, you did," she asserted. "You said it was her fault. You took Marcie. Marcie was never Mama's baby, she was always yours."

"June never took care of herself very well. You really have to look after yourself when you're carrying a baby. It's very important."

Michelle looked at him steadily. Justin looked down at the coffee.

"It's my fault as much as June's. I was out of town. I shouldn't have left. I should have stayed with her."

"But you had to travel, to work. To support her."

"She told me the baby had moved down. That she would be born soon. We actually thought it was a boy at the time. I ignored what June said and figured I had plenty of time for another run. Especially since I could just turn around and go home if I needed to."

"But she was right."

"Yes. She went into labor that day. The baby was in trouble, but June wouldn't let them do a C-section. She was too scared. She didn't believe the baby could die. I guess she thought they were just trying to pressure her. I don't know. I talked to her on the phone. I tried to talk her into it. But she wouldn't listen."

Michelle stared at him, fascinated with the story she had never heard before. It had always been taboo, with both June and Justin avoiding any mention of what had happened.

"So they didn't do a C-section and that's why Marcie was born brain-damaged?"

"She wouldn't consent to a C-section and Marcie's heart stopped beating. Then June said go ahead and take her."

"And they revived Marcie after?"

"Yeah. But her brain had been without oxygen for several minutes."

"Wow. So if she had just done the C-section, Marcie would have been fine."

Justin made a face, frowning and pursing his lips. "I know a lot more about CP now than I did when she was born, or even when you guys were little. There are a lot of other possible causes. She might have had CP anyway. It might have been a stroke or infection before she was born. Or a genetic problem... a chance mutation..."

"So it might not have been Mama's fault?"

He shrugged and stared off. Michelle pondered this, staring down at her coffee and swirling it a little in her cup.

When she looked back at Justin's face, his expression had changed. He was looking past her, angry. His brows were drawn down, and one hand had clenched into a fist while the other snaked toward his pocket. Michelle looked quickly behind her to see what he was looking at. An enemy of Justin's? Some other trucker he had a grudge with? A cop? No one she saw in the restaurant behind her seemed to be a threat.

"What?" Michelle asked. "What's wrong? What are you looking at?"

Justin slid off of the stool to his feet, his body tense. "There was a boy. Watching us. I noticed him before, he came in behind you."

Michelle looked behind her again, this time looking for a rival gang member. "Where did he go?"

"I don't know. There were people coming and going, he might have gone outside. But he was watching you, and he was... I don't know. Not happy about something. It looked like he was going to come over here, but then he changed his mind."

Michelle scanned for any sign of him. She had a sinking feeling she knew exactly who it was. "Dark blond, about your height?" she asked.

Justin looked once more at the door and got back onto his stool. "Sounds like you know him."

Michelle nodded and took a couple gulps of her coffee.

"Yeah. I know him."

CHAPTER
Fifty

"Dammit, Tanner, why can't you just leave me alone?" Michelle stormed into Tanner's recently-acquired squat and slammed the door behind her. A few of the other Jags were there and they drew back from Tanner as if afraid of being caught in the line of fire.

Tanner laughed and held up his hands defensively. "Whoa, what bit you? I'm not doing anything to you."

Michelle slid her knife out of its sheath and put the point against Tanner's throat. "You quit following me! I don't want to turn around and see your face unless we're here or out with the Jags. You keep showing up other places and I'm going to put an end to it. Permanently."

Michelle was expecting the others to heckle her or Tanner, but they were silent. The room was quiet enough to hear a pin drop. Tanner swallowed, his Adam's apple pushing against the tip of the knife. He forced a smile.

"You didn't see me," he pointed out.

"Justin did. You just stay out of my business!"

"Who is this Justin?" he moved his head back and forth, trying to ease the pressure of the knife from his throat. "I want to make sure you're not seeing Dan on the side and I find you with another guy? How many of them have you got on the string?"

"What's it to you?"

MICHELLE

He struggled for an answer. He knew he couldn't assert that she was his girlfriend. She had agreed to stay on with him to be with Kenny. A smile flitted across his face before he schooled it into a concerned expression. He touched her arm.

"I've seen you get hurt too many times, Michelle. These older guys get too close to you and you end up getting hurt. You don't even see it coming."

Michelle's blood boiled at his audacity. "That's not how it was!" she insisted. With Stan, she had thought he would respect her wishes, that she could protect herself. The store cop had been another story. She hadn't gone into anything with her eyes shut. And Carter... she should have listened to her first instinct that he was a cop. She shouldn't have let down her guard.

"You can see why I'd be concerned..." Tanner spread his hands apart in a shrug.

Michelle hit him with her closed fist. With her hand still clutching the dagger. The crack of her fist across his jaw rang out, and Tanner went over, laid full out on the floor. A cheer went up from the other Jags.

"Nice one, Michelle!" Clyde whooped. "He ain't gonna forget that for a while."

Michelle kicked Tanner to make sure he was still conscious. He groaned and pulled away from her, but didn't manage to crawl to his feet. "I'll see whoever I want," she growled. "And it isn't any of your business! Just stay away from me."

Tanner groaned again, propping himself up on his elbows, his eyes moving back and forth as he watched the room spin around him. Michelle caught a handful of his hair and held him still. "I'll see Dan, or my daddy, or whoever I want, and you won't say a word about it!"

He didn't argue any further. Michelle let him go, shoving his head back down to the floor with a dull thump. The other Jags respected her space, not getting too close. Michelle looked around at them.

"Where's Kenny?"

"He went out for drinks," Clyde offered.

Michelle grunted. She turned and walked back out of the apartment. She was going to need a long walk before she could cool down again.

Michelle stepped in the door of the cafe and took a wary look around. There weren't any Jags around, nor anyone in colors from the other gangs. It seemed safe enough. She looked behind her, checking the sidewalk outside for anyone who might have followed her. Even though she'd already checked several times and was sure no one would be able to follow her.

Dan wasn't there yet. Irritated, Michelle selected an empty table and sat down. A red-headed waitress walked up. "Hi, honey. Get you a coffee?"

"Yeah, thanks."

"Do you want a menu?"

Michelle shook her head. "No, not yet."

"Waiting for someone?"

"Yeah." Michelle readjusted her chair so she could watch the street outside the window and the door without having to twist around. "Yeah, he should be here soon."

Maybe. He was reliable when it came to his job, the people he lectured for. He always showed up at schools and other events on time. But when Michelle wanted to see him, he was almost always late. She could find the time to see him, arrange to be there alone, away from the gang, but Dan was busy, and she was supposed to excuse it.

Michelle's coffee was just about gone when Dan finally walked in. He spotted her and flashed her a cheerful grin as he walked up to the table. "Hey, Michelle. How's it going? Sorry, I'm a bit late."

"You were a bit late an hour ago," she pointed out.

Dan frowned and looked down at his watch. "Really? I'm sorry, Michelle. I know I finished on time because I knew I had to come here after…"

"And you didn't stay to chat with everybody after?"

"Well…" Another frown and look at his wrist. "I guess I must have. But—"

"Hey!" A couple of girls came over, smiling at Dan. "It's Dan, right? I told you it was him!"

MICHELLE

Dan sat with his mouth open, looking at them. He glanced at Michelle, then back at the girls again. Teenagers. His fans. "Sorry, I don't remember where we've met," Dan offered.

They immediately went into a spiel, telling him which school they went to, when he had come to speak, and how his presentation had had such an impact on them.

"It's so different, having someone who's really been through it tell you how it is," one of the girls gushed. "Especially when it's someone close to you in age, like you are."

Dan smiled politely and tried to indicate Michelle. "Well, it was nice to see you again. I—"

"Could we sit with you? It would be so cool to just sit down and have a heart-to-heart with you…"

"I'm here with a friend—"

The girls pulled out chairs and sat down. "Hi, what's your name?" one of them asked Michelle.

Michelle looked at Dan in disbelief. He just sat there like a lump, as if he didn't know how to take charge of the situation and send them away. "Excuse me! We're having a private discussion here," Michelle said loudly, drawing attention from the other diners in the cafe. The girls fell silent and looked at each other, then back at Michelle, eyes wide. As one, they got up, scowling at Michelle.

Dan got pink. "Sorry…" he apologized to the girls.

"Don't tell them you're sorry," Michelle snapped. "They're the ones barging in on us. They're the ones that should be sorry."

They didn't apologize, but walked away, heads bent together, looking back at Michelle.

Michelle turned her eyes back to Dan. "You're not a celebrity. You can't let people barge in. I wanted to get together with you, not the fangirls!"

"Michelle, I'm sorry. I can't help it if people come up to me…"

"You can help it if you let them sit down and impose on our dinner!"

"Yeah, okay. I'm sorry." He reached across the table and grabbed her hand, giving it a comforting squeeze. "Really, I am. I'm here now. I was late and I was rude, but now you have one hundred percent of my attention."

Michelle looked out the window at the street, watching for anyone suspicious. Dan looked back over his shoulder to see what she was staring at.

"Nothing," Michelle said. "Just making sure. I've been having some trouble lately…"

He took a glance around. "We're alone. It's safe."

Michelle sighed. She motioned for the waitress to refill her cup, and the woman got one for Dan as well. "Menus?" she offered.

"I don't need one," Dan said. "Burger and fries for me. How about you?"

Michelle considered, then shrugged. "Yeah, okay," she agreed. "Same."

The waitress nodded and went to pass the order on to the kitchen. Michelle looked down at her hand in Dan's. "Your work is going good," she suggested. "You're happy with it?"

A smile spread across Dan's face, replacing his anxiety. "Yes. It's amazing to me, how this could all happen. That something good could come out of it all. I feel like I'm making a difference."

"Good."

They were silent for a few minutes. Michelle felt the tension building. They used to be able to sit and just be with each other. Now, the silence was uncomfortable. Even his touch was uncomfortable, and she didn't know when it would be acceptable to pull her hand out of his.

"I know you're not happy doing what you are," Dan said. "You could go back to school. Or break with the Jags. Or do both."

"Why would I go back to school? You think I should be like the cheerleaders? You spend so much time with these girls, you think everybody should go to school?"

Dan's eyebrows rose at this. He released her hand, sitting back a little further in his chair. "I'm not telling you what you should do. You have to find your own path. I'm just saying I know you're not happy."

"What is there to be happy about? Things haven't exactly been going my way."

Dan traced a circular burn mark on the table top. After a few more minutes of silence, the waitress brought their plates to them. "Anything else?"

Michelle shook her head and watched the waitress walk back away again. Dan followed Michelle's eyes. "You know, her life probably isn't that great either, but she manages to put on a smile and get through the day. She's probably a single mom. Maybe with teenagers. Husband ran off and she's been working a dead end job for ten years. Nothing to show for it. Everybody has tough times, Michelle. But some people can pick themselves up and make the best of it and be happy with what they've got." He pushed a few greasy fries into his mouth and prepared to take a bite of the hamburger. "You're alive. Kenny's alive. You got your mom and your aunt to help you out if you want. You've got your dad and Marcie, but you won't even go see her."

Michelle chewed on her burger. She stared down at her plate with her eyes stinging and couldn't think of how to argue it with him. He thought just because he'd climbed out of his addiction, that anyone could pull themselves out of anything. He had no idea how deep a hole she was in.

"I'm sure going to school would solve all my problems," she sneered. Her throat was hot and constricted and the words came out in an unpleasant screech. "I could just become a normal kid if I went to school."

"I'm not saying that. I'm not telling you what to do."

"Except to cheer up and get over myself."

He shrugged and went on eating.

"I didn't come here to fight," Michelle said finally.

"No. I didn't either. I'm sorry."

"Yeah. Forget it."

"Is there anything I can do to help you? Anything?"

"No. I guess... maybe we should stop seeing each other."

"Because of Tanner?" Dan's brows drew down in a scowl.

"No... just because we're making each other miserable. You've got your thing now." Michelle peered out the window, making Dan turn and look again. "And I got my own issues."

"I don't think we have to quit being friends, just because we have other interests."

Michelle couldn't think of how to explain it to him. She ate her burger in silence, watching out the window.

Michelle winced at the bright sunlight when she stepped outside. She blinked a few times, waiting for her eyes to adjust to the light. Tears had collected in the corners of her eyes and she pretended they were from nothing other than the sun.

She headed for the bus stop for the bus that would take her back into Jag territory, keeping a lookout for anyone hanging around looking suspicious. Kenny was leaning up against a lamppost, his arms crossed in front of him. Michelle scowled.

"What are you doing here?"

"Looking for you."

"Did you follow me here?" she demanded. "I told Tanner nobody had better follow me!"

"I didn't see where you went."

His eyes didn't go to the cafe Michelle had come from and Michelle thought he was telling the truth. He might have managed to follow her to the area, but he hadn't seen where she had gone, and had just remained there, waiting for her to reappear. One thing about Kenny, he really couldn't lie. He didn't have the cunning for it. He was like a child; you could see right through any attempt at deception.

"Kenny, you can't follow me. Even if Tanner tells you to. If you want to hang out together, we can, but you can't follow me around."

Kenny didn't make any response.

"I mean it. Do you understand me?"

Kenny was looking past Michelle and she turned her head, knowing with a tight coil of dread already settling in her stomach what she was going to see. Dan was coming up behind her.

"Michelle, I just wanted to say I'm sorry—"

Michelle swore.

Dan looked at her, frowning. He saw Kenny. "Oh, hey Kenny. How's it going?"

"You were meeting Dan." Kenny's fists clenched. His mouth was an ugly scowl.

"No, I wasn't," Michelle insisted, glancing aside at Dan, hoping he'd catch on quickly. "I was just shopping and ran into him. He thinks I'm mad because I won't do anything with him." She rolled her eyes dramatically at Kenny. "But *you* know…"

"I know?" Kenny echoed.

MICHELLE

"Kenny knows what?" Dan demanded. "Kenny knows why you've been avoiding me?"

Michelle breathed out slowly, relieved he'd picked up the hint. "Why I won't do anything with you anymore," she agreed. "Kenny understands that."

Kenny was looking back and forth at them like he was watching a tennis match. His face showed confusion.

"I told you I can't hang out with you anymore," Michelle insisted. "You're not a Jag anymore and I'm with Tanner now. So stop showing up and expecting me to do stuff with you."

She saw Kenny's mouth form the words 'I'm with Tanner now' silently. He focused on Dan. "You leave Michelle alone. Quit following her," he ordered.

Michelle swallowed and nodded at Dan. He gave a wide shrug to Kenny. "Fine. If that's the way you're gonna be."

As he turned away, he touched Michelle the briefest touch on the small of her back and then walked away down the street. Michelle stood, watching him go, still feeling his hand on her back. It was amazing how one brief touch could convey so much. More than their entire conversation at the cafe.

"You're with Tanner now," Kenny repeated, watching Dan walk away.

Michelle looked at him. "Yeah, I am," she agreed.

Michelle felt Tanner moving around beside her and rolled over to see what was wrong. Light was filling the room, but the gang hadn't gotten in until sunrise, so she couldn't judge how long they had been in bed.

"Go back to sleep," she murmured to Tanner, wanting him lying close against her again, holding her to help her sleep.

He moved closer again, so his face was close to her ear. "You're still seeing Dan," he whispered.

Michelle was instantly wide awake. She tried not to let her body tense. He would feel that. She kept her voice low-pitched and sleepy. "What're you talking about?"

"I told you to stay away from him. You're with me. Dan is out."

"Kenny told you we saw him? Then he musta told you I told Dan to leave me alone, too. I wasn't meeting with him. He just showed up while I was talking with Kenny."

Tanner put his arm around her, holding her firmly.

"You might be able to fool Kenny, but he ain't playin' with a full deck. Don't think you can snow me."

Michelle clutched for her knife, but it wasn't there. She'd taken it off when she got ready for sleep. Her belt and sheath were on the other side of the mattress, on the other side of Tanner. He tightened his grip on her.

"Not this time," he whispered. "Do you think I'd make that mistake twice?"

Michelle sat up, squirming away from his grip. "What are you talking about?" she asked briskly, trying to use a normal tone so others would hear her and Tanner couldn't do anything without them knowing. "Since you're awake, I think I'm gonna get some breakfast. You want coffee?"

Michelle was wearing a long t-shirt for a nightshirt. She grabbed her pants from beside Tanner and pulled them on quickly. But her belt and sheath were not attached to them. She looked around. Tanner rose to his feet and pulled on a t-shirt, his eyes drilling into her. Michelle tried to make light of it. To pretend she didn't notice his attitude.

"You seen my blade?"

"Like I said, you think I'd make that mistake again?"

She had hoped she had just misunderstood him. That she'd given his words a meaning he didn't intend. But she was getting nervous now. Really scared of his low, warning voice. Why had he taken her dagger? Because he didn't want a fight with her? Because he didn't want to give her an advantage? Michelle took a step toward the kitchen. Tanner's hand shot out and he grabbed hold of her arm, his grip tight and painful. Michelle tried to pull back, but it was no use.

"Tanner! I just want some coffee."

"We'll go out for coffee. That stuff's crap."

She was only slightly reassured by his words. She couldn't understand why he was holding onto her. But if he agreed to go out for coffee, she would at least be out in public, where he wouldn't dare try anything.

"Where do you want to go, then?" she asked, trying to casually pull out of his grip. But he wouldn't let go.

"Down the street," Tanner offered, his voice sounding almost normal. Maybe he'd had a nightmare that had put him into an angry mood, but now that he was waking up, he was okay. Tanner pulled Michelle to him and put his arm around her. Pasted close together, they walked out of the bedroom, into the communal kitchen and TV area. Glancing around, Michelle was disappointed to see it was deserted. No one was there to see or hear what was going on. The tiny clusters of bedrooms fashioned out of what had once been spacious apartments were full of people. Some of them families, some gang members or junkies. People who couldn't afford a real apartment, but were happy for a roof over their heads and a few plywood divider walls, even if there were no amenities. And the flophouse did offer pirated TV and an ancient coffee maker in each cluster. If she screamed, hundreds of people would hear her. But Michelle didn't know whether to scream. If Tanner was calm and they were just going to the coffee shop, what did she have to be worried about?

She walked with him out of the building. A couple of times she tried to wiggle out from his grip, but he kept her at his side.

"Tanner…"

"Shh."

"Where are we going?"

"Come here."

He pulled her over to a car. She didn't recognize it. Tanner didn't usually drive a car of his own. Jacked one occasionally or borrowed one from one of the other boys, but since they usually stayed within Jag territory, none of them had much use for a car.

"Yours?" Michelle asked, studying it with a frown.

In answer, Tanner reached down and opened the passenger door. Michelle got in, looking at him once more, trying to figure out what was going through his head. As he walked around the car to the driver's side, Michelle surveyed the street around them. It was definitely full daylight, so she must have been asleep for a while. The street was busy, but not crowded. She could smell the coffee from the coffee shop Tanner had said they were going to. And various deep-fried goods from food carts that served the street crowd. Michelle wasn't hungry. All the smells mixing together made her feel nauseated. She touched her waist where her knife usually hung, feeling undressed without it. Vulnerable. Tanner climbed into the driver's seat and started the engine.

"Where are we going?" Michelle repeated.

He turned to her. Without any warning he punched her in the face. Michelle tried to jerk back at the last instant to avoid it, and also hit the back of her head on the interior of the car. Before she had a chance to recover from the first blow, he punched her twice more.

The pain was blinding. Lights flashed in front of Michelle's eyes and she swayed in her seat, dizzy and confused. There was a gasping, sobbing sound she didn't think came from inside of her, but she couldn't figure out why Tanner would be crying. She felt his hands on her and didn't know what he was going to do. Drag her back out of the car? Assault her? She raised her hands to defend herself, but she was too weak. She couldn't even see him in front of her. Tanner buckled Michelle's seatbelt around her.

He pulled away from the curb. Michelle's throbbing head wobbled and she was glad he had done up the seatbelt to keep her from falling over. Foul blood was draining down her throat and she tried to balance herself so she could lean forward, but her head just hit the car's side window, sending another lightning flash through her brain.

Tanner was muttering under his breath, but Michelle couldn't tell what he was saying. She didn't know where they were going. Everything faded out and in again. She tried to hold onto the door handle. Onto reality.

The combination of her spinning head and the blood running down her throat made her sick to her stomach. She tried to tell Tanner to stop the car, but only groans came out. She was sorry for punching him in the face the other day. She had no idea how it felt. And she had kicked him when he was down and humiliated him in front of the gang. That had to be why he was acting like this now. Getting back at her. Showing her what it felt like. But she couldn't apologize, even if she wanted to.

Unable to get control of her lolling head, Michelle wasn't even able to bend over or turn aside when the vomiting started. The warm fluid washed down her chest, soaking into her t-shirt. She felt distant and disconnected, with no control over her own body.

MICHELLE

Tanner swore and rolled down his window. "Just stop that," he muttered.

Michelle tried to protest, but couldn't. He didn't touch her or ask her if she was okay. The vomiting continued to come in uncontrollable waves. At one point, she breathed in the combination of blood and bile and it burned in her lungs and made it hard to get enough air. She coughed and choked but couldn't get it all out.

She didn't know how long it was before Tanner stopped the car. He touched her gingerly, swearing about the slick vomit that coated everything. He unbuckled her seatbelt and pulled her out of the car, stretching her arm around his neck and putting his arm around her body to take her weight. Michelle wanted to ask him where they were going, but she still couldn't speak. She wondered if it was all just a nightmare and in a few minutes she would wake up to find she was just badly hung over.

There were stairs. Tanner made his way up them slowly, stopping to rest every few steps. He opened a door. A few steps later, he laid her down on a mattress. Not on the floor, but a couple of feet up, on a bed. Michelle tried to speak, but her grunts and coughs were incomprehensible. She closed her eyes, trying to clear her brain. When she opened them, blinking to clear her vision, she wasn't sure if she had passed out or no time had passed. Tanner was there. He removed the puke-soaked shirt and replaced it with one that didn't quite fit, and was scratchy and stiff. He threaded her arms through the sleeves and buttoned it up. Michelle groaned.

"Shh. Enough of that. You're all right. It's not that bad."

He pulled her around until she was lying curled up on her side. Her bleeding nose stopped draining down her throat and it was easier to breathe, though the fluid already in her lungs still burned and made her cough. Tanner pulled her hands around behind her and she heard the ripping noise of tape being pulled off of a roll before he wrapped the wide tape around her wrists to pin them together. She struggled to free herself from his grip, but it was too late. When he pressed another piece over her mouth, Michelle panicked, afraid if she threw up again, she would drown in her own vomit. She thrashed.

"Settle down. You want me to do your feet too? Hog tie you?"

Michelle stopped struggling. Tanner waited for a few minutes, then she heard him walk away. She closed her eyes. The shapes around her were too fuzzy and jumbled to make any sense of. She just rested her throbbing head and tried to breathe comfortably.

~

When Michelle next awoke, she had a pounding headache. Her swollen face throbbed in time with her pulse. But the nausea was gone and when she pried her eyes open, as far as the swelling would allow, she could make out some of the shapes around her. Not that there was much to look at. The mattress under her. The closed door. What she thought might be a window that had been boarded over.

She closed her eyes again, concentrating on her body and sorting out the messages it was sending her. Her head and face were the worst. Her arms and shoulders also nagged with a combination of numbness and stretched-out soreness. Her chest still burned and was heavily congested. She coughed every few minutes, but couldn't clear it properly.

The door opened and closed again. Michelle squinted through her swollen lids at Tanner.

"Are you awake?"

She grunted in response. He came and sat on the edge of the bed, looking down at her. "You look a little worse for wear."

He had a bowl and a washcloth and he carefully dabbed at her face, where her skin felt tight from the blood and saliva and all the gunk dried there. He grasped the corner of the duct tape and pulled it quickly off. Michelle yelped at the sting.

"Best to pull it off fast," Tanner said apologetically. "Are you okay?"

Michelle worked her mouth and cleared her throat, not sure if she was able to speak. She coughed for a few minutes, unable to either clear her lungs or settle them down. When she was finally able to stop, she lay there still, breathing shallowly, trying to avoid triggering another spasm.

"What the hell?" she whispered. "You kidnap me, and beat me up, and then you want to know if I'm okay?"

She started coughing again and wasn't able to say all the things she wanted to, which was probably a good thing. Tanner reached over and started to rub her back. She wanted to pull away from him and fight back. But her wrists were still tied, her body a wreck, and she was afraid if she fought him, he would kill her. Tanner had already gone way further than she'd ever expected from him. She sensed he was teetering on the edge, stuck somewhere between his desire to hurt her and revenge the way she'd made a fool of him, and the twisted sort of affection he had for her. He had always been obsessive, right from the start when he'd gotten into that first fight with Kenny and decided he liked Michelle. And it hadn't been the kind of obsession that burned out quickly; it had drawn on for years.

Besides, the rubbing felt good, relaxing her aching muscles and soothing the uncontrollable spasms of coughing. She let her body just sink into the mattress, exhausted. She felt like she'd been fighting for hours or running a marathon. Michelle had almost drifted off to sleep when he leaned in to kiss her on the cheek, startling her and making her flinch back.

"Don't!" she protested, without thinking. The word just came out in a reflex. She forced her mouth closed, not wanting to aggravate him any further. She knew she needed to cooperate with him, to do whatever he wanted, if she was going to survive. He had said once he would never force her like Stan had, but it seemed the time for patient waiting had passed. He was no longer willing to stand by and watch her make a fool of him. He had decided it was time for him to take what he wanted.

This time, at least, he didn't push. He withdrew, looking unhappy. Michelle heard him tear another strip of tape off the roll, and watched him put it over her mouth again, not trying to move away or fight it. Tanner walked back out of the room.

CHAPTER Fifty-One

Dan was exhausted after his long work day, but exhilarated at the same time by the response he was getting from the kids he spoke to. They really got it. And they really identified with him. He wasn't some old fogey telling them not to have any fun. He was a kid like they were, warning them what could happen, explaining how they could get help before something so disastrous happened to them. He was starting to get notes and e-mails from students who said he had made a difference in their lives. Kids who were now working on recovery, because of something he had said to them during one of his talks. Or as he talked with them afterward. He really felt good, knowing he was having a positive effect. Maybe he could prevent some of these kids from having to go through what he had gone through with George. Maybe he could protect some of the brothers and friends and innocent bystanders that would otherwise be injured or killed by drunk or high drivers.

A movement in the hallway outside of his apartment caught his eye and made him realize he had been walking with his head in the clouds, paying no attention to what was going on around him. Not a good idea in the hood. He hung back for a moment, letting his eyes adjust to the dimness of the hallway. He recognized the big figure hanging around his door and smiled.

"Hey, Kenny. What's up?"

Kenny watched him juggle out his key and open up the apartment door. Dan didn't invite him in, but Kenny trailed Dan into the front room. Dan put down his books and looked at Kenny, raising his eyebrows and cocking his head.

"Well, what's up, bud?"

Kenny didn't answer, but instead went to the bedroom that used to be Michelle's and looked around. Then he went to Dan's and looked around it as well. He walked back into the living room, frowning at Dan.

"Where's Michelle?"

"Michelle? Not here. I thought maybe you came to visit me."

Kenny shook his head ponderously back and forth, glaring at Dan as if Dan were trying to fool him.

"I'm looking for Michelle," he insisted.

"Well, I'm sorry. You're not going to find her here. I haven't seen her for a while. Not since that time when I ran into you on the sidewalk. Remember that?"

"I remember." Kenny didn't look pleased with the memory. "Tanner said you're lying."

"You've looked around. You can see Michelle isn't here. I haven't got her hidden in the closet."

Kenny went back into the bedrooms and Dan heard him opening the closet doors and checking. He came back out again.

"Where is she?"

"I don't know where she is. She hasn't been here."

"Where is she?" he repeated.

"Kenny. How long have you been looking for her? When did you see her last?"

"She's not at our place."

"For how long?"

"I dunno." He shook his head again, his thick, dark eyebrows pushing even closer together. "I dunno, a long time."

"Did she and Tanner have a fight?"

"No. I don't know where they are."

"Wait." Dan tried to hold Kenny's gaze, concentrating on what he was saying. "Tanner is missing too? Are they together?"

"I dunno. Where is Michelle?"

"When did they leave? Today? Yesterday?" Kenny shook his head. "Last week?"

Kenny walked over to the fridge and opened the door. He looked inside, and finding no beer, closed the door again.

"Kenny? How long?" Dan persisted.

Kenny turned back to him. "Don't know. Three days."

"You haven't seen Tanner or Michelle for three days?"

Kenny shrugged. Dan thought it through. Maybe Kenny was wrong on the number of days, but he certainly knew the difference between a few hours and a few days.

"Did they tell you where they were going? Did they say they were going on a trip or vacation?"

Kenny just looked at him with blank, vague eyes and gave no response.

"What were they doing? Did they hold up a store? Get scooped by the cops?"

"Nobody knows."

"None of the Jags?"

Kenny just waited for Dan to get his thoughts together and tell him where to find Michelle. Dan considered. Michelle hadn't called him to say she'd been arrested. Obviously, none of the Jags had gotten calls either. Not from her or from Tanner. Michelle would at least have told her brother what was going on. And despite Dan's own suggestion, he couldn't see Michelle and Tanner just taking off on some honeymoon without telling Kenny or anyone from the Jags.

"We'll find her, Kenny. I don't know what happened, or where they went, but we'll find out. Someone must have seen them. Someone knows something."

There were several loud knocks on the door, just about scaring Ruby right out of her chair. Catching her breath, she looked toward the door and then at June. June's face was as white as a sheet.

"Who is it?" June whispered.

"I'm sure it's nothing to worry about," Ruby assured her, getting up. She glanced at the window to begin with, even though she knew without doing so it was dark out. Not an hour visitors normally came by the house. "If it's not someone we know, we can call Charlie. Nice thing about a cop in the family."

MICHELLE

The porch light was already on, triggered by motion detectors. Ruby went to the door and looked out the peephole. There she saw Kenny, squinting angrily in the assault of lights in his face.

"It's Kenny," she said over her shoulder to June.

June didn't look reassured. "Charlie's not here..."

"I'm going to see what he wants. If you're worried, you'd better go into the bedroom. Lock the door."

"Do you have to let him in?"

"It could be important. He could be in trouble and need help. He won't bother with you if you're out of sight."

June hurried out of the room. Ruby waited until she heard the bedroom door shut before opening the door. Kenny pushed in without an invitation.

"Where's Michelle?"

Ruby moved back and watched him make a quick circuit of the living room and kitchen, his head going back and forth as he looked for his sister.

"Michelle is not here," Ruby said.

"Where is she?"

"I don't know. Why don't you tell me what happened? Is she missing?"

He paced restlessly around the room. He went into the hallway and started checking the bedrooms. Ruby pulled out her phone and dialed Charlie. She didn't think Kenny would do anything when he reached the locked bedroom door where June was hiding. But he was obviously agitated. If he decided to force it, Ruby wanted Charlie or one of the other policemen they knew there to keep things calm.

"Hi, honey."

"Charlie, we might have a little problem."

Kenny reached the locked door and after trying the handle, knocked loudly on the door. "Michelle? Michelle, come out!"

"What's going on?" Charlie asked, hearing Kenny.

"Are you close by? Or could you send someone? It's Kenny. I'm sure everything will be okay, but just to be safe..."

"I'm on my way. What's going on? Did he and Michelle have a fight?"

"I don't know what happened. He just showed up here looking for

Michelle. She's not here. But June is in the bedroom with the door locked."

"So he thinks Michelle is locked in the bedroom?"

"Something like that."

Kenny came back into the living room. "Get Michelle out," he insisted. "Get her out of there."

"Kenny, Michelle isn't here. She isn't in the bedroom. It's just June. You're not looking for June."

He shook his head. "Michelle. I want Michelle."

"I know you do. Do you want to come into the kitchen? I'll get you a snack and you can tell me what's going on."

"No! Unlock the door!"

"Michelle isn't here. Maybe she's still coming. Why don't we wait for her in the kitchen? Do you want a cookie?"

He shook his head again, but followed her into the kitchen and watched her put a handful of cookies on a plate. He sat down to eat them at the table. Ruby poured a glass of milk for him to wash the cookies down and he shook his head.

"I want beer."

"Have you already been drinking?"

"Gimme a beer."

Ruby went to the fridge and grabbed a can of cola. She put it beside his plate. Kenny looked at it for a moment and didn't make any further demand for alcohol. Ruby still had her ear to the phone.

"You're doing great, Ruby," Charlie assured her. "You're keeping him calm. That's good."

By the time Kenny picked up the last cookie, Charlie was there. Kenny heard the front door open and took the cookie with him to see who it was. His face fell when he saw it was Charlie.

"Where's Michelle?" he demanded, frustrated.

"I haven't seen Michelle," Charlie said. "Why don't you come sit down, and tell me what happened. Did Michelle say she was coming here?"

Kenny followed Charlie over to the couch and sat down looking at the TV as if waiting for Charlie to turn it on.

"Kenny, why did you think Michelle was here?" Charlie asked, glancing at Ruby and then back at Kenny again.

Kenny looked at him. "She's not with the Jags. She's not with Dan. Maybe here or the cops got her."

"Maybe," Charlie agreed. "She's not here. But I can call in and see if she's been arrested."

Kenny nodded. "Call her now."

Charlie pulled out his cell phone and called in, initiating a search. After a few minutes, he shook his head at Kenny. "No. Doesn't look like she's been arrested."

"Where is she?"

"I don't know. How long has it been since you saw her?"

Kenny hung his head and covered his face with his hands. "I don't know," he moaned. "Where is Michelle?"

Charlie patted Kenny on the back. He looked over at Ruby. "I think maybe we'd better start some inquiries."

Ruby nodded.

Michelle awoke slowly, groggy, her head thick. At first, she was confused. She couldn't remember where she was or what had happened. But Tanner was there. She could feel his arms around her, hugging her close and keeping her safe. When had things gotten to the point where the only time she could sleep soundly was with him?

Gradually, as she lay there, she became aware of the aching strain across her shoulders, and the uncomfortable position her arms were in. She couldn't seem to move them. She opened her eyes and saw the bare room around them. Michelle stiffened as it all rushed back. Tanner had hit her. Had taken her away. Was holding her, bound and gagged.

"Shhh," Tanner had felt her go rigid and he rubbed her back. "It's okay."

Michelle made a sound through the tape and squirmed for a better look at his face. Tanner's eyes were still closed, half-asleep. Automatically calming her like he had done other nights, without even fully waking up. Michelle nudged him with her knee. He pulled away.

"Shh..."

She nudged Tanner harder and his eyes opened. She watched

awareness enter them as he looked at her face and he too remembered what had happened. His expression darkened. Michelle nudged him again, barely applying pressure this time. He reached over and ripped off the tape.

"What?"

"I gotta pee."

She didn't, but it was the only way he would get her up off of the bed. She needed to put some weight on her feet. Get some kind of movement. She didn't have to pee because he still hadn't given her anything to drink. Her body was parched, dry as a desert. She hadn't had to pee in hours. Maybe days. In the tiny, dim room, she couldn't accurately judge the passage of time. But Tanner didn't challenge her claim. He grunted. He released his hold on her and got stiffly to his feet. Tanner had to help her get to the edge of the bed. He pulled her to her feet, but Michelle just about collapsed on the floor. Her knees were weak as a baby's. Tanner took her weight and stood there for a minute, waiting for her to get control and walk upright. Michelle tried to push herself straight and then to put one foot in front of the other, but it was no use.

"Come on, Michelle." Tanner gave her an impatient shake. "You gotta help me out here. Stand up. Walk."

"I can't."

"You can. Come on."

She tried valiantly and still failed. "My legs are asleep."

Tanner snorted and started to walk her to the bathroom, having to take all her weight, while Michelle twitched her legs and tried to remember how to walk. In the bathroom, he jerked her pants down clumsily and sat her down. Michelle just about toppled off of the toilet. Tanner held her shoulders and waited for her to get her balance back. Every time he tried to withdraw, Michelle started to cant to the side again.

"What's wrong with you?" he snapped.

Michelle could hear the faucet next to her dripping. She turned her face toward it. "Would you get me a drink? Water?"

He scowled. "How am I supposed to get it, when I can't let you go? Just sit up for a minute."

"I can't. Put me on the floor."

"You said you had to pee." Tanner's eyes narrowed.

"I... I don't anymore. A drink...?"

He eventually hauled her upright again to pull up her pants and lowered her to the floor. Michelle lay there exhausted, her face inches from the foul toilet, yellow streaks down the outside of the bowl and, she was sure, in dried puddles under her cheek. She could smell the rank urine. But she could also smell the water in the tank and bowl and it was driving her crazy with thirst.

Tanner left the room for a minute and returned with a cup. Michelle listened to him fill it at the sink. Listened to the level of the water rising in the cup, getting higher in pitch as the water reached the top. Her breathing sped up. Tanner shut the faucet back off and knelt down beside Michelle, pulling her back into a sitting position. Once she was up, he took the cup from the counter and held it to her lips. Michelle sucked at the cup greedily. She hardly even let the water touch her cracked lips, gulping it down as fast as Tanner tipped the cup. It hurt her stomach to drink so much all at once, but she kept going anyway, desperate for water.

"Another one?" she gasped when the cup was drained.

Tanner looked at her. "That's enough for now. Or I'm gonna be taking you to the bathroom every ten minutes."

Michelle didn't argue. Tanner pulled her back to her feet and Michelle was able to take a little of her weight this time as he walked her back to the bedroom and deposited her on the bed. Michelle breathed heavily, but it made her cough again, trying to clear the congestion still sitting in her chest. She tried to quiet it and breathe more shallowly. When the coughs quieted, Tanner picked up the big roll of silver-gray duct tape and prepared to tape her mouth again.

"Why are you doing this?" Michelle asked before he could cover it up. "Can't we just go home?"

"This is home now."

"But... can't you leave the tape off? And get it off my arms? It hurts."

"No."

"I'll stay with you. I promise. It will be nice, just you and me..."

Tanner gazed into her eyes for a long time. She didn't say anything else, not wanting to make him think she was too eager and would try to escape. "No," Tanner said finally. "We had years to make that work. It never did."

"I just wasn't ready then… now, I am."

Tanner shook his head and applied the tape over her mouth.

∼

"You can't cancel," Steve protested over the phone. "You're lined up for four more schools this week."

Dan tried to be patient. "Look, it's an emergency, or you know I wouldn't cancel out on you."

"You're not sick."

"No. My friend is missing. I'm trying to help to find her."

"But you could do that on your off-hours. You don't need to cancel your presentations."

"I can't try to juggle both. I can't give the presentations my attention when I'm looking for Michelle. And I need to give this my time. We'll just have to reschedule."

Steve was silent. Dan knew he wasn't happy, knew he didn't understand. But he was going to have to get it. Dan couldn't just ignore Michelle's disappearance and go on as if nothing had happened.

"Look," Steve said in a careful, measured tone. "This is that girl who hangs out waiting for you sometimes, right?"

"Yeah. Michelle. I've introduced you guys."

"She's a gang-banger, right? She could be anywhere. The drunk tank, off making trouble with the gang, whatever. She'll come back on her own. Someone like that isn't reliable. You can't schedule around her issues. You need to take charge of your own life."

"You don't know Michelle. Her brother says she hasn't been with the gang for a few days. I already checked with the cops. She hasn't been arrested. She could be in real trouble."

"She's just off with a guy. Come on. You can't let her issues control your time."

"Steve… I've said all I'm going to. Cancel the rest of this week. I'll let you know on the weekend what to do about next week."

"Dan…"

"What?"

"Are you sober?"

Dan clutched the medallion around his neck. "Yeah, I'm sober."

"You're sure? No setbacks? Are you canceling because you're off the wagon?"

"No. This isn't about my sobriety. It's about a friend being in trouble."

"Okay... but if you cancel too many engagements, we're going to have to take you off of the circuit. And I'd hate to do that. You've been doing really well with these kids. You know how much of a difference it's making."

"I know. And I'll get back to it as soon as I can."

"Uh-oh."

Butch looked up. Artis swore. Butch followed everyone's eyes toward the approaching figure. Dan Thompson. Butch echoed the other Jags' sentiments. As Dan got closer, he held up both hands, open and empty, signaling he wasn't armed or looking for trouble.

"What's this all about?" Clyde growled.

"I'm not here to rattle anybody's chain," Dan said. "I'm looking for Michelle."

Clyde's eyes flashed to the other boys. "Well, you can see she ain't here."

"Does anyone know where she is?"

"We kind of figured she must have run to you. She and Tanner both disappear..."

"Tanner wouldn't have come to me," Dan pointed out, frowning.

"If he went after Michelle, you might have... er... taken care of him."

Dan made a motion indicating he conceded the point. "But she's not with me or I wouldn't be here looking for her. Kenny came to find her, but I haven't seen her."

They looked at Dan and Dan looked at them. Clyde motioned for Dan to join them. Dan sat down but didn't reach for any of the drinks available. Instead, he pulled out a cigarette and lit it.

"When is the last time you saw her?" he asked.

"Friday?" Derry suggested. "They were at the rumble by the school." He looked around at the others.

"After that," Butch disagreed. "Shooting pool at Mike's and tagging after that. They were both there."

"Wasn't that Friday?"

Butch shook his head. "Saturday."

Dan looked around at them. "What about Sunday, then? Anyone see them?"

No one offered any information. Dan chewed on his lip. "Four days. Did they have a fight? Or say they were going anywhere?"

Head shakes. Dan looked at their faces carefully. "Were they getting along? No trouble?"

"Getting along?" Butch snorted. "Tanner's been crazy paranoid about Michelle lately. Jealous if she even looks toward another guy. Like he's tripping out. And since she hit him, he's been... well..." he looked at the other Jags for input. "He's been fuming... just quietly seething..."

It took a minute for Dan to process this. "Since Michelle hit him?"

"Man, you should have seen it!" Derry crowed. "Tanner had followed her somewhere and she was steamed. Held him at knifepoint and then punched him right in the kisser with the dagger still in her fist. He went over like a log."

Dan looked around at the other boys. He met Clyde's gaze. "And you think they went off together? After that?"

"They made up," Clyde said, shifting around in his seat and taking another drink. "They were still sleepin' together after that, so how mad could he be?"

He and Butch looked at each other. Butch shook his head. "They hadn't made up," he said. "It was more of a stand-off."

Dan scratched his jaw. "Don't like it. Don't like it at all. Where's Kenny?"

"Kenny ain't with them," Derry dismissed.

"I know. He came to my place looking for Michelle. But where is he now? I thought he'd be back here."

"He didn't show last night," Clyde advised. "Don't know where he is. Maybe he got himself cooled."

"Maybe he found them."

"Where would he find them?" Derry asked, waving his hand in dismissal. "How could he? He's not exactly... the brightest bulb..."

"I don't know. He didn't say where he was going?"

The Jags looked at each other.

"Kenny don't say much," Butch said. He shrugged.

"Where else would he go?" Derry said. "I mean, who does he know other than the Jags? And you."

"Their mom and their aunt. Maybe he went there."

"Maybe that's where Michelle went."

Dan shook his head. His chest was tight with anxiety. He knew she hadn't just gone back to her mom for a couple of days. Especially now that he knew about how Tanner had been acting. He had to find them quickly. Assuming Tanner hadn't already done something stupid.

Ruby looked in on Kenny watching TV in the living room, before going into the kitchen where June was sitting and Charlie had just finished brewing some coffee. She got her mug and sat down with June. Her eyes were itchy and ached.

"No word?" she said to Charlie.

"Nothing yet. They're putting out some alerts, but they won't do a whole lot about a teen who's already living on the streets. Hard to persuade anyone that she is really missing or in danger. She could just have decided to take off. Moved on somewhere else."

Ruby looked back toward the living room. "And left Kenny behind to fend for himself? You know she wouldn't do that."

"*I* know that. I'm just saying it's hard to convince anyone that she is a missing person. Or to devote any manpower to it."

Ruby nodded and sipped her coffee. June was still nervous about being in the same house as Kenny, but he had settled down since his initial arrival and was distracted by the television.

"What should I do?" June asked. "I should be doing something. Going out and looking for her."

"Where would you look?"

June shook her head. "I don't know."

There was a knock at the front door. Glancing at his watch, Charlie went to get it. He came back into the kitchen with a young man.

"Oh, Dan!" Ruby stood up to greet him. "I'm glad you came. Help yourself to a cup of coffee."

Dan nodded and did so. He turned back around and nodded his head toward the living room. "I wondered if Kenny had come here."

"He was pretty agitated," Charlie acknowledged. "We kept him overnight and he's calmer now. But I don't know how long that will last if we don't turn up some trace of Michelle."

"No luck?"

"Nothing yet. She's not in police custody. I have BOLOs out, but they're not going to be looking too hard for her."

Dan stood next to Charlie, leaning on the counter, rather than sitting down at the table with Ruby and June.

"I think it's Tanner," he said. "I think he's... done something."

Ruby and June were pale. The resemblance between the two of them was remarkable.

"What do you think he's done?" Charlie asked. His voice was low and even. None of them protested that Tanner couldn't have done anything to Michelle.

Dan didn't answer the question directly. "I've been talking to the Jags. I don't know if you know I'm not with them anymore. Not since I got jumped. Tanner squeezed me out."

"What did the Jags say?" Ruby looked at Dan over her mug.

"They've been on the outs. Tanner's always been jealous of Michelle spending too much time with any other guy, but he's gotten worse. And they've been arguing. Had some kind of altercation where Michelle ended up laying Tanner flat out in front of some of the Jags."

"Oh, no..."

It was June that the words escaped from, but they were all thinking it. Ruby and June were gang chicks and Charlie was a cop. They all knew how important a guy's rep was in front of his gang. A guy who allowed himself to be pushed around by his girl, no matter how tough she was, wasn't a man.

"Tanner's crazy about Michelle," Dan said as if it would soften his words.

"Crazy being the operative word," Charlie said. "Even before, he was obsessed with her. He followed her here. Had to be with her all the time. Well... hopefully, I can use some of this information to get

Missing Persons to sit up and take notice. A jealous boyfriend on the scene does raise the risk assessment level."

Dan nodded. "So what can I do to help?"

"You talking to the Jags was a big help. I'm sure they told you more than they would have told any police officer. Kenny took me to the flophouse he and Michelle were staying at since they left your place. The place is bare. We'll get an investigator to look it over anyway, ask neighbors questions, see if anyone saw anything or can pinpoint the time they left there last. You've got your ear on the street... if there's any talk, you'll hear it before the police will. Someone will have to see Tanner sooner or later unless he's left town. And Kenny says he doesn't have a car."

"No. But he can steal one as easily as anyone. If he's done anything to hurt her..."

"Let's just pray he hasn't," Ruby said.

"I've checked the hospital and morgue," Charlie said. "So far nothing. Let's hope it stays that way."

June was looking at Ruby. "I can go to the church and pray," she offered.

Ruby raised her eyebrows. She shrugged. "I don't see how it could hurt."

"It could help."

"If you say so."

Charlie looked Dan in the eye. "Keep your ear to the ground. Let me know if you hear anything or have any ideas."

"Okay... you'll let me know if you find anything out? If there's a direction I should be listening?"

"I'll tell you what I can."

CHAPTER
Fifty-Two

Something gnawed at the back of Dan's mind. He knew he needed to get some sleep if he was to be of any use tracking Michelle down, but his brain wouldn't stop circling like some crazy hamster wheel. If he could rely on chemicals, it would have been the night to take some kind of tranks or downers to dull the activity of his brain so he could make himself sleep.

He tossed and turned, trying to find a comfortable position. He wasn't used to sleeping where it was so quiet. He'd always had other members of the gang around, George, Michelle and Kenny, Tanner... sleeping in the apartment all by himself was disconcerting. It was too quiet. There were distant noises in other apartments. Water running. A baby crying. But it was muffled and he felt like he was buried in a tomb.

Where was Michelle? Where would Tanner take her if he hadn't killed her in a jealous rage? It was hard to picture Tanner being violent toward Michelle. But the Jags had said his jealousy had gotten out of hand. He acted like he was high. He had been boiling mad about the way she'd treated him.

Dan started to drift in and out of sleep, dozing off for a few minutes and then waking up with a start, his brain still searching desperately for an answer. How was he going to track down where Tanner had taken Michelle? It was a needle in a haystack. Tanner had never really hung out anywhere except for with the Jags. There was no secret retreat. No special place he returned to. He knew the Jags, and that was it. But none of them admitted to knowing where he might go. He wasn't staying with any of them. Not while he was holding Michelle hostage.

Dan awoke with a start and stared at the darkness, his heart thumping hard.

Tanner acted like he was tripping out.

What if he wasn't just *acting* high? Tanner liked his pharmaceuticals as much as any other banger. Maybe more.

There was one thing Tanner was going to need, no matter where he went. He could find food at the nearest corner store anywhere in the city. But drugs... Tanner would need a connection. And without being able to rely on the Jags, he didn't have a way to be properly introduced. Getting a good source without references was prohibitively expensive. Nobody was going to sell to an unknown who just walked up demanding his fix. Too many narcs around.

Dan knew who Tanner's dealer was, and though morning wasn't generally a good time for tracking down drug dealers, Dan managed to find him.

"I don't inform on clients," Squeegee responded to Dan's queries. "It wouldn't be good for business."

Dan set his jaw and tried to figure out how he was going to get the information he needed. "Look, you know Michelle, Tanner's... girlfriend."

"I'm not sharing any information about her either."

"No, I know Michelle doesn't use—" Dan cut himself off, seeing the gleam in Squeegee's eyes. "Michelle doesn't use," he repeated.

"Like I said, I'm not informing on any clients."

Dan rubbed his temple, frowning. "Seriously? What's *she* been buying?"

"I don't—"

"You don't inform on clients." What could Michelle be buying from a pusher like Squeegee? She knew how Dan felt about drugs and alcohol. She claimed she didn't like to lose control. She showed no compassion toward the addicts Dan dealt with. But what about something to help her sleep at night? Or uppers to try to treat her depression? Or had she planned another suicide attempt? What if she'd already done something desperate? Maybe her disappearance had nothing at all to do with Tanner.

Dan tried to tear his mind away from the dozens of scenarios that started to tumble through his brain. He had a job to do and he was getting more desperate, not less.

"I don't need to know what either of them buys," he said. "Nothing like that. I'm just trying to track them down. The last few days... you meet either of them? Or make an introduction to a dealer in another part of the city? Or out of town?"

Squeegee continued to eyeball Tanner as if he was trying to pull a fast one. "It's like being a doctor," he explained. "Doctor-patient privilege. I can't disclose—"

Dan's calm exterior broke. It just busted wide open and the temper he'd been struggling to keep suppressed made an appearance.

He grabbed Squeegee by the neck and shoved him back against the wall. "You're no doctor," he snapped. "So spill! I want to know who he's buying from now. Still from you? Or did he move out of your territory and need an introduction? Quit with the nonsense. You know I'm no cop."

The small man's eyes bulged and Dan wasn't sure if it was because he was scared or because Dan's hand was squeezing his windpipe too tightly. He loosened his grip a little.

"Tell me."

Squeegee's hands clawed at Dan's. Dan shook his head. "I'm not letting go until you tell me," he warned. "I'm tired of games. You tell me what you know about Tanner."

"He did move," Squeegee croaked out. Dan loosened his grip a little further and waited. "I had to reach out to Tyler, let him know Tanner was legit."

"Where's Tyler's territory? Where do I find him?"

"I can't..."

"You tell me, Squeegee. Or I'm just going to squeeze." Dan demonstrated. Squeegee struggled. Dan released his grip. "Now. Where do I find Tyler?"

Squeegee rubbed his throat tenderly and told Dan where to find Tanner's new supplier. Dan nodded. "That wasn't so hard, was it?"

MICHELLE

∼

Dan had been forced to move a couple of times when people had started to look at him, wondering what he was doing hanging around with no apparent purpose. But from each position he took up, he kept an eye on Tyler, Tanner's new drug dealer. Tyler was more flamboyant than Squeegee, who no one would take for a drug dealer if they didn't know it from other sources. But Tyler, with his studded leather and fedora, fairly screamed 'dealer.' Even so, the police didn't appear to be taking any active interest in his trade, and he continued to ply his drugs in plain view.

There was no guarantee Tanner would show up. He might have enough of a stash for several days. But Dan didn't think approaching Tyler for information would work out as well as squeezing Squeegee had. He would be tougher to get information out of, and Dan noticed there were a couple of heavies who hung around up and down the street and were keeping a pretty close eye on Tyler. He wasn't vulnerable like Squeegee.

The morning passed without any luck. But Dan hadn't really expected to see Tanner in the morning. Like the rest of the gang, he was a night owl and he wouldn't be getting ready for the day until noon or later. As the afternoon drew on, he started to doubt himself. Tanner wasn't going to show. Maybe he already had enough drugs for a few days. Maybe he didn't have any money. Maybe Squeegee had sent Dan on a wild goose chase.

Dan's eyes were tired and he rubbed them, trying to soothe the scratchiness. He opened them wide, looking back at the dealer. In the time he'd closed his eyes, Tanner had appeared. Tanner approached Tyler tentatively, looking around for any cops, checking on the guards. Apparently satisfied with the set-up, he turned to Tyler and conversed with him. The transaction was brief, money and drugs changing hands, and then Tanner was walking away.

Dan moved quickly after him. His heart pounded hard in his chest. If he lost Tanner, he lost his one chance to find Michelle. Who knew how much longer she had. Or if it was already too late and Tanner had killed her. Dan stayed back as far as he dared. Tanner didn't seem to suspect anything. He didn't look back over his shoulder or survey the street. He just headed—Dan hoped—straight back home. Tanner approached a dilapidated old building and started to look around for any trouble. Dan stepped back into the doorway of a shop, out of sight. He waited a few seconds before peeking out. Tanner was moving into the apartment building.

Dan rushed to catch up. When he stepped into the building, he heard footsteps on the stairs. He stood at the bottom, trying to estimate how far Tanner had gone up. He listened closely to each step and followed, keeping his own footsteps as silent as possible. A door opened and closed above him, and he tried to get up to it before Tanner could disappear. He made it just in time to peek through the narrow window and see Tanner open the door to his apartment.

Before Tanner could close the door, Dan was on top of him. Tanner let out a yell and fought back desperately. Dan was bigger and more experienced, but Tanner fought like a wildcat and Dan struggled to keep him down and get him under control. Almost lying on top of Tanner, Dan finally managed to get a sleeper hold around his neck and in a few seconds Tanner went limp. Dan released him slowly, watching for any sign Tanner was just playing possum. But Tanner didn't move, didn't try to jump up and attack him. Dan got to his feet and looked around. The apartment was tiny. There really wasn't anywhere to hide. He opened the door to the bedroom.

Michelle was lying on the bed, her back to the door, her hands bound behind her. She didn't move at the sound of the opening of the door. Dan hurried to her.

"Michelle? Michelle, are you okay?"

She didn't stir when he touched her. Dan bent over Michelle to look at her face. It was bruised and swollen. Her eyes were shut. She seemed thinner, her skin dry and papery. But she was warm to the touch. Dan felt for her pulse and was relieved when he found it, ticking the seconds away.

"It's okay, Michelle," he told her, even though she couldn't hear him. "You're safe now. Everything is going to be okay."

He pulled out his cell phone and dialed Charlie.

Charlie looked in the door, taking a quick glance and ducking back again. The front room of the apartment appeared to be empty.

"Dan, you there?" he called.

"Yeah. In here."

Charlie moved slowly into the room, a couple of officers he had called for backup trailing in behind him. After looking around to be sure there was nowhere Tanner could be hiding, Charlie pushed the door to the bedroom open. Dan was sitting on the bed next to Michelle's supine body.

"Where's Tanner?" Charlie questioned.

Dan looked at him, the color draining from his face. "He was out there... I left him unconscious on the floor."

He got up and went to the door as if he thought Charlie might just have missed Tanner lying in the middle of the floor. Dan swore and leaned on the doorframe.

"He must have woken up... and sneaked off."

Charlie holstered his weapon and secured it. "It looks that way."

Dan looked around on the floor for some clue. He picked up a couple of squares of paper that looked like miniature postage stamps. He handled them by the edges and showed them to Charlie.

"Everybody kept saying he's been acting different. Crazy paranoid."

Charlie opened up a small size evidence bag and dropped the stamps into it. "LSD could explain that."

"Yeah."

Dan led Charlie back into the bedroom. "She hasn't woken up... but she has a pulse."

"Thank goodness for that."

Charlie leaned over Michelle and pried her eyelids open. He also felt her pulse and nodded confirmation to Dan. "I already have EMTs on their way. They should be here any second." He realized he hadn't yet advised the scene was cleared and pulled out his phone to report it so the EMTs could come up.

CHAPTER
Fifty-Three

Michelle came to gradually, one fraction of consciousness at a time. Something was different. It took a long time for her to realize she could move her arms and hands. She moved restlessly in the bed, stretching the muscles that had been forced to be still for so long.

"Michelle. Michelle, are you awake?"

Michelle pushed the voice away at first. But later she realized the voice meant something. Female, not male. Not Tanner. Had she finally woken up from that nightmare? Michelle tried to pry her eyes open. If the nightmare was done, she should be able to open her eyes now. She rubbed them with her fists. Her face still felt bruised and swollen, her own touch sending lightning bolts of pain through her nose and cheeks.

"Michelle."

She blinked toward the sound but wasn't able to sort out the input from her eyes yet. Michelle lay there for a long time, staring without comprehension at the light and white shapes around her before it finally started to coalesce into something that made sense.

"Ruby?"

Ruby smiled at her. "Hi, there. I'll bet you're feeling like crap."

Michelle tried to look around, but her head was too heavy to move. "Where am I?"

"You're in hospital. You're safe now."

Michelle swallowed. Her throat hurt. And her lips were cracked and swollen. It hurt to talk, but she pushed on, so relieved to have someone other than Tanner to talk to, even if it was just a dream or hallucination.

"Where's Mama?"

"She just went to the chapel for a few minutes to pray. She'll be back up before long."

Michelle wondered fleetingly whether it was true or whether June had gone somewhere private to shoot up. The whole religion thing couldn't last long.

"Justin is on his way," Ruby said.

"Kenny?"

"Kenny's right here. Kenny, come around so Michelle can see you."

There was a noisy sigh and Michelle heard him get to his feet. In a minute, Kenny's face swam into view in front of Michelle. She reached out and tried to touch him. "Kenny. Are you okay?"

She couldn't reach him, but he grabbed her hand, squeezing it too tightly. "I'm not hurt," he said. "You're the one who got hurt."

"He didn't do anything to you?"

"Tanner?"

Michelle nodded the best she could, but her head pounded and vertigo threatened to send her back into the darkness.

"Yeah, Tanner. Did they catch him?"

Kenny made a derisive snorting noise. "Dan let him get away."

"Dan? Where is he?"

"He's at the police station with Charlie," Ruby contributed. "Filing a statement and seeing if he can help them track Tanner down before he can hurt anyone else."

Michelle let her eyes close. "Who else would he hurt?"

"Well, you're probably right there. It was always you he was interested in, wasn't it?"

"Yeah."

Michelle just breathed. Her chest still hurt, but not as much as it had.

"Is she awake?" another female voice asked tentatively.

Michelle tried to turn toward the sound. "Mama?"

"Come around here," Ruby told June, getting out of her seat. "Come sit where she can see you."

Michelle saw Kenny's eyes dart toward June. He didn't threaten her, but he moved out of the way, disappearing from sight again as June moved in.

"Oh, my baby," June said, touching Michelle's hair. "We were so worried! How are you?"

"Thirsty."

June looked around and found a cup. She held the straw to Michelle's mouth and Michelle sucked down as much as she could until her stomach hurt and she had to stop. June put the cup aside and continued to stroke Michelle's hair.

"There, sweetie. It will be okay."

Michelle closed her eyes, drifting back to those early days. It hadn't all been bad. There had been times... June taking them out for a walk to the park... comforting Michelle when she was sick... Michelle had loved trips to the library. And June had taken her, even though Michelle knew June could barely read and Kenny had no interest in anything beyond looking at pictures. Those trips to the library had been just for Michelle.

She wasn't sure whether she had been asleep or not when Justin arrived.

"Has she been awake? Is she okay?" he asked Ruby in a low, urgent voice.

"She'll be okay," Ruby said. "She's dehydrated and a little worse for wear, but she'll recover. Is she awake, June?"

Michelle opened her eyes to look at June. June smiled at her and nodded. "Yes. She's awake."

June's eyes followed Justin as he walked across the room. Justin came into Michelle's vision, but instead of looking at her, he was looking at June.

"Hi, June."

"Justy—Justin," June's voice cracked. "How are you?"

It took Michelle a few seconds to process their awkwardness and to realize that even though she had seen each of them, they hadn't seen each other. Not since that painful parting long ago when Michelle was eight.

"Daddy," she said.

MICHELLE

His eyes turned from June to Michelle. He reached down to ruffle her hair. "Hi, pumpkin. You know, you gave us all a pretty good scare."

"Sorry."

He perched on the edge of the bed, looking down at her. "Was it that boy who was following you? At the truck stop?"

"Yeah."

"I hope they lock him up and throw away the key!"

"He managed to get away," Ruby said, in her calm, even voice. "The police have put up roadblocks and are searching, hoping they can still catch him."

"They'd better find him," Justin growled. "You can't let someone like that just go wandering around."

Michelle closed her eyes to rest them and to try to think things through, but her lids were so heavy she couldn't open them again.

When Michelle awoke again, she was no longer lying on her side, facing the visitor chair and the wall, but was lying on her back. The head of the bed was elevated so she was partially sitting up. It gave her a better view of the hospital room and she could breathe more easily. She wanted to rub her eyes to clear them, but remembered how much it had hurt last time. Ruby and Kenny were gone. June and Justin were there but had fallen asleep. June was leaning with her head on Justin's shoulder, and Justin's head was tipped back at an uncomfortable-looking angle. He was snoring occasionally, a long raspy sound. Michelle was surprised either of them could sleep in the positions they were in. The window showed it was dark outside.

She choked up a little, looking at them. The reuniting of her parents. Of the twins who had once been so close, but had been estranged for almost as long as she could remember. She knew when they woke up, they wouldn't be looking nearly so comfortable and at home with each other. The awkwardness and the stress and the bitterness between them would return.

The other person in the room was Dan. He was sitting on the other side of her bed. His eyes were shut and his head was nodding. Michelle reached over to touch his arm. Her aim wasn't quite true, but she managed to make contact. Dan straightened and opened his eyes.

"Well, hey, sleeping beauty," he whispered. He cleared his throat, but kept his voice quiet, glancing at June and Justin and obviously not wanting to wake them. "How are you doing?"

Michelle moved her shoulders around, trying to ease the stiffness of her body and wake herself up a bit more. "I'm alive."

"I..." he swallowed and started again. "I wasn't sure you would be."

Michelle could see the pain in his eyes. Fear still lurked there. She looked away, not wanting to feel it. "Don't you have a meeting to go to?" she asked flippantly.

Dan reached over and held her hand for a moment, then wove his fingers through hers.

"Don't you have a boyfriend?" he countered.

Michelle's anger flashed. It was a struggle to keep her mouth shut and not respond to the jab. She supposed it had been a low blow on her part to goad him about his meetings. She just didn't know where to go, how to get around the issues that separated them like an insurmountable wall.

"I canceled all of my appearances to look for you," Dan said. "Nothing else was more important than finding you."

She turned her gaze back toward him and searched his face. The words were just what she wanted to hear, but she had to be sure they were sincere. She didn't want to be tricked into believing he cared. Like Tanner had said *he* cared. Dan's face was open. She saw no sign of deception there. Michelle thought about it, looking down at their hands.

"I can't believe Tanner would do something like that," she said, skirting their personal issues. "I thought... I didn't think he'd ever hurt me."

"Did you know he was taking LSD?"

Michelle raised her eyebrows in disbelief. "Acid? Tanner?"

Dan nodded.

"No... I mean, he's always done pot and booze. And some pills... but never hard stuff. Crack or meth. Acid? You're sure?"

"That's what he bought today. That's how I found you. Found his dealer and waited for him. Followed him back to where he had you."

"I didn't know. I guess... that's why he changed... I never saw him act like that before. I mean, he'd get a bit pushy, but he'd never... physically... he'd never hurt me." She touched her bruised face.

"Did he... uh...?" Dan cleared his throat again and shrugged, not wanting to finish the sentence.

Michelle looked away from him, swallowing and trying to keep her breathing normal and her voice perfectly even. "It's not like I haven't been with him before, so what difference would it make?"

Dan didn't say anything for some time. Michelle watched June and Justin, sleeping peacefully cuddled up against each other. Eventually, she looked back at Dan.

"All I can say," Dan said darkly, "is that Tanner had better hope the cops find him before I do."

Charlie was framed in the hospital room door. "We got him!" he announced.

Michelle wasn't sure how she felt. She saw the open relief on Dan's face. He'd felt guilty for having had Tanner in his control and then having allowed him to escape. But Michelle didn't feel relief. She felt like it was her fault Tanner was going to jail. Why had she resisted him for so long? She knew he was a nice guy. He cared about her and wanted to take care of her. So why had she refused to commit to him? She didn't have a serious relationship with Dan. And she shouldn't have let Carter split them up. So what if he had beaten Tanner in a fight? She didn't have to abide by the whims of a couple of hormonal boys. She should have just stayed with Tanner in the first place. Then none of this would have happened.

"Michelle?" Charlie was looking at her with concern. "Are you okay?"

"Yeah, I'm fine. That's good. That's really good. Tell the arresting officer 'good work' for me."

Charlie nodded, a crease between his eyebrows.

"What?" June had woken up. "Did you say you caught him? The guy who hurt Michelle?"

"Yes," Charlie agreed. "He didn't get very far. You'll testify against him?" he said to Michelle, his eyes narrow.

Michelle bit her lip. It had all ended up being such a mess. She had never really liked Tanner. Had never wanted to end up with him. But he was—or at least had been—a nice guy, up until the end.

"You know you gotta," Dan said quietly.

"But what if—I mean, the only reason he acted like that was the LSD. He's not really... responsible."

Dan's eyes went to the ceiling. "I was responsible for what happened to Georgie," he said. "Even though I was totally plastered. If I hadn't chosen to drink and drive, it wouldn't have happened. Nobody made Tanner take acid. That was his own choice. And he's gotta be responsible for it."

"But you didn't have to go to prison and George was hurt a lot worse than me." Michelle gestured to her face. "This will heal."

"I did serve time," Dan said. "They just arranged so I could serve it around respite services for George, so I didn't have to be away from him for too long. And they counted taking care of him toward service hours."

"The penalties for DUI are different than for kidnapping," Charlie inserted. "If Tanner was under the influence of LSD, then his lawyer will have to decide whether to use that as part of his defense."

"I don't know what to do." Michelle shook her head. "Is he okay? Did he... did he resist arrest?" She was sure they all knew what she meant. Had the cops beaten him up? If they considered Michelle one of their own, due to her relationship with Ruby and Charlie, they could have hurt Tanner pretty badly in retribution for the way he'd hurt Michelle.

Charlie shifted his stance. "He didn't go quietly. But I don't think they used undue force. He's got some bruises. Nothing as bad as yours."

Michelle nodded, staring down at her hands.

Later, it was just Dan and Michelle. The room was quiet and still, the only sound the muted noises of the nursing station and the PA system pages in the hall outside.

"I don't know what I'm going to do," Michelle said.

Dan raised his eyebrows. "About what?"

"I can't really go back to my place... it's Tanner's flop, not mine and I don't exactly want to stay there."

"You don't have to go back there. In fact, you don't have to go back to the Jags at all. You can come back to my place. *Our* place."

Michelle looked Dan in the face. "Really?"

"We got it together. Wasn't Tanner the only reason you moved out? Because he was threatening to take Kenny away?"

Michelle nodded. That was why she had left. But she knew in her heart that Tanner hadn't been the only problem. She and Dan had never discussed their relationship and it was a big question mark in her mind. Did he care about her? That way? Did she care about him? Would all the other things always end up getting between them? Tanner and Carter, their siblings, Dan's work, and the other girls? She and Dan didn't exactly have a good track record for putting each other first. Michelle suspected they needed that if things were going to work out.

"Michelle..." Dan took her hand and wrapped his warm, strong fingers around hers. "I know there's an age difference and you don't think much of my work... but we could try... if you wanted to. If not... we could just be roommates. If that's what you want."

"I'm not against your work," Michelle said, eyes down. "I know it's important. It's just... it doesn't leave a lot of time... and I don't know where I fit into it all."

"If I watched my hours and made sure we had time together... what do you think? Could we do it?"

She studied their hands and didn't raise her eyes. "I don't know."

"Could we try?"

Michelle finally looked up at his face.

"Yeah," she said. "I think we could try."

CHAPTER Fifty-Four

Charlie and Kenny were glued to the TV. The girls had been in the kitchen getting the final meal preparations done. June was awkward in the kitchen, completely useless at food preparation. But Ruby was patient with her, trying to show her what to do. Michelle could tell June was trying. Michelle's skills weren't much better than June's. It came easier to her and she'd read through the recipe books before starting, but she wasn't any more experienced at preparing a traditional Christmas dinner than June was.

Michelle had one eye on the clock, watching it count down to dinner time. The boys shouted and booed at the TV and she looked into the living room. Kenny threw a TV Guide on the floor, booing more loudly, obviously trying to make a bigger fuss than Charlie. Michelle shook her head. She loaded the warm buns into the bread basket and covered them up.

The doorbell rang. Michelle swallowed and looked at Ruby, her heart racing.

"It's okay," Ruby reassured her. "It will be fine."

Michelle nodded. Ruby went to the door. Michelle glanced over at June. June was white around the mouth. Her eyes were widely dilated. Michelle didn't know what to say to her, so she said nothing. She heard Ruby greet the visitors cheerfully. Michelle walked from the kitchen to the living room with a lead weight in her chest.

Justin came into the house first, turned around backward to pull the wheelchair up the steps. He saw Michelle and gave her a tight smile. Michelle licked her lips and swallowed. Justin turned the wheelchair around and Michelle saw Marcie's wide, open-mouthed smile. Marcie babbled a greeting, and Michelle gave her a genuine smile.

"Hi, Marcie," she greeted around a big lump in her throat.

She felt June push by her. Before Michelle could process what was going on, June was bent over the wheelchair, wrapping her arms around Marcie's slight form.

"My baby girl!" she exclaimed, pressing her cheek against Marcie's face. "Oh, my baby girl! I haven't seen you for so long. You don't even know who I am, do you?"

She backed off a little so she could look Marcie in the face. Marcie's mouth closed and Michelle could see she was struggling to form a word. Marcie's eyes went to Justin, and he was focused on her to help interpret. Marcie's drooly mouth opened and closed again and she pushed the word out.

"Ma."

Tears started down June's cheeks. She didn't need Justin to interpret for her. "Yes, it's Mama," she agreed with a sob.

The rest of the family was coming into the house. Michelle looked up from the tender reunion to look at them. She recognized Sondra. The younger children were an unfamiliar, noisy mob.

"Welcome," Ruby was saying to them. "Nice to meet you. Merry Christmas!"

Charlie had gotten up from the couch and he also came over and shook hands, smiling and greeting Sondra and each of the kids. Kenny stood up and looked at the crowd of newcomers, his mouth slightly open. His eyes went to June and Marcie, then for an instant to Justin, and then to Sondra. Sondra was helping her kids off with their coats and noticed his stare.

"Hello, Kenny."

Kenny looked over at Michelle, his brows drawn down. She walked around the outside of the group to his side. "That's Sondra. Justin's girlfriend."

He shook his head. "I don't know her."

But his voice said he remembered something. "We used to," she said. "A long time ago, before Daddy left. We used to go to the zoo and stuff."

His jaw worked as he ground his teeth. "I don't remember."

"It's okay." Michelle looked at Ruby. "Are we ready to eat now? Should we get dished up?"

Ruby nodded. "Why don't you help Kenny get ready and Sondra and I can get her kids dished up?"

Michelle led Kenny into the kitchen. He looked over the heaping buffet with big eyes. "It's like Christmas on TV!" he blurted. "Wow!"

Michelle laughed. "Yeah. Here, what do you want? Turkey and mashed potatoes. And do you want veggies? Sweet potato?"

"Everything." He took the plate from her and held it while she loaded it up, his eyes enormous. When she was done, he went back into the living room and sat down in front of the TV.

"Hi, Michelle," Sondra said, as she started on plates for her kids.

Michelle glanced sideways at her and swallowed.

"It's nice to see you again," Sondra ventured.

"Yeah." Michelle clenched her teeth, holding back all the bitter accusations. Sondra had known what she was doing, had kept them apart all those years ago. But Michelle was trying to keep things happy and relaxed for Christmas. She had been prepared to deal with June and Justin, but seeing Sondra had thrown her for a loop. She hadn't worked out how to deal with Sondra. She looked for something to say that wouldn't bring up their past. "Your kids are cute."

"Thanks!" Sondra bit her lip, looking over the spread. "This all looks so good. Did you help?"

"Yeah. A bit."

The doorbell rang again and Michelle breathed a sigh of relief. She knew who it would be. Ruby stepped out of Michelle's way as Michelle made her way to the door. Michelle opened it to Dan. He grinned and handed her a package of bakery cookies.

"Merry Christmas."

"You too."

He leaned in and gave her a quick peck on the cheek. "You okay?" he murmured.

"Yeah." Michelle nodded, breathing out a long sigh. "I think it'll be okay."

Did you enjoy this book? Reviews and recommendations are vital to making a book successful.

Please leave a review at your favorite book store or review site and share it with your friends.

Don't miss the following bonus material:
Sign up for mailing list to get a free ebook
Read a sneak preview chapter
Other books by P.D. Workman
Learn more about the author

DON'T MISS A THING! GET THE LATEST NEWS AND A FREE EBOOK

PDWORKMAN.COM/SIGNUP

Preview of Chloe

CHAPTER
One

Chloe was dragged out of sleep by shouting and by someone shaking her violently. Her head and shoulders flopped around, out of control, and she tried to go back to sleep instead of having to wake up and face whatever was going on. She thought maybe it was a family fight. She was no stranger to yelling in the middle of the night, to fights between her parents or between her mother and one of the other kids.

But the shaking and the shouting didn't stop. Even when they fought at night, they didn't come and shake her awake. She was supposed to be asleep in her bed. She didn't get up in the night. It was against the rules. And Chloe always followed the rules, no matter how unreasonable they might seem.

"Wake up!" a harsh voice yelled. "You need to wake up! Right now!"

He pulled the blankets off of her and dragged her to the edge of the bed. Chloe put her feet on the floor, her head so foggy and thick that she still couldn't force her eyes open enough to see what was going on.

The thick, strong fingers pulled her upright. Chloe's knees sagged, refusing to take her weight. Why wouldn't they just let her sleep? She was supposed to be sleeping. She wasn't supposed to be getting out of bed. He continued to shake her and hold her upright while Chloe tried to find her feet and give her legs the command to hold her up.

"Come on. Open your eyes now," the voice yelled in her ear. Chloe turned her head away from him, but he let go of one arm and grasped her chin, forcing her head to turn back, shaking it, slapping her lightly on the cheeks. "Open your eyes. You need to wake up. You need to get up now!"

Chloe blinked sluggishly. The bedroom light was on. The window was still dark. It was the middle of the night. The man holding her wasn't her father. She had known that, but she hadn't stopped to wonder who he was. Now as she blinked, she saw it was some kind of policeman. A dark blue uniform. Gold decorations. A heavy utility belt with a gun holster on one side and a baton on the other.

"Wha—?" Chloe's tongue was clumsy, and she couldn't slur out the question. "What's…?"

"You need to come with me now. Can you walk?"

Chloe looked down at her feet. They were on the floor now, and apparently holding her weight. She concentrated on getting them to move. On getting her right foot to slide forward so that she could take a step.

The policeman put an arm around her waist, dragging her arm around his shoulder to support her. With him taking most of her weight, he took a step toward the door of the bedroom. Chloe stumbled along with him. Her feet were moving, but her steps were the wrong length or timed wrong because nothing felt natural and right. There were other voices yelling back and forth. Too many people in the house. Why had the police come? Was there a fire? A fight? Why would they be taking Chloe out of her room?

He kept encouraging her, dragging her along by force and acting as if she was walking of her own volition. "Come on… that's right… keep going…"

He walked her through the living room, which was swarming with people. When Chloe turned her head groggily to look around at them, the cop turned her head back the other direction, away from the living room, toward the kitchen.

But Chloe had already seen, and as the policeman walked her out the front door, her brain was trying to process it. Trying to assemble the pieces of what she had seen in the living room, the fragments of voices, all the strange things going on, to try to understand what had happened.

He took her right out the front door, and Chloe was distracted momentarily by the frigid concrete under her bare feet. It helped to wake her up a little, and she suddenly wondered why she was still wearing her nightgown and had nothing on her feet. Why hadn't she changed before going outside? Why hadn't she gotten on her socks and shoes, at least? And a sweater. It was cold outside.

She was blinded by flashing, strobing lights. Red and blue. And more people outside. Chloe could finally hear her mother's voice as she screamed and railed at someone. She and Chloe's father must have gotten into a fight. The police had come to break it up. Her father was still in the house, in the living room, and her mother, Mim, was outside complaining to the police about the whole thing.

She could hear Justin's and June's voices too. June crying and screaming. Justin's voice calm and even. But all the noise and activity broke everything up and made it impossible for Chloe to understand. There were more sirens, cops yelling back and forth, an ambulance driving up to the house, siren screaming away. Chloe swayed on her feet with a wave of vertigo. But the policeman still held onto her firmly and she didn't fall down.

"It's okay," the policeman assured her. "Everything is going to be okay. We will take you somewhere safe, and everything will be fine."

"I want..." Chloe was still struggling to tame her sluggish tongue. "Want to go to bed. What's... what's going on?"

"There's been an accident. We'll explain more to you when we get somewhere quiet. Let's get you somewhere you can sit down."

He walked her through the cold, wet grass with no regard to her bare feet. He was wearing socks and shoes; why would he notice how damp the grass was? He took her to one of the police cars pulled in front of the house at random angles and opened the front door. He lowered her gently into the front passenger seat. Chloe pulled her feet into the car and placed them on the warm, dry carpet. It was gritty with gravel, but at least it was dry. She closed her eyes.

"When can I go home?"

"Don't worry about that right now, okay? Everything will be taken care of. They'll take you somewhere safe tonight."

"Who will? You?"

"No, it won't be me." Chloe looked up at his face and blinked, trying to adjust to all of the flashing lights and force away the afterimages. Why was she trying to memorize his face when he said he wouldn't be the one that would take her somewhere safe? He had other things to do. She would never see him again.

Chloe closed her eyes again. "So sleepy."

"Try to stay awake. There are going to be questions for you to answer."

He stood there for a moment longer, not saying anything, but not leaving her alone. Then she heard his footsteps as he retreated. Or at least she imagined she did. Probably she couldn't, over all the chaos raging around her. Chloe tried to just retreat into sleep again. Maybe when she woke up, she would find that it had all just been a dream. A very realistic dream.

She couldn't remember whether she had fallen back asleep in the police car, or whether she had just sat there, watching all of the police running back and forth outside. She wasn't sure whether hours had passed or only minutes. Everything seemed out of step. It had to be a dream. That would explain why it didn't make any sense.

A cop got into the driver's seat beside her, introduced himself, and talked all the way to wherever they were going. But Chloe didn't hear a single word he said. She didn't look at him. Didn't ask him to repeat his name, and didn't introduce herself. She didn't know whether he asked her any questions, or if he just chattered on to fill the silence without expecting any answer from her. They got to the police station. Chloe was pretty sure it was the police station. Red brick, set low to the ground; it looked like a police station. The cop pulled into the parking lot and got out of the car, then went around to Chloe's side and opened her door.

"Come on, sweetheart," he encouraged, putting a hand under her elbow and easing her out of the car. Chloe swung her feet out of the car and stepped on gravel atop concrete. She winced. It was as bad as stepping on Lego bricks when she had to get up to go to the bathroom.

The policeman said something to her, and Chloe directed her gaze at his face, wondering what he had asked. He was obviously waiting for some kind of answer.

"Is that how they took you out of the house?" he asked, shaking his head. "In your nightgown? Don't you have any other clothes?"

Chloe shook her head. He led her through the parking lot, stepping gingerly over the sharp gravel and onto the smooth tile of the police station hallways. Chloe rubbed her arms, trying to rub away the goosebumps.

A few minutes later, they were at a counter with another cop.

"Chloe Simpson," the officer who was escorting her said. "Age twelve or so? They'll be bringing in the mom and the brother."

"Thirteen," Chloe said. "I'm thirteen."

She rubbed her eyes with her fists, trying to focus on what was going on. But her brain was still too fuzzy to pull everything together.

"Where's…? What's…? What's going on?"

"All your questions will be answered soon," her escort assured her.

He stuck a red-bordered 'visitor' label with her name on it to the front of her nightgown. Then he was guiding her through the hallways again.

Chloe was taken to a bare conference room, with just a table and a few chairs. He nudged her into one of the chairs.

"Have a seat, please, Chloe."

She was happy to get off her feet again, but the metal of the chair was cold enough to feel through the nightgown. Chloe hugged herself tightly, trying to stop the shaking that started deep down in her stomach.

"What can you tell me about what happened tonight?" the policeman asked her.

Chloe studied him for a moment and then closed her eyes, wanting to go back to sleep and not have to think about anything. What had happened tonight? She'd been pulled out of bed because her parents had gotten into a fight. That was all. It was nothing to do with her. Nothing to do with any of the children.

"Chloe."

She ignored him. As uncomfortable as she was, she was going to go back to sleep sitting in the cold chair. Block him and anyone else out. Not think of anything.

"Chloe."

His hand closed around her arm to get her attention, then released her abruptly. "You're cold as ice!" The backs of his fingers brushed her cheek. "Wake up. You have to stay awake, Chloe. Come on."

Chloe opened her eyes again and blinked at him. The shaking inside was getting worse and so was the desire to just shut everything out. The cop moved across to the door of the conference room. Chloe heard him call to someone, and they had a muttered conversation.

"All she's wearing is a thin nightgown..." one of them growled. "...blankets, clothes... going to need a social worker..."

Chloe roused herself, rubbing her eyes. "No social worker," she insisted. "I don't need any social worker."

They ignored her. Within a few minutes, the officer was wrapping a dark wool blanket around her. It was scratchy like a camp blanket, but at least it provided a little warmth. Chloe lifted her feet off the floor to her chair, pulling her knees up to her chest so that she could enclose her whole body in the warm cocoon.

"Wait, are you hurt?"

Chloe followed his gaze to the floor where her feet had been. There was a smudge of dirt and what looked like blood. Chloe rubbed her feet.

"Maybe I cut them on the gravel," she suggested.

More dirt and blood transferred to her hands and she rubbed it away with the blanket. The cop bent over her and used the blanket to wipe her feet, examining them for cuts from the gravel. Maybe there had even been broken glass in the gravel. Where in the city could you walk through loose gravel uncontaminated by bits of broken glass?

"I don't think it's your blood," he said.

Then whose blood was it?

"There was blood in the living room." Chloe pinned down one of the fragmented impressions from walking through the house. "Why was there blood? Who got hurt?"

Her mother and June and Justin had all been outside, seemingly well. But Chloe remembered the ambulance and June crying.

The policeman let her feet be and wrapped the blanket back around her.

"You can't go back to sleep," he told her. "I know you're too young for coffee, but do you want a cola? A little bit of caffeine to help wake you up?"

"I drink coffee," Chloe said. She remembered how she used to criticize Ruby for drinking coffee when she was a young teen—while secretly envying her for being so daring. It hadn't been very long before coffee had replaced Chloe's customary juice and dry cereal breakfast.

"You want a cup? That would help you to be more alert."

"I was sleeping," Chloe said defensively. She looked around the room, but there were no windows or clocks. "It's the middle of the night."

"I know. You want to be able to sleep. And you will be able to when we're done. But right now, I need you to be awake and answer some questions."

Chloe rubbed her temples. "I drink it black," she announced. She wasn't a little kid, diluting it with milk and cutting the bitterness with spoonfuls of sugar. She drank it straight, like a grown-up.

"Okay. Give me a minute to get you some."

Chloe nodded her heavy head. She clutched the edge of the table, the movement of her head making her dizzy and causing a moment of stomach-dropping vertigo. The policeman noticed nothing amiss and went back to the door to ask someone to bring a couple of cups of coffee, black. In a few minutes, he was seated across from Chloe, a steaming mug in front of each of them. It was too hot to drink, but even just the smell perked Chloe up a little. Her heart sped in anticipation of the stimulant.

"Who got hurt?" she asked. "Was it June?"

"June is going to be okay. All of you kids are going to be just fine," he assured her.

Chloe shook her head at the answer. "But whose blood was it? What happened?" She rubbed her arms. "Why did you bring me here?"

"Chloe... I'm sorry to have to tell you this, but there has been an accident. Your father has been killed."

Chloe stared at the depths of the black coffee, trying to process this. There was no immediate pang of regret or sadness. Just a blank, unfeeling sense of unreality.

"My dad? How? I don't understand." She tried to think of how it might have happened. An accident? Did he fall? Maybe someone pushed him. He tripped over something and hit his head. The blood had leaked from his head into a pool...

But she knew from the fragmented memories of walking through the living room that the blood hadn't pooled anywhere. It had been spattered over everything. Small droplets. She watched enough TV to know that that didn't happen when someone fell and hit their head. Maybe if they were hit over the head repeatedly. Bludgeoned. Or stabbed, hitting an artery that pulsed and sprayed.

An accident?

"What happened?" she asked numbly.

"I'm afraid that what it looks like right now is... Justin shot him."

Another whirl of images and memories that made Chloe dizzy with their rapidity. Justin's and June's childish faces. They were eight. How could Justin possibly have shot anyone? It didn't make any sense.

Chloe took a sip of the coffee. It was still too hot to drink, but she had to get it down somehow or she was going to faint. She wished now that she had told him to put sugar in it. Maybe sugar would help to keep her from blacking out.

"Are you okay, Chloe?" the cop asked in a sympathetic tone.

"I'm... no... what...?"

"Did you know that there were problems between Justin and your father?"

"No."

"Did they fight?"

Chloe rubbed at her eyes and took another drink of the coffee. "Fight...? No... Justin talked back sometimes, maybe got—uh—spanked for it, but they didn't... fight... He's only eight!"

"It's pretty hard to comprehend, isn't it? I'm sorry, I know this must be a shock. How about your mom? Did Justin fight with her?"

Chloe shook her head.

"Was there any other trouble? There have been calls to your house in the past."

"No. Nothing. What do you mean?"

"Disturbance calls. Possible domestic violence. Your sister, a couple of years ago, being admitted to the emergency room."

"Ruby?" Chloe said blankly. Then she remembered. "Oh, Ronnie. Before she... when she went to that foster family."

He nodded. "Do you want to talk about it?"

Chloe's head whirled. "About what?"

"About the situation at home. It sounds like things have been pretty rough."

"No." Chloe shook her head and took another drink, trying to counteract the dizziness. "It wasn't. Things are just normal. There wasn't any trouble."

"You didn't see any problems cropping up between June and Justin and your father?"

"No."

"There hasn't been any increased tension? Unusual behavior from Justin?"

"No." She concentrated. "He acts like he's older than he is. Admires the boys in the gangs and wants to be grown up like them. That must be it. He just wanted people to think he's grown up. Doing something that would make them think he wasn't just a little kid."

"That seems like an unlikely reason to shoot his father."

"You just don't get how it is. He just wanted to look grown up."

The cop didn't say anything for a few minutes. The coffee was starting to do its job. Chloe didn't feel like falling asleep again as soon as he went quiet. She rubbed the back of her neck. Her head hurt.

"Justin says that your father was molesting June."

Chloe's jaw dropped. She sat there staring at the cop. It was even more unbelievable than the news that Justin had killed their father. Their father molesting June? She couldn't even conceive of the possibility. He wouldn't ever touch June. He couldn't. The idea was so unbelievable that Chloe couldn't even wrap her mind around it.

"No. That never happened."

"You never saw anything… that didn't seem appropriate between the two of them?"

"No!"

"No touching or kissing that might not have been as innocent as it looked?"

"No! No, he wouldn't ever do that."

"Did he ever do anything… that made you feel uncomfortable? Sort of icky inside?"

Chloe shook her head, tears escaping the corners of her eyes. He was talking to her like a child. Like she didn't know what molesting meant. And she could see by his kind, compassionate gaze that he didn't believe a word she said. They were automatically taking Justin at his word. Why would they believe an eight-year-old over a thirteen-year-old? Chloe was old enough to be responsible for the twins. She took care of them every day, supervised their comings and goings. She knew everything that went on in the house. It was impossible to even conceive of what the cop had said.

"You can't believe Justin," she said. "He's just making it up."

"Okay. I'm sorry to upset you. How have things been with June and Justin lately? Generally speaking?"

"Where's my mom?" Chloe looked at the closed door. "I want my mom. I want to see her."

"Someone else is talking to your mom right now. You'll see her later."

Chloe pulled the blanket more tightly around her, a shudder running through her body.

"Please. I want to see her."

There were tears running down Chloe's cheeks. She wasn't playing a game; they were real tears. She wanted to make sure that her mother was okay. Mim would be upset, crushed at her husband's demise. Chloe wanted her mother to tell her what to do. She didn't know what she should say to the cop. Maybe she had already said things that she shouldn't.

"I'm sorry, you can't see her right now, Chloe. There will be a social worker here in a few minutes to sit with you."

"I don't want any social workers! I don't need a social worker. I'm going to be with my mom. She didn't do anything wrong! I didn't do anything wrong! We're going to go home."

"You won't be able to go back to the house today, or in the near future."

"I'm going to be with my mom. Not with a social worker or foster family."

"You may need respite care for a day or two—"

"No!" Chloe insisted, her voice breaking. "I'm not! I'm not going to anyone else!"

"Tell me about June," the cop said, changing the subject. "What is June like?"

Chloe sniffled. "I dunno. She's eight. She's got dark hair like

Daddy and Justin." Chloe raked her fingers through her own thick, dirty-blond mane. "She's in grade three." She wiped her nose with the back of her hand. "She's not doing so good at school."

"No? Why not?"

"I don't know. She's been skipping a lot."

"Skipping school?"

"She doesn't feel good in the morning, so she thinks she doesn't have to go to school. I feel sick some mornings too, but I still go to school."

"She's been sick how?"

"Just her stomach. Mom says it's nothing, she's just putting it on. So I make her go to school."

"It's good that you help to look after the younger kids."

Chloe nodded. "Someone has to be responsible. I always look after them if Mom's not home."

"I'm sure she appreciates your help. How about Justin? What's he like?"

Chloe wrinkled her nose. There were a lot of words that she could use to describe Justin, none of which she would use in polite company. "He's a brat. Doesn't want to listen. Wants to be a hood. He and June..."

The policeman raised his eyebrows. "Yes...?"

"Well, they're twins," Chloe offered. "So they're really close. Always together, even a lot of the time at school. Eat lunch together and walk home together and stuff. Justin's always looking after her. Protective," Chloe finished lamely. She bit her lip. Had she said too much? Mim always said that family business stayed in the family. They weren't supposed to talk about family stuff to others.

Chloe needed to watch herself. Cops and social workers were dangerous. They broke up families. Chloe had seen it over and over again. Cops and social workers couldn't be trusted.

She recognized the social worker who was eventually shown into the little conference room. He was Ruby's and Ronnie's social worker. The last year or two. Chloe had seen him a couple of times when he came to the house to talk to her parents about something to do with one of the girls. But they didn't like to talk to him. They said he didn't need to come to the house to deal with Ruby's and Ronnie's cases. The girls didn't live there anymore; their parents didn't have anything to do with their lives.

When he walked in, Chloe gave him no sign of recognition. She just slouched back in her chair as much as the straight-backed seat would allow and pulled the blanket tightly around herself, arms wrapped protectively around her body.

"Hi, Chloe," the social worker greeted gravely. "I don't know if you remember me. My name is Mr. Clive."

Chloe just raised her eyebrows.

"How are you doing? This must all have been a big shock to you."

She didn't say anything. Mr. Clive looked her over.

"Are you okay?" he persisted.

"I'm fine."

"You need warm clothes and sleep. I'm here to make sure that you're being treated okay, and I'm working on getting you a place to move into for now until everything gets straightened out."

"I'm not going to some foster home," Chloe snapped. "I'm staying with my mom."

"Your mom is tied up right now. It might be a few days before she can really give you the attention that you need."

"If it was Justin that shot my daddy, then why are they holding Mom? They can't arrest her when he's the one that did it."

"She hasn't been arrested. But she is a witness. Both to the shooting... and to the events that led up to it. It's going to take a few days for the police to sort that out."

"They can't keep her here if she isn't arrested," Chloe said stubbornly. "They have to let her go, and I'm going with her."

Clive considered this, studying Chloe with slightly lowered lids.

"Social Services would like to take a few days to make sure that you are going to be safe going back to her," he said finally.

This, at least, was more honest. It wasn't the police. It was Social Services. They wanted to apprehend Chloe. The family had already lost two girls, and Chloe wasn't going to be the third.

"I'm not going. If Social Services takes me out, they're never going to let me go back." He opened his mouth to object, and Chloe continued, speaking over him. "Ruby and Ronnie never came back."

"Ruby's and Ronnie's cases are different. We just want to make sure you're safe."

"Safe from what? What has Mom done?"

"Possibly she allowed abuse to go on under her own roof. Allowed children access to firearms. She may have been a participant in the abuse, for all we know."

"She didn't do any of that. You can't take me away. Just because Justin's making stupid accusations about my dad, that doesn't make it true. And even if it was, he's not there anymore. What's going to happen?"

"I'd really appreciate your cooperation, Chloe. Let's work this out together. Sort out a solution."

"I'm not going to respite. I'm not going to a foster home. If you put me in one… I'm going to run away. I'm not going to be like Ronnie, a little sheep going wherever you say."

"You know why Ronnie is in foster care. She was hurt pretty badly."

"And no one ever proved it was Daddy who hurt her. He was never charged with anything. But you kept Ronnie, even though there was no proof. That's not going to happen to me. You're not going to take me away."

"It's not up to you, Chloe."

"I've got two feet."

Clive knew Ruby's history. Knew that they hadn't been able to do anything to keep her from running away. He knew that no matter what he said about who was in charge, Chloe could run the first chance she got, just like her sister. They couldn't physically force her to stay. They couldn't put her in detention for her own good. Not until she had done something other than threaten to run away.

He looked at his watch. "I still have to see the others. I'm not sure what we're going to do with you… I'll have to make some phone calls."

"I'm not going to foster care," Chloe maintained.

He gave a little grimace and got up. He snapped a business card down on the table in front of her.

"If you need to reach me, for anything—"

Chloe swiped the business card off the table, and it fluttered to the floor. Clive didn't pick it back up. He just walked out of the room.

CHAPTER Two

It was morning before they wrapped everything up. Chloe knew it was morning, not because she could see the daylight out a window or could accurately calculate the passage of time, but because they brought her breakfast. Chloe had shifted between groggy and wakeful states in turn, sometimes falling asleep in the chair and other times so uncomfortable she could hardly sit still. It had been a weird, disrupted night, and she felt a little like she was hallucinating the whole thing.

A policeman brought her a plate of food. She didn't know whether it was the same cop who had brought her in. She supposed he had since clocked out and gone home. But their faces were all a blur. She couldn't keep track of which cops had come and gone throughout the night, and hadn't heard any of their names.

The meal consisted of scrambled eggs, two slices of white toast, and two strips of oily bacon. Chloe's stomach twisted, and she didn't know whether the smell of the food made her hungry or nauseated. She poked at it with the fork, not sure what to do.

"I brought you some clothes, too," the cop said, depositing a white plastic shopping bag on one of the other chairs.

Chloe looked at it, then prodded with a finger to look at the contents. "Whose are those?"

"They are for you."

"Yeah, I get it, but... whose were they before? Somebody else wore them."

"They are clean. You can eat and get changed, and then I'm sure you'll be feeling much better."

"Where's my mom?"

"She is still being questioned."

"How come it takes so long when she didn't do anything? It was Justin that shot my daddy."

"These things take time."

Chloe looked at the clothes. "Are they from some dead person? Or the lost and found? Where did they come from?"

"I don't know," he said in a firm, measured tone.

Chloe looked back at her food.

"Can I have coffee? And I gotta pee."

"I'll take you to the restroom. You can change in there," he offered.

"I don't want to wear someone else's clothes."

"Well, you can't go back to your house to get your own clothes, and neither can I. You can't walk around here or leave here wearing just a nightgown. You can't go to the store to buy new clothes looking like that. So you may as well put them on."

He picked up the bag and handed it to her. Chloe stood up, keeping the blanket wrapped around her, and took the bag. He was right about that. She couldn't go anywhere in her nightgown, no matter how gross it was to wear someone else's clothes. And better to change in the bathroom than in the conference room with its surveillance cameras and a window in the door.

People looked at Chloe curiously as she was escorted through the halls to a restroom. Chloe felt her face flush in embarrassment.

"It's okay," the policeman told her. "Don't worry about anyone else. We've all seen some pretty bizarre things. A girl in her pajamas is pretty normal."

That just made her feel more awkward. The cop gestured to the bathroom door. Chloe hesitated, then gave him the blanket. "Uh—here, I guess."

He took it.

In the bathroom, Chloe looked at herself in the mirror. What a mess. She'd been dragged out of bed in the middle of the night, and her hair looked like it. It was a tangled rat's nest of stringy blond hair. There were dark shadows under her eyes. The nightgown was practically see-through. Chloe quickly pulled on the stranger's clothes. The pants were tight around her butt and baggy everywhere else. The t-shirt pulled tight across her bust, and not in a flattering way. Chloe tugged at the clothes to try to make them look better, but she didn't have much to work with. She washed her face with cold water and finger-combed her hair, which didn't make it look much better. Eventually, she stepped back into the hallway to meet her escort.

"Are you going to take me to see my mom now?" she demanded.

～

Chloe thought it was just before noon when they finally took her back to Mim.

"Mommy!" Chloe ran to her mother and threw her arms around her. "Mom, are you okay? Did they hurt you? Did they give you something to eat?"

Mim thumped her on the back and pushed her away.

"What they call breakfast around here," she complained. "They certainly don't know how to feed a body properly."

She indicated her ample body as if it had somehow been desecrated by the trash food. Chloe grabbed her arm and snuggled close.

"Can we go now, Mom? Where are we going to stay?"

Mim looked at the policemen. "They said we can't go back to the house. I don't know where we can go. A hotel, I guess, for today. Then after that... I don't know. We'll have to find something. There's not much money in the bank."

Chloe cuddled against her mother. Mim pushed her away in irritation.

"Don't do that. You're a big girl, not a baby. Come on, then."

～

Things were tense. Chloe's mother was obviously upset and still tense over everything. A policeman had dropped them at the house to allow them to pick up the car, but there was yellow tape all around the house and sealing the door and they were not allowed to go in, even to retrieve personal items or important papers. The policeman stayed there watching them until Chloe and Mim got into the car and drove away. Chloe watched out the back window until the police car was out of sight.

"Are you okay, Mom?" she asked worriedly. "Everything will be all right, won't it?"

"Does it look like everything is all right?" Mim demanded. "My whole family is gone! I have no home, nowhere to go. I need to find somewhere to lay down. I need to sleep." She blinked her eyes and rubbed her forehead. "I didn't sleep all night. They kept me up, questioning me, the whole time. Like this was my fault! I'm not the one who shot him. There's something wrong with that boy. How could he do such a thing? There must be something wrong with his head."

Chloe nodded. She knew it wasn't time to ask questions. As confused as she was by everything, there was a time and a place, and she was good at recognizing what her mother needed and when it was okay to ask questions. They had to find somewhere to sleep first.

"How about... the motel over by the dentist's office?" she suggested. "That one doesn't look too expensive."

"It's a rat trap! Of course it doesn't look expensive. It's a wonder they haven't shut that place down."

"Oh." Chloe nodded her understanding. "What about... the one that your friend stayed at, when she came to visit?"

"The Palisade?" Mim considered this, her red-lipsticked lips pursed. "Yes, that might do the trick. Not too upscale, but it's not a fleabag. I don't want to stay somewhere with bedbugs!"

"No," Chloe agreed with a shudder.

"I don't need your approval, miss."

Chloe closed her mouth. It only took a few minutes to get to the motel. Green, with a red roof. Chloe stayed in the car while her mother went in to the reception desk. Mim didn't look at her or say a word, acting as if Chloe wasn't even there. Chloe watched her through the glass doorway, though she couldn't see much with the reflection. Mim didn't turn to look at her. Maybe it cost extra to check in with a kid, and she didn't tell the manager that she had one.

When she finished registering and got the key, Mim marched out of the lobby and headed for her room. Chloe scrambled to get out, locked the car, and ran to catch up with her. Mim didn't look at Chloe or say anything to her. She opened the door of room fifteen with the key and went in. Chloe caught the door and entered behind her. Mim did not flip the light on, and Chloe left it alone. There was one bed: a double, not a queen. There was no couch or cot. Mim groaned, pulling off her shoes, and stretched out on the bed with a noisy sigh. Chloe moved slowly, using her toes to remove the flimsy tennis shoes. She crept over to the bed as silently as she could. Mim took up most of the space with her bulk. Chloe carefully slid into the remaining space.

"Do you want me to rub your back, Mom?"

Chloe knew that Mim's back hurt most of the time. It would be worse after staying up all night at the police station. The hard chair had hurt Chloe's tailbone and back, and she was young and flexible. Her mother didn't say anything. Chloe took it as a yes. If it were no, Mim would have snapped at Chloe. Told her not to touch her. Chloe touched Mim's back tentatively. There was no objection. Chloe started to rub, very gently at first, and then harder, focusing on Mim's neck, the small of her back, and the bottom near her tailbone. Mim groaned a few times when she hit a tender place, but she didn't say anything to stop Chloe. Eventually, she started to snore.

Chloe cuddled up behind her, giving her mother a hug and closing her eyes, soaking up the warmth of Mim's body. They were safe. She was with her mother, and they were safe together. Everything was going to be okay.

It was growing dark when Mim started to stir. Chloe had been awake for a while, but lay very still, not wanting to disturb her mother's sleep. It wasn't like there was anything to do. She couldn't turn on the TV, or it would wake Mim up. She didn't have a book to read, or the inclination to read even if she had. For a while she was hungry, but she just lay there cuddled up to her mother until the hunger eventually died away again.

Mim groaned. "What time is it?" she demanded.

Chloe pulled away from her slightly to turn around and look at the clock.

"It's seven."

"Seven o'clock?" Mim stretched and sat up, rubbing her eyes and twisting her neck while grimacing. "I can't believe I slept that long. We need to get something to eat."

Chloe's stomach growled. "Yeah, I'm hungry."

"I'll bet you are. You kids are always hungry."

There was no more 'you kids.' There was only Chloe.

"What's going to happen to Justin and June?"

"They'll go to jail. That's what happens to murderers."

"June too? She didn't do anything."

"Spreading lies like that! They'll have to put her somewhere. You can't have a kid like that just running around, making accusations about good, decent people. They'll have to put her away."

Chloe tried to picture the kind of place that they would put an eight-year-old murderer and a little girl who spread lies. Would it be like a jail? With bars instead of walls? Or would it be like a boarding school? Would they really lock June away somewhere or would they just put her in a foster home? Chloe decided it was best not to pursue it yet. Certainly not while Mim was hungry. It was bad to ask her questions while she was hungry. And she looked like she had a headache from sleeping all afternoon too, kneading her forehead with her knuckles.

"Do you need a pill, mom? I'll get you a glass of water," Chloe offered.

"Yes. Yes, get me a pill," Mim agreed.

Chloe took a cup out of its paper wrapping and went into the dingy, stained bathroom, where she ran the water for a few minutes to make sure it was nice and cold and wouldn't taste of rust. She rifled Mim's purse to find the pill container and took out two for her. Chloe presented the pills and glass of water to her mother solicitously.

"Here, Mom. These will help you feel better."

Mim took them and gulped down the water without a word of thanks.

"We'll go find something to eat," she said. "And stop by the store for a few things." Her eyes went over Chloe, brows drawn down. "What are you wearing?"

"They gave me clothes at the police station. Because all I had was a nightgown." Chloe tried to readjust the shirt so it wasn't so tight around her bust. "It doesn't fit real well."

"No. You look like you've been stuffed into a sausage casing."

Chloe didn't know whether to be hurt or to laugh at the image. She *felt* like she'd been stuffed into a sausage casing.

~

When they returned from eating supper and shopping, with everything charged on the credit card, Chloe judged that Mim was in as good a mood as she was going to get. Mim turned on the TV and was surfing through channels, looking for something good.

"Mom…"

"Mmm-hmm?"

"Why… why did Justin do it?"

Mim flashed a glare at Chloe and then turned her eyes back to the TV to continue looking for a program to watch.

"I told you. He must be wrong in the head. What kind of an eight-year-old shoots his father?"

"Was it an accident? Maybe he didn't mean to."

"It wasn't an accident," Mim maintained.

"Then… why did he do it? Did he really think that…" Chloe lowered her voice and tried to think of how to word the question. "Did he think that Daddy would… hurt June?"

"He's crazy. Don't ask me what he thinks."

"But Daddy wouldn't hurt June. He wouldn't do anything like that to her. Would he?"

"Of course not," Mim snapped.

Chloe hesitated to go on. She knew she shouldn't press Mim too hard. She should just back off and let Mim watch TV. But the questions burned inside of Chloe. Whenever she thought about it, there was a heavy, ten-pound knot in her stomach. She insisted to herself, over and over again, that there was no way that her father would ever do such a thing. But other thoughts, unwanted thoughts, kept cropping up, pressing their way into her consciousness.

"What about Ronnie?" Chloe asked. "She got hurt, and they thought it was Daddy."

Mim turned her head and looked at Chloe, her face flushing an angry red. "What did you say?"

"I just thought... something *did* happen to Ronnie. You took her to the hospital. I remember. But that... that wasn't Daddy. Daddy wouldn't hurt any of us."

Mim slapped her. The impact cracked like a whip and Chloe's head snapped back, hurting her neck. Chloe put her hand over the burning skin.

"Mom! Mommy, I didn't say he did it. I said he *wouldn't* do that!"

Mim was up on her feet, the TV forgotten. She looked around the little hotel room, her eyes afire. "You little minx! We've always done everything for you. Protected you and took care of you, and you have the gall to ask questions like that? You cast aspersions on your father? On me?"

"No, no!" Chloe protested, tears starting in her eyes. "No, Mommy!"

Mim thrust her hand into the narrow closet and came out with several thin wire coat-hangers. Grabbing Chloe by the hair with her other hand, Mim wrenched her around and pushed her face-down into the bed.

"No, I'm sorry," Chloe begged. "Please..."

The coat hangers whistled through the air and landed on Chloe's backside, almost making her shout with the pain of the impact. She pressed her face into the pillow, strangling her cries, willing herself to be silent. The coat hangers struck several more times, and then Mim, apparently not satisfied with the severity of the punishment, grabbed Chloe's pants and yanked them down so that she could strike bare skin. Chloe cried out into the pillow. As the blows continued to fall, she tried to protect her bottom, and the hot, stinging stripes burned her hands instead. Chloe jerked them back out of the way, putting her fingers into her mouth; until it hurt too much and she again had to block the blows with her hands to get relief from the repeated lashes.

All throughout, she choked back her cries. The walls of the motel were paper-thin, and she didn't have any desire to bring the cops down on them yet again. She muffled the screams that she couldn't keep inside with the pillow and pressed her hand over her mouth or bit her fingers, willing herself to be quiet.

When she couldn't take the pain anymore, she felt herself leaving her body, and she was floating up at the ceiling of the motel room instead, watching Mim whip the girl on the bed, feeling nothing but pity for both of them.

Finally, Mim flung away the hangers. Back in her body again, Chloe heard them all clatter to the floor. Then Mim sat down on the bed, picked up the TV remote, and started thumbing through the channels again.

"I'm sorry, Mommy," Chloe sobbed. "I'm sorry."

"Move your fat butt out of the way. You're taking up the whole bed."

Chloe pulled her pants back up over her hips and moved to the far side of the bed, squeezing herself onto the edge.

"I'm sorry," she sobbed again.

"You're usually such a good girl," Mim growled. "I don't know what's come over you. Why are you such an ungrateful little witch?"

"I was just mixed up. I'm sorry, Mom. I'll be better. I'm sorry. I didn't mean to be bad."

"See that you are," Mim snapped.

Then she said nothing more, watching the TV.

Chloe, Book #4 of the *Between the Cracks* series by P.D. Workman can be purchased at pdworkman.com

About the Author

P.D. Workman is a USA Today Bestselling author, winner of several awards from Library Services for Youth in Custody and the InD'tale Magazine's Crowned Heart award, and has published over 100 mystery/suspense/thriller and young adult books, including stand alones and these series: Auntie Clem's Bakery cozy mysteries, Reg Rawlins Psychic Investigator paranormal mysteries, Zachary Goldman Mysteries (PI), Kenzie Kirsch Medical Thrillers, Parks Pat Mysteries (police procedural), and YA series: Tamara's Teardrops, Between the Cracks, and Breaking the Pattern.

Workman loves writing about the underdog, who the reader may love or hate. She has been praised for her realistic details, deep characterization, and sensitive handling of the serious social issues that appear in all of her stories, from light cozy mysteries through to darker, grittier young adult and mystery/suspense books.

> P. D. Workman, does not shy from probing the deep psychological scars of childhood trauma, mental illness, and addiction. Also characteristic of this author, these extremely sensitive issues are explored with extensive empathy, described with incredible clarity, and portrayed with profound insight.
>
> —KIM, GOODREADS REVIEWER

Some of Workman's titles have been translated into Spanish, French, Portuguese, German, and Italian.

Workman began writing at an early age and is a prolific reader as well as writer. She is also passionate about teaching and learning, expresses her creativity through art and cooking, and loves exploring the Calgary parks and green spaces where the Parks Pat Mysteries are set. She was a legal assistant for many years and has done extensive charitable work.

Workman was born and raised in Alberta, Canada, and is married with one adult son.

∼

Please visit P.D. Workman at pdworkman.com to see what else she is working on, to join her mailing list, and to link to her social networks.

∼

If you enjoyed this book, please take the time to recommend it to other purchasers with a review or star rating and share it with your friends!

tiktok.com/@pdworkmanauthor
facebook.com/pdworkmanauthor
x.com/pdworkmanauthor
instagram.com/pdworkmanauthor
amazon.com/author/pdworkman
bookbub.com/authors/p-d-workman
goodreads.com/pdworkman
linkedin.com/in/pdworkman
pinterest.com/pdworkmanauthor
youtube.com/pdworkman
patreon.com/pdworkmanauthor
reamstories.com/pdworkmanauthor

Find P.D. Workman's books at

PDWORKMAN.COM

Scan the QR code below

www.ingramcontent.com/pod-product-compliance
Lightning Source LLC
Chambersburg PA
CBHW031425160426
43195CB00010BB/616